Collaboration for Sustainable Tourism Development

Edited by

Janne Liburd and Deborah Edwards

 Goodfellow Publishers Ltd

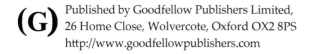 Published by Goodfellow Publishers Limited,
26 Home Close, Wolvercote, Oxford OX2 8PS
http://www.goodfellowpublishers.com

British Library Cataloguing in Publication Data: a catalogue record for this title is available from the British Library.

Library of Congress Catalog Card Number: on file.

ISBN: 978-1-911635-00-0

 Design and typesetting by P.K. McBride, www.macbride.org.uk

Printed by Baker & Taylor, www.baker-taylor.com

Cover design by Cylinder

Contents

Contributors

Bodil Stilling Blichfeldt, Department of Design and Communication, University of Southern Denmark

Peter Devereux, Curtin University Sustainability Policy Institute, Perth, Western Australia

Larry Dwyer, Griffith University, Australia; University of Ljubljana, Slovenia; University of Technology Sydney, Australia

Deborah Edwards, University of Technology Sydney

Carmel Foley, University of Technology Sydney

Jaume Guia, University of Girona, Spain

Bronwen Harrison, University of Technology Sydney

Chris Heape, Department of Design and Communication, University of Southern Denmark

Anja Hergesell, University of Technology Sydney

Anne-Mette Hjalager, Department of Entrepreneurship and Relationship Management, University of Southern Denmark

Kirsten Holmes, Faculty of Business and Law, School of Marketing, Curtin University, Perth, Western Australia

Michael Hughes, School of Veterinary and Life Sciences, Environmental and Conservation Sciences, Murdoch University

Gayle R Jennings, Imagine Consulting Group International Pty Ltd, and Griffith University, Australia

Janne Liburd, Centre for Tourism, Innovation and Culture, University of Southern Denmark,

Dagmar Lund-Durlacher, Department of Tourism and Service Management, MODUL University Vienna

Angus Morrison-Saunders, Edith Cowan University, Australia; North West University, South Africa

Andreas H. Zins, Department of Tourism and Service Management, MODUL University Vienna

About the editors

Janne Liburd is Professor of Tourism and the director of the Centre for Tourism, Innovation and Culture at the University of Southern Denmark. By ministerial appointments, Janne is the Chair of the UNESCO World Heritage Wadden Sea National Park, and serves on the Danish National Tourism Forum, charged with developing the first strategy for tourism in Denmark. She is a cultural anthropologist: her research interests are sustainable tourism development, innovation, national parks, and tourism higher education.

Deborah Edwards is an Associate Professor and Director (Postgraduate Research) in the Business School, University of Technology Sydney. She has published extensively in a wide variety of areas including tourism sustainability, business events, and visitor experiences. Deborah's research interests are in sustainable tourism management, festival and event impacts and the legacies of business events, tourist's spatial behaviour, and urban tourism precincts.

Preface

This is our third book that has a focus on sustainability in tourism. The three books have evolved from our interest to drive change in sustainable tourism practices. Janne's interest in sustainability was activated during the two years in which she took a gap period between high school and higher education. During her travels, she wondered about the local community's relation to place of residence, nature and other people. Later whilst studying anthropology, the 'impact studies' of the 1980s and 1990s championed by Valene Smith were inspiring to her. However, she was surprised that anthropologists rarely wrote about encountering tourists during their field work and wondered how they were able to judge what tourism 'did' to a culture, and how these findings could be applied to sustainable development. Since then her research has changed focus to sustainable tourism development, and to working with stewards who care beyond selfish interests. Janne's philosophy is to educate with students, to bring forth their individual potentials, taking them into unsettling territory, and to create space for transformations of the self, so they can engage in future world-making.

Deborah's journey to this point is somewhat more pragmatic. Following high school, she eschewed higher education to explore the world and expand her familial boundaries. It was some 15 years later when she decided to upskill (she had made enough beds, and teaching others how to make beds no longer interested her) that she found herself in class with Professor Larry Dwyer. Week by week he opened her eyes to the implications of global warming on tourist destinations and the importance of involving the community in the tourism planning process. Community participation and collaboration are now core to her philosophy and like Janne, she believes that today's students are the world-makers of the future and she encourages them to examine, consider, and reflect on the implications of their decision-making – before and after decisions are made and implemented. Indeed, she is heartened by the social conscience of today's youth, feeling that this bodes well for positive futures.

It is easy to become cynical about tourism and its promise of contributions to sustainability with communities in destinations complaining of being overwhelmed by tourist numbers, weekly reports of tourists behaving badly and disrespecting cultures, the expansion of tourism prostitution, and tourists knowingly or unwittingly participating in the drug trade, if not media reports telling yet another horror story of terrorist acts aimed at familiar destinations. BUT there are other, compelling narratives. There are many positive stories of individuals and groups working in collaboration to aspire to better outcomes for people and planet. This book has progressed because we want to address these inspirations – not just of activity but also of new advances in thinking.

We so much enjoyed writing the first two books and the collaborative opportunities of working with colleagues who share similar passions for sustainability, that we decided to invite authors to work with us in this new edition. Each of the contributing authors has responded to our request for centralising their chapters in new imaginings for the sustainable development of tourism. We are very appreciative of their rigour and timeliness. The book visits the main protagonists of sustainable tourism development: education, (ir-)responsible tourists, volunteerism, innovations, corporations, governance, branding and communication, climate change, suppliers, the sharing economy, and unpredictable futures. Our hope is that those who read our book will draw insights from which they will critically reimagine the now, to contest unrelenting consumption, ponder upon desirable futures, and take action that collaboratively addresses the wicked problems facing tourism at the dawn of the Anthropocene. We are only beginning to realise the scale of human induced changes to the ecological limits of a finite planet. Many of these are irreversible. We call for collaborative transformations of tourism and societies, which challenges dominant thinking and doings of economic growth and development. There is an urgent need to envisage new norms and forms of living well with others, of prosperity without growth, and of sustainability, safety and security for all.

The book cover illustrates a phenomenon known as 'Black Sun'. Looking closer you will see starlings in flight captured just before sunset in the UNESCO World Heritage Wadden Sea National Park in Denmark. Right before they settle for the night, the starlings gather in large flocks, of which some may count several hundred thousand birds. The starlings' appreciative awareness of each other enables them to promptly shift direction. They navigate in unknown territory while identifying latent opportunities. Thereby the sustain not only their individual being, but the group of participants for the betterment of the whole. In short, they collaborate! They accomplish what no single bird could do alone, namely fend off much larger, predatory birds. Their eloquent formations, which resemble a ballet in the sky, have become a major tourist attraction, which by virtue calls for collaboration to underpin sustainable tourism development in the National Park.

We have been working in the global field of sustainable tourism development research for more than 20 years. We are convinced that collaboration for sustainable tourism development ultimately should identify positive options for how tourism can be other-regarding and re-imagined to attain its full potential in the world. As such, this book is a critical and optimistic undertaking intended to stimulate critical thought and actions for living well with others.

Janne Liburd & Deborah Edwards

Introduction

Janne Liburd and Deborah Edwards

More than one century ago, in a revolutionary piece of prose, D. H. Lawrence wrote:

"And barrenly, the professors in their gowns offered commercial commodity that could be turned to good account in the examination room; ready-made stuff too, and not really worth the money it was intended to fetch; which they all knew" *([1914] 1995: 367).*

One of the most important challenges facing the world today is educating the leaders of today and tomorrow. In order to avoid blind reproduction, as implied in the opening quote by D.H. Lawrence, and to create challenging vistas, these leaders should be equipped with a holistic understanding of the concepts, values and principles of collaboration and sustainable tourism development.

The reader is hereby challenged not only to think about the means to current problem solving but to reflect philosophically upon processes and ethics in the context of desirable futures with others. Reflecting upon the kind of tourism we wish to have does not imply moving away from one's own, or industry's, needs and demands of the market place, nor of meeting those of society. More fundamentally it raises the issues of stewardship, the kind of tourism to be developed, by whom, how it should be governed, and what the objectives behind these activities should be.

This book positions itself among recent contributions to sustainable tourism development. Its original contribution lies in its critical focus on collaboration and the juxtaposition of conceptual and practical themes, and to open up for new possibilities for sustainable tourism development. The overarching purpose is to provide an original textbook based on robust research in the area of sustainable tourism development, which is framed by cutting edge understandings of collaboration. We aim to help identify positive options for how sustainable tourism development can be re-imagined as a collaborative endeavour in the 21st century to attain its full potential in the world. Aspects of this may already be seen in current and experimental practices of sustainable tourism development. These can be gleaned from case studies of industry practice, discourses, new learning approaches and collaborative communities.

Collaboration for Sustainable Tourism Development is an optimistic and critical undertaking. New visions for the sustainable development of tourism are needed to learn from past mistakes, to fully seize its possibilities, and to meet its responsibilities, and to embrace complexity and chaos in collaborative efforts for resilient action. The latter suggest that tourism has responsibilities not only to itself as an industry, but to its customers, investors and staff, to governance, to society, to other nations, and over time. Tourism is more than a hedonistic phenomenon. Tourism is a lens through which we can begin to understand contemporary society, e.g. in the organisation of free time, in representations of self to others, in interpretations, in perceptions of risk and safety. Tourism shapes parts of the world into sites of work and play, places to be revered and preserved, or turned into production and development. Tourism affects design, aesthetics, buildings and food. Tourism challenges the boundaries of the world and where tourism can take 'place'. Consider, for instance, tourism enabled by virtual reality, tourism in (lower orbit) space, and whether tourism should be in fragile areas and nature conservation zones.

As a field of study, tourism contributes to critical knowledge about the past and present, for transformations, for engagement in future world-making, for collaboration with and for society. This should not be mistaken for a demonstration of the importance of tourism, or tourism's usefulness as a global industry. Rather, and without losing sight of tourism as fun, it sets an ambitious scope for how such a far reaching phenomenon must contribute to resolving current societal problems and global challenges.

The UN *2030 Agenda for Sustainable Development* recognizes the insufficiency of more sustainable accomplishments for people, planet, peace and prosperity. Tourism is accentuated in three of the seventeen UN Sustainable Development Goals (SDGs), and partnerships are seen as central tenets for action. The global problems addressed by the SDGs are 'wicked', in as much as there is no one resolution to be found. And if a solution is identified, it may well be that it causes unforeseen consequences creating new problems to be solved. We are deeply concerned that partnerships and conventional development approaches based on economic growth and historically unequal relations of cooperation and partnerships are futile. Moreover, the SDGs reduce sustainability to a static, achievable goal by 2030, whether for cities, communities, the oceans, or the planet. The Earth has entered a new geological epoch, the Anthropocene. The Anthropocene is characterized by the extent of long-lasting, if not irreversible human degradation of the biosphere. More of the same will not meet the urgency for transformation.

Collaboration for intentional change with others is needed to gain advantages in an unpredictable world. Human preferences, practices and actions are the main drivers of planetary change in the 21st century (Holm & Brennan, 2018). However, we are not likely to change individual behaviour, even when pressed into realization that our powers of creation, including technological advancements, may lead to the destruction of life as we know it. Imagine if we all turn vegetarian, fly less (or not at all), don't smoke, ban single use plastics, and only use public transport. The planet would suffer less from methane gasses and CO_2 emissions and we would arguably be healthier. But many of us love to travel and to eat meat, and as researchers we readily fly across the world to attend conferences on climate change and sustainable tourism development.

Intentionally transforming human behaviour is a realistically optimistic and imaginative endeavour that must be grounded in current realities, global inequalities and power struggles. A transformation of such magnitude cannot be accomplished by a single individual, but may arise in the micro detail of interactions between people. We have yet to realise the power of collaboration, stewardship and ethics that are 'other-regarding' in order to guide our actions for more resilient futures. This resonates well with Holm & Brennan (2018) who insist, in the *Humanities for the Environment,* to help us transform our perception and imagination for the Anthropocene as new human condition:

"humans use language, narrative, imagination and cognitive models to cope and take action" (p. 3).

The fundamental interdependence between human behaviour, regions and socio-economic activities must be acknowledged in order to embrace collaborative efforts for resilient action over time. Only then can tourism become a significant contributor to broader societal transformations *with* civic society and *with* stewards who care beyond selfish interests.

Throughout this volume, authors argue that collaboration may leverage sustainable tourism development between diverse groups of agencies, organisations, businesses and people with many different values and agendas. We explore the role of collaboration in sustaining livelihoods, meaningful experiences, profitable partnerships, cultures and the environment through tourism in thirteen distinct chapters.

Chapter 2 provides conceptual framing of collaboration and sustainable tourism development. Liburd calls attention to how collaboration does not imply a division of labour, which is often the case in co-ordination, co-operation, co-creation, etc. Collaboration implies that the creation of joint outcomes could not be engendered by a single organisation or individual, which may be the epitome of competition. Liburd explores how collaboration across multiple dimensions can help bridge the gap between sustainable tourism and development, and she ultimately challenges whether sustainable tourism development is enough.

Blichfeldt in Chapter 3 introduces the notion of sustainable tourism development communication and discourses as complex and dynamic meaning making processes that transcend what individual actors bring to the conversation. She argues that sustainability discourses are informed and collaboratively constructed by a plethora of actors. Blichfeldt criticizes traditional communication models and destination branding. She illustrates the different, sometimes opposing, versions of destinations arising from tourists' active participation in constructing knowledge on destinations and sustainable tourism development. Vignettes are presented in a most amusing manner that capture ten compelling examples, including travel agencies' use of new media, (misunderstood) viral marketing processes, the (lack of) control by Destination Marketing Organizations, conflicting place interests, notions of over-tourism, greenwashing and green-hushing. The chapter demonstrates how tourism actors should not see branding and strategic communication as simply sending messages that emphasize sustainable tourism development, but should instead define this as actively partaking in the discursive performances that inform and collaboratively construct sustainability.

Guia in a comprehensive review of the literature on tourism collaboration in Chapter 4 finds that this literature has explored three broad areas: collaborative structures for sustainable tourism; stakeholder identification and involvement; and the obstacles faced in pursuing collaborative processes. Guia argues that these obstacles continue to be persistent despite the various development and application of practices, models and tools. Guia's focused analysis of the literature leads him to note that while many tourism destinations have attempted to move toward sustainability, their attempts have been hindered by a lack of collaboration among stakeholders. This leads him to develop a conceptual framework for the management of uncertainties in governance networks for sustainable tourism. He guides the reader through the framework simultaneously mapping the research field on governance of sustainable tourism while identifying neglected areas for future research.

Hergesell, Edwards and Zins in Chapter 5 examine the influence and interrelations of sociodemographic, psychological and situational factors on tourists' environmental behaviors. Their findings are not heartening. They contend that the 'responsible tourist' may be a dream as "tourists' personal interest will always take precedence", potentially leading to irresponsible environmental behaviors. Business as usual and cooperative approaches, they maintain, fall short of realizing desired change in tourists' behavior. The authors argue that destination managers must be realistic in designing collaborative initiatives, giving greater thought to the development of environmental infrastructures that demand collaboration and foster habitual pro environmental behaviors from the tourist.

A business as usual response is critiqued by Devereux and Homes (Chapter 6) who explain that voluntourism practice is evolving, and can play a prominent role in achieving the Sustainable Development Goals (SDGs). They present five rationales for linking SDGs and Agenda 2030 to volunteering and voluntourism. These are: recognition of volunteering's role in facilitating new interactions; universality of voluntourism to tackle neo-colonial approaches; voluntourism's ability to bring together the educational elements required to deliver SDG 4.7; voluntourism's capacity to deliver collaborative citizen science for collective responses to issues of concern; and voluntourism's capacity to provide opportunities for collaboration by connecting people within and between nations. Finally, they reason that voluntourism can facilitate partnerships within and between nations that can lead to deeper understandings for collaborative relationships.

Hughes and Saunders (Chapter 7) explore theoretically sustainable tourism development and collaboration asking the reader to consider – 'whose needs'?. In drawing on illustrated examples from practice, they propose an alternative definition of sustainable tourism development that prioritises 'host community' needs and thereby better aligns with the spirit of the definition endorsed by the World Commission on Environment and Development (1987). A matrix that takes account of spatial and temporal dimensions is used as a framing device for collaboration so that allowances are made for communities in both "the here and now as well as there and then".

In Chapter 8, Dwyer and Lund-Durlacher comprehensively tackle the systemic issue of corporate social responsibility (CSR). The chapter explores CSR from the perspective of large organisations, and small and medium enterprises, highlighting the many benefits that organisations gain from proactively adopting and implementing CSR initiatives. These benefits, they explain, are particularly enhanced when collaboration between corporations and their stakeholders act as catalysts for sustainable tourism development. However, they warn us that collaboration is challenging, because it requires processes to integrate and engage different stakeholders, the establishment of codes of practice, addressing the main concerns/issues of stakeholders, organisations accounting for their activities, and ensuring positive initiatives are recognized. Throughout the chapter, the restraints of CSR are highlighted in relation to its strategic and collaborative implications.

Chapter 9 maintains the business perspective by focusing on the work life balance (WLB) of employees in the hospitality sector. Deery, Jago, Harris and Liburd find that an absence of WLB leads to lower levels of retention, increased stresses at work and home, and less time to fulfil aspirations/interests. They put forward suggestions for a number of collaborative human resource practices that could assist in shaping employees' motivation and capacity to meet work and family demands.

Dredge and Meehan (Chapter 10) explore in detail a relatively new area in tourism, the collaborative economy, which is a socio-economic system underpinned by the sharing of human and physical resources. They argue that collaboration is an important cornerstone of any economic organisation. They show that as a form of collaborative exchange the collaborative economy is not as new as current thought would suggest, and should take account of the diversity and depth of alternative collaborative economic forms irrespective of the technologies by which it is currently underpinned. As meaningful definitions are difficult, Dredge and Meehan summarise alternative conceptualisations of the collaborative economy and go on to critically discuss the effects and consequences of the collaborative economy, focusing on four key areas: its role in reducing hyper-consumption; its ability to attract consumers interested in sustainability; its capacity to reshape demand; and its contribution to democratising economies. A final cautionary note is given regarding the ability of the collaborative economy to address sustainability as they note that deeper engagements with other models, such as the collaborative commons and the circular economy, are required if sustainability is to be fully addressed in tourism.

In Chapter 11, Hjalager explores how suppliers are key collaborators for innovation and sustainable tourism development. Based on a conceptual approach to understanding driving forces for innovation in sustainable tourism development, she turns to the role of suppliers. Hjalager introduces a four-field model that aims at stimulating new forms of collaboration between tourism firms and their suppliers in the upstream supply chain, which also challenges traditional perspectives on value chains in tourism. Hjalager argues that suppliers to the tourism sector are indispensable allies for leaders who want to commit themselves to work towards the sustainable development of tourism.

In Chapter 12, Foley, Edwards and Harrison present a case study of collaborative partnerships in a backward supply chain. The largest convention centre in Australia, the International Convention Centre Sydney (ICC Sydney), adopts sustainable, inclusive and collaborative practices as part of its Feeding Your Performance program. The case study details a sustainability strategy that incorporates *inter alia* social targets for sourcing fresh, seasonal, and ethically sourced local produce direct from the producer. To achieve their goals the ICC Sydney established relationships with 65 small, local and regional, food producers by visiting the producers on their farms or premises. The details of the program's outcomes are set out under four themes: environmental sustainability, knowledge sharing, economic development, and social contributions. The case study epitomises many of the sentiments in this book, in particular that collaboration and partnerships can form a basis for good business practice and resilience. But the authors, problematize the future and caution the reader to think beyond the now as long term collaborative relationships and knowledge continuity require the implementation of strategies in the now.

In Chapter 13, Heape and Liburd explore how complex and critical understandings of sustainable tourism development can be collaboratively designed with students, tutors and teachers. The notion of *designing-with*, instead of *developing-for*, is intentionally applied to leverage the participatory nature of learning and doing sustainable tourism development. They describe a principal pedagogical thrust in that students have far greater resources than they realise, which include basic human resources of empathy, imagination, association, metaphor, narrative and the ways in which we navigate the world. The authors demonstrate how the initial processes of collaborative learning for sustainable tourism development are about building trust and establishing a safe zone for the students' project, their process of inquiry and their budding transformation to an altered sense of self as philosophic tourism practitioners.

All of the chapters in this book present critical reflections on research actions undertaken in the spirit of fostering sustainable tourism development. In Chapter 14, Jennings offers critical insights into the consequences and effects of those research actions by considering the suite of research paradigms with regard to their ability to support collaboration for sustainable tourism development. She systematically argues that the participatory paradigm serves to champion most considerations. The participatory paradigm is action–oriented, predicated on the principles of collaboration and resiliency and its methodologies embrace the majority of considerations for resiliency. She makes a compelling case for critical consideration and deep reflection of the impact of (often concealed, we add) researcher values and positionalities. This includes, but is not limited to levels of and competencies in communication skills; critical thinking, reflection and reflexivity, types of learning, creativity, innovation, and imagination; power relationships; potential for agency, empowerment, and emancipation; expected research outcomes—social action, policy, practice, levels of impact, adaptation, and transformation.

This book would not be an exemplar of research cooperation in the field of sustainable tourism development, if it was not complemented by a final chapter. Chapter 15 is our critical and joint effort of drawing together the collective outcomes generated by colleges who inspired and collaborated with us in realising this book. We are grateful that the final product is indeed much more than what could have been generated by any one of us, which bodes well for engendering more collaborative, desirable futures with others.

Understanding Collaboration and Sustainable Tourism Development

Janne Liburd

Introduction

This chapter will provide conceptual clarifications of collaboration and sustainable development, and their application to tourism. Collaboration is not new in the contexts of tourism research, tourism higher education or the tourism industry. Academic life thrives on selection, classification and informed judgement, which are not at odds with collaboration. Without argument and counterargument, knowledge cannot be advanced. Tourism destinations are made up of many industry actors and stakeholders who are engaged in a myriad of networks and collaborative efforts. Tourists readily choose between destinations in a globally competitive field. Many travel to over-crowded destinations, where the tourism sector drives the destination to accommodate its demands, which may be at odds with sustainably living within the needs and wants of the destination and its local inhabitants. This chapter will attempt to overcome the all too frequent gap between sustainability in tourism theory and practice, by focusing on collaborative dimensions and possible critical engagements. The overall objective is to add three aspects to the current literature and appreciative understanding of the importance of collaboration for sustainable tourism development.

First, it is of pivotal importance to emphasise that collaboration distinguishes itself from cooperation and other forms of coordination. Collaboration does not imply a division of labour, which is often the essence of cooperation. It rests on the hypothesis that the sum of the work is more than its individual parts (Huxham, 1993; Liburd, 2013). The concept of collaboration suggests that the creation of joint outcomes could not be engendered by a single organisation or individual. Collaboration is not a neutral undertaking. It implicates interests and power, which are easily diluted in the abbreviated use of co-operation, co-creation, co-ordination, etc.

Second, I advance conceptual understandings of sustainable tourism development in order to embrace dynamics, complexity and the human dimension in the sustainable development of tourism. It is humans who care for the sustainable development of tourism – or not.

Third, by reflecting on the present dimensions of collaborative engagement and sustainable tourism development, I will question whether sustainable tourism development is sufficient, and if ethics can help to advance understandings of how caring that lies beyond selfish concerns can be used to identify latent opportunities for stewardship. The UN *2030 Agenda for Sustainable Development* recognizes the shortcomings of sustainable accomplishments for people, planet, peace and prosperity. As tourism is accentuated in three of the seventeen UN Sustainable Development Goals, I will also argue that collaboration – not just partnerships – should be seen as a central tenet for resilient action. The fact is that we consume and destroy natural resources at an unprecedented rate, with material and environmental impacts that will outlive us by tens or hundreds of thousand years. Impacts that are met with policy exercises and planning horizons of only three to five years. This represents not only a futile exercise by regional and national governments, but also an urgent call for system transformation where civic society, businesses and governments collaborate beyond selfish gains and build resilience across a range of scales (Morton, 2010; Schellhorn, 2010; Liburd, 2013; Higham & Miller, 2017).

Conceptualising collaboration

Conceptual research is generally concerned with typologies, definitions, past and current usage, discourse, deconstruction, and synthesis of concepts, which need not mobilise direct, empirical evidence (Xin, Tribe & Chambers, 2013). In the following, I will provide definitions and syntheses, which are complemented by empirical evidence of collaboration that have been gleaned from collaborative dimensions of tourism education and research. This is to ensure that the concept and importance of collaboration does not sit as a castles-in-the-air proposition. Empirical grounding will serve to ambitiously engage tourism's possibilities and responsibilities as a global phenomenon in the joint creation of better futures.

In the most basic terms, collaboration can be said to take place when two or more parties join forces to achieve a shared objective, whether the parties are individuals, groups, businesses, institutions or nations. Originating from the Latin word *collaborare*, meaning to work together, the concept of collaboration appears uncomplicated. Mattessich, Murray-Close and Monsey (2001) define collaboration as a mutually beneficial and well-defined relationship entered into by two or more organisations to achieve common goals. Since the Second

World War, collaboration has nevertheless carried highly negative connotations. During World War II, collaborators were those who worked with the enemy. Offering goods and services for ideological and non-ideological pursuits, some of the worst crimes and atrocities against humanity, including the Holocaust, were assisted by collaborators. In linguistic terms, collaboration implies more or less equal partners working together, which is clearly not the case when one party is an army of occupation. The positive form of working together for some form of mutual benefit will be pursued in the following, where the concept of collaboration suggests the joint effort of individuals to achieve a common objective, whether in institutions, organisations, businesses, with the state or other nations.

Collaboration often increases boundaries of knowledge (Anandarajan & Anandarajan, 2010), which is particularly evident in research collaboration, where scientific knowledge is advanced through argument and counterargument. In a bibliometric review of research collaboration, Subramanyam (1983) identified the following types: teacher–pupil collaboration, collaboration among colleagues, supervisor–assistant collaboration, researcher–consultant collaboration, collaboration between organisations, and international collaboration. These types of collaboration seem to overlap, and can be summarized in five dimensions: collaboration within and across the institution, with the state, with industry, across nations, and over time (Liburd, 2013: 57). Collaboration across all five dimensions will be illustrated through practices in tourism education and research.

Tourism attracts academic attention as a phenomenon and by the sheer diversity of subject areas jointly involved in its construction. Disciplines such as economics, geography, anthropology, psychology, sociology and history, among others, have contributed to the development of a dynamic and productive field of higher education and research. I shall refrain from entering into how sustainable tourism development informs teaching and learning in higher education, or how sustainable tourism development education may inform research, as this is compellingly addressed in Chapter 3 (Heape & Liburd, 2018). The development in higher tourism education and research since the 1950s is captured in Figure 2.1, which illustrates the defining characteristics and the relations between stages, research platforms, and the disciplines informing the tourism curriculum.

Jafari's (1989, 1990) four research platforms are based largely on motives as the key rationale by scholars in tourism, hence the classifications as advocacy, cautionary, adaptancy, and knowledge. As noted by Airey (2008: 2), it was not until the "knowledge platform" that a mature state of tourism as a field of study was arrived at by means of gradual, collaborative efforts. The four development stages represent artificial divides, which does not adequately depict overlapping practices and epistemologies in the development of tourism education and research. Figure 2.1 indicates aspects of ongoing cooperation during the 'industrial' and 'fragmented' stages, notably with industry and the state, characterized by cooperation within institutions offering business and economic studies. The 'benchmark' and 'matur' phases represent multi-disciplinary cooperation, which may evolve into inter-disciplinary collaboration within and across institutions, with industry, with the state, across nations and over time.

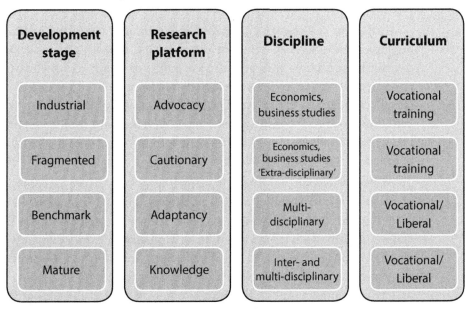

Figure 2.1: Stages in the development of tourism education and research. (Adapted from Jafari 1989, 1990; Airey, 2008 in Liburd, 2013: 87).

In order to understand the differences and complexity in multi-, inter-, and even extra-disciplinary approaches, a few examples may help illustrate the dimensions of tourism research collaboration. The development of an inter-disciplinary focus hinges not only on multiple disciplines but intentional collaboration across disciplines within and across institutions, and perhaps across nations, which often evolves over time. The inter-disciplinary frame may involve a blending of research philosophies, so that none stand apart but are brought together and explicitly seek a synthesis (Echtner & Jamal, 1997: 879), and whereby epistemic transfer is facilitated (Strathern, 2006). Still in 2007, Pritchard and Morgan argued that:

"positivist discourses and a commitment to empiricism, quantification, neutrality, objectivity, distance, validity, and reliability continue to be the appropriate markers of the authoritative voice in much tourism research". (Pritchard & Morgan, 2007: 18).

Jamal and Everett (2007: 58) confirm that cooperation based on a business oriented approach has dominated tourism studies, led by the 'economics-externalities camp' over an 'impacts-internalities camp' cognizant of social and cultural aspects. The 'camps' are indicative of early cooperation and some collaborative research efforts fraught by epistemological competition, which also framed the curriculum space within institutions. For a deeper understanding of the epistemology and ontology of tourism, the reader is referred to Tribe and Liburd (2016) who developed a comprehensive model of 'the tourism knowledge system'.

Turning to collaborative dimensions within and across the institution, the organisational effects of different departments, schools and research centres (e.g. business schools at large, or more contrived ones such as departments of parks and recreation, or centres for sustainable tourism) direct time, funds, and corral research to fit a particular institutional strategy (Tribe, 2006). Within the institution, one of the most pervasive social vehicles to facilitate collaboration between tourism researchers involves the formal unit of organisation and norms of collaboration, which I will return to shortly.

At state level, national research councils have come to play an important role in promoting collaboration across institutions and with other nations (Lowe & Phillipson, 2009). Research agendas are set at state (including the European Union) level through thematic and/or disciplinary calls for competitive grants. And research agendas and grants are often supported by a neo-liberal drive for measurable efficiency where the state is also instrumental in defining research quality and impact. These are, among other, measured through accreditation exercises and journal rankings, in addition to applying a range of bibliometric indicators, e.g. citation analysis, total research outputs, research income, and research recognition based on esteem measures (Hall, 2011a: 19). In the United Kingdom, research impact is defined as "the demonstrable contribution that excellent research makes to society and the economy" (Research Councils UK, 2017), where the relationship between collaborative research and impact is heralded:

"Through evaluation and commissioned work on knowledge exchange, we have found that more co-productive forms of research (i.e. research undertaken with rather than on people in a collaborative, iterative process of shared learning) offer particular potential for impact academically and socially".

The concept of collaboration *with* others resonates well with the approach to sustainable tourism development addressed below. Other authors, such as Florida and Cohen (1999) argue that collaboration with industry comes at the expense of basic research. Concerned that industry collaboration appears counter-productive over time, Banal-Estanol, Jofre-Bonet and Meissner (2010) demonstrate how research collaborations, in the forms of contract research, consultancy, and conferences, are far more important channels of knowledge transfer than patents, licenses, and spin-offs. These are, however, more difficult to measure empirically and even more difficult to compare across institutions and time.

So why do people collaborate? Presented with the option to engage in collaboration, individuals or groups will have to decide with whom to collaborate, if at all. The choice to collaborate entails the exclusion of other individuals or institutions from the inner circle of collaborative practice (Walsh & Kahn, 2010: 197). Notwithstanding differing objectives, language, procedures, and culture (Huxham, 1996), perceived and real power differences may exacerbate collaborative difficulties. Power relations and competition can be augmented through collaborative practice. At the simplest level, collaboration can increase a collaborator's own power, and collaboration may be used to empower the weaker partner. But self-interest need not be at the expense of others. Individuals or organisations may enter into collaboration to achieve something they could not generate alone. As such collaboration may represent the essence of competition. Huxham (1993: 599) refers to "collaborative advantage" arising from people working together and how the unusual outcome could not be generated by a single organisation or individual.

The element of freedom to collaborate also carries limitations. It may have repercussions on the level of commitment of individuals, organisations and the industry, and to the effort, energy, and time they may spend on any given undertaking (Walsh & Kahn, 2010). The establishment of consensual norms are of importance to ensure commitment and trust in collaboration. Collaboration is substantiated by reciprocal norms and exchanges that require trust for their consummation. At the same time, mutual relations create trust (Boisot, 1998: 141). A failure to re-engage in a just and reciprocal manner implies that collaboration and trust in others may be impeded. Following from Aristotelian ethics I recognise a virtuous aspect of collaboration, which must be 'other-regarding' (Jamal & Menzel, 2009: 234). One cannot expect oneself to be able to flourish without reciprocity and responsibility. Whilst collaboration thus offers opportunity for re-engagement, it also comes with a duty to others (not only the self) in Kantian terms. I will explore the ethical aspects in greater detail in the context of sustainable tourism development.

Still, to not reciprocate need not have personal implications (e.g. loss of honour, status) due to the freedom of collaboration, which does not necessarily represent a social bond. The lack of a social bond is even more noticeable if research collaboration is conducted in virtual environments by groups of potentially unrelated participants. Benkler explains:

"It enforces the behavior it requires through appeal to the common enterprise that the participants are engaged in, coupled with a thoroughly transparent platform that faithfully records and renders all individual interventions in the common project and facilitates discourse among participants about how their contributions do, or do not, contribute to this common enterprise" (2006: 73).

Failure to deliver when engaged in collaboration, whether face to face or online, may simply reduce trust in individuals, or in leadership, and will likely inhibit future engagements. Collaboration requires reciprocity, trust, a duty to self and others, and without specifying what collaborative acts might be, they contain the possibility of re-engagement. Whilst collaboration is a multifaceted, complex phenomenon that enables engagement across numerous domains, collaboration is hardly ever a goal in itself. In the following I explore how the concept and practice of collaboration is of key importance for meaningful engagement in tourism development, sustainability and future world-making.

Conceptualising development and sustainability

First, the concept of development will be deconstructed by reference to historical events, power and knowledge constructions in the form of specific development theories. Past and present usage is related to tourism development and underlying notions of cooperation, and subsequently to the concept and definitions of sustainable tourism development. Complex systems thinking will be introduced. This will serve to move beyond narrow sector focus in favour of dynamic, holistic understandings of sustainable tourism development that are informed by peoples' values and perceptions (McDonald, 2009) whereby the conceptualisation of sustainability becomes more about the way things are done by those engaged in travel and tourism than an achievable goal.

The concept of sustainable development can be traced to a variety of antecedents. Liburd (2010) points to Western environmental and conservation movements, international organisations and conferences, such as the 1972 *UN Stockholm Conference on the Human Environment*, the 1980 *World Conservation Strategy*, and the 1992 Rio Earth Summit (UN Conference on Environment and Development, 1992) which addressed the critical relationship between development and the environment. Influential publications, such as Carson's *Silent Spring* (1962) and Hardin's *Tragedy of the Commons* (1968) also inspired Rothman (1998: 34) to describe how "taming rivers in the United States was both sport and mission". These publications reflect in different ways how dominating Western views of nature have shifted substantially from a hostile view of nature to be controlled by man, followed by a 19th century romantic view in awe of nature, to one of wise use or conservation (Larrère, 2008; Liburd & Becken, 2017). For example, the so-called Wise Use movements in America are renowned anti-environmentalist lobbyists for expansion of mining, logging and ranching by reference to traditions of American frontier mentality. The reader is referred to Sachs' (1995) *Eco-justice: Linking Human Rights and the Environment* for a more detailed account.

The above examples reveal how the notion of wise use of nature is firmly rooted in modernity's unprecedented belief in human rationality and instrumental reason (e.g. valuing something because of the economic benefit it holds (Fennell, 2018: 177)). It is reflected in economic growth models (Rostow, 1952) and in the political agenda following World War II, captured below in President Truman's inaugural address to the US Congress in 1949.

Truman's inaugural address to US Congress 1949

More than half the people of the world are living in conditions approaching misery. Their food is inadequate, they are victims of disease. Their economic life is primitive and stagnant. Their poverty is a handicap and a threat to both them and more prosperous areas. For the first time in history, humanity possesses the knowledge and skill to relieve the suffering of these people… I believe that we should make available to peace-loving peoples the benefits of our store of technical knowledge in order to help them realise their aspirations for a better life… What we envisage is a program of development based on the concepts of democratic fair dealing… Greater production is the key to prosperity and peace. And the key to greater production is a wider and more vigorous application of modern scientific and technical knowledge.

With issues of underdevelopment, elimination of poverty and economic growth dominating the international development agenda during the 1950s and 1960s, more direct and disciplinary practices of development were institutionalised. Examples of such institutions are the World Bank, the International Monetary Fund, the United Nations Development Program, and bilateral aid agencies. Institutional power was complemented by development theories of modernisation and underdevelopment. Modernisation theory visualises development as a progressive movement toward more institutionalised complex forms of 'modern' industrialised society, which can be facilitated by a series of economic and technological interventions. The benefits of these, Rostow (1952) professed, will eventually 'trickle down' via the middle class to the underdeveloped masses.

Highly critical of modernisation theory and capitalist penetration into the 'underdeveloped' world, theories of dependency and neo-imperialism evolved during the 1960s and 1970s. Dependency theorists, notably A.G. Frank (1967) argued that development is a judgemental, unequal process through which wealthy, so-called 'centre' or 'core' nations become richer and the poor 'peripheries' of the world even poorer. Underpinned by Marxist ideology where capitalism is seen as exploitative, dependency theory recognises underdevelopment as embedded in particular political structures. It points to the inherent expansionist nature of capitalism and the continuous need for new markets and increased capital accumulation. Processes of exploitation are entrenched in the constant supply of raw materials from the 'peripheries' to the 'centers', which corroborate unequal trade relationships.

The post-World War II geo-political imagery was ordered in binary oppositions: the developed and underdeveloped world; the north and the south; and the centre and the periphery. As a term, 'development' is inherently judgmental and requires something or someone for comparison. It is at odds with the concept of collaboration between equal partners. It is important to note that references to modernisation and dependency theory are also testaments to how theoretical knowledge is not to be mistaken for neutral facts. Rather, theoretical works are instruments of power and persuasion, and associated policies may profoundly affect who benefits and who loses (Foucault, 1980; Bramwell, 2015).

Theories of modernisation and dependency can be illustrated through tourism development in the post-World War II era. Tourism was typically seen as an economic panacea that would lead to modernisation of underdeveloped, peripheral areas as foreign exchange would filter through the economy and elevate standards of living, education, health, etc. The potential negative impacts were largely unquestioned as the 'industry without chimneys' was highly reproducible. Generally, little upfront investment was required by local authorities who, lured by fascinating profitable potentials, provided lucrative incentives to foreign investors and multinational corporations to set up operation in their destination (Poon, 1993; Patullo, 1996). In their seminal works, tourism researchers Smith (1977), Cohen (1978), de Kadt (1979) and Britton (1982) argued that tourism, instead of benefiting peripheral destinations, in many cases led to new forms of dependency and acculturation. Parallels between service and servitude in neo-colonial contexts were drawn and the economic value of tourism was fundamentally questioned. Frank (1967) and other dependency theorists (e.g. Emmanuel, 1972; Wallerstin, 1974; Amin, 1976) lamented that exploitative practices and unequal relations result in peripheral countries failing to establish their own manufacturing basis and market relations, which accelerate environmental degradation and the gap between rich and poor.

The UN responded to the intertwined, global problems of development and nature degradation by establishing three independent commissions in less than a decade (1977-1984). Chaired by three former prime ministers, Germany's

Willy Brandt, Sweden's Oluf Palme and Norway's Gro Harlem Brundtland, the UN Commissions were established with distinct mandates to report on aspects of "the interlocking crisis of the global commons" (World Commission of the Environment and Development [WCED], 1987: 4). In addition to the growing awareness of environmental degradation and major discrepancies between the rich, industrialised nations and the poor, developing countries trapped in (depth-creating) poverty, the three commissions identified a number of factors that would have profound negative effect on the ability of all people to sustain continued development for generations to come. Factors included the increasing world population, ecological depletion of the ozone layer, air and water pollution, soil degradation, deforestation, loss of biodiversity, hunger, poverty, illiteracy and uneven development. Some tourism researchers argued that impacts from mass tourism, characterised by rigidly standardised package holidays, appeared to not only capture but directly contribute to global tribulations (Turner & Ash, 1975; McElroy & de Albuquerque, 1996).

Entitled *Our Common Future*, the WCED (1987) identifies two sources – both cause and effect – of the interlocking crisis: Third World poverty and over-consumption by the First World. Frequently referred to as the *Brundtland Report* by reference to its chairperson, *Our Common Future* (WCED, 1987) builds on the core recommendation of the two Brandt Reports to increase industrialisation, production, and economic growth in the Third World. This was arguably a surprise given the apparent failure of kindred development schemes and well-established critique of the underlying modernisation theory and unequal exchange (Frank, 1967; Sachs, 1974; Wallerstin 1974; Escobar, 1995). The Brundtland Commission also carried through Palme's participatory approach and concerns of security, which were not limited to global disarmament. Civil and ecological survival were emphasised *through* the importance of inter-and intra-generational equity, combating poverty, creation of intersectoral linkages, maintenance of the ecological resource base and empowerment of smallholders, women, indigenous people, rural farmers and local communities (WCED, 1987: 63, 116, 143). Importantly, the Brundtland Report affirms a need for an integrated understanding of the world as a whole, where the wellbeing of man and nature, future development and environmental issues are inextricably linked. Given this lens, the Brundtland report introduces limits to growth and defines sustainable development as:

> *"development that meets the needs of the present without compromising the ability of future generations to meet their own needs"* (WCED, 1987: 43).

Effortlessly embraced as a good idea of making things last, the report was met with enthusiastic support by governments, non-government organisations and academics alike. The well-established definition of sustainable development hinges on a holistic integration of economic, environmental, social and cultural development. The Brundtland report emphasises that meeting present and future needs not only involves economic growth in poor countries, but being able to sustain it through the strengthening of international, *cooperative* efforts. The concept of sustainable development implies both equity and ethics within and between generations, emphasised in the overview entitled "From one Earth to one World" (WCED, 1987: 1). Unfortunately, the issues of ethics, equity and collaboration have received very limited attention in the growing volume of publications on sustainable development and sustainable tourism development, which I will critically address next.

Sustainable tourism development

It is important to note that the Brundtland Report concentrates on sustainable development through economic growth, effective international *cooperation*, strategic long-term planning and maintenance of the resource and productivity base beyond narrow institutional and national concerns (WCED, 1987). This implies that tourism is not mentioned in *Our Common Future*, despite being a hallmark of modern society and having a vested interest in protecting the very resource base on which it depends.

Following Jafari's (1989) conceptualisation of academic platforms occupied by tourism researchers, the late 1980s were characterised by a quest for knowledge about the impacts of tourism, namely the environmental, social, cultural and economic positive and negative effects of tourism development around the world (Smith, 1977, 1989). The relation between tourism and sustainable development received scant attention until the 1997 *Agenda 21 for the Travel and Tourism Industry* [Agenda 21] by the World Travel and Tourism Council, the World Tourism Organization and the Earth Council.

Setting out the priorities for sustainable development in the 21st century, *Agenda 21* recognises tourism as a model form of economic development that should improve the quality of life of the host community, provide a high quality of experience for the visitor, and maintain the quality of the environment on which both the host community and the visitor depend. Agenda 21 identifies several measures and objectives that can be undertaken by governments and the tourism industry worldwide. These include strengthening of institutional *cooperation*, improved water waste management, training and education favouring minorities, and the exchange of information, skills and technology related to travel and tourism.

The interrelated environmental and socio-economic elements are captured in the definition by the World Tourism Organization (1998: 21):

"Sustainable tourism development meets the needs of present tourists and host regions while protecting and enhancing opportunities for the future. Sustainable tourism is envisaged as leading to management of all resources in such a way that economic, social and aesthetic needs can be fulfilled while maintaining cultural integrity, essential ecological processes, biological diversity, and life support systems".

Conceptual definitions and practical concerns of sustainable tourism development and sustainable tourism have received considerable academic and government attention and have been exposed to substantial criticism (Bramwell & Lane, 1993; Mies, 1997; Butler, 1998; Hall & Lew, 1998; Mowforth & Munt, 1998; Cohen, 2002; Dwyer & Sheldon, 2005; Miller & Twining-Ward, 2005, Wheeller, 1993; Weaver, 2009; Bramwell, 2015). A few of the principal concerns will be addressed here to set the scene for a more holistic and dynamic approach that is linked to collaboration.

In relation to practicality, there has been a relative neglect of how to implement the laudable principles in tourism and to address the very reasons why individual tourists, businesses and governments should consider their environmental, social and cultural performance, rather than only an economic bottom line. A simple, but most persuasive example is the dominance of economic indicators used by the UN World Tourism Organisation and the World Travel and Tourism Council, such as tourist arrivals, annual growth averages, direct contribution of tourism to GDP, and size of direct employment used to document tourism's importance worldwide (Budeanu et al., 2016). Critically documented in *Jamaica for Sale* (Figueroa & McCaulay, 2008), the single bottom line and industrial sector focus on tourism have become entrenched practices that may easily be attributed to corrupt or ill-informed destinations, but globally it remains a powerful discourse.

A conceptual perplexity exists within the literature where narrow sectoral concerns and tourism's contribution to broader sustainable outcomes are at odds. It is important to distinguish between sustainable tourism and sustainable tourism development. Sustainable tourism is centred on the viability of tourism and balancing industry and environmental impacts (Hunter, 1995). Sustaining tourism implies that management of the net productive value of the 'natural' capital can be calculated in order to implement compensating resource replacement and substitution strategies (Hughes, 1995). Paradoxically, conservation efforts to maintain equilibrium mean that the environment, and social and cultural aspects, should be kept in an unimpaired state for tourism over time. Such an anthropocentric approach rests on static conceptualisations that neglect knowledge about the dynamics of the environment, culture and society at large. Sustainable tourism is hereby reduced to maintaining a 'natural' equilibrium as a measurable state toward which intervention strategies can be applied as an economic (and tourism) trade-off between present utilisation and presumed future needs. But who has the power and ability to determine what to preserve, on behalf of whom, and where tourism should be developed?

Regulation and conservation efforts tie closely into this managerial perspective where irregularities and problems are addressed in causal, linear relationships. Fennell (2018: 6) referring to McKercher (1999) points to the ineffectiveness of traditional tourism models because they imply that: tourism can be controlled; its players are formally coordinated; service providers achieve common, mutually agreed goals; tourism is the sum of its parts; and an understanding of the parts will allow us to understand the whole. An exemplar model is Butler's (1980) adaptation of Plog's (1974: 4) life-cycle model into the *Tourism Area Life Cycle* that demonstrates how "destinations carry within them the potential seeds of their own destruction". The much cited Tourism Area Life Cycle model represents both a cautionary approach and also a belief in managerial intervention techniques to avoid decline. Without repeating Habermas' (1987) comprehensive deconstruction of the value-laden progress of Western science, the role of objective science in ideas about environmental management and sustainable tourism persevere. Hunter (1997) warned against the tourism-centric and often marginal concerns of sustainable tourism that appear to be separated from the sustainable development debate. When the tourism industry is considered in isolation, its activities may run counter to other sustainable development initiatives, preservation efforts and overall quality of life issues. These are noticeable, among other, in the industry's notorious low-skill, low-wage structures and long working hours (Deery et al., 2012). Referring to Butler (1999), Moscado (2008: 6) argues that "tourism cannot be sustainable in its own right". Tourism does not operate in a spatial vacuum and must be understood as a total social and economic phenomenon (Theobald, 2005), and as part of other elements of society, the environment and the economy. When the fundamental interdependence between human behaviour, regions and socio-economic activities are acknowledged, tourism is a potential contributor to the broader societal aims of sustainable development.

There continue to be frequent debates in the sustainability literature as to whether sustainable tourism outcomes are actually sustainable and claims that sustainable tourism development can be achieved (Cater & Lowman, 1994; Cater & Goodall, 1997; Swarbrooke, 1999; Holden, 2005; Bricker et al., 2013). Yet to argue that sustainability is achievable over a period of time fails to understand that change and ever-evolving processes are the norm rather than the exception. Consider, for example, how choice in travel, life style, cultural preferences and patterns of consumption and communication are not the same between or across generations, and that these are unpredictable. Similarly it is not feasible to assume that "tourism that stays the same will go on forever" (Hall & Butler, 1995: 202). The very idea of striking a balance in which the environment, economy and social and cultural elements are in equilibrium appears to be an oxymoron. Instead deeper, interrelated understandings of how socio-cultural values, quality of life aspirations, and the biophysical and economic systems in which tourism takes place change over time are needed.

Bramwell (2007, 2015) argued that studies of sustainable tourism development would be strengthened if they engaged more fully in wider debates and contestations around social theory. Excellent scholarly examples are: Cohen, Higham and Cavaliere on tourists' behavioural addiction to flying. Dredge and Jamal (2013) discuss destination governance and fluid mobilities. Hughes and Moscardo (2016) focus on customer engagement in corporate social responsibility. Miller and Twining-Ward (2005), Gössling et al. (2012), Gill and Williams (2014), and Williams (2013) discuss public-private sector transition management, structural lock-in and sustainability pathways. Scott and Becken (2010) address climate change adaptation and policy. And innovation is investigated by Hjalager (1997; 2010a & b); Gössling et al. (2009) and Liburd et al. (2013). These and other recent publications on tourism and sustainability continue to highlight absences, problems and gaps in both research and practice (e.g. Bramwell & Lane, 2011 & 2013; Hall, 2011b). Such queries about the viability of the sustainability concept to tourism are instrumental for advancing critical understandings and facilitating transformation towards sustainable tourism development. In due course, by discarding the conceptualisation of sustainable development as a goal that can be achieved, especially by reference to itself and non-mass types of tourism/tourists, I propose that dynamic and more complex conceptualisations of sustainable tourism development deserve further attention.

Complex systems

Tourism can be seen as operating within a complex system of dynamically interacting components that influence outcomes, such as the sustainable development of tourism. McDonald (2009) argues how reductionist approaches to sustainable tourism development have hitherto acknowledged, but failed to recognise, its inherent complexity. She positions complexity science and complex systems thinking to better capture value-laden concepts, such as sustainable development, which involves processes that rely on stakeholder values (McDonald, 2009: 456). In sustainable tourism development, stakeholder perceptions and values will inevitably influence actions that may facilitate transition processes.

Values can be seen as determining priorities, as internal compasses or as springboards for action, resembling moral or ethical imperatives that guide action (Oyserman, 2001). It is important to recognise that the dominant values and the power relations and paradigms, in which they are embedded, may change over time (Becken, 2016). This further implies that the component parts and their shifting inter-relationships are time-, topic- and context-sensitive. Demonstrated in a study of the Great Barrier Reef, Liburd and Becken (2017) reveal how shifting ideologies and government policies increased pressures on nature, and forged new alliances between the marine tourism sector, national and international organizations in a time of systemic crisis. The alliances were built over time on shared nature conservation values and, in 2016, they success-fully reduced development pressures.

McDonald (2009) explains that the component parts within a complex system are hierarchical in nature. Many subsystems exist, but they are influenced by underlying, unpredictable behaviours and connections both within and outside of the system. By implication, causal explanations and management action cannot control or predict behaviour, even though common behaviours are exhibited throughout the system. Equilibrium is therefore not a desirable state, as complex system stability is "always a matter of more/less rather than either/or" (Cooksey, 2001: 81). Liburd and Becken (2017) further argue that a future system crisis is likely to engender new alliances. This is to be expected in a com-plex adaptive system, which may, once again, be prompted by the continued degradation of the Great Barrier Reef – an iconic UNESCO World Heritage site. Indeed, in complex systems conflicts are inevitable and will expose inherent, underlying values. Identification of these will provide important information, possibilities for intervention, and show how best to utilize conflicts when, and not if, they emerge. Conflicts stemming from complex patterns of interaction need to be identified, understood and considered as latent resources in adapta-tions toward sustainability.

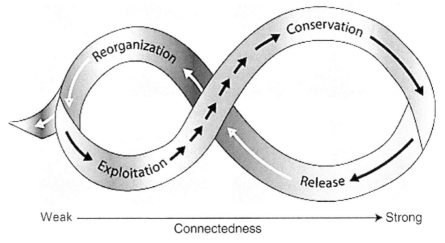

Figure 2.1: Complex adaptive systems (Gunderson *et.al*, 2005).

Illustrated in Figure 2.1 by a reclining figure eight, Holling's (1986) adaptive cycle illustrates how a complex system of ongoing transitions works, and how it can be adapted into sustainable tourism development (Malanson, 1999; Gunderson *et al.*, 2005; Miller & Twining-Ward, 2005).

The cycle explains how the 'sudden surprises' that have various effects on a destination may affect the destination's resilience and/or vulnerability. These changes might reinforce the destination after 'the incident' or make it weaker. In this case, the destination managers and stakeholders learn from the event and rebuild the destination through, for example, the introduction of supplier collaboration and innovation (Hjalager, 2018). Butler's (1980) Tourism Area Life-Cycle model mentioned earlier (p. 20), can be recognised in the 'exploration' and 'conservation' stages of Holling's (1986) adaptive cycle. Coupled with the collapse of the system, entitled 'release' and 'reorganisation', it becomes a dynamic model well suited for understanding chaos, transformational processes, power and unpredictability in sustainable tourism development. One can infer that the illustration resembles a never-ending structure, instead of a multi-dimensional, continuously evolving system.

The embedded ability of tourism to adapt to change, which includes occurrences outside the system, implies that the system is in a constant learning process to improve the system's resilience and capitalise on phases of self-organisation and reorganisation (Miller & Twining-Ward, 2005). This is not the same as saying that change is easily attained, nor socially desired, despite the new morality that has emerged regarding different ecological, social and ethical issues (Fennell, 2018). Complex adaptive systems thinking encourages critical reflection about tourism's history and performative ability, memories within the system, relations between elements, and coping with uncertainty. It effectively escapes causal, linear explanations and simple accounts of tourism's impacts. Moscado and Pearce already in 1999 demonstrated that only too often 'impacts' are imposed on respondents by those conducting research or undertaking development.

A dynamic conceptualisation of sustainable tourism development can be feasibly strengthened by recognising systems thinking's ability to provide insights to underpinning values and behaviours influencing a system and to identify latent opportunities for intervention that can ensure sustainable outcomes prevail (McDonald, 2009: 469). Such a holistic and inter-relational understanding of sustainable development cannot be determined by single components (e.g. economics over environmental or socio-cultural sustainability). The inter-relational understanding must not be mistaken for one of impact that resembles billiard balls colliding and reacting – and one could add cooperating – without affecting the interior properties of the entities in question. Rather, a relational and holistic understanding sees sustainable tourism development and the entities of analysis as constituted in and through constantly unfolding processes in which social interaction, power relations, knowledge and values are always at stake.

By embedding the dynamic concept of sustainable development into everyday tourism practices, it changes from being an 'add-on' to being more about the way things are 'always' done by those engaged in travel and tourism. I also find inspiration in Heidegger's notion of being, which at all times is a matter of 'being-possible' ([1927] 1998: 183). The being of sustainable tourism development hereby becomes a matter of becoming, of transformational changes, and of unfolding potentials in tourism's contribution – not to itself, but to better world-making.

Ethics and stewardship

Visions for better state of affairs, for a more just world, enjoy a long trajectory of philosophical contributions, including John Rawls (1971) and Paul Ricoeur (2002) who both offer perspectives of relevance to issues of stewardship and desirable futures. Inspired by the works of Aristotle, Immanuel Kant, David Hume, John Locke, Jean Jacques Rousseau, among others, Ricoeur contends that justice does not spring from a Kantian, deontological sense of duty (Liburd, 2013: 288). Justice is an integral part of the ethical intention "to live a good life with and for others in just institutions" (Ricoeur, 1992: 172).

Ricoeur consistently rejects any claim that the self is immediately transparent to itself, or fully master of itself. This is an idea pursued by Rawls (1971) arguing that human beings understand justice behind a veil of ignorance that will lead to principles that are fair to all. Self-knowledge therefore only arises from our relation to the world, our life with and among others, and attributing actions to some person or persons as worthwhile, or not worthwhile, according to Ricoeur (1992). Contemplating desirable futures may thus involve developing self-esteem within an interpretation of self, mediated by ethical evaluation of our actions by self. Aiming at the good life with and for others, in just institutions, Ricoeur puts forward a "three-cornered ethics" (Muldoon, 2002: 84). Ricoeur emphasises the necessity to see the self, the other and institutions as intimately connected. Acknowledging these connections, which imbue numerous dimensions for collaboration, and based on the need to be good as part of our genetic and cultural fabric (Fennell, 2018: 349), it becomes necessary to question: How might I act, and what might we want for the future?

By now it should be clear that it is insufficient to consider merely sustaining the world (through tourism) in the sense of finding a balance, or maintaining equilibrium. The definition of sustainable development being "the ability of present generations to meet their own needs without jeopardising the ability of future generations to meet their needs" (WCED, 1987) here becomes susceptible to a two-fold critique. First, a vast percentage of present generations across the world do not meet their daily, basic needs. Nor do they fulfil their right to education and independent, free research to a better civic society. Second, suggesting that future generations would want the same as the present generation is not only unrealistic, but blind to global inequalities and technological innovations.

I propose that stewardship transcends sustainability in its concern with caring for, shaping the interests of, and advancing society. It implies taking responsibility for the changing world. Liburd & Becken (2017) argue that the concept of stewardship differs from stakeholder and agency theories, which find their justification in self-preservation, economic motives and a pragmatist, rational approach to management (Donaldson & Davis, 1991; Freeman et al., 2004; Bernstein et al., 2016). Both stakeholder and agency theories have a strong individualistic focus that may easily jeopardize greater environmental and societal good. Neubaum (2013: 2) defines stewardship as "caring and loyal devotion to an organization, institution, or social group". Stewardship theory does not reject individual motivations, but suggests that those involved benefit from putting the interests of others above their own and pursuing actions that generate their own intrinsic rewards (Neubaum, 2013). The difference from instrumental reason and utilitarian ethics is noteworthy. Stewardship resonates well with the concepts of collaboration and complexity theory because stewardship puts an emphasis on the people involved in conservation efforts, and recognises intrinsic as well as personal values and dynamic interrelations beyond selfish gain, while not excluding the latter. Collaboration enables latent opportunities to emerge in the creation of joint outcomes that could not be generated by a single organisation or individual.

This is of relevance to the *2030 UN Sustainable Development Goals*, which mentions tourism in three of the 17 Goals. The SDG aims are described as follows:

"The new Goals are unique in that they call for action by all countries, poor, rich and middle-income to promote prosperity while protecting the planet. They recognize that ending poverty must go hand-in-hand with strategies that build economic growth and addresses a range of social needs including education, health, social protection, and job opportunities, while tackling climate change and environmental protection. While the SDGs are not legally binding, governments are expected to take ownership and establish national frameworks for the achievement of the 17 Goals." (UN, 2016)

I note that the development discourse is recognizable from the Brundtland Report and previous UN Commissions charged with addressing the vexing problem between development and the environment. The insistence on "building economic growth in all countries" makes me wonder if the unequal exchange, and by default lack of collaboration, criticized by the dependency theorists in the 1970s was made in vain? What about the obvious lack of intergenerational equity as professed by the Brundtland Commission and not the least a 15 year UN horizon to solve matters against the Anthropocene as the new human induced age (Lewis & Maslin, 2015)? According to Carrington (2016) Anthropocene manifestations include: accelerated loss of biodiversity, plant and animal extinction rates; climate warming CO_2 increasing the atmosphere at the fastest rate in 66 million years; plastic pollution and concentration of plastics that likely will be identifiable in fossil records in the future; double levels of nitrogen and phosphorous in our soils due to fertiliser use; and a permanent layer of airborne particulates in sediment and glacial ice such as black carbon from burning of fossil fuels!

These problems and challenges confront the current and new generation of tourism scholars and practitioners (Higham & Miller, 2017). I am afraid that if growth and human progress are limited to traditional measures such as gross domestic products (GDP), visitor arrivals in tourism, actions allocated to "governments to take ownership" and to create "partnerships to achieve the SDGs" (UN, 2016), the scale and urgency of transformations will not be met. SDG partnerships simply signify cooperation and concerted management efforts, and sustainability is once again reduced to an achievable, static outcome (by 2030), whether for cities, communities, the oceans, or the planet. In order to fully embrace complexity and nuanced understandings of the SDGs as wicked problems at multiple, interrelated scales, the ambitions of the laudable SDGs beacon response beyond conventional solutions, such as "governance and national leadership" (Higham & Miller, 2017: 3).

The global problems addressed by the SDGs are 'wicked', or 'fuzzy' in as much as there is no one resolution to be found. Collaboration for intentional change with others will be needed to gain advantages in an unpredictable world. Inspiration may be gleaned from Boston (2017, in Higham & Miller, 2017: 3) who calls for adoption of a holistic system approach based on new measures. These may include collective, intergenerational well-being, social cohesion and equity, and the recognition of biophysical limits. I propose that these must be met by new collaborative approaches by stewards who care beyond selfish interests, and who will embrace complexity and chaos in collaborative efforts for resilient action. Collaboration must be broadened beyond traditional domains and sectors *with* civic society, which has hitherto been missing in the current literature on collaborative dimensions in tourism and sustainability research (Liburd, 2013). It is *people* who care for each other, nature and planet Earth – or not!

Conclusion

This chapter sets out to add three aspects to the current literature and appreciative understanding of the importance of collaboration for sustainable tourism development, in addition to providing conceptual framing for the contributions of this volume. I first emphasised that the concept of collaboration suggests that the creation of joint outcomes could not be generated by a single organisation or individual, and that collaboration is not a neutral undertaking. Easily diluted in the abbreviated use of co-operation, co-creation, co-ordination, etc., collaboration implicates interests and power. Second, I exposed how development has been subjected to cooperation between unequal partners in the so-called First and Third Worlds since World War II. The concept of sustainable development and its application to tourism has suffered from static conceptualizations that sought to achieve sustainability despite its inherent dynamics. Third, I questioned whether sustainable tourism development is enough, and pointed to the role of ethics in tourism and collaboration. Collaboration hinges on a virtuous aspect of collaboration, which must be other-regarding. This implies that one cannot expect oneself to be able to flourish without reciprocity and responsibility, which resonates well with the concept of stewardship. Duly, I also criticised the UN *2030 Agenda for Sustainable Development* for reverting to static notions of achieving sustainability through economic growth everywhere, by evoking (historically unequal) relations of cooperation and partnerships.

> *"Growth has delivered its benefits, at best, unequally. A fifth of the world's population earns just 2 per cent of global income. The richest 20 per cent by contrast earn 74 per cent of the world's income. [...] Such disparities are unacceptable from a humanitarian point of view"*. (Jackson, 2009: 5)

Mindful of Anthropocene manifestations as wicked problems where there is no one resolution to be found, the Anthropocene epoch is adversely addressed by incremental innovations that extend what it currently is, which may easily lead to blind reproduction. Sustainable tourism development is a collaborative space to engage in future world-making where radical, other-regarding innovations should be envisaged. Only when the fundamental interdependence between human behaviour, regions and socio-economic activities are acknowledged, is tourism a potential contributor to the broader societal aims of sustainable development. Collaboration for sustainable tourism development gives way for new imaginations and conceptualisations of more desirable futures, which should be explored across numerous dimensions. I have proposed to put emphasis on engaging the latent potentials *with* civic society and *with* stewards who care beyond selfish interests to embrace complexity and chaos in collaborative efforts for resilient action over time.

References

Airey, D. W. (2008) *Tourism education: Life begins at 40.* Paper. School of Management, University of Surrey. Retrieved on February 14, 2018 from http://epubs.surrey.ac.uk/1136/1/fulltext.pdf

Amin, S., (1976). *Unequal Development: an essay on the social formation s of peripheral capitalism.* New York: Monthly Review Press.

Anandarajan, A. & Anandarajan, M. (2010) *e-Research Collaboration.* Springer-Verlag Berlin Heidelberg.

Banal-Estanol, A., Jofre-Bonet, M. & Meissner, C. (2010) *The Impact of Industry Collaboration on Research: Evidence from Engineering Academics in the UK.* Available URL http://www.econ.upf.edu/docs/papers/downloads/1190.pdf Accessed on April 4, 2011.

Becken, S. (2016). Evidence of a low-carbon tourism paradigm? *Journal of Sustainable Tourism.* DOI 10.1080/09669582.2016.1251446

Benkler, Y. (2006). *The Wealth of Networks. How Social Production Transforms Markets and Freedom.* New Haven and London: Yale University Press.

Bernstein, R., Buse, K. & Bilimoira, D. (2016). Revisiting agency and stewardship theories. *Nonprofit Management & Leadership,* **26**(4), 489-498.

Boisot, M. (1998) *Knowledge Assets: Securing competitive advantage in the information economy.* Oxford: Oxford University Press.

Bramwell (2007) Opening up new spaces in the sustainable tourism debate. *Tourism Recreation Research,* **32**(1), 1-9.

Bramwell, B. (2015). Theoretical activity in sustainable tourism research. *Annals of Tourism Research,* **54**, 204-218.

Bramwell, B. & Lane, B. (1993). Sustainable tourism: an evolving global approach. *Journal of Sustainable Tourism,* **1**, 1-5.

Bramwell, B. & Lane, B. (2011). Critical research on the governance of tourism and sustainability *Journal of Sustainable Tourism,* **19** (4&5) 411-421.

Bramwell, B. & Lane, B. (2013). Getting from here to there: Systems change, behaviour change and sustainable tourism. *Journal of Sustainable Tourism* **21**(1), 1-4.

Bricker, K., Black, R. & Cottrell, S. (Eds.) (2013). *Sustainable Tourism & The Millennium Development Goals. Effecting Positive Change.* Burlington, MA: Jones & Barlett Learning.

Britton, S. (1982) .The political economy in the Third World, *Annals of Tourism Research,* **9**, 331-358.

Budeanu, A., Miller, G., Moscardo, G. & Ooi, C.S. (2016). Sustainable tourism, progress, challenges and opportunities: an introduction. *Journal of Cleaner Production,* **111**, 285-294.

Butler, R.W. (1980). The concept of a tourism area cycle of evolution: implications for the management of resources, *Canadian Geographer,* **25**, 5-12.

Butler, R.W. (1998). Sustainable tourism – looking backwards in order to progress? In C.M. Hall and A. Lew (Eds.), *Sustainable Tourism: A Geographical Perspective,* New York: Addison Wesley Longman, 25-34.

Butler, R.W. (1999). Problems and Issues of Integrating Tourism Development. In: Pearce, D.G. and Butler, R.W. (Eds.) *Contemporary Issues in Tourism Development.* London: Routledge, 65-80.

Carrington, D. (2016) The Anthropocene Epoch: Scientists declare dawn of human-influenced age. *The Guardian Online.* Retrieved February 8, 2018 from https://www.theguardian.com/environment/2016/aug/29/declare-anthropocene-epochexperts-urge-geological-congress-human-impact-earth

Carson, R. (1962) *Silent Spring,* Greenwich: Fawcett.

Cater, E. & Goodall, B. (1997). Must tourism destroy its resource base? In: L. France (Ed.) *The Earthscan Reader in Sustainable Tourism.* London: Earthscan.

Cater, E. & Lowman, G. (Eds.) (1994). *Ecotourism: A sustainable option?* Chichester: John Wiley & Sons.

Cohen, E. (1978). The impact of tourism on the physical environment, *Annals of Tourism Research,* **5**, 215-237.

Cohen, E. (2002). Authenticity, equity and sustainability in tourism, *Journal of Sustainable Tourism,* **10**(4), 267-276.

Cohen S.A., Higham, J.E.S. & Cavaliere, C.T. (2011). Binge flying. Behavioural addiction and climate change. *Annals of Tourism Research,* **38**(3), 1070–1089.

Cooksey, R. (2001). What is complexity science? A contextually grounded tapestry of system dynamism, paradigm diversity, theoretical eclecticism, and organizational learning. *Emergence,* **3**(1), 77-103.

Deery, M., Jago, L., & Fredline, L. (2012). Rethinking social impacts of tourism research: A new research agenda. *Tourism Management,* **33**(1), 64–73.

de Kadt, E. (Ed.) (1979) *Tourism – Passport to Development? Perspectives on the Social and Cultural Effects of Tourism in the Developing Countries,* Oxford: Oxford University Press.

Donaldson, L. & Davis, J.H. (1991). Stewardship theory or agency theory: CEO governance and shareholder returns. *Australian Journal of Management,* **16**(1), 49-65.

Dwyer, L. & Sheldon, P. (2005). Introduction: sustainability and mass destinations: challenges and possibilities, *Tourism Review International,* **9**, 1-7.

Dredge, D. & Jamal, T. (2013). Mobilities on the Gold Coast, Australia: implications for destination governance and sustainable tourism. *Journal of Sustainable Tourism,* **21**(4), 557-579.

Echtner, C.M. & Jamal, T.B. (1997). The disciplinary dilemma of tourism studies. *Annals of Tourism Research,* **24**(4), 868-883.

Emmanuel, A. (1972) *L'échange inégal: Essai sur les antagonismes dans les rapports économiques internationaux; Préface et "remarques théoriques" de Charles Bettelheim.* Paris: Maspero.

Escobar, A. (1995) *Encountering Development. The Making and Unmaking of the Third World.* Princeton NJ: Princeton University Press.

Fennell, D. (2018). *Tourism Ethics* 2nd edition. Bristol: Channel View Publications.

Figueroa, E. & McCaulay, D. (2009). *Jamaica for Sale* DVD Video, Vagabond Media, Jamaica Environment Trust.

Florida, R. & Cohen, W.M. (1999) Engine or Infrastructure? The University Role in Economic Development. In Branscomb, L.M., Kodama, F., and Florida, R. (Eds.) *Industrializing Knowledge: University–Industry Linkages in Japan and the United States.* MIT Press, London: 589–610.

Foucault, M. (1980). *Power/Knowledge: Selected Interviews and Other Writings 1972–77.* Brighton: Harvester Press.

Frank, A.G. (1967) *Sociology of Development and Underdevelopment of Sociology,* Stockholm: Zenit.

Freeman, E.R., Wicks, A.C. & Pamar, B. (2004). Stakeholder theory and "the corporate objective revisited". *Organization Science,* **15**(3), 364-369.

Gill, A. & Williams, P.W. (2014). Mindful deviation in creating a governance path towards sustainability in resort destinations. *Tourism Geographies,* **16**(4), 546-562

Gössling, S., Hall, C. M., Ekström, F., Engeset, A.B. & Aall, C. (2012). Transition management: a tool for implementing sustainable tourism scenarios? *Journal of Sustainable Tourism,* **20**(6), 899-916.

Gunderson, L.H., Holling, C.S., Pritchard, L. & Peterson, G.D. (2005). Resilience of large-scale resource systems. In: L.H. Gunderson and L. Pritchard, Jr. (Eds.), *Resilience and the Behaviour of Large-Scale Systems,* Washington DC: Scope 60. Island Press, 3-18.

Habermas, J. (1987) *The Philosophical Discourse of Modernity,* Cambridge: Polity Press.

Hall, C. M. (2011a) Publish and perish? Bibliometric analysis, journal ranking and the assessment of research quality. *Tourism Management,* **32**, 16–27.

Hall, C.M. (2011b). A typology of governance and its implications for tourism policy analysis. *Journal of Sustainable Tourism,* **19**(4-5), 437-457.

Hall, C. M. & Butler, R.W. (1995). In search of common ground: reflections on sustainability, complexity and process in the tourism system – a discussion between C. Michael Hall and Richard W. Butler, *Journal of Sustainable Tourism,* **3**(2), 99-105.

Hall, C.M. & Lew, A. (1998) *Sustainable Tourism: A Geographical Perspective,* New York: Addison Wesley Longman.

Hardin, G. (1968). Tragedy of the Commons, *Science,.* 162, 1243-1248.

Heape, C. & Liburd, J.(2018). Collaborative learning for sustainable tourism development. In J.Liburd and D. Edwards (Eds.) *Collaboration for Sustainable Tourism Development.* Oxford: Goodfellow Publishers.

Heidegger, M. ([1927] 1998) *Being and Time.* Oxford: Blackwell.

Higham, J. & Miller, G. (2017). Transforming societies and transforming societies: sustainable tourism in times of change. *Journal of Sustainable Tourism* DOI:10.1080/0966 9582.2018.1407519.

Hjalager, A.-M. (1997). Innovation patterns in sustainable tourism – an analytical typology. *Tourism Management,* **18**(1), 35–41.

Hjalager, A-M. (2010a). A review of innovation research in tourism. *Tourism Management,* **31**(1), 1-12.

Hjalager, A-M. (2010b) Supplier-driven innovations for sustainable tourism In: J. Liburd and D. Edwards (eds) *Understanding the Sustainable Development of Tourism.* Oxford: Goodfellow Publishers: 148-162.

Hjalager, A-M. (2018). Suppliers as key collaborators for sustainable tourism. In J. Liburd and D. Edwards (Eds.) *Collaboration for Sustainable Tourism Development*. Oxford: Goodfellow Publishers.

Holden, A. (2005). Achieving a sustainable relationship between common pool resources and tourism: The role of environmental ethics. *Journal of Sustainable Tourism*, **13**(4), 339-352.

Holling, C.S. (1986). The resilience of terrestrial ecosystems: local surprise and global change. In: Clark, W.C. and Munn, R.E. (eds) *Sustainable Development of the Biosphere, International Institute for Applied Systems Analysis*. Cambridge University Press, Cambridge, 292-317.

Hughes, C. (1995). The cultural construction of tourism, *Tourism Management*, **16**(1), 49-59.

Hughes, K. & Moscardo, G. (2016). United we stand, divided we fall: Strategies for engaging customers in Corporate Responsibility Programs. *Conference proceedings BEST EN Think Tank XVI Corporate Responsibility in Tourism – Standards Practices and Policies*. www.besteducationnetwork.org/Outstanding_Paper_Award. Accessed Aug 1, 2017.

Hunter, C. (1995). On the need to re-conceptualize sustainable tourism development, *Journal of Sustainable Tourism*, **3**, 155-165.

Hunter, C. (1997). Sustainable tourism as an adaptive paradigm *Annals of Tourism Research*, **24**, 850-867.

Huxham, C. (1993). Pursuing collaborative advantage. *Journal of the Operational Research Society*, **44**(6), 599-611.

Huxham, C. (Ed.). (1996). *Creating Collaborative Advantage*. Sage.

Jackson, T. (2009). *Prosperity Without Growth*. London: Earthscan.

Jafari, J. (1989). Structure of tourism. In *Tourism Marketing and Management Handbook*, S.F. Witt and Lou Moutinho, eds., pp. 437-442. London: Prentice Hall.

Jafari, J. (1990). Research and scholarship: the basis of tourism education. *Journal of Tourism Studies*, **1**(1), 33-41.

Jamal, T.B. & Everett, J. (2007). Resisting rationalisation in the natural and academic lifeworld: critical tourism research or hermeneutic charity? In: Ateljevic, I., Pritchard, A & Morgan, N.: *The Critical Turn in Tourism Studies: Innovative Research Methodologies*. Amsterdam: Elsevier Ltd., 57-76.

Jamal, T. & Menzel, C. (2009). Good actions in tourism. In: J. Tribe (Ed.) *Philosophical Issues in Tourism*. Bristol: Channel View Publications: 227-243.

Larrère, C. (2008). Scientific models for the protection of nature, pp. 28-31. In: Garnier, L. (Ed.) *Man and nature-making the relationship last*. Biosphere Reserves – Technical Notes 3. UNESCO, Paris.

Lewis, S.L. & Maslin, M.A. (2015). Defining the Anthropocene. *Nature*, **519**, 171–180.

Liburd, J. (2013). *Towards the Collaborative University. Lessons from Tourism Education and Research*. Odense: Print & Sign.

Liburd, J. (2010). Sustainable tourism development, In: J. Liburd and D. Edwards (Eds.) *Understanding the Sustainable Development of Tourism* pp. 1-18. Oxford: Goodfellow Publishers.

Liburd, J. & Becken, S. (2017). Values in nature conservation, tourism and UNESCO World Heritage Site stewardship. *Journal of Sustainable Tourism* DOI:10.1080/09669582.2017.1293067

Liburd, J. , Carlsen, J. & Edwards, D. (Eds.) (2013). *Networks for Innovation in Sustainable Tourism. Case studies and cross-analysis.* Melbourne: Tilde University Press.

Lowe, P. and Phillipson, J. (2009). Barriers to research collaboration across disciplines: scientific paradigms and institutional practices. *Environment and Planning,* **41,** 1171-1184.

Malanson, J.P. (1999). Considering complexity, *Annals of the Association of American Geographers,*. 89, 746-753.

Mattessich, P. W., Murray-Close, M., & Monsey, B. R. (2001) *Collaboration: What makes it work,* 2nd edition. St Paul, MN: Amherst H. Wilder Foundation.

McDonald, J.R., (2009). Complexity science: an alternative world view for understanding sustainable tourism development. Journal of Sustainable Tourism, **17,** 455–471.

McElroy, J.L. & de Albuquerque, K. (1996). Sustainable alternatives to insular mass tourism: recent theory and practice. In: Briguglio, L., Archer, B., Jafari, J. And Wall, G. (Eds.) *Sustainable Tourism in Islands and Small States: Issues and Policies.* Pinter, London, 47-60.

McKercher, B. (1999). A chaos approach to tourism. *Tourism Management,* **20,** 425-434.

Mies, M. (1997). Do we need a new moral economy? *Canadian Women Studies,* **17**(2), 12-20.

Miller, G. & Twining-Ward, L. (2005) *Monitoring for a Sustainable Tourism Transition: The Challenge of Developing and Using Indicators,* Wallingford: CABI Publishing.

Moscado, G. (2008). Sustainable tourism innovation: challenging basic assumptions, *Tourism and Hospitality Research,* **8**(1), 4-13.

Moscado, G. & Pearce, P.L. (1999). Understanding ethnic tourists, *Annals of Tourism Research,* **26**(2), 416-434.

Morton, T. (2010). *The Ecological Thought.* Cambridge: Harvard University Press.

Mowforth, A. and Munt, I. (1998) *Tourism and Sustainability: New Tourism in the Third World,* London: Routledge.

Muldoon, M. (2002). *On Ricoeur.* Wadsworth philosophers series. Belmont, CA Wadsworth.

Neubaum, D.O. (2013). Stewardship Theory, pp 768-769. In: E. Kessler (Ed.) *Encyclopaedia of Management Theory.* Thousand Oaks, CA, Sage.

Oyserman, D. (2001). Values: Psychological perspectives. In: N. J. Smelser, J. Wright & B. Baltes (Eds.) *International Encyclopaedia of the Social and Behavioural Sciences.* Oxford: Pergammon.

Patullo, P. (1996) *Last Resorts: The Cost of Tourism in the Caribbean,* London: Cassell.

Plog, S. (1974). Why destination areas rise and fall in popularity, *Cornell Hotel and Administration Quarterly,* **14,** 55-58.

Poon, A. (1993). *Tourism, Technology and Competitive Strategies,* Wallingford, CABI International.

Pritchard, A. & Morgan, N. (2007). De-centring tourism's intellectual universe, or traversing the dialogue between change and tradition. In I. Ateljevic, A. Pritchard and N. Morgan (Eds.) *The Critical Turn in Tourism Studies: Innovative Research Methodologies.* Amsterdam: Elsevier: 11-28.

Rawls, J.B. (1971) *A Theory of Justice,* Cambridge, Mass: Belknap Press.

Research Councils UK (2017). What is impact? Retrieved on February 14, 2018 from http://www.esrc.ac.uk/research/impact-toolkit/what-is-impact/

Ricoeur, P. (1992) *Oneself as Another.* (K. Blamey Transl.) Chicago: University of Chicago Press.

Rostow, W.W. (1952). *The Process of Economic Growth,* New York: W.W. Norton.

Rothman, H. K. (1998) *The Greening of a Nation: Environmentalism in the United States Since 1945,* Fort Worth: Harcourt Brace College Publishers.

Sachs, A. (1995). *Eco-justice: Linking Human Rights and the Environment.* Washington DC: World Watch Paper 127.

Schellhorn, M. (2010) Development for whom? Social justice and the business of ecotourism. *Journal of Sustainable Tourism,* **18**(1): 115–135.

Scott, D. & Becken, S. (2010). Adapting to climate change and climate policy: progress, problems and potentials. *Journal of Sustainable Tourism,* **18**(3), 283–295.

Smith, V.L. (ed.) (1977) *Hosts and Guests. The Anthropology of Tourism,* Philadelphia PA: University of Pennsylvania Press.

Smith, V.L. (ed.) (1989) *Hosts and Guests: The Anthropology of Tourism,* Philadelphia PA: University of Pennsylvania Press.

Strathern, M. (1996) Cutting the Network. *The Journal of the Royal Anthropological Institute,.* 2(3), 517-535.

Subramanyam, K. (1983) Bibliometric studies of research collaboration: A review. *Journal of Information Science,.* 6(1), 33–38.

Swarbrooke, J. (1999). *Sustainable Tourism Management.* Wallingford: CABI Publishing.

Theobald, W.F. (Ed.) (2005). *Global Tourism,* Burlington, MA: Elsevier Butterworth Heinemann.

Tribe, J. (2006). The truth about tourism. *Annals of Tourism Research,* **33**, 360–381.

Tribe, J. & Liburd, J. (2016). The tourism knowledge system. *Annals of Tourism Research,* **57**, 44–61.

Truman, H.S. (1949) *Public Papers of the Presidents of the United States: Harry S. Truman,* Washington DC: U.S. Government Printing Office.

Turner, L. and Ash, J. (1975). *The Golden Hordes: International Tourism and the Pleasure Periphery,* London: Constable and Co.

United Nations Environment Programme (1972). *Report on the United Nations Conference on the Human Environment,* Retrieved on 2 November 2009 from http://www.unep.org/Documents.Multilingual/Default.asp?documentID=97.

United Nations (2016). 2030 Sustainable Development Agenda. Retrieved on February 8, 2018 from: http://www.un.org/sustainabledevelopment/development-agenda/

Wallerstin, I. (1974). *The Modern World System,.* 1&2, New York: Academic Press.

Walsh, L. & Kahn, P. (Eds.) (2010). *Collaborative Working in Higher Education. The Social Academy*. New York and London: Routledge.

Weaver, D. (2009). Reflections on sustainable tourism and paradigm change. In: S. Gössling, M. Hall & D. Weaver (Eds.) *Sustainable Tourism Futures. Perspectives on Systems, restructuring and innovations*. New York: Routledge, pp. 33-40.

Wheeller, B. (1993) Sustaining the ego. *Journal of Sustainable Tourism*, **12**, 121-129.

Williams, A. (2013). Mobilities and Sustainable Tourism: Path-creating or path-depending relationships? *Journal of Sustainable Tourism,* **21**(4), 511-531.

World Commission of the Environment and Development (1987). *Our Common Future,* Oxford: Oxford University Press.

World Travel and Tourism Council, World Tourism Organisation and the Earth Council (1997). *Agenda 21 for the Travel and Tourism Industry: Towards Environmentally Sustainable Development,* Madrid: WTO.

World Tourism Organization (1998). *Guide for Local Authorities on Developing Sustainable Tourism,* Madrid: WTO.

Xin, S, Tribe, J. & Chambers, D. (2013). Conceptual research in tourism. *Annals of Tourism Research*, 41, 66-88.

Co-branding and Strategic Communication

Bodil Stilling Blichfeldt

By means of collaboration, the sum of the work becomes more than its individual parts (Liburd, 2013). This also goes for communication about sustainable tourism development, where meanings created on the basis of the sum of communication exceed the meanings introduced by individual communicators' messages. This chapter introduces the notion of sustainable tourism development communication and discourses as complex and dynamic meaning-making processes that transcend what individual actors bring to the conversation, thus emphasizing such discourses as informed and co-constructed by the plethora of actors that communicate about this issue. Hereby, communication becomes more than a matter of *giving* or *sending* information; it becomes an issue of *sharing* information and by doing so, creating and advancing knowledge through collaborative meaning-making processes.

The chapter first introduces and criticizes traditional communication models, paving the way for understanding branding and communication of sustainable tourism development as an issue far more complex than that of converting sustainable tourism development branding and communication strategies to flashy ads and catchy taglines. Thereafter, interactive branding and communication models are introduced to acknowledge that sustainable tourism development is not only a matter of what is 'done', but also a matter of what is 'said' by different actors. This leads to discussions of different, sometimes opposing, versions of destinations as well as of tourists' active participation in constructing knowledge on sustainable tourism development and destinations. The chapter ends with reflections on the wider implications for sustainable tourism development of seeing branding and communication not as something 'done' by someone to someone, but as collaborative meaning making processes.

Many definitions of communication ignore the interactive and collaborative nature of communication and emphasize the *sending* of messages. The popular *transmission model of communication* conceptualizes communication as one-directional transmission of messages and assumes that communication is about the transmission of information, ideas, attitudes, emotions etc. from one person, group or organization to others (Theodorson & Theodorson, 1969). The classical Shannon and Weaver (1949) model emphasizes the sender's transmission of messages through a channel and reduces other elements to either 'noise' or 'feedback' from receivers. At its core, the transmission model of communication is thus concerned with how 'we' get 'our information' passed on to largely passive recipients. This take on communication is highly relevant insofar we wish to understand what one actor brings to a conversation. But this traditional take on communication under-prioritizes the critical role of interactivity in the communication process; predominantly because it casts one actor as an active sender and reduces the performances of other actor(s) to that of listening. Bauer (1964:319) points to understandings of advertising (and branding, I propose) based on the transmission model to be imbued with notions of "the exploitation of man by man" where "the communication does something to the audience, while to the communicator is generally attributed considerable latitude and power to do what he pleases to the audience".

The notions of senders as powerful and effectively 'doing something' to receivers, and of receivers as subdued to whatever senders inflict on them, are imbued with ideas of communication as asymmetrical in terms of power, impact and activity levels. Bauer's (1964) criticism of the transmission model and its underlying notion of senders 'doing something' to largely passive recipients can also be extended to classical understandings of branding. Traditionally, branding was seen as images marketers 'put' into consumers' minds by means of advertising and promotion. However, according to associative network memory theory, and as applied by Keller (1993) and Aaker (1991), brands are represented in consumers' minds as sets of nodes and links that form the associations that give meaning to a brand. Accordingly, brand value (or equity) is not something that marketers 'make' as brand values and meanings are actively formed by, and reside in the minds of individuals (Keller, 1993). The following explores branding and strategic communication as grounded in co-creation and interaction.

Interactive and collaborative communication

In contrast to the transmission model of communication, the *interactive model of communication* (Blumer, 1969) is based on the fundamental assumption that communication involves not only *exchange*, but also *creation* of meaning. Communication hereby becomes a symbiotic process through which messages and meanings are co-created, constructed, re-constructed, de-constructed and often transformed as dialogues between actors inform both parties and lead to more advanced understandings. At its core, the interactive model of communication thus focuses on how shared understandings, meanings, realities and cultures evolve as actors engage in, shape and construct communication, hereby portraying communication as a more symmetrical process where it becomes less relevant which party initiated the communication process (i.e. by being the 'original sender' or the 'marketer') and far more relevant how communication evolves and creates new, possibly more informed, meanings about issues such as sustainable tourism development.

Although the transmission model of communication has been highly influential, today, the dominant discourse is that communication is not simply a matter of one-way transmission of intended (and consequently rather 'fixed' and static) meanings, but a matter of interactive communication between agents. Therefore, contemporary research (e.g. Blichfeldt & Smed, 2015; Gyimothy, 2013; Rosengren, 2000) first and foremost points to communication as multi-directional processes of collaborative meaning-making that are interactive and participatory. Complexities increase dramatically when communication is defined as interactive and as 'new' media make it easier for actors to join online conversations, social media may fundamentally change the asymmetrical power relationships that have traditionally characterized mass communication. Traditional theories of mass communication and branding originate from a time and context where media institutions (such as radio and television networks) were the only actors with the capacity to disseminate messages and content to large (mass) audiences. Furthermore, these traditional media institutions used channels that allowed for information to flow in only one direction. However, with the development of the Internet, "individuals and organizations of only modest means become content selectors and editors in their own right. Opportunities for self-expression once denied by the old media are celebrated by the new media" (Chaffee & Metzger, 2001:370). In practice, this means that communication through 'the new media' potentially redistributes power from 'elite' senders to users and as the number of users that may join on-line conversations is large, "Internet content is literally unbound" (Chaffee & Metzger, 2001:372). The following vignette exemplifies how communication through new media may fundamentally change messages and content as viewers comment on, and add new meanings to a video launched by a travel agency.

Vignette 1: Do it for Denmark or Do it to Denmark?

In 2014, the Danish travel agency Spies launched the video 'Do it for Denmark' (available at: http://doitfordenmark.parseapp.com/), aiming to increase Danish customers' awareness of Spies' city break holidays. The video claims that Spies is on a mission to 'save the future of Denmark with romance'. Falling birth rates and an aging population are introduced as problems, which the Danish government has not been able to solve. With the video, Spies offers a solution as people are more likely to have sex (and consequently 'make babies') when they are on holiday. The video 'went viral' and soon featured more than 10 million viewings on Youtube (a number almost twice the size of the entire Danish population).

On the basis of a content analysis of 780 comments on the video, Blichfeldt and Smed (2015) found that what happens as people comment on the video is not simply that Spies' original message is spread. Instead they identify six different discourses that are introduced in the commentary. These range from the theme 'This is fun' (144 comments), 'Sexism' and 'Antifeminism' (196 comments), 'Nationalism' and 'Racism' (231 comments) and 15 comments that present strong and negative attitudes towards Denmark on the basis of mass media coverage of euthanization of animals in Danish Zoos and legality of animal brothels in Denmark. On the basis of the analysis of the 780 comments, Blichfeldt and Smed (2015:299) conclude that online commentators bring a welter of associations (from anti-feminism, sexism, nationalism and racism to a giraffe killing and animal sex) into the online communication, hereby suggesting that "viral processes create unforeseeable associations and meanings that may have little to do with the original message and meanings – in the present case changing meanings from 'do it for Denmark' to 'do it to Denmark'".

Vignette 1 exemplifies how opportunities for self-expression are extensively used in on-line contexts, thus unbounding content and making it go beyond the narrative and discourses introduced by the original sender. Spies' 'Do it for Denmark' video qualifies as an example of strategic communication as it is communication infused with an agenda (in the Spies' case, spurring attention, interest, desire and/or action for the Spies' brand, its city break holidays and urging viewers to engage in certain practices (whether it is to go on a city break holiday or 'to make babies')). However, Spies is not the only actor communicating on the basis of the video and Blichfeldt and Smed's (2015) analysis shows how other actors contribute with messages beyond those initially introduced by Spies, hereby pointing to the potential of 'everybody' to actively contribute to the content of the 'Do it for Denmark' storyline. But if everybody can join the conversation, a critical question is what the difference between *communication* and *strategic communication* is. Communication is often defined as strategic when it involves *deliberate* spread of information, ideas, principles, doctrines etc. and it is a concept almost exclusively used when discussing communication within, between and about organizations and institutions, such as governments, national agencies, businesses, non-profit organizations etc. However, this does not mean that only organizations engage in strategic communication. On the contrary, all communicators who *deliberately spread* information, values, ideas, principles, doctrines etc. inherently engage in strategic communication and therefore, this chapter tries to cover both (a) strategic communication in the form of branding and communication initiated by organizations and (hopefully) consistent with those organizations' goals, values and strategies and (b) communicators that are not traditionally enacted as doing strategic communication (particularly tourists as well as local residents and communities).

The tendency to define strategic communication as only covering communication initiated by organizations is deeply anchored in the transmission model of communication. Adopting a more interactive view on communication, it would however be more correct to define strategic communication as communication that is strategic in that it is *not* random, unintentional or done without having the sender's mission, vision or fundamental values in mind. Consequently, and in an interactive perspective, strategic communication is multi-directional communication processes in which organizations engage in order to create meanings *together with* other actors while letting the organization's strategic goals, mission and brand values consistently inform the organization's contributions to communicative meaning-making processes. Hereby, branding becomes a term that points to organizations' communication as informed by, but not dictated by, managerial decisions, where organizations not only present and promote themselves, but also interact with other actors while intentionally trying to communicate meanings that align with organizational strategies, goals, values and 'reasons-to-be'. In an interactive communication perspective, branding and strategic communication are consequently *not* simply a matter of defining organizational goals and brand values and transforming such goals and values to branding and communication strategies and messages transmitted to passive recipients. On the contrary, contemporary branding and strategic communication are about understanding how organizations interact with other actors (e.g. customers, employees, suppliers, investors, government agencies, mass media and society at large) and how they present themselves as social actors that engage in meaning-making processes with these other actors. In contemporary society the successful brands are those that are best at engaging in interactive communication whereas those that enact communication and branding as making flashy or catchy advertising that triggers viral marketing processes may have misunderstood the kind of relationships consumers wish to form with brands.

Vignette 2: Brands that thrive

"People are connecting with brands in an increasingly two-way relationship. Brands that thrive are no longer simply trying to publicise themselves in a monolithic way, they are inviting consumers to join them in creating meaning and being a part of the process".

[Hodder, 2002:16]

Due to the immerse importance of co-creation of communication and brands, tourism researchers have taken a genuine interest in defining who it is that actively co-creates brands and meanings, and many researchers have embraced the notion of stakeholders in order to address this question (e.g. Allen et al., 1993; Davis & Morais, 2004; Markwick, 2000; Ryan, 2002; Robson & Robson, 1996; Sautter & Leisen, 1999). Tourism is a conglomerate product consisting of a number of distinctive products, services and experiences that are grouped together. The grouping of these products and services might be done by tourism suppliers; such as it is the case when tourists take a packaged tour and spend the entire holiday at a resort that caters to all of these tourists' needs and wants. But mostly, the tourist is responsible for the grouping of products and services into an overall 'holiday package', especially when doing independent travel, making their own travel and accommodation arrangements *en route* and/or choosing between different peak and supporting products, services and experiences *in situ*.

As products, services and experiences are grouped together, so are the brands behind (or beyond) these entities. In the branding literature, the concepts of co-branding, joint branding and brand alliances have been used to describe situations, in which two or more brands are linked together. However, these concepts are traditionally used to describe situations, where two or more brands (or more correctly, the marketers behind these brands) strategically collaborate to reach certain objectives. Park et al. (1996) argue that co-branding is the *intended* pairing of two or more brands, both in the form of physical product integration and in the form of, for example, joint promotion or joint advertising. This means that albeit the grouping of brands may take many different forms, the co-branding literature emphasizes *intended linking* of brands, thus ignoring all the situations where co-branding is not intended. However, as Swait et al. (1993) remind us, brands are cues for customers and represent images formed on the basis of customers' past experiences with the brand and/or information they have obtained on the brand, and consequently, brand equity consists of constellations of associations in consumers' minds triggered by brand names. Applying the notion of co-branding to tourism, where the conglomerate product is often the result of tourists' grouping of brands, co-branding becomes a matter of destination, and tourism brands being linked, grouped and co-constructed (as well as de- and re-constructed) actively by individuals on the basis of communication from many different actors. Therefore, the identification of actors that communicate about touristic brands becomes a critical element of strategic communication in touristic contexts and the notion of stakeholders can aid us in the quest to identify these actors.

Stakeholders as brand co-constructors

Traditionally, a stakeholder is defined as "any group or individual who is affected by the achievement of the organization's objectives" (Freeman, 1984:46). Tailoring this definition to the special characteristics of the tourism industry, tourism stakeholders can be defined as any groups or individuals who are affected by tourism (not a specific organization's objectives) in a specific area (whether this is a village, a city, an island, a national park, a region, a country etc.). However, this means that stakeholders are not only actors with a commercial interest in tourism, but also actors with no direct commercial interests in tourism, who are nevertheless affected by tourism – such as residents, local communities, cultural heritage sites or nature.

Many different ways of identifying and listing tourism stakeholders have been suggested, but which stakeholders are included in, or excluded from, these lists depend on the more specific objectives behind each list. However, one thing that most lists of tourism stakeholders have in common is that they include groups of central stakeholders in the form of the private sector (including tourism service providers, tour operators, tourism-related businesses and trade associations); the public sector (national government institutions as well as regional and local authorities); civil society (e.g. NGOs); citizens (often referred to as host communities); and consumers (often referred to as tourists, but also including people not included in the official UNWTO definition of tourists, such as one-day nearcationing tourists). The fact that so many different actors have 'a stake' in not only promoting or branding, but also in using, working with, doing good for, living in and taking a keen interest in destinations, means that branding and strategic communication become rather complex in a tourism context, particularly as the number of actors who strategically communicate about a destination is relatively high. Furthermore, as exemplified by vignette 3, different actors might communicate about a specific destination/place in very different ways and may emphasize very different aspects, or versions, of the destination/place in question.

Vignette 3: CPH – One place (?) and many voices

"Copenhagen is not only the coolest kid on the Nordic block, but also gets constantly ranked as the happiest city in the world. Ask a dozen locals why and they would probably all zone in on the hygge which generally means coziness, but encompasses far more." [Lonely Planet]

"I've lived in Copenhagen for a while now, and I must say that spending every day coping with the endless tide of bearded, elitist, single-speed bikers inhabiting the most pretentious village in the world kind of makes Copenhagen seem like a terrible provincial shit hole." [Vice.com]

"There are way more people than apartments in Copenhagen. That's why it becomes almost a privilege to pay a rent so high it would make your grandma scratch out her eyes for a room in a concrete block in the outskirts of town." [cbslife]

"Copenhagen – the first carbon neutral capital in the world." [DenmarkDK – the official website of Denmark]

"The EU commission could be preparing legal action to force the government to finally address Copenhagen's air pollution." [The Local]

"If you have the drive, a good idea or an ambition to be an entrepreneur, Copenhagen is a good place to start a business." [The city of Copenhagen website]

"The 2011 GEM report marks Denmark as having the second lowest entrepreneurial activity of any country in the developed world." [Articstartup.com]

"Copenhagen is in general a safe city to visit." [visitcopenhagen]

"Police kill Copenhagen gunman suspected of terror attacks." [The National]

"Copenhagen is a playground for the whole family." [visitdenmark]

"Copenhagen has a great selection of adult locations." [WikiSexGuide]

As exemplified by vignette 3, not only do many actors communicate about Copenhagen, but these actors voice very different, oftentimes conflicting, ideas about what Copenhagen 'is', leaving it to the receiver/interpreter of all of these messages to build his/her own understanding of Copenhagen as a place – an understanding that we may define as the place (or destination) image. Crompton (1979:18) defined destination image as "the sum of beliefs, ideas and impressions that a person has of a destination", hereby pointing to destination images, as all other brand images, being formed by individuals on the basis of the meanings and associations they generate over time.

Furthermore, Papadopoulos & Heslop (2002:295) argue that:

"whether positive or negative, focused or diffuse, held widely or by only a few, developed deliberately or by default, and formed from education, the media, travel, immigration, product purchases, business experiences or any combination of sources, every place has an image".

As Papdopoulos and Heslop (2002) remind us, place images may be based on a multiplicity of sources and tourism actors are but a few of the many voices that articulate their specific understandings and enactments of a particular place. Apart from pointing to ways in which different actors voice very different, often conflicting, ideas about what places such as Copenhagen 'are', vignette 3 also exemplifies how places are defined more broadly than destinations, as places are available for/being used by many different actors for many different reasons (including living or working there), whereas destinations are traditionally defined as places that tourists go to. The difference between these two notions is the reason why we sometimes differentiate between place and destination branding and, why – when using the later notion – we deliberately emphasize the touristic dimensions of places.

Destination marketing organizations (DMOs) and versions of destinations

Destination marketing (or management) organizations usually have branding of destinations as one of their key tasks and they therefore aim to be(come) powerful and credible sources of information that tourists (and other actors) use when forming destination images. However, as exemplified by vignette 4, these are not easy tasks to complete.

Vignette 4: DMOs as managers and marketers without mandate?

"… although any DMO would probably prefer that all local tourism enterprises at all times use logos and brand values promoted by the DMO, thus allowing the destination to market a coherent image across all target groups, most DMOs do not have any legitimate right to interfere with promotional material using other logos and/or values." [Blichfeldt, Hird & Kvistgaard, 2014]

As vignette 4 points out, DMOs have a more difficult task than marketers of traditional brands as DMOs are not 'in control' of the branding and communication of the various products, services and experiences tourists consume while visiting a destination. Therefore, several researchers (Blichfeldt, Hird & Kvistgaard, 2014, Zach, 2011; Wang & Pizam, 2011) argue that DMOs should be defined as entities *marketing* destinations as well as *managing* relations between local actors, who are the ones actually 'producing' and delivering the conglomerate tourism product, hereby facilitating *cooperation, collaboration* and *coordination* between these actors in order to fulfil the destination brand promise that (hopefully) pulls tourists to the destination. However, tourism actors may not agree on what the destination, or the destination brand promise, should be, nor may their communication align with that of other actors or the DMO. As destinations are defined as places that tourists travel to, at the core of the destination concept we find nested commercial interests in the form of the revenues that tourism can generate by means of its ability to pull tourists to the destination that will spend money on various products, services and experiences during their stay. Which products, services and experiences tourists can consume during their holidays is not dictated by the DMO, but by the various tourism operators at the destination and different tourism actors may have very different ideas about what products should be offered to which tourists and what destination identity (or identit*ies*) should (not) be promoted. Discussing this issue, Morgan et al. (2003:289) argue that "many organizations and groups have vested interests in the promotion of particular identities (many of which may be in direct conflict with the interests of others)". As vignette 3 showed, very different actors communicate about Copenhagen and what these actors communicate reflect their diverging vested interests in the promotion of particular place identities. For example, both 'official Denmark' and 'green' tourism operators may have vested interests in promoting Copenhagen as carbon neutral whereas the City of Copenhagen may have vested interests in promoting Copenhagen as a good place for entrepreneurial enterprises, including entrepreneurs that are not especially carbon neutral. On the other hand, VisitDenmark, along with amusement parks such as Tivoli and Bakken, are likely to have vested interests in promoting Copenhagen as an attractive destination for families with children. The WikiSexGuide is likely to have vested interests in communicating about the aspects of Copenhagen that relate to its identity as an adult location. In the same vein, a hotel in Copenhagen that caters to the needs of families with children may emphasize Copenhagen's identity as a 'safe city' whereas a hostel catering to the needs of backpackers may emphasize Copenhagen's identity as a vibrant and buzzling city.

But is it a problem that different actors emphasize different versions of Copenhagen? Traditional branding theory and more functionalistic takes on communication would suggest that the answer to this question is 'Yes!', because the purpose of destination branding is to create a coherent and unique destination identity (i.e. to develop and communicate an unambiguous picture of what the destination 'is'). Destination brand image (i.e. how tourists 'see' the destination) is often said to be, at least partially, based on destination brand identity (Pike, 2004; Daye, 2010) and therefore, coherent and clear communication emphasizing a unique identity is often seen as necessary in order to establish a clear destination image that makes the destination stand out from the crowd (Therkelsen, 2007). Drawing in these kinds of arguments, it would be a problem if different tourism stakeholders accentuate different identities or versions of the destination in their communication as this will contribute to blurred and/or multiple brand identities. However, vignette 5 presents an alternative understanding of destination identities and images.

Vignette 5: Challenging simplicity in place and destination branding

"By exploring the possibility of the existence of several destination versions, 'the' identity and henceforth 'the' image of the destination is revealed as a simplistic and unproductive reduction. The clear identity of destination branding neglects and omits a variety of destination identities, actors, discourses, performances and artefacts. This suggests that branding, or in broader terms the cultural communication, staging and construction of a tourism destination is not an innocent enterprise but contains the capacity to normatively define and represent the place, people and activities of tourism in a certain place. Place branding does not just reflect a place, but actively takes part in creating what it is – and is not. When considering the aspects of power in relation to a tourism destination, one must direct attention not only to the abundant representations and identities of the destination, but also to the dynamics and complexities of the place." [Ren & Blichfeldt, 2011:430]

Place identity relates to definitional processes, in which only some subjects, objects, activities, practices and discourse are included when connecting certain identities to certain places. As stakeholders discursively position themselves and their versions of 'the' destination in a variety of ways, places are not 'empty containers' into which people, practices and objects can be placed (Murdoch, 2006), but are negotiated and contested 'turfs' (Modan, 2007) where actors struggle to define what the place is or should be (Ren, 2006; Ren & Blichfeldt, 2011). Branding and strategic communication in a tourism context are therefore, first and foremost, matters of identifying the welter of stakeholders and including their voices in the study of what is being communicated about a certain place, a certain destination or a certain issue (such as 'green' tourism or sustainable tourism development). Seeing tourism not as an industry, but as groups of stakeholders including not only those that have a commercial interest in tourism, but also actors with no direct commercial interests in tourism, who are nevertheless *affected by tourism*, makes branding and strategic communication in a tourism context complex matters.

From a commercial perspective, local residents are sometimes reduced to being seen as important insofar they are part of the 'product' that tourists 'consume' when visiting a destination, a perspective underlying much of what has been said and written about locals as *host* communities. But destinations are not only places that tourists visit, they are also places where people live, work, start businesses, love, build families, grow up, grow old etc. – and tourism is but one of the many, often conflicting, interests within a given place, as exemplified by vignette 6.

Vignette 6: Barcelona no esta en venda

"Barcelona is not for sale" and "We will not be driven out" - these were messages on banners that protestors carried on the Rambla in Barcelona in January 2017. The protest was organized by resident and community groups in Barcelona and the aim was, amongst others, to point out how the massive upsurge in tourism and tourist apartments had driven up rents and driven residents out of Barcelona.

Source: *The Guardian*
https://www.theguardian.com/world/2017/jan/29/barcelona-residents-protest-high-rents-fuelled-by-tourism
https://www.theguardian.com/technology/2017/jun/02/airbnb-faces-crackdown-on-illegal-apartment-rentals-in-barcelona

Branding with, not to, tourists

Having introduced both more traditional tourism stakeholders and locals as actors communicating about destinations, one critical stakeholder within tourism has, this far, been unfairly silenced in this chapter. Therefore, we now turn to the roles that *tourists* (including both potential tourists and those that have already visited the destination in question) play in branding and strategic communication and we start this discussion by introducing a story about an international kite flying festival on a small island.

Vignette 7: Some Danish island starting with 'F' and ending with oe

BBC news, June 18, 2017 aired a video showing hundreds (thousands?) of spectacular kites flying in the air under the headline: "5,000 kite enthusiasts from around the world have come to Fanoe in Denmark and they're flying high". 2 days later, the video had 1.3 million views, 40,000 likes and had triggered 1,400 comments, including Iwo Gross' comment: 'I'll visit Faroe Islands when they stop slaughtering whales'.

The BBC video presenting the Fanoe International Kite Fliers Meeting is a short 'feel good' video that is imbued with pathos and does little more than show the many different kites 'flying high in Denmark'. Most of the commentary is posted by people, who find the event interesting, voice they would like to go to see the event, tag their friends and/or make references to childhood memories of kite flying (some even mentioning the video speaking to their 'inner child'). However, comments such as the one posted by Iwo Gross touch upon very different issues and triggered a fair amount of responses. Some of these responses sought to 'rectify' the commentator's mistaking the Fanoe Island for the Faroe Islands (pointing to 'wrong island' and the 1,500 kilometer distance between these islands). However, if we take the matter of co-creation of meanings and messages seriously, it is problematic to reduce Iwo Gross' comment to something that is 'wrong' or 'mistaken'. After all, both the media coverage of the pilot whale killings at the shores of the Faroe Islands and the BBC video of the kite festival on Fanoe trigger associative links to Denmark, making it quite likely that audiences activate associations to the Faroe Islands (and whale killings) when seeing the Fanoe video. Simplistic as this example is, it nevertheless points to audiences not as passive recipients of messages, but at people linking new information to existing nodes in their memories when making sense and actively creating meaning. This illustrates how complicated it is to 'do' branding and strategic communication that work in more interactive and dynamic contexts as – given the audience(s)' active co-creation of meanings and messages – strategic communication is not only a matter of creating the 'right' messages and delivering them in the 'right' way, it is also a matter of taking into account which associations in others' minds our communication might trigger and subsequently trying to avoid signs, symbols, metaphors etc. that trigger undesired associations and, instead, emphasize elements that activate desirable associations. However, even a seemingly unproblematic slogan such as 'fly the friendly skies' can easily become a subject of undesirable associations under the right (or perhaps more correctly, wrong) circumstances – as exemplified by vignette 8.

Vignette 8: Suggestions for new United Airlines mottos

After a disturbing video of a man being dragged out of a United Airlines' overbooked flight was released on social media, on Twitter, people began to suggest new mottos that could replace United Airlines'"Fly the friendly skies". Some of the suggestions were …

So much for flying the friendly skies.

Let us re-acccommodate you.

We can re-accommodate you the easy way … or the hard way.

We put Hospital in Hospitality.

Fight or Flight – We decide.

We treat you like we treat your luggage.

United. Because flying is always a drag.

http://www.boredpanda.com/united-airlines-motto-twitter/?page_numb=4

Branding and communicating sustainable development

Sustainable tourism is often argued to be "applicable to all tourism ventures, regardless of scale" although "a precise definition of sustainable tourism is less important than the journey towards it" (Hardy et al., 2002:483). The purpose of this section is *not* to discuss what sustainable tourism development is. Instead, the purpose is to discuss sustainable tourism development, not only as something that is 'done' or 'practiced', but something that is also *made sense* and *meaning(s)* of through branding and strategic communication. Tourism actors at many different levels in many different ways and in many different contexts use (and sometimes misuse) sustainability for branding purposes and tourism actors' strategic communication about sustainability actively contributes to constructions of what sustainability 'is' (not) as exemplified in vignette 9.

Vignette 9: Tourism development in (un)protected areas

Coastlines in Denmark have traditionally been protected from development and construction, hindering construction of 'front row' hotels, resorts etc. However, in 2014 Danish government softened the regulation of the Danish coastline and invited municipalities and other actors to propose tourism development projects within these hitherto protected areas. In the call for development projects, it was explicated that the projects should be sustainable (although this requirement was omitted from the subsequent selection process). Andersen et al. (2017) compared the written project proposals to academic discourses on sustainability, identified a series of discrepancies and concluded the following:

"It is unclear how Danish policy makers envisaged sustainable development of tourism in coastal areas or why sustainability vanished during the selection process. What is clear, though, is that without a clear communication of how decision-makers define sustainable tourism development, there were no clear guidelines for tourism actors to follow when writing sustainability into their project proposals. The result of this, it seems, is that the definitions of sustainability used when proposing tourism development along the Danish coastline in many ways differ from academic discourses on sustainable tourism development."

As vignette 10 shows, how governments communicate about sustainable development can have vast implications for how tourism actors enact sustainability, or at least, lead to enactments of the concept that do not align with the knowledge we already have accumulated, opening up for a wide variety of activities (and projects) that are not necessarily sustainable. Wight (1993) argued that sustainable tourism might, as ecotourism, suffer from the potential of being little more than a marketing label. Though Wight might have been overly pessimistic, there is certainly much 'greenspeak' going on – as exemplified by vignette 10.

Vignette 10: Greenspeak

Doing a rhetorical analysis of print media advertisements, Dann (1996) points to 'Greenspeak' as a promotional discourse which focuses on the environment and the corresponding motivations of green tourists. One of his main findings is that Greenspeak tries to convert the conventional mass tourism themes (sun, sea, sand and sex) to those of eco-tourism (nature, nostalgia, nirvana and narcissism).

Whereas Dann's (1996) *greenspeak* simply points to 'green' as what is being communicated, without assessing the truth of such communication, others more critically point to discrepancies between 'sayings' and 'doings' when it comes to sustainability (e.g. Self, Self and Bell-Haynes, 2010). Such critics often use the word *greenwashing* to describe situations, in which businesses, governments or other groups promote green/environmentally friendly initiatives or images, but actually operate in ways that are not environmentally friendly, or may even be damaging to the environment etc. Vignette 11 introduces a piece of research that tries to determine the extent to which a series of tour operators in the Galapagos Islands engage in greenwashing.

Vignette 11: Greenwashing

Self, Self and Bell-Haynes (2010:111) argue that "because there is no universally adopted certification program for ecotourism, tourism operators may market their operations as 'ecotourism' while in reality they are 'greenwashing'" and they define greenwash as to "promote ecotourism while effectively doing the opposite".

Using the criteria established by the Mohonk Agreement for responsible ecotourism, the authors did a content analysis of fifteen websites of ecotourism operators in the Galapagos Islands to determine the extent to which they are "ecotours" or "greenwashed tours." Although the websites suggest that the companies operate in concordance with many of the criteria for responsible eco-tourism, "greenwashing is evident when it comes to sustainable practices" and "only one company [...] is eco-certified through an outside, performance-based audit" (p. 122).

The study referred to in vignette 11 attempts to uncover acts of greenwashing. However, greenwashing is not only a matter of what is strategically *communicated*, but also a matter of what is (not) *done* by the organizations in question. We should always be careful not to equate what is communicated strategically with what is actually done as there might be many (and sometimes very good) reasons why organizations do not communicate about all they do. Self, Self and Bell-Haynes (2010: 122) touch upon this issue as they immediately follow up on their claim that only one company is eco-certified with the sentence: "While the companies may actually engage in these practices [being eco-certified], their websites do not specifically mention them". Discrepancies between what is 'said' and what is 'done' may consequently not only be the result of greenwashing and/or organizations pretending to be 'better' or 'doing more good' than they actually do. As exemplified in vignette 12, quite other rationales can be decisive for how organizations (do not) strategically communicate about sustainability or other socially desirable actions.

Vignette 12: Greenhushing

Font et al. (2017) argue that greenhushing refers to the situation where fewer pro-sustainability actions are communicated than practiced by businesses. Their analysis of gaps between the communication and practices of sustainability of 31 small rural tourism businesses in the Peak District National Park (UK) suggests that these businesses only communicate 30% of the sustainable actions they practice. On this basis, Font et al. (2017) suggest that greenhushing is a form of public moralisation that adopts communication practices similar to those at work in relation to greenwashing, reflecting the social norms expected from a business; however, in the case of greenhushing reflecting moral muteness, rather than moral hypocrisy.

Font et al.'s (2017) study is rather interesting from a strategic communication perspective, because it is a case of deliberate *under-communication* of sustainable initiatives (i.e. engaging far more in sustainable practices than what is communicated). In a broader perspective, pointing to deliberate under-communication of (positively laden) actions, practices and doings opens up for a more nuanced and advanced understanding of strategic communication, where organizations and businesses not only create and transmit messages intended to emphasize the most positive aspects of their business, but where they may be reluctant to use moral expressions in their communication even if they act morally (what Font et al. refer to as *moral muteness*). There are many different reasons why organizations engage in moral muteness, but one of these could be intentionally trying to not reduce sustainability to a marketing label. Another could be that these organizations do not wish to partake in public discourses inscribed with political correctness. However, the simple reason could also be that these organizations do not have sufficient knowledge about strategic communication to make a website that sends messages that align with organizational values.

This chapter has sought to demonstrate that strategic communication is not a matter of 'doing' something to passive audiences. It is a symbiotic process through which more informed understandings of sustainable tourism development can develop. However, in order for such symbiotic processes to succeed, tourism actors need to avoid publicising themselves in a monolithic manner and (re)define themselves as parts of multi-directional communication processes where meanings about sustainable tourism development are created *with* other actors. This also means that they should revise understandings of what co-branding is and see it as something that inevitably happens as they take part in dialogues on sustainable tourism development, *not* as strategic alliances based on intended pairing with carefully selected partner brands. As it becomes easier and easier for everyone to communicate and construct different versions of sustainable tourism development, it is simply not enough to communicate about the sustainability of tourism development in 'our' destination, nor is it enough to brand 'our' offers as sustainable. Or, in the words of Tom Robbins:

Closing vignette: Alarm bells are ringing

Suddenly, it seems that every hotel, tour operator and even airline is bending over backwards to do its bit for the planet. Adverts and websites are full of claims about the good that choosing a particular holiday will do for the environment and local communities. And amid such a profusion of green claims, it's becoming increasingly hard to tell who is genuinely concerned about the planet and who is just cashing in on our eco-guilt.

Tom Robbins, July 6th

https://www.theguardian.com/travel/2008/jul/06/green.ethicalholidays

Although the stakes may seem particularly high for traditional tourism actors, everybody has a stake in regard to sustainable tourism development. Unfortunately, the 'profusion of green claims' entails that the nature of sustainable tourism development is up for debate and contested all the time – and as long as some (even if it is only a few) actors apply this notion to 'cash in', then lack of credibility and trustworthiness may undermine any and all attempts to communicate about sustainable tourism development. Therefore, those that will 'do best' in terms of sustainable tourism development will be those that are able to embrace opportunities to engaging in dialogues *with* other actors. However, this changes the responsibility for each actor from strategically communicating about their own sustainable doings to also actively partaking in the wider conversations on sustainable tourism development. Hereby, issues such as engaging in wider discussions of what sustainable tourism development is (not) and/or actively fighting green washing and greenhushing, becomes the collaborative responsibility of all communicators who wish for more sustainable developments within tourism. This, it seems, is the only way to ensure that sustainability stays everything *but* a marketing label.

Conclusion

Branding and strategic communication in tourism – including everything from photos posted by tourists on social media as well as photos included in a travel brochure over promotional videos to strategy documents or how companies respond to customer complaints – are not 'innocent', nor value-free, but define and inscribe themselves in certain ways of *seeing* tourism and hereby actively contribute to the *making* of tourism by prescribing certain ways of *doing* tourism and *being* tourism actors. As a result, strategic communication and branding are not only something tourism suppliers do in order to brand, market or position themselves as sustainable. Instead their communication and branding initiatives become parts of wider discourses on, and constructions of, what sustainable tourism development 'is'. Within a tourism context, the notions of collaborative communication processes and cobranding are extremely important as many other actors than tourism businesses take part in creating discourses and constructions of sustainability. Therefore, tourism actors should not see branding and strategic communication as simply sending messages that emphasize sustainable tourism development, but should instead define this as actively partaking in the discursive performances that inform and construct sustainability.

The study of strategic communication and branding of sustainability is not simply a matter of understanding or discussing the qualities of a specific touristic text. It is also something that sensitizes and extends understandings of what sustainable tourism development is (and is not) and how it relates to wider society and human being. In order to create more sustainable futures, tourism actors need to understand that branding and strategic communication are inherently collaborative endeavours, where it is more important to actively engage in dialogues with other actors than it is to make flashy websites or catchy promotional videos. Sustainable tourism development is *not* created by transmitting carefully crafted messages about sustainability to passive audiences. On the contrary, sustainable development should be seen as dynamic processes where actors do all they can to be valuable and trustworthy partners in collaborative communication processes that discursively construct and frame sustainable tourism development.

References

Aaker, D. A. (1991). *Managing Brand Equity: Capitalizing on the value of a brand name.* New York: Free Press.

Allen, L., Hafer,H., Long, P. & Perdue, R. (1993). Rural residents' attitudes toward recreation and tourism development. *Journal of Travel Research,* 31(4), 27–33.

Andersen, I. M., Blichfeldt, B. S. & Liburd, J. (2017): *Sustainable Tourism Regulation and Development. The Case of the Danish Coastline.* TIC TALKS no. 2. SDU, Kolding. Retrieved from http://www.sdu.dk/en/om_sdu/institutter_centre/c_tik/publikationer

Bauer, R. A. (1964). The obstinate audience: The influence process from the point of view of social communication. *American Psychologist,* 19(3), 319–328.

Blichfeldt, B. S. & Smed, K. M. (2015). 'Do it to Denmark': A case study on viral processes in marketing messages. *Journal of Vacation Marketing,* 21(3), 289–301.

Blichfeldt, B., Hird, J. & Kvistgaard, P. (2014). Destination leadership and the issue of power. *Tourism Review,* 69(1),74–86.

Blumer, H. (1969). *Symbolic Interactionism: Perspective and method.* Englewood Cliffs, NJ: Prentice-Hall.

Chaffee, S. H. & Metzger, M. J. (2001). The end of mass communication? *Mass Communication & Society,* 4(4), 365-379.

Crompton, J. (1979). An assessment of the image of Mexico as a vacation destination and the influence of geographical location upon that image. *Journal of Travel Research,* 17(4), 18-23.

Dann, G. (1996). Greenspeak: An analysis of the language of eco-tourism. *International Journal of Tourism Research,* 2(3-4), 247-259.

Davis, J. S. & Morais, D. B. (2004). Factions and enclaves: Small towns and socially unsustainable tourism development. *Journal of Travel Research,* 43(1), 3–10.

Daye, M. (2010). Challenges and prospects of differentiating destination brands: The case of the Dutch Caribbean brand. *Journal of Travel Research,* 27(1), 1–13.

Font, X., Elgammal, I. & Lamond, I. (2017). Greenhushing: The deliberate under-communicating of sustainability practices by tourism businesses. *Journal of Sustainable Tourism,* 25(7), 1007-1023.

Freeman, R. E. (1984). *Strategic Management: A Stakeholder Approach.* Boston: Pitman.

Gyimothy, S. (2013). Symbolic convergence and tourism social media. In A. M. Munar, S. Gyimothy & L. Cai (Eds.): *Tourism Social Media: Transformations in Identity, Community and Culture.* Bingley: Elsevier Science, Tourism Social Science Series, vol. 18, pp. 107-131.

Hardy, A., Beeton, R. &. Pearson, L (2002). Sustainable tourism: an overview of the concept and its position in relation to conceptualisations of tourism. *Journal of Sustainable Tourism,* 10(6), 475-496.

Hodder, C. (2002). God and Gap: What has Asda got to do with Jerusalem? Branding and being a Christian in the 21st century — some reflections. Available at: http://www.instituteforbrandleadership.org/Chris_HodderBrands_and_Theology.htm.

Keller, K. L. (1993). Conceptualizing, measuring, and managing customer-based brand equity. *Journal of Marketing,* 57(1), 1-22.

Liburd, J. (2013). *Towards the Collaborative University: Lessons from Tourism Education and Research*. Odense, Denmark: University of Southern Denmark.

Markwick, M. (2000). Golf tourism development, stakeholders, differing discourses, and alternative agendas: The case of Malta. *Tourism Management, 21*(3), 515–524.

Modan, G.G. (2007). *Turf Wars. Discourse, diversity, and the politics of place*. Malden, MA: Blackwell Publishing.

Morgan, N., Pritchard, A. & Piggott, R. (2003). Destination branding and the role of the stakeholders: the case of New Zealand. *Journal of Vacation Marketing, 9*(3), 285-299.

Murdoch, J. (2006). *Post-Structuralist Geography: A guide to relational space*. London: Sage.

Park, C. W., Jun, S. & Shocker, A. (1996). Composite brand alliances: An investigation of extension and feedback effects. *Journal of Marketing Research, 33*(4), 453-466.

Papadopoulos, N. & Heslop, L. (2002). Country equity and country branding: Problems and prospects. *Journal of Brand Management, 9*(4/5), 294–314.

Pike, S. (2004). *Destination Marketing Organizations*. Amsterdam: Elsevier.

Ren, C. (2006). After inventing the trail. The staging and consumption of outdoor recreation. *Ethnologia Scandinavica, 36*, 5–20.

Ren, C. & Blichfeldt, B. S. (2011). One clear image? Challenging simplicity in place branding, *Scandinavian Journal of Hospitality and Tourism, 11*(4), 416-434, DOI: 10.1080/15022250.2011.598753

Robson, J. & Robson, I. (1996). From shareholders to stakeholder: critical issues for tourism marketers. *Tourism Management, 17*(7), 533–540.

Rosengren, K. E. (2000). *Communication: An introduction*. London, England: Sage.

Ryan, C. (2002). Equity, management, power sharing and sustainability — issues of the new tourism. *Tourism Management, 23*(1), 17–26.

Sautter, E. & Leisen, B. (1999). Managing stakeholders: a tourism planning model. *Annuals of Tourism Research, 26*(2), 312–328.

Self, R., Self, D. & Bell-Haynes, J. (2010). Marketing tourism intThe Galapagos Islands: ecotourism or greenwashing? *International Business & Economics Research Journal, 9*(6), 111-126.

Shannon, C. E., & Weaver,W. (1949). *The Mathematical Theory of Communication*. Urbana: University of Illinois Press.

Swait, J., Erdem,T., Louviere, J. & Dubelaar, C. (1993). The equalization price: A measure of consumer-perceived brand equity. *International Journal of Research in Marketing, 10*(3), 23-45.

Theodorson, G. A., & Theodorson, A . G. (1969). *A Modern Dictionary of Sociology*. New York: Crowell.

Therkelsen, A. (2007). Branding af turismedestinationer - muligheder og problemer. In A. Sørensen (Ed.), *Grundbog i Turisme* (pp. 215–225). Copenhagen: Frydenlund.

Wang, Y., & Pizam, A. (2011). Destination marketing and management: Theories and applications. Cambridge: CAB International.

Wight. P. A. (1993). Sustainable ecotourism: Balancing economic, environmental and social goals within an ethical framework. *Journal of Tourism Studies, 4*(2), 54-66.

Zach, F. (2010). Partners and innovation in American destination marketing organisations. *Journal of Travel Research, 51*(4), 412-425.

4 Managing Uncertainties in the Governance of Sustainable Tourism Networks

Jaume Guia

Introduction

At the turn of the millennium, the *Journal of Sustainable Tourism* special issue on collaboration and partnerships (Bramwell & Lane, 1999), and the book *Tourism Collaboration and Partnership: Politics, practice and sustainability* (Bramwell & Lane, 2000), set the agenda for research about the role of collaboration in sustainable tourism. Since then, many more articles on the topic have been published and as a result a solid corpus of knowledge has emerged over the years. This literature can be divided into three main blocks according to whether the focus is on collaborative structures for sustainable tourism (partnerships, networks and governance), on stakeholder identification and involvement, or on the obstacles that these collaborative processes may face.

This chapter draws on this established stock of knowledge to identify the areas that need further research in order to better understand the origin and reason of those obstacles and how they seem to be persistent despite the use and application of practices, models and tools that in particular cases have proven to be effective. Further research on the processes of change to the adoption of sustainable tourism values, on the strong political nature of the governance of these processes, and on the singularity of each local context, is thus identified (Fadeeva, 2005, Nunkoo, 2017; Robertson, 2011) and a clear critical approach is recommended (Bramwell, 2010; Bramwell & Lane, 2014).

This is done after identifying three types of uncertainties underlying governance and presenting a conceptual framework adapted from Governance Network Theory (Klijn & Koopenjan, 2012; Koopenjan & Klijn, 2004), which explains the development of governance networks and the management of such processes in the case of sustainable tourism. In the subsequent section a literature review of collaboration and governance of sustainable tourism is presented. Next, a conceptual framework of how uncertainties are managed in governance networks for sustainable tourism is outlined. Some guidelines for further research are derived from the model and later discussed in the last section of the chapter.

Collaboration and governance of sustainable tourism

The implementation of sustainable forms of tourism calls for collaboration among a variety of interdependent stakeholders, encompassing public administrations, businesses, local communities and visitors. In practice, this collaboration is shaped in the form of partnerships and collaborative networks of different sorts, and is achieved and sustained through governance mechanisms and structures.

Partnerships, networks and governance for sustainable tourism

The first stream of literature focuses on analyzing both successful and complex cases of collaboration for sustainable tourism, to show how multi-stakeholder partnerships and networks and participatory governance can be effective mechanisms for the adoption and implementation of sustainable tourism practices. Selin (1999) developed a typology of partnerships for sustainable tourism on the basis of the geographical scale, the top-down or bottom-up origin of the partnership, the locus of control, the degree of organizational diversity, or the timeframe of the collaborative arrangement. Later, Bramwell (2010) highlighted the importance of the participation of destination communities in decision-making for sustainability and advocated for critical perspectives and a greater attention to the broad range of contexts and activities of tourism governance. Robertson (2011) studied a cross-sectorial organizational network created to promote sustainable tourism through collaborative governance and discussed the network formation process, the role of public managers, and the features of the local context that may influence the network's likelihood of success. In the same vein, Graci (2013) explored the implementation of a multi-stakeholder partnership as a case of successful collaboration leading to the implementation of innovative sustainability initiatives. Finally, Dredge and Jamal (2013) analyzed the challenges of tourism destination governance and sustainability in complex places where multiple types of mobility coalesce. For this purpose they explored the tensions between these mobilities and established sustainable tourism principles, and suggested that governance should be grounded in local community dialogue and values. Multi-stakeholder and cross-sectorial partnerships, collaborative governance, and participatory community involvement, are thus common mechanisms for the success of tourism sustainable development in all the cases analyzed by these authors.

Some papers have adopted a network approach to the study of these part-nerships and governance structures, focusing on the structural and positional aspects of relational networks to diagnose and guide the management of collaborative initiatives for sustainable tourism. For instance, Fadeeva (2005) studied how tourism networks contribute to the adoption of sustainable practices through the discussion, implementation and dissemination of sustainability as a new value or idea to be promoted and adopted. Later, Timur and Getz (2008) adopted a network approach to collaboration for sustainable tourism and illustrated the use of social network analysis for diagnosing structural and positional aspects of collaborative networks, the knowledge of which can contribute to a more effective design and management of partnership development processes. Finally, Albrecht (2013) proposed a research agenda for networks and networking for sustainable tourism, and noted that while substantial progress had been made in the investigation of private sector networks, networks involving public sector stakeholders and cross-sectorial networks remained limited.

Managing stakeholders and their involvement in collaborative processes

This stream of literature focuses on collaboration and governance of sustainable tourism from a stakeholder approach and with a more managerial perspective. The main concern is the identification of relevant stakeholders, how they can become involved in collaborative networks, and what role each of the stakeholders may play for the development and sustainability of the partnership and the adoption and implementation of sustainable tourism practices.

In the first place, the research by Araujo and Bramwell (1999) focused on how the stakeholders of a tourism project, who might participate in collaborative tourism planning, can be identified. Byrd (2007) also focused on the identification of relevant stakeholders in tourism but with particular emphasis on sustainable tourism initiatives, and highlighted the relevance of four categories of stakeholders, some of them still neglected: present and future visitors, and present and future host communities. The same research also analysed how these stakeholders can become involved in the projects.

Other authors have made important contributions by proposing models or frameworks for the implementation of collaborative practices in sustainable tourism projects, which managers can borrow in their efforts to develop collaborative partnerships for sustainable tourism. For instance, Getz and Timur (2005) studied the involvement of stakeholders in sustainable tourism by balancing their different voices. These authors proposed a process that commences with a legitimate focal group of stakeholders, identifies all the relevant stakeholders, determines their potential interests and prioritizes sustainable issues through consensus building; and ends determining how each group of expectations are met and modifying the destination's priorities, strategies and policies to integrate each stakeholder's sustainability issues. Similarly, Waligoet al. (2013) emphasized the relevance of stakeholders' involvement to facilitate the implementation of sustainable tourism, and proposed a multi-stakeholder involvement management framework that consists of three strategic levels: attraction, integration and management of stakeholder involvement; and six embedded stages: scene-setting, recognition of stakeholder involvement capacity, stakeholder relationship management, pursuit of achievable objectives, influencing implementation capacity and monitoring stakeholder involvement.

Still other researchers have paid attention to the role that particular types of stakeholders – public administration, businesses, local communities and visitors – play in processes of collaboration for sustainable tourism. Regarding public administration, Vernon et al. (2005) identified the role of the public sector in promoting bottom-up forms of governance in the adoption of sustainable practices by tourism businesses. Similarly, Ruhanen (2013) in an investigation of the role of local government in facilitating sustainable development objectives in a destination, discovered that, due to the absence of strong industry leadership and top-down directives from state and federal governments, it was local government that took responsibility for facilitating the sustainable tourism agenda.

In regard to the role that destination businesses play in the development of collaborative networks for sustainable tourism, there are limited results. Halme and Fadeeva (2000) explored the role of small and medium-sized enterprises in sustainable development networks, and Sigala (2008), Schwartz, Tapper and Font (2008) and Adriana (2009) studied the role of tour-operators within business supply chains in collaborative initiatives for sustainable tourism.

As for local communities, Sofield (2003) studied the effects of community empowerment for sustainable tourism development. Later, Blackstock (2005) wrote a critical article on community-based tourism, and found out how a functional approach to community involvement, the treatment of the host community as homogeneous, and the neglect of structural constraints to local control of the tourism industry are major problems in attempts to involve or empower local communities in the development of sustainable tourism. Other contributions have also been made regarding community involvement for heritage sustainable tourism (Li and Hunter, 2015). More recently, Mayaka, Croy and Cox (2018) made a relevant contribution focusing on how and why communities participate in CBTs, as informed by practice theory. The findings highlight community participation as a recurrent practice, where its different forms are fully influenced by local contexts. Thus, these results inform of the possibilities for enhancing tourism-led community development strategies where participation management is no longer subject to Western standards.

Finally, the role of the most neglected category of stakeholder, the visitors, has been explicitly studied by Sigala (2014), who demonstrated various ways in which customers are contributing to sustainability at various points in the supply chain. It has also been implicitly discussed in a few articles, which analyzed how tour operators and their mediating role between the destination and the visitor markets can contribute to the development of sustainable tourism initiatives and practices in the destinations. For instance, Sigala (2008) analyzed the role of these tour operators and their collaboration within tourism supply chains for the development of sustainable tourism. Farmaki (2015) found that the effectiveness of regional tourism governance is often limited by continuing dependence on foreign tour operators. Further, Bertella and Rossi Romanelli (2018) explained how responsible practices in Cuba have emerged through tourism initiatives developed through collaboration with foreign NGOs and tour operators. Finally, Parkh and Kholer (2018) have investigated the case of travel-2change, a company that connects travellers and local organizations through a crowdsourcing platform to facilitate concerted efforts for sustainable tourism in Hawai. Their findings shed light on actions stakeholders can take, so that the constituents can mobilize, synchronize, and synthesize their resources and efforts toward a sustainable tourism destination.

Obstacles to collaboration for sustainable tourism

This stream of research emphasizes the difficulties and barriers that hinder the development, emergence and sustainability of collaborative networks and governance structures for sustainable tourism. Jamal and Stronza (2009) drew attention to the challenges of implementing collaboration for sustainability and success: the complexity of the task, the scale, structure and scope of collaborations; and the long-term timeframe of the process.

More particularly, Dodds and Butler (2009), in their study on the barriers to successful implementation of sustainable tourism policy in mass-tourism destinations, found the lack of collaboration as one of the main obstacles. Dinica (2009) noted that the recommended governance of partnerships and networks for sustainable tourism is largely missing due to a design approach that follows neo-liberal principles. Ruhanen (2013) identified power struggles, tokenistic public participation and the strong influence of the local government authority in local governance structures as inhibitors to sustainable tourism development. Farmaki (2015), in her study on the effectiveness of regional tourism governance, found obstacles in a system of mutual favours among some stakeholders, and in the growing emphasis on economic interests. Further, Bramwell (2015) and Nunkoo (2017) have recently pointed out at the relevance of trust, power and social capital in the governance of sustainable tourism. They note that behind policies there is always politics, and understanding the politics is a prerequisite to overcoming these obstacles to sustainable tourism (Meadowcroft, 2011; Mihalic et al., 2016). Finally, Robertson (2011) and Mayaka et al. (2018) emphasized how the features of each local context influences the collaborative network's likelihood of success, and therefore implicitly alerted of the dangers of exporting best practices from one context to another.

Therefore, a predominant neo-liberal agenda, politics and power relations, and the singularities of local contexts can be singled out as the main types of obstacles for the creation of effective collaborative partnerships for sustainable tourism development.

Managing uncertainties in governance networks

Types of uncertainties in networks

The three types of obstacles identified in the literature above are conceptually correlated with the three types of uncertainties (Figure 4.1) identified by Koopenjan and Klejn (2004) as relevant for the governance of networks: substantive uncertainty (neo-liberal vs sustainability agendas), strategic uncertainty (diversity of interests and micro-politics), and institutional uncertainty (the singularities or local contexts).

Figure 4.1: Three types of uncertainties in networks

Substantive uncertainty is eminently concerned with the availability and allocation of information and knowledge within a network, but since different actors might have different perceptions of problems and interpret them from different frames of reference, they may also understand the available information differently. The interpretation of the meaning of information is thus a highly relevant source of substantive uncertainty. Only when actors are aware of the existence of different frames of reference, will it be possible to detect the real substantive questions that need to be addressed. It then becomes conceivable that a joint frame of reference is established from which shared meaning is conferred to facts and research results.

Strategic uncertainty refers to the strategic decisions actors make to deal with their mutual interdependences with other actors, and has its source in the diversity of goals and interests of the different actors in the network. By engaging in interaction, actors learn about others' objectives and interests and a negotiated organizational setting gradually emerge, where certainties are created through agreements that will facilitate joint action and common solutions.

Institutional uncertainty stems from the fact that interaction between actors is difficult since each of them will have their behavior guided by the practices, opinions, rules and language of their own organizations, their own position in them, and their own institutional context. Moreover, some players trust each other while others may not, which makes interactions more unlikely and increases uncertainty about the behavior of the other actors.

Governance Network Theory

Governance Network Theory lies at the crossroad of three main research streams in social science: policy networks, service delivery and network management (Kljn & Koopenjan, 2012). The policy networks tradition focuses on the relation between public administration and different interest groups; the service delivery stream is concerned with the coordination problems in delivering public services in fragmented settings; and the perspective of network management is to address complex policy problems through horizontal coordination among interdependent actors. Despite these differences, the three traditions largely use the word 'network' and rely on horizontal coordination mechanisms. Three main concepts can be identified in this theory: frames of reference and interpretation; actors, interdependencies and interests; and institutional features.

Frames of reference and interpretation

Actors in networks select their strategies on the basis of their frames of reference of the world and thus have different perspectives on problems and solutions (Schön & Rein, 1994). Knowledge makers are increasingly seen as sectarian and taking part in policy advocacy (Nowotny et al., 2001). Moreover, social media communication makes it more difficult to discern between evidence- and non-evidence-based statements, producing contending truths and thus contributing to information overload and uncertainty (Bekkers et al., 2011). As a result, there is a departure from reason, and a rise of populism (van Zoonen, 2012).

Actors, interdependency and interests

Policy and service delivery are both created and implemented in a network of interdependent actors, and interdependency is the core factor that initiates and sustains networks (Hanf & Scharpf, 1978; Rhodes 1997; Koppenjan & Klijn, 2004). As a consequence of the interdependencies between actors and the variety of interests and strategies that they rely on, complex interaction and negotiating patterns emerge in problem solving, policy implementation and service delivery. Governance network theory draws attention to the interaction of many actors rather than to the action of one single actor (Mandell, 2001; Kickert et al., 1997). Moreover, multi-stakeholder interaction processes do not develop in a linear way, through determined sequential stages, but are non-linear and erratic. They may result in win-win outcomes, but they may also fail, take a lot of time, and/or have large transition costs. They may result in dialogues of the deaf, or they may even be aborted (Mandell, 2001; Marcussen and Torfing, 2007).

Institutional features

Interaction patterns in networks result in institutionalization of relationships between actors. Institutions can be understood as patterns of social relations (rules, norms, social practices, shared language, power relations etc.). They facilitate interaction in networks, thus reducing transaction costs and influencing the performance of networks (Ostrom, 1986; Koppenjan & Klijn, 2004). Trust is a most valuable institutional feature of network governance, but it is not intrinsic to networks. It reduces strategic uncertainty, and thus facilitates investments in uncertain collaboration processes among interdependent actors with diverging and sometimes conflicting interests. But in the end trust has to emerge or be built.

These three elements of Governance Network Theory have a direct correspondence with the three types of uncertainties in networks identified above, as depicted in Figure 4.2: frames of reference and interpretation determine the substantive content of relational networks, actors' interdependencies and interests shape the strategic aspects of the networks, and the institutional features of the relational context determine the institutional make-up of the network.

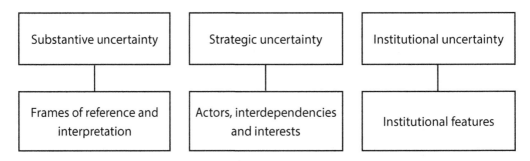

Figure 4.2: Types of uncertainties in networks and related concepts of Governance Network Theory

In what follows, these correspondences are used to underpin a conceptual framework that enables a re-mapping of the research field on governance of sustainable tourism and later identify relevant avenues for further research.

Deadlocks and breakthroughs in governance network development

Deadlocks and breakthroughs are characteristic phases of governance network development processes. Deadlocks hinder collaboration and are produced by the rise of any type of uncertainty. On the other hand, breakthroughs foster collaboration and are the result of the dissolution of those uncertainties. Understanding the sources of uncertainties will thus be relevant for the management of these deadlocks and breakthroughs. Substantive uncertainties have cognitive causes, strategic uncertainties have social causes, and institutional uncertainties draw on institutional causes (Koopenjan & Klijn, 2004).

Cognitive causes for stagnation can be found in the varying perceptions about the nature, origin and effects of problems and their solutions (Termeer & Koopenjan, 1997). They are, thus, concerned with the diversity of opinions about the nature of a problem and the quality of the available knowledge and solutions. Characteristic of this kind of discussion is that actors talk past each other and are, actually, discussing different things. There is a dialogue of the deaf. Since each actor conducts their own research, the differences of opinion are intensified. Instead of diminishing knowledge conflicts and substantive uncertainty, the results of the research serve to enhance them. A substantive breakthrough calls for joint image building. Cognitive learning is thus possible and substantive uncertainty is reduced through a convergence of ideas and perceptions, and a mutual understanding of the meaning of situations and problems. This requires frame reflection and cross-frame discussions where problems and solutions are developed afresh (van Hulst & Yanow, 2016). The availability of new substantive ideas and their inclusion in the debate play an important role in this discussion and reflection. An additional important factor is the degree to which actors are able to search for new knowledge so that instead of reinforcing the advocacy role of one party, it benefits the process of joint image building.

Social causes of deadlocks emerge when the strategies of actors, whose resources for dealing with the problem are crucial, are not coordinated, are in conflict or when there is no interaction between actors. Conflicting strategies are generally a consequence of the differing objectives and interests of actors. Limited coordination may be originated by the fact that actors are not well enough aware of their mutual dependency or they have failed to find a mutual interest. It might also be caused by the uncertainty of how to approach the problem at hand, by who will play what role, and by how much the cost will be. If the risks of joint action are considerable, actors might decide not to aim for it. As a result, actors may be unwilling to contribute with their resources. A breakthrough can thus emerge when actors find the way to coordinate their strategies, so that their individual actions are no longer in conflict and joint action becomes possible. For this to occur, the reduction of strategic uncertainty is essential. This can be done by engaging in interaction, by linking arenas, and by mitigating the risk of strategic behavior through agreements (van Bueren Klijn, & Koppenjan, 2003). Actors have to come up with a solution that makes it possible to link their goals and, when costs are not even for all actors, offers opportunities for compensation (Koopenjan, 2008).

Institutional causes of stagnation include the absence of common institutions (norms, rules, shared language, etc.). Institutions that help reduce the risks of participating in collaborative networks usually have a mitigating effect upon conflicts, and provide procedures for creating interaction and managing conflict. A weak institutional structure might explain why deadlocks occur. It is not that there are no institutions but that they are not tuned to each other. Instead of supporting interaction, they prevent it. Institutional causes of deadlocks can also result from the nature and level of trust. Networks with strong patterns of distrust will have difficulty cooperating. To sum up, a strong institutional structure, such as discernible rules and strong trusting relations between actors, might result in low transaction costs since arrangements for furthering cooperation do not need to be developed from scratch, and actors can rely on already existing arrangements. Such a structure however may also have negative effects when interaction takes place in arenas situated in more than one network. This is the case when institutional norms favor cooperation inside the network but condemn collaboration with external actors and networks.

Institutional breakthroughs take place when deterring institutions are changed or dissolved. Also, the creation of new organizational structures and formal rules can support the interaction between parties that are involved in long-term processes of problem solving and thus result in a breakthrough. The creation of institutions supporting collaboration, however, is not something that can be accomplished in the short term. They are usually the consequence, rather than the cause of interaction processes. At issue are the ad hoc rules, which actors only progressively come to share during a long-term process. In the end, they may end up part of the institutional structure.

Network management as managing uncertainties

The complexity of governance processes within networks requires guidance and management of interactions. This is usually referred to as network management (Gage & Mandell, 1990; Kickert et al, 1997; Meir and O'Toole, 2007), which is aimed at facilitating collaborations, exploring content and organizing interactions between actors.

Conceptually, governance refers to the self-regulation of actors within networks. However, governance is also used to refer to strategies of governments and non-governmental organizations aimed at initiating, facilitating and mediating collaborative network processes, that is: network management. As depicted in Figure 4.3, network management operates on the three elements of Governance Network Theory to overcome the deadlocks produced by uncertainties, whose origin might be cognitive, social and/or institutional.

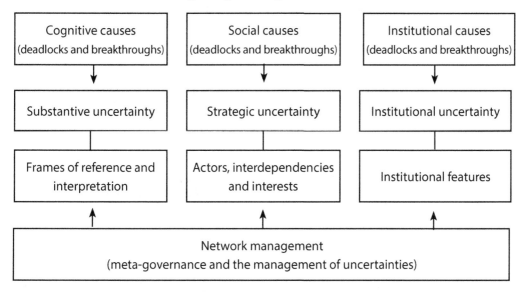

Figure 4.3: Causes of uncertainty in networks and network management as managing uncertainties

Therefore, network management strategies will consist of creating new content, by exploring new ideas, or by, organizing joint research and joint fact finding (Koppenjan & Klijn, 2004); initiating and facilitating interaction processes between actors (Kickert et al., 1997); and/or creating and changing network arrangements to enhance coordination (Rogers & Whetten, 1982). It is thus clear that network management requires another type of managerial approach compared to traditional management, since network managers do not possess hierarchical means to intervene in the network. It requires negotiating skills, skills to bond actors together and skills to devise new solutions that appeal to the various actors whose resources are required to implement solutions.

Guidelines for future research on the governance of sustainable tourism networks

The conceptual framework described above is here applied to the governance of sustainable tourism networks. Therefore, in the first place we focus on substantive uncertainty, the concept of frames of reference, and the cognitive causes of the deadlocks and breakthroughs that occur in the development of networks for sustainable tourism. The focus is then on strategic uncertainty, the concepts of actor interdependencies and interests, and the social causes of deadlocks and breakthroughs. Finally, we proceed in a similar vein in what concerns institutional uncertainty, the institutional features of networks, and the institutional causes of deadlocks and breakthroughs of sustainable tourism network development.

Substantive uncertainty, frames of reference and interpretation, and cognitive issues in the governance of sustainable tourism

The focus on the shared meaning of sustainability values by actors of a network and on the collective negotiation of this meaning for the governance of sustainable tourism networks has been neglected. The exceptions are Fadeeva (2005), who studies how tourism networks contribute to the adoption of sustainable values and practices through the discussion, implementation and dissemination of sustainability as a new value or idea to be promoted and adopted; and Gill and Williams (2014), who focus on understanding how the shift from growth models to models based on sustainability principles evolve.

Therefore, either a shared notion of sustainable tourism by the different actors has been assumed, or the relevance of substantive uncertainties has been underestimated. This problem has, nonetheless, been implicitly acknowledged by Dinica (2009), Ruhanen (2013) and Farmaki (2015) who emphasize how much neo-liberal principles, tokenistic participation and economic interests affect the way some actors frame and interpret sustainability, and are presented as an obstacle for the development of governance networks of sustainable tourism.

Further research is thus needed, which gives central attention to the diversity of actor's frames of reference and the interpretation of the meaning of sustainable tourism, sustainable values and sustainable practices: What are these frames of interpretation? How are shared meanings negotiated? How do knowledge conflicts around this meaning affect the development of governance networks for sustainable tourism? How much does collective cognitive learning decrease substantive uncertainty and foster the development of the networks? How many effective external and expert sources of knowledge are required to produce reflection, cross-frame debate and joint image building of sustainable tourism in the network?

These questions can be approached by studying existing, effective, sustainable tourism governance networks; but the analysis of destinations and supply chains where sustainable tourism is not their characteristic attribute, or where both sustainable and non-sustainable forms of tourism coexist, can also produce valuable contributions. Additionally, as the focus is here on interpretation, the interpretive approach to governance by Bevir and Rhodes (2007) and Bevir (2011) can be given prominent attention. According to these authors, governance is created by individuals' construction of meanings through their local practices, based on their beliefs, traditions, and responses to dilemmas. This approach aims to examine the ways through which actors act on their beliefs in relation to creating, sustaining, and changing governance patterns and structures. When individual actors perceive deficiencies in governance, or new situations that cannot be accommodated by their existing beliefs and frames of interpretation, a conflict of meanings emerges and gives rise to interpretation dilemmas. Change in governance is therefore driven by these contested meanings that arise in practice and that underlie the construction of networks. As activities of governance occur in local practices, a complex and continuous process of interpretation, reconciliation, and change of meanings can contribute to a change in the frames of reference (Sørensen & Torfing, 2007).

Strategic uncertainty, actors' interdependencies and interest, and social issues in the governance of sustainable tourism

This element of the governance of sustainable tourism networks has received the most attention so far. It concerns the identification and involvement of interdependent actors in processes of governance network development, as well as the structure of these collaborative networks. Three main weaknesses are noted here.

The attention to the stakeholder category of visitors is clearly underrepresented and neglected, with only a few exceptions (Parkh & Kholer, 2018). Moreover, it is implicitly assumed that each category of stakeholders (public administration, businesses, and communities) is uniform in their shared interests and goals (which is seldom the case). Furthermore, the focus is only on what binds or should bind actors together, that is, on their interdependencies around sustainable tourism. They have hitherto disregarded that parties in a governance network can also have multiple and often conflicting interdependencies and interests in other arenas, or relations of exteriority (Deleuze & Guatarri, 1980, Van Wezemael, 2008)

Further research is thus needed in this area. Such research should give central attention to the inclusion of all relevant stakeholder groups, to the lack of uniformity of interests within each of these categories, and overall, to the intertwinement of multiple interdependences, goals and interests by all the relevant actors of sustainable tourism governance networks. Research questions which can address gap include: How can visitors be involved in the governance of sustainable tourism? How much visitors can contribute to the effectiveness of governance networks for sustainable tourism? Do 'clusters' of interests differ within each stakeholder group in relation to the adoption of sustainable tourism practices in a governance network? How does mutual dependency or lack of mutual interest affect coordination? How do actors with diverging or conflicting interests deal with the uncertainty about roles and investment of resources?

How is participation affected by the perception of unequal costs and how can these perceptions be overcome by providing opportunities for compensations? What are the different arenas in which each actor has interdependences and participates and how do the goals and interests in one arena conflict with those in another? Can active engagement and the linking of arenas mitigate the risk of strategic behavior? How much does the fact that multi-actor interaction processes do not develop in a linear way affect the involvement of actors and the development of governance networks?

The questions about the inclusion of all relevant stakeholder groups must be approached by increasing the research on visitor involvement. This may follow a similar path to that of community inclusion and participative processes of governance. Research on supplier-consumer co-design and co-innovation (Hjalager, 2018), as well as the field of customer relationship management within marketing can be taken as potential avenues to approach those questions. Questions with respect to uniformity of interests within each stakeholder group, and the entwinement of multiple interdependences, goals and interests of relevant actors, may benefit from the adoption of more critical approaches, such as Actor Network Theory (Callon, 1986; Latour, 1999; Van der Duim, 2005; Van der Duim et al., 2013; Dedeke, 2017) and Assemblage Theory (Deleuze & Guatari, 1980; Van Wezemael, 2008; Anderson & McFarlane, 2011). Actor Network Theory pays attention to micro-politics, translations as processes of change, and individual actors (instead of stakeholder groups). Assemblage Theory focuses on relations of exteriority (and thus the multiplicity of arenas and potentially conflicting interests faced by actors). The foci of these theories make promising perspectives to further the knowledge on strategic uncertainty, actors' interdependencies, trust and interest, including social issues in the governance of sustainable tourism.

Institutional uncertainty, institutional features of networks, and institutional causes in the governance of sustainable tourism

Attention to the institutional aspects of governance in sustainable tourism networks has been under-researched and it was not until Bramwell (2015) and Nunkoo (2017) emphasized the relevance of trust and social capital in the governance of sustainable tourism, that this area started to receive increasing attention. Regarding other institutional features in addition to trust, Robertson (2011) and Mayaka et al. (2018) found out how each local context influences a network's likelihood of success, implicitly putting the focus on institutional uncertainty.

Further research is thus needed on the role of institutional features in the development of governance networks for sustainable tourism. Particularly, the focus must continue on the role of trust and social capital, and much attention is needed to better understand the role that 'local' rules, norms and practices play in the governance of sustainable tourism. Therefore, relevant research questions are: How is the governance of sustainable tourism affected by different and/or conflicting institutional contexts and the absence of mutual institutions? How to diagnose network contexts where different institutions are not attuned to each other, preventing supportive interaction? What are the roles of norms and practices in mitigating conflicts and promoting interaction? What particular types of norms are more favorable to the development of effective governance networks for sustainable tourism? How to adapt or abolish blocking institutions? Can new organizational structures and formal rules be created to support interaction between parties that are involved in long-term processes of governance of sustainable tourism? How may the long-term nature of institutional change affect the commitment of actors to keep involved? What is the role of trust in delivering successful governance of sustainable tourism?

These types of questions about institutional uncertainty in the governance of sustainable tourism networks emphasize the need to be more cautious at the time of importing and exporting best practices of governance management from one institutional context to another. With respect to trust in the governance of sustainable tourism, further developments can draw on the framework, approaches and agenda set up by Kramer and Cook (2004) and the framework proposed by Nunkoo and Smith (2015). Additionally, institutional theory (Powell & DiMaggio, 1991; Scott, 1995) provides a conceptual background for furthering research in the understanding of rules, norms and other institutional mechanisms in the governance of sustainable tourism. Moreover, for questions concerning institutional change we suggest the adoption of Practice Theory (Reckwitz, 2002; Nicolini, 2012), which takes social practices as the unit of analysis. Generally, practices can be understood as routinized 'doings and sayings' performed by knowledgeable and capable human actors, also referred to as carriers of the practice, involving material objects and infrastructures. Lamers, Van der Duim & Spaargaren (2017) suggests three ways in which practice theories could particularly contribute to the agenda of tourism studies and policy, i.e. by allowing for in-depth analysis of performed tourism consumption or production practices, by facilitating the understanding of change in tourism through the analysis of tourism practices over time, and by unravelling the embeddedness of tourism practices in extensive networks of practices. This makes Practice Theory a promising avenue for furthering research on the management of institutional uncertainty in the governance of sustainable tourism networks.

The effectiveness of network governance and management in sustainable tourism

Finally, further research is needed regarding the understanding of effectiveness in the management of sustainable tourism governance network development. As seen above, most of the research on the governance of sustainable tourism networks has been carried out from cases that have previously been identified as successful or effective, or cases where a process of governance network development was in place, from where some researchers identified both obstacles to collaboration and best practices. Nonetheless, there is no research specifically focused in studying and measuring the effectiveness of these processes.

Koopenjan and Kljn (2004) provide a framework that could be imported to the case of sustainable tourism governance network development. These authors assert that when governance processes are seen as activities addressed to reduce initial uncertainties and conflicts through interaction, it seems that their effectiveness could be measured by the degree to which learning occur. These collective learning is thus defined as "the sustainable increase in shared knowledge, insights and methods and working between parties" (p. 125), and refer to a change of shared mental models among members of an organization, group or network.

Learning outcomes in the three areas of content (cognitive learning), process (strategic learning) and institutions (institutional learning) must be distinguished. Success or failure might, then, depend upon the degree to which parties have collectively learned in each of these three areas. Therefore, this evaluation can be exported to further the research in the evaluation of the effectiveness of governance for sustainable tourism and of the outcomes of managerial efforts to reduce the three types of uncertainties in collaborative networks.

Conclusions

Collaboration, specifically through multi-stakeholder partnerships and networks, has been seen as an effective way to support initiatives in tourism development in general and in sustainable tourism in particular. Thus, many tourism destinations have attempted to move toward sustainability, but unfortunately, have been hindered in their attempts by a lack of collaboration among stakeholders. Knowledge has been developed about the relevance of partnerships, collaborative networks and participative forms of governance for sustainable tourism, about how these networks may be activated and their stakeholders identified and involved, and about the main obstacles behind the lack of an effective collaboration for sustainable tourism. Nonetheless, we do not seem to fully understand yet the change processes towards the adoption of sustainable tourism (Fadeeva, 2005), the strong political nature of these processes (Nunkoo, 2017), and the determining quality of each local context (Robertson, 2011), and therefore new perspectives of further research have been called forth (Bramwell, 2010; Farmaki, 2015).

It is also relevant to note that research on collaboration and governance of sustainable tourism networks started as an extension of the wider research on collaboration and governance of (conventional) tourism partnerships and networks. Focus on sustainability was thus achieved but unfortunately, it mostly consisted of studying existing networks that operated in protected areas and within the sustainable tourism realm, or networks that had developed over time to adopt sustainable tourism practices. In both cases though, the approach consisted in mimicking the research already done on the processes of (conventional) tourism governance. As a consequence, emphasis was mostly placed on the identification and involvement of actors and the development of strong partnerships and cohesive networks, which we have seen consist of dealing with strategic uncertainties in networks. A shared understanding of, and commitment to sustainability values and practices in tourism by the actors in the network was implicitly taken for granted and therefore the chance to further research on the role of substantive uncertainties around the meaning of sustainable tourism, and on the corresponding managerial implications for the effective development of governance networks in sustainable tourism, was lost. For similar reasons, opportunities to put more attention to the role of institutional uncertainty and particularly trust and social practices in the governance of sustainable tourism were also missed, as sustainable tourism is substantially different from other types of (conventional) tourism practices.

Moreover, the few researchers who have studied the obstacles that sustainable tourism governance network development face, have indirectly identified these same shortcomings. Yet, a conceptual framework, which provides for the many research findings and which, enables the mapping of the most neglected areas requiring attention, has been missing. This chapter contributes to the aforementioned framework. It builds on Koopenjan and Kljn's (2004) typology of uncertainties in networks and on the concepts of Governance Network Theory (Klejn & Koopenjan, 2011). Taking this conceptual framework as a reference the chapter ends by identifying where the existing literature fits within it and suggesting guidelines, avenues and approaches for future research. In doing so the chapter amends the lack of attention paid to the management of substantive and institutional uncertainties in the governance of sustainable tourism.

Finally, the need of more critical approaches to further the research on the topic has also been recognized in the literature (Bramwell & Lane, 2014). This chapter contributes to this need by identifying particular theoretical approaches, and the specific areas where their application can be more effective. Notably, further avenues of research can incorporate Actor Network Theory (Callon, 1986; Latour, 1997; Van der Duim, 2005; Van der Duim et al., 2013; Dedeke, 2017) and Assemblage Theory (Deleuze & Guatari, 1980; Van Wezemael, 2008; Anderson

& McFarlane, 2011) in exploring the management of strategic uncertainty, and Practice Theory (Reckwitz, 2002; Nicolini, 2012, Lamers et al., 2017) in analysing institutional uncertainty and how it can be managed in sustainable tourism governance networks.

References

Adriana, B. (2009). Environmental supply chain management in tourism: The case of large tour operators. *Journal of Cleaner Production*, **17**(16), 1385–1392. doi.org/10.1016/J.JCLEPRO.2009.06.010

Albrecht, J. N. (2013). Networking for sustainable tourism – towards a research agenda. *Journal of Sustainable Tourism*, **21**(5), 639–657. doi.org/10.1080/09669582.2012.721788

Anderson, B., & McFarlane, C. (2011). Assemblage and Geography. *Area*, **43**, 124-127. http://dx.doi.org/10.1111/j.1475-4762.2011.01004.x

Araujo, L. M. de, & Bramwell, B. (1999). Stakeholder assessment and collaborative tourism planning: The case of Brazil's Costa Dourada Project. *Journal of Sustainable Tourism*, **7**(3–4), 356–378. http://doi.org/10.1080/09669589908667344

Bekkers, V. J. J. M., Edelenbos, J., & Steijn, A. J. (2011). *Innovation in the Public Sector : Linking capacity and leadership*. Palgrave Macmillan.

Bertella, G., & Rossi Romanelli, C. (2018). Tourism initiatives developed through collaboration with foreign organizations: the emergence of responsible practices in Cuba. *Tourism Planning & Development*, **15**(3), 260–276. doi.org/10.1080/21568316.2017.1349688

Bevir, M. (2011). Interpretive theory. In M. Bevir (Ed.), *The SAGE Handbook of Governance*. (p. 593). SAGE Publications.

Bevir, M., & Rhodes, R. A. W. (2007). Decentred theory, change and network governance. In Sørensen E. & Torfing J. (Eds.), *Theories of Democratic Network Governance* (pp. 77–91). London: Palgrave Macmillan UK. doi.org/10.1057/9780230625006_5

Blackstock, K. (2005). A critical look at community based tourism. *Community Development Journal*, **40**(1), 39–49. http://doi.org/10.1093/cdj/bsi005

Bramwell, B. (2010). Participative planning and governance for sustainable tourism. *Tourism Recreation Research*, **35**(3), 239–249. doi.org/10.1080/02508281.2010.11081640

Bramwell, B. (2015). Trust, governance and sustainable tourism. In *Trust, Tourism Development and Planning* (Taylor & Francis, pp. 40–59). Routledge. doi.org/10.4324/9780203537817-8

Bramwell, B. & Lane, B. (1999). Editorial. *Journal of Sustainable Tourism*, **7**(3–4), 179–181. doi.org/10.1080/09669589908667335

Bramwell, B. & Lane, B. (2000). *Tourism, Collaboration, and Partnerships : Politics, practice, and sustainability*. Clevedon: Channel View Publications.

Bramwell, B., & Lane, B. (2014). The 'critical turn' and its implications for sustainable tourism research. *Journal of Sustainable Tourism*, **22**(1), 1–8. doi.org/10.1080/09669582.2013.855223

Byrd, E. T. (2007). Stakeholders in sustainable tourism development and their roles: applying stakeholder theory to sustainable tourism development. *Tourism Review*, **62**(2), 6–13. doi.org/10.1108/16605370780000309

Callon, M. (1986). The sociology of an actor-network: the case of the electric vehicle. In Callon M., Law J., & Rip A (Eds.), *Mapping the Dynamics of Science and Technology* (pp. 19–34). London: Palgrave Macmillan UK. doi.org/10.1007/978-1-349-07408-2_2

Dedeke, A. (Nick). (2017). Creating sustainable tourism ventures in protected areas: An actor-network theory analysis. *Tourism Management*, **61**, 161–172. doi.org/10.1016/J.TOURMAN.2017.02.006

Deleuze, G. & Guattari, F. (1980). *A Thousand Plateaus : Capitalism and schizophrenia*. University of Minnesota Press.

Dinica, V. (2009). Governance for sustainable tourism: a comparison of international and Dutch visions. *Journal of Sustainable Tourism*, **17**(5), 583–603. doi.org/10.1080/09669580902855836

Dodds, R. & Butler, R. (2009). *Barriers to implementing sustainable tourism policy in mass tourism destinations*. Retrieved from https://mpra.ub.uni-muenchen.de/25162/

Dredge, D. & Jamal, T. (2013). Mobilities on the Gold Coast, Australia: implications for destination governance and sustainable tourism. *Journal of Sustainable Tourism*, **21**(4), 557–579. doi.org/10.1080/09669582.2013.776064

Fadeeva, Z. (2005). Translation of sustainability ideas in tourism networks: Some roles of cross-sectoral networks in change towards sustainable development. *Journal of Cleaner Production*, **13**(2), 175–189. doi.org/10.1016/S0959-6526(03)00124-0

Farmaki, A. (2015). Regional network governance and sustainable tourism. *Tourism Geographies*, **17**(3), 385–407. doi.org/10.1080/14616688.2015.1036915

Gage, R. W. & Mandell, M. P. (1990). *Strategies for Managing Intergovernmental Policies and Networks*. Praeger.

Getz, D. & Timur, S. (2005). Stakeholder involvement in sustainable tourism: Balancing the voices. In W. F. Theobald & S. Timur (Eds.), *Global Tourism* (pp. 230–247). Elsevier Butterworth-Heinemann. Retrieved from espace.library.uq.edu.au/view/UQ:161613

Gill, A. M. & Williams, P. W. (2014). Mindful deviation in creating a governance path towards sustainability in resort destinations. *Tourism Geographies*, **16**(4), 546–562. doi.org/10.1080/14616688.2014.925964

Graci, S. (2013). Collaboration and partnership development for sustainable tourism. *Tourism Geographies*, **15**(1), 25–42. doi.org/10.1080/14616688.2012.675513

Halme M., & Fadeeva, Z. (2000). Small and Medium-Sized Tourism Enterprises in Sustainable Development Networks – Value-Added?, *Greener Management International*, **30**: 97-113.

Hanf, K. & Scharpf, F. W. (1978). *Interorganizational Policy Making : Limits to coordination and central control*. Sage Publications.

Hjalager, A.M. (2018). Suppliers as key collaborators for sustainable tourism development. In Liburd, J. and Edwards, D. *Collaboration for Sustainable Tourism Development*. Oxford: Goodfellow Publishers.

Jamal, T. & Stronza, A. (2009). Collaboration theory and tourism practice in protected areas: stakeholders, structuring and sustainability. *Journal of Sustainable Tourism*, **17**(2), 169–189. doi.org/10.1080/09669580802495741

Kickert, W. J. M., Klijn, E.-H. & Koppenjan, J.F.M. (1997). *Managing Complex Networks : Strategies for the public sector*. Sage.

Klijn, E.-H. & Koppenjan, J.F.M. (2012). Governance network theory: past, present and future. *Policy & Politics*, **40**(4), 587–606. doi.org/10.1332/030557312X655431

Koppenjan, J. (2008). Creating a playing field for assessing the effectiveness of network collaboration by performance measures. *Public Management Review*, **10**(6), 699–714. doi.org/10.1080/14719030802423061

Koppenjan, J. F. M. & Klijn, E.-H. (2004). *Managing Uncertainties in Networks : a network approach to problem solving and decision making*. Routledge.

Kramer, R. M. & Cook, K. S. (2004). *Trust and Distrust in Organizations : Dilemmas and approaches*. Russell Sage Foundation.

Lamers, M., van der Duim, R. & Spaargaren, G. (2017). The relevance of practice theories for tourism research. *Annals of Tourism Research*, **62**, 54–63. /doi.org/10.1016/J.ANNALS.2016.12.002

Latour, B. (1999). On recalling ANT. *The Sociological Review*, **47**(1_suppl), 15–25. doi.org/10.1111/j.1467-954X.1999.tb03480.x

Li, Y. & Hunter, C. (2015). Community involvement for sustainable heritage tourism: a conceptual model. *Journal of Cultural Heritage Management and Sustainable Development*, **5**(3), 248–262. doi.org/10.1108/JCHMSD-08-2014-0027

Mandell, M. P. (2001). *Getting Results Through Collaboration : Networks and network structures for public policy and management*. Quorum Books.

Marcussen, M. & Torfing, J. (2007). *Democratic Network Governance In Europe*. Palgrave Macmillan.

Mayaka, M., Croy, W. G. & Cox, J. W. (2018). Participation as motif in community-based tourism: a practice perspective. *Journal of Sustainable Tourism*, **26**(3), 416–432. doi.org/10.1080/09669582.2017.1359278

Meadowcroft, J. (2011). Engaging with the politics of sustainability transitions, *Environmental Innovation and Societal Transitions*. **1**(1) 70-75. doi.org/10.1016/j.eist.2011.02.003

Meier, K. J. & O'Toole, L. J. (2007). Modeling public management. *Public Management Review*, **9**(4), 503–527. doi.org/10.1080/14719030701726630

Mihalič, T., Šegota, T., Knežević Cvelbar, L. & Kuščer, K. (2016). The influence of the political environment and destination governance on sustainable tourism development: a study of Bled, Slovenia. *Journal of Sustainable Tourism*, **24**(11), 1489–1505. doi.org/10.1080/09669582.2015.1134557

Nicolini, D. (2012). *Practice Theory, Work, and Organization : an Introduction*. Oxford University Press.

Nowotny, H., Scott, P. & Gibbons, M. (2001). *Re-thinking Science : Knowledge and the Public in an Age of Uncertainty*. Polity.

Nunkoo, R. (2017). Governance and sustainable tourism: What is the role of trust, power and social capital? *Journal of Destination Marketing & Management*, **6**(4), 277–285. doi.org/10.1016/J.JDMM.2017.10.003

Nunkoo, R. & Smith, S. L. J. (2015). *Trust, Tourism Development and Planning*. Taylor & Francis.

Ostrom, E. (1986). An agenda for the study of institutions. *Public Choice*, **48**(1), 3–25. doi.org/10.1007/BF00239556

Park, S.-Y. & Kohler, T. (2018). Collaboration for sustainable tourism through strategic bridging. *Journal of Vacation Marketing*, 135676671775042. http://doi.org/10.1177/1356766717750422

Powell, W. W. & DiMaggio, P. (1991). *The New Institutionalism in Organizational Analysis*. University of Chicago Press.

Reckwitz, A. (2002). Toward a theory of social practices. *European Journal of Social Theory*, **5**(2), 243–263. doi.org/10.1177/13684310222225432

Rhodes, R. A. W. (1997). *Understanding Governance : Policy networks, governance, reflexivity, and accountability*. Open University Press.

Robertson, P. J. (2011). An assessment of collaborative governance in a network for sustainable tourism: the case of RedeTuris. *International Journal of Public Administration*, **34**(5), 279–290. doi.org/10.1080/01900692.2010.550078

Rogers, D. L. & Whetten, D. A. (1982). *Interorganizational Coordination : Theory, research, and implementation*. Iowa State University Press.

Ruhanen, L. (2013). Local government: facilitator or inhibitor of sustainable tourism development? *Journal of Sustainable Tourism*, **21**(1), 80–98. doi.org/10.1080/09669582.2012.680463

Schön, D. A. & Rein, M. (1994). *Frame Reflection : Toward the resolution of intractable policy controversies*. BasicBooks.

Schwartz, K., Tapper, R. & Font, X. (2008). A Sustainable supply chain management framework for tour operators. *Journal of Sustainable Tourism*, **16**(3), 298–314. doi.org/10.1080/09669580802154108

Scott, W. R. (1995). *Institutions and Organizations*. Thousand Oaks, CA: Sage.

Selin, S. (1999). Developing a typology of sustainable tourism partnerships. *Journal of Sustainable Tourism*, **7**(3–4), 260–273. http://doi.org/10.1080/09669589908667339

Sigala, M. (2008). A supply chain management approach for investigating the role of tour operators on sustainable tourism: the case of TUI. *Journal of Cleaner Production*, **16**(15), 1589–1599. doi.org/10.1016/J.JCLEPRO.2008.04.021

Sigala, M. (2014). Customer involvement in sustainable supply chain management. *Cornell Hospitality Quarterly*, **55**(1), 76–88. doi.org/10.1177/1938965513504030

Sofield, T. H. B. (2003). *Empowerment for Sustainable Tourism Development*. Pergamon.

Sørensen, E. & Torfing, J. (2007). Theoretical approaches to metagovernance. In E. Sørensen & J. Torfing (Eds.), *Theories of Democratic Network Governance* (pp. 169–182). London: Palgrave Macmillan UK. /doi.org/10.1057/9780230625006_10

Termeer, C.J.A.M. & Koppenjan, J.F.M. (1997). Managing perceptions in networks. In W. J. M. Kickert, E.-H. Klijn, & J. F. M. Koppenjan (Eds.), *Managing Complex Networks: Strategies for the Public Sector* (pp. 79–97). Sage.

Timur, S. & Getz, D. (2008). A network perspective on managing stakeholders for sustainable urban tourism. *International Journal of Contemporary Hospitality Management*, **20**(4), 445–461. doi.org/10.1108/09596110810873543

van Bueren, E. M., Klijn, E. & Koppenjan, J. F. M. (2003). Dealing with wicked problems in networks: analyzing an environmental debate from a network perspective. *Journal of Public Administration Research and Theory*, **13**(2), 193–212./doi.org/10.1093/jpart/mug017

van der Duim, R. (2005). Tourismscapes: An actor network perspective on sustainable tourism development. Wageningen Universiteit (Wageningen University). Retrieved from https://www.cabdirect.org/cabdirect/abstract/20053123321

van der Duim, R., Ren, C. & Thor Johannesson, G. (2013). Ordering, materiality, and multiplicity: Enacting Actor-Network Theory in tourism. *Tourist Studies*, **13**(1), 3–20. doi.org/10.1177/1468797613476397

van Hulst, M. & Yanow, D. (2016). From policy 'frames' to 'framing'. *The American Review of Public Administration*, **46**(1), 92–112. doi.org/10.1177/0275074014533142

Van Wezemael, J. (2008). The contribution of assemblage theory and minor politics for democratic network governance. *Planning Theory*, **7**(2), 165–185. doi.org/10.1177/1473095208090433

van Zoonen, L. (2012). I-Pistemology: Changing truth claims in popular and political culture. *European Journal of Communication*, **27**(1), 56–67. doi.org/10.1177/0267323112438808

Vernon, J., Essex, S., Pinder, D. & Curry, K. (2005). Collaborative policymaking: Local Sustainable Projects. *Annals of Tourism Research*, **32**(2), 325–345. doi.org/10.1016/J.ANNALS.2004.06.005

Waligo, V. M., Clarke, J. & Hawkins, R. (2013). Implementing sustainable tourism: A multi-stakeholder involvement management framework. *Tourism Management*, **36**, 342–353. doi.org/10.1016/J.TOURMAN.2012.10.008

5 Personal Interest: (Ir-)Responsible Tourists

Anja Hergesell, Deborah Edwards, and Andreas H. Zins

Introduction

One of the key factors shaping the future of tourism is climate change (Becken & Hay, 2007; Dwyer et al., 2009; Nordin, 2005). Burns and Bibbings (2009) even predict "the end of tourism" should current consumption patterns prevail. There is an alternative to this future, but to develop "new imaginations for the sustainable development" of tourism we must understand the wicked problem of tourists' environmental behavior. Tourists' environmental behavior impacts on sustainable development to varying degrees (Becken et al, 2003; Metz et al., 2007) depending on whether they behave responsibly or irresponsibly. People consider holidays as a break from everyday life (Becken, 2004; Dolnicar & Grün, 2009) which suggests that people may behave differently when they are tourists. For this reason, this chapter explores tourists' uptake of environmental behaviors by examining their propensity to responsible environmental behavior while travelling. A better understanding of tourists' environmental behavior can lead to strategies that support collaborative actions "towards facilitating tourism development that is inherently sustainable" (Jennings, 2018). Environmental behavior is a very complex field of research (Hergesell, 2017). Such behavior is determined by a range of internal and external factors with the significance of these factors differing dependent on the person, the context and the type of behavior under study. The question is hence how to reduce 'irresponsible' behavior.

This chapter examines the influence of sociodemographic, psychological and situational factors on tourists' environmental behaviors and their interrelations on two levels: 1) the relationship between environmental behaviors in the home and holiday context; and 2) the relationship between general environmental behaviors and environmentally friendly holidaying behaviors. Following a presentation of the results, the chapter discusses the implications of collaboration for sustainable destination management.

The complexity of tourists' environmentally friendly behavior

There has been a growing interest among tourism researchers in studying the interplay between tourist behavior (Dolnicar & Grün, 2009) and the determinants of environmental behavior (Dolnicar, 2010). Normative models of behavior such as the one by Stern (2000) suggest the existence of common origins for environmentally friendly behaviors in the form of values. Based on this idea, current environmental policies assume "that small pro-environmental behaviours can spill over into motivating more ambitious and environmentally significant behaviours" (Thøgersen & Crompton, 2009: 143). Such positive spillover effects are intrinsic to models like self-perception theories, consistency theories and knowledge theories (Thøgersen & Crompton, 2009). According to self-perception theory, internal dispositions are inferred from behavior, meaning that undertaking an environmentally friendly behavior may change how one perceives oneself thus increasing the likelihood of engaging again in the same behavior and also in other environmentally friendly behaviors. Consistency theories (e.g. Festinger, 1957) suggest that people strive to behave consistently, i.e. they feel a cognitive dissonance behaving environmentally friendly in one area but not in another. One of the strategies to resolve this dissonance is to behave consistently. Knowledge theories propose spillover effects through learning. The engagement in one environmentally friendly behavior builds knowledge or skills that facilitate the uptake of other environmentally friendly behaviors.

While theoretical models suggest mechanisms that could explain positive spillover, these mechanisms are not certain to occur. Thøgersen and Crompton (2009) criticize the idea of positive spillover effects and its uptake in environmental campaigning, arguing that empirical studies could frequently not establish such effects, and that, in contrast, negative spillover effects could occur as noted in a range of studies (Barr et al., 2010; Becken, 2007; Hares et al., 2010; Randles & Mander, 2009; Stoll-Kleemann et al., 2001). The idea of negative spillover effects is also supported by cognitive dissonance theory, suggesting that denial and displacement mechanisms are frequently applied to deal with the dissonance in behavior. This means the environmental contribution of current behavior is exaggerated, the environmental commitment is displaced to another context, and powerlessness or external constraints are claimed.

While several focus group studies in tourism have underpinned the existence of denial mechanisms (Barr et al., 2010; Hares et al., 2010; Randles & Mander, 2009), empirical evidence for positive spillover effects are predominantly limited to behaviors that are somewhat easy to exert (Thøgersen & Crompton, 2009). This may be because they are most common or habitualized. Thøgersen (2004) concluded that dissimilarities in various behavior components can preclude a feeling of dissonance and hence prevent positive spillover. Determinants include: 1) the amount of effort and resources needed; 2) the physical actions involved; 3) the setting (space/time); 4) the specific outcome; and 5) its perceived contribution to a superior goal.

Undertaking environmentally friendly behaviors for other reasons than to protect the environment, such as contributing to an alternative superior goal, has frequently been recognized (Stern, 2000; Whitmarsh, 2009). In other words, engaging in environmentally friendly behaviors to protect the environment has been found to arise from different underlying values. Stern (2000) differentiated 1) the egoistic, 2) the altruistic/social, and 3) the biospheric value orientation in which people behave based on the benefit for the environment. Each value orientation may encourage environmentally friendly behaviors dependent on the person's beliefs about adverse consequences (AC). The first type describes people who undertake environmentally friendly behaviors when perceived personal benefits outweigh perceived costs. The second type behaves environmentally friendly if this is believed to be for the good of a group of people even if it means a personal sacrifice. The third orientation describes people who behave environmentally friendly for the good of the environment regardless of the perceived costs and/or benefits to themselves or others. While these value orientations could be empirically identified (Axelrod, 1994), all value orientations coexist in a person. They may not only shift throughout a person's lifecycle, but also vary in dominance dependent on situational conditions (Jackson, 2005).

Behavioral studies provide inconsistent clues in regards to the stability of behaviors across contexts. The repetition of past behavior may encourage the development of habits, while the context is frequently a more important determinant of behavior than internal forces (Klöckner & Blöbaum, 2010). The former relates to the idea that repetitive behavior includes the use of heuristics, i.e. cues, which limit the control one exerts on a decision, acting 'habitual' (Jackson, 2005; Verplanken et al., 1997). The importance of situational factors is stressed by integrated models of consumer behavior which show that the inclusion of context-related constructs increases the explanatory power of models (Guagnano et al., 1995; Klöckner & Blöbaum, 2010).

The influence of situational conditions on the engagement in environmentally friendly behaviors was also stressed in tourism studies, e.g. by Barr and colleagues in their focus group interviews (Barr et al., 2011; Barr et al., 2010) and by Dolnicar and colleagues in their quantitative study on the stability of behaviors across lifestyle domains (home and holidays) (Dolnicar & Grün, 2009; Dolnicar & Leisch, 2008). The latter study segmented respondents based on their level of engagement in selected behaviors at home (recycling/waste avoidance, mobility behavior/car avoidance, reading about the environment, donating) and examined the influence of the change in context. They discovered that while a part of each segment remained within their segment in the holiday context, a varying proportion of each of the segments demonstrated characteristics of other segments, especially of the least environmentally friendly segment. This change towards lower frequency of environmentally friendly behavior on holidays was linked to differences in moral obligation towards a place with a higher sense of responsibility for the home environment. Barr and colleagues' (2010) study explored self-reported commitments, attitudes and intentions across behaviors and contexts. The discussions revealed that the holiday context is perceived as a contrast, a break from daily life, in which hedonic motives like relaxing, having fun, etc. dominate, all of which may negatively affect the uptake of environmental behaviors.

Studies in tourism and environmental psychology suggest that consumers act inconsistently both on the individual level, comparing the performance of one specific behavior across lifestyle domains, and on a cumulated level, comparing the uptake of a number of environmentally friendly behaviors. While earlier studies have investigated (in)consistencies within one specific behavior or (in)consistencies between behaviors, the present study incorporates both levels taking a stepwise approach. This chapter contributes original insights on relationships between tourists' environmentally friendly behaviors, differences in underlying value orientations, and underlying motives. With a better understanding of tourists' environmental behavior, we make suggestions for supporting tourists' environmental behavior through collaborative strategies.

Methodology

The primary research was carried out at the Slovenian coast in July 2010. The study took a stepwise approach examining the relationships: 1) between general environmentally friendly behaviors in the home and holiday context, and 2) between environmentally friendly behaviors and environmentally friendly holidaying behaviors. The relationships across contexts and types of behavior were further explored by considering underlying value orientations and self-reported motives for stability or divergence in behavior.

A questionnaire was used which incorporated five sections covering questions on the respondents' current and past travel behavior, their beliefs about the human-environment relationship, their engagement in selected behaviors in the home and holiday contexts, their engagement in environmentally friendly holidaying behaviors and demographic characteristics. Respondents' value orientation was assessed indirectly by measuring beliefs about the adverse consequences (AC) of the human-environment relationship as developed by Stern and colleagues (Stern et al., 1993). Nine questions addressed three dimensions ACegoistic, ACaltruistic/social and ACbiospheric. In accordance with previous research (Barr et al., 2010; compare Dolnicar & Grün, 2009; Whitmarsh & O'Neill, 2010) nine behaviors exemplified by a variety of environmental behaviors related to resource consumption, purchase decisions, mobility and political activism were chosen for comparison between contexts. Respondents were asked to indicate how often they undertake these activities at home. The frequency of undertaking the same activities in the holiday context was measured relative to home context differentiating less often, same like at home and more often.

In addition, the primary reasons for undertaking the behaviors at home and on holidays were noted. Respondents could choose from eight reasons (Table 5.1) developed from the literature (Blake, 1999; Kollmuss & Agyeman, 2002).

Table 5.1: Classification of primary reasons

Types	Reasons
Environmental reasons	Environmental reasons
Internal reasons (other)	Personal (dis)interest Health concerns Convenience considerations Because of other people (perceived social influence)
Habit	Habit
External reasons	(Non)availability of (infra)structures / means
Socio-economic reasons	Financial reasons

Finally, nine behaviors related to environmentally friendly holidaying were included. Used in an earlier tourism study by Fleischhacker et al. (2009), the behaviors relate to much-discussed environmental aspects of holidaying: the frequency of undertaking trips, the choice of destinations, travel modes and accommodation. The respondents were asked whether they undertake these behaviors at present.

An administered survey was distributed in four languages (English, German, Slovenian and Italian) to accommodate the majority of the tourists visiting the Slovenian coast. Tourists were randomly approached and asked to participate resulting in 434 usable responses. Table 5.2 presents a profile of respondents.

Respondents, who checked the not applicable option for a specific behavior or did not answer a question, were excluded from the analysis for this particular behavior but they were included in the analysis of all other questions. The influence of value orientations on uptake of environmentally friendly behaviors were tested with ANOVAs, in other words the groups of respondents who engage never, occasionally or frequently in the nine selected environmentally friendly behaviors were tested for significant differences. Post hoc analyses were undertaken to further characterize the differences. To investigate whether the reasons for undertaking a behavior with a certain frequency are changing if people engage either less or more frequently in environmentally friendly activities on holidays, a transitional analysis was undertaken.

Table 5.2: Profile of respondents

Characteristics	Proportion of sample	Characteristics	Proportion of sample
Nationality		*Occupational status*	
Slovenia	33%	Studying/training	24%
Austria	22%	Employed/self-employed	62%
Germany	21%	Not employed	3%
Italy	20%	Retired	11%
Other	4%		
		Educational attainment	
Age		Primary and lower secondary education	13%
18 to 24	23%	Upper secondary (high school certificate)	54%
25 to 44	47%	Tertiary education	33%
45 to 64	25%	*Gender*	
65 and over	5%	Female	51%
		Male	49%

Differences in uptake of environmental behaviors by type of behavior and reasons

Almost all respondents engaged in some environmentally friendly behaviors at home. The behaviors adopted by over ninety percent of respondents were turning off lights, followed by separating waste (Figure 5.1). Using public transport to go to events constituted the approximate overall mean in difficulty. Behaviors to its left were on average more popular suggesting that they are considered easier, while those to its right were on average less popular suggesting that they are considered more difficult (Figure 5.1). The least popular behaviors among respondents were engaging in environmental organizations and abstaining from taking a car for shopping (coding reversed for analysis). The much lower uptake of environmental activism in contrast to private-sphere environmentalism has been noted by earlier studies (Dolnicar, 2010; Stern, 2000; Whitmarsh, 2009).

The level of engagement in seven out of nine environmental behaviors at home was significantly different by strength of underlying value orientation. In most cases, biospheric or altruistic value orientations were significantly stronger as respondents engaged in a behavior more frequently or egoistic value orientations were stronger as respondents engaged in a behavior less frequently. This suggests that the behavior uptake of most of the behaviors studied here are positively related to altruistic or biospheric value orientations, or negatively related to egoistic value orientation. Significant correlations between individual behaviors also support the idea of common underlying roots between some of the behaviors.

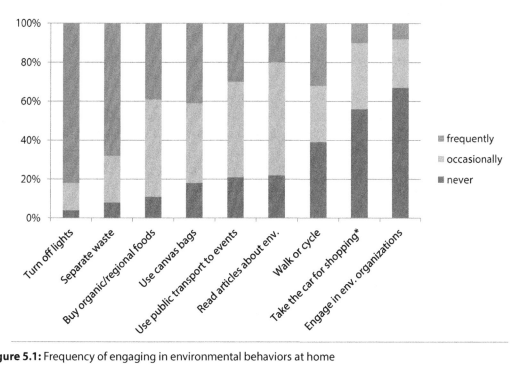

Figure 5.1: Frequency of engaging in environmental behaviors at home

In contrast to environmental behaviors in the home context, few environmental holidaying behaviors were undertaken by respondents, supporting the hypothesis that tourists are taking a break from everyday life (Becken, 2004; Dolnicar & Grün, 2009) desiring to enjoy their holidays unencumbered by the need to think about the impacts they may be having (Miller et al., 2010). Indeed, the only somewhat popular environmental holidaying behavior was choosing destinations closer to home, which half of the respondents endorsed. None of the other behaviors were undertaken by the majority of the respondents. Possible relationships between environmental behaviors at home and environmental holidaying behaviors were examined. Although the relations are unspecified, the frequency of significant links gives some indication of relationships. Overall, choice of ground transport mode and accommodation showed the highest number of links with environmental behaviors at home. In contrast, behaviors related to vacation frequency and plane use had few significant links to environmental behaviors at home suggesting that these behaviors are not systematically related to an environmentally friendly lifestyle.

Stability of environmental behaviors across contexts and reasons

The majority of the respondents undertook some of the behaviors consistently across contexts. Among them were popular behaviors such as turning off lights, using canvas bags, and buying organic/regional foods. Indeed, these behaviors could be considered those that are most habitualized and hence of little surprise that they remain stable across contexts.

Other behaviors were only undertaken consistently across contexts by approximately half of the respondents. Interestingly, there were positive changes from an environmental point of view in regards to mobility behaviors with about half of respondents abstaining from using the car more often for shopping, walking / cycling more, and one third of the respondents using more public transport to attend events. This suggests that mobility behavior at the destination might be less of a problem (given the necessary infrastructure and tourist information).

Table 5.3: Relative count of reasons for engaging in environmental behaviors at home (relative count of activities = occurrence per activity)

Engaging in 9 different activities	Never	Occasionally	Frequently	Overall
Financial reasons	.09	.07	.08	.08
Habit	.28	.25	.23	.22
Environmental reasons	.05	.20	.28	.21
Health concerns	.02	.07	.11	.07
Convenience considerations	.09	.13	.10	.12
Because of other people	.04	.06	.03	.04
(Non)Availability of (infra)structures / means	.15	.07	.05	.08
Personal (dis)interest	.29	.15	.12	.18

Table 5.4: Relative count of reasons for engaging in environmental behaviors on holidays

Engaging in 9 different activities	Never	Occasionally	Frequently	Overall
Financial reasons	.07	.05	.07	.06
Habit	.18	.33	.27	.27
Environmental reasons	.09	.15	.17	.14
Health concerns	.02	.07	.10	.06
Convenience considerations	.16	.11	.13	.12
Because of other people	.05	.03	.06	.04
(Non)Availability of (infra)structures / means	.26	.08	.09	.13
Personal (dis)interest	.16	.18	.14	.18

Habit was found to be one of the most cited reasons given by respondents to explain their behaviors regardless of the frequency (Tables 5.3 and 5.4). Of critical importance is that environmental reasons were the most frequently mentioned type of reason for engaging in a behavior frequently, while personal disinterest explains why respondents exert little effort to participate in environmental behaviors.

Habit was also the most frequently noted reason when examining environmental behaviors in the holiday context (Table 5.4). Interestingly though, habit was not only the primary reason for consistency across context but also the top reason for engaging more frequently in a behavior on holidays. This might be related to these behaviors generally being undertaken more frequently on holidays compared to at home (e.g. more frequent entering and leaving of room with switching off of lights). Interestingly, the most frequent reason for not engaging in a behavior was the non-availability of (infra)structures, suggesting that there is a lack of structures in place at the destination and/or a lack of awareness of these structures. This, in turn, suggests that destinations could do their share in promoting certain environmental behaviors on holidays.

Next to habit, the main reasons for undertaking the behaviors as frequently as/more frequently than at home were the same as for the uptake of the behaviors at home. These were: convenience and health considerations for mobility behaviors, health reasons for purchasing regional produce, environmental reasons for energy saving and waste reduction/management, and personal interest for engagement in environmental issues (reading, supporting organizations).

Next to habit, the main reasons for engaging less frequently in a behavior were the non-availability of (infra)structures / means and personal disinterest. The former was the major inhibitor for waste reduction / management behaviors as well as for purchasing regional produce. It also seemed to influence mobility behaviors in positive and negative ways (e.g. own car not available at destination), as did convenience considerations. A less frequent engagement in environmental issues (reading, supporting organizations) was also linked to the non-availability of means (e.g. no reading material on the topic in tourist language) as well as to personal disinterest. The latter seems surprising given that 77% of these respondents engaged occasionally, and the remainder engaged frequently in such behavior at home, with 73% mentioning personal interest as the key reason. This might suggest that their interest does not concern the environment per se, but rather certain issues related to the environment. Environmental issues at the destination might not awake the same degree of interest. Though further research is needed on the issue, some studies have suggested a disparity in the degree of moral obligation towards environmental issues at home versus on holidays (Dolnicar & Grün, 2009).

Furthermore, a transitional analysis was undertaken to investigate whether the types of reasons are changing if people engage either less or more frequently in environmentally friendly activities on holidays. For this purpose the eight reasons were aggregated into five types of explanations: socio-economic, internal, habit, environmental and external (Table 5.2). It was then explored whether the underlying type of reason remained the same or changed as the context changed. In total, 25 transitions of reasons were defined.

In the situation of less frequent engagement in environmental behaviors in the holiday context, the primary reasons for this heterogeneity remained internal, i.e. within the person, for almost all of the environmental behaviors. This means that the primary reason cited for engaging in an environmental behavior less often in the holiday context remained internal to the person (e.g. convenience, health). The only exceptions relate to separating waste, using canvas bags, and switching off lights. In the former cases, the most cited transition was from environmental considerations in the home context to external constraints in the holiday context (20% and 14% of all transitions respectively). In the latter case, the lower frequency in the holiday context was linked to a transition from socio-economic reasons to internal reasons such as convenience considerations and personal disinterest (20% of all transitions). Other plausible transitions towards a lower frequency in the holiday context were buying organic/ regional products and reading articles about the environment (18% and 13% of all transitions from internal drivers to external constraint), and engaging in environmental organizations (27% of all transitions from environmental reasons to external constraints).

The arguments for undertaking behaviors more often in the holiday context also predominantly remained internal. Again, the most notable exceptions were separating waste, using canvas bags and turning off lights. In the former cases, the most frequent transition remained environmental reasons (42% and 23% of all transitions respectively), while in the latter case, the most frequent transition remained habit (28% of all transitions). Interestingly, abstaining from using the car for shopping more frequently was linked equally to constant internal reasons and the transition from internal dispositions to external constraints (each 21% of all transitions). The latter suggests that the travel to the destination by other transport modes (e.g. train, bus) frequently determines mobility behavior at the destination towards a lower environmental impact.

Discussion

The findings reinforce the literature (e.g. Thøgersen, 2004) that environmentally friendly behaviors are diverse, which can explain the lack of spillover or relationship between them. Communicating expectations of the destination community may not be enough to affect changes in tourists' environmental behaviors. This means that behaviors that are expected from tourists have to be first carefully assessed in terms of their characteristics (associated effort, underlying motives, etc.) before deciding on policy approaches to encourage desired behaviors. Choosing to attract tourists that display desired behaviors in the home context will not guarantee environmentally friendly outcomes for a destination; nor can one expect destinations to be able to assess tourists' behaviors at home in order to identify whether they will be 'environmentally friendly tourists' in the destination. Other approaches are going to be required and this is where collaboration could be useful. Participating in collaborative approaches that create group standards for environmentally friendly behavior may assist in overcoming the opposing dilemmas of what is best for the individual in the short term versus what is best for long-term societal outcomes (Miller et al., 2010).

The analyses indicate that value orientations can explain some environmentally friendly behaviors, but their relevance depends on the type of behavior and the context. As already noted by Stern (2000), many private sphere behaviors are explained by value orientations while environmental activism is not. The study also affirms that the context affects the influence of value orientations as competing values co-exist in a person and change priority with the change in context (Jackson, 2005). Particularly the holiday context has been recognized for the prominence of hedonic values (Decrop, 2006) with these values shown to be negatively related to environmental behavior uptake (Steg et al., 2012). It is therefore doubtful if appeals on environmental or altruistic/social grounds are effective in the holiday context. Yet Liburd and Becken (2017) found that value-based collaborations can tap into local and global networks via the media and by telling environmentally friendly behavior success stories.

The challenge of appealing to people's environmental concern is further reinforced by the study of the primary reasons underlying environmentally friendly behaviors. The findings assert that several of the environmentally friendly behaviors are not motivated by environmental concern but by reasons such as personal interest, financial considerations, health concerns or habit. Moreover, inconsistencies in behaviors across contexts seem to be predominantly caused by intrinsic factors other than environmental considerations as also noted in earlier studies (Barr et al., 2010; Dolnicar & Grün, 2009).

The results are not encouraging. Peoples' bias towards satisfying their needs compounds negative environmental outcomes (Persson & Savulescu, 2012), and more so when there are large numbers of people travelling. Perhaps the responsible tourist as defined by Dwyer (2018: 15) is but a dream, as the tourists' personal interest will always take precedence. We argue that to assume the "responsible tourist" exists in numbers that can make a difference sets up destination managers for planning failure. Instead, if we accept that all tourists will behave (ir)responsibly (at least at some point) we can create a more realistic focus for developing appropriate strategies that can lead to improved environmentally friendly behaviors. It is argued in this book that collaboration is a key condition for sustainable tourism development. These results would suggest collaboration may only occur when personal interests can be aligned. That is, any sort of collaboration is going to be difficult to achieve while individuals address their own personal interests ahead of others.

Only the separation of waste and use of canvas bags indicated a significant role of environmental considerations. In those cases, the transition towards a lower frequency of undertaking the behavior is predominantly related to perceived external constraints. Thus, efforts should focus on improving environmental infrastructure that supports the consistent uptake of environmentally friendly behaviors across contexts and create awareness for these among tourists.

The difficulties in encouraging environmentally friendly behavior in the holiday context are also related to the dominance of habit as an underlying reason, which can be both a curse and a blessing. Habits may encourage behavioral stability over contexts, hence increasing the ability to predict certain behaviors in other contexts (like the holiday context). However, this study found support that behaviors based on habits are very limited in terms of positive spillover effects (Thøgersen & Crompton, 2009), i.e. even though such behaviors may be well predicted, they cannot serve as indicators for the engagement in other behaviors. Cohen et al.(2011: 1073) note "that the 'deep problem' within the tourism supply and consumption chain is of such a scale that habits...must be challenged and changed".

Based on the findings, the only area in which such spillovers could possibly be imagined, is mobility behavior. However, there is too little data to substantiate this association. Moreover, it may be convenience considerations (the other frequently cited reason) that play a role in mobility decisions. Indeed, other studies have found that tourists enjoy alternative modes of mobility (i.e. walking, cycling, bus tours) at the destination as such modes enable the tourist to engage intimately with a destination (Edwards and Griffin, 2014).

Perhaps destination managers have relied too much on more cooperative approaches (such as hanging up towels) 'hoping' that tourists will make environmentally friendly choices. Given the role of habit in predicting tourist behavior in the destination (Miller et al., 2015) we pose the question: Could the destination help foster habits of environmental collaboration with tourists? Collaborative approaches to environmental issues have been used to address problems that have failed to be effectively resolved by independent action (Graci, 2013). Gray (1985: 912) defined collaboration as "the pooling of appreciations and/or tangible resources, e.g., information, money, labor, etc., by two or more stakeholders, to solve a set of problems" which in turn may generate outcomes beyond what any individual or organization could achieve on their own. Redmond and colleagues (2016: 431) argue that "previously dormant (or secondary) pro-social motives can be 're-booted' through a contextual change, and can have greater weighting on subsequent behaviors in comparison to more stable self-interest motives". Such collaboration can be in the form of tourists working with and "respecting community needs" (Hughes & Morrison-Saunders, 2018; Miller et al., 2010). Destination managers can take advantage of tourists' personal disinterest by offering reciprocal exchanges for environmental collaboration (Hughes & Morrison-Saunders, 2018). With this strategy, "there will be an incentive to collaborate for the purpose of pursuing common or mutually beneficial goals or interests" (Fielder & Deegan, 2007: 419). Moreover, destinations can capitalize on visitors' pro-environmental interests by using them as evaluators and reporters for environmental reporting programs. Collaborative exchanges that require the sharing of skills and resources can then "foster the habit of collaboration, mutual support, and a willingness to put the good of the team first" (Gardner, 1991: 6).

Conclusion

Overall, the results verify earlier critiques on current environmental policy (Barr et al., 2011; Thøgersen & Crompton, 2009). Encouraging environmentally friendly behaviors based on behavior at home does not ensure environmentally friendly behaviors in the holiday context nor the uptake of environmental holidaying behaviors. The findings on the transitions suggest that managers and policy makers will have to develop alternative approaches that appeal to internal forces rather than environmental considerations (e.g. health, personal interest or social influence) and develop collaborative activities that encourage environmentally friendly behaviors.

The destination has an important role to play in the development of environmental infrastructures that demand collaboration from the tourist. Without such structures, we can only expect tourists to behave in their own personal interest. Linked to managerial implications there is a need for further research on environmentally friendly behaviors and their determinants to holistically understand possible relationships. The findings reported here are based on a limited set of environmentally friendly behaviors and did not measure the reasons for (not) engaging in environmental holidaying behaviors. Cultural differences that can affect value orientations (Holden, 2000) were not considered. Future studies could thus expand on the number and types of environmentally friendly behaviors considered. They could also include more respondent characteristics in order to further explore opportunities for segmenting tourists in regards to their behavior on holidays. More research is also needed on the key determinants of environmental holidaying behaviors to develop effective collaborative initiatives that bring about lasting behavioral change. Whilst in the destination, can tourists be encouraged to undertake collaborative activities that foster habitual behaviors that lead to ongoing environmentally friendly behaviors? Especially in light of current climate change discussions, the associations shown between mobility behaviors should be examined further. In conclusion, this study provides support for the need for further research on environmentally friendly behaviors and the types of collaborative approaches that will be required to promote responsible tourist behavior.

References

Axelrod, L. J. (1994). Balancing personal needs with environmental preservation: identifying the values that guide decisions in ecological dilemmas. *Journal of Social Issues*, **50**(3), 85-104.

Barr, S., Gilg, A. & Shaw, G. (2011). 'Helping people make better choices': exploring the behaviour change agenda for environmental sustainability. *Applied Geography*, **31**, 712-720.

Barr, S., Shaw, G., Coles, T. & Prillwitz, J. (2010). 'A holiday is a holiday': practicing sustainability, home and away. *Journal of Transport Geography*, **18**, 474-481.

Becken, S. (2004). How tourists and tourism experts perceive climate change and carbon-offsetting schemes. *Journal of Sustainable Tourism*, **12**(4), 332-345.

Becken, S. (2007). Tourists' perception of international air travel's impact on the global climate and potential climate change policies. *Journal of Sustainable Tourism*, **15**(4), 351-368.

Becken, S., & Hay, J. E. (2007). *Tourism and Climate Change: Risks and opportunities*. Clevedon: Channel View Publications.

Becken, S., Simmons, D. G. & Frampton, C. (2003). Energy use associated with different travel choices. *Tourism Management*, **24**, 267-277.

Blake, J. (1999). Overcoming the 'value-action gap' in environmental policy: tensions between national policy and local experience. *Local Environment*, **4**(3), 257-278.

Burns, P. & Bibbings, L. (2009). The end of tourism? Climate change and societal challenges. *21st Century Society*, **4**(1), 31-51.

Cohen, S. A., Higham, J. E. & Cavaliere, C. T. (2011). Binge flying: Behavioural addiction and climate change. *Annals of Tourism Research*, **38**(3), 1070-1089.

Decrop, A. (2006). *Vacation Decision Making*. Oxfordshire: CABI Publishing.

Dolnicar, S. (2010). Identifying tourists with smaller environmental footprints. *Journal of Sustainable Tourism*, **18**(6), 717-734.

Dolnicar, S. & Grün, B. (2009). Environmentally friendly behavior: can heterogeneity among individuals and contexts/environments be harvested for improved sustainable management? *Environment and Behavior*, **41**(5), 693-714.

Dolnicar, S. & Leisch, F. (2008). An investigation of tourists' patterns of obligation to protect the environment. *Journal of Travel Research*, **46**, 381-391.

Dwyer, L. (2018). Saluting while the ship sinks: the necessity for tourism paradigm change. *Journal of Sustainable Tourism*, **26**(1), 29-48. doi:10.1080/09669582.2017.1308372

Dwyer, L., Edwards, D., Mistilis, N., Roman, C. & Scott, N. (2009). Destination and enterprise management for a tourism future. *Tourism Management*, **30**(1), 63-74.

Edwards, D., & Griffin, T. (2013). Understanding tourists' spatial behaviour: GPS tracking as an aid to sustainable destination management. *Journal of Sustainable Tourism*, **21**(4), 580-595.

Festinger, L. (1957). *A Theory of Cognitive Dissonance*. Stanford: Stanford University Press.

Fiedler, T. & Deegan, C. (2007). Motivations for environmental collaboration within the building and construction industry, *Managerial Auditing Journal*, **22**(4), 410-441.

Fleischhacker, V., Formayer, H., Seisser, O., Wolf-Eberl, S. & Kromp-Kolb, H. (2009). *Auswirkungen des Klimawandels auf das künftige Reiseverhalten im österreichischem Tourismus*. Forschungsbericht im Auftrag des Bundesministeriums für Wirtschaft, Familie und Jugend. Retrieved https://meteo.boku.ac.at/report/BOKU-Met_Report_19_online.pdf

Gardner, J. W. (1991). *Building Community* (p. 5). Washington, DC: Independent Sector.

Graci, S. (2013). Collaboration and partnership development for sustainable tourism, *Tourism Geographies*, **15**(1), 25-42.

Gray, B. (1985). Conditions facilitating interorganizational collaboration. *Human Relations*, **38**(10), 911-936.

Guagnano, G. A., Stern, P. C. & Dietz, T. (1995). Influences on attitude-behavior relationships: a natural experiment with curbside recycling. *Environment and Behavior*, **27**(5), 699-718.

Hares, A., Dickinson, J. & Wilkes, K. (2010). Climate change and the air travel decisions of UK tourists. *Journal of Transport Geography*, **18**, 466-473.

Hergesell, A. (2017). Climate-Friendly Tourist Behavior (Unpublished doctoral dissertation). Vienna Unviersity of Economics and Business, Vienna, Austria.

Holden, A. (2000). *Environment and Tourism*. New York: Routledge.

Hughes, M. & Morrison-Saunders, A. (2018). Whose needs and what is to be sustained? In Liburd, J. and Edwards, D. (2018) *Collaborations for Sustainable Tourism Development*. Goodfellow Publishers, Oxford, UK.

Jackson, T. (2005). Motivating sustainable consumption: a review of evidence on consumer behaviour and behavioural change. Retrieved from Guildford: http://www.sd-research.org.uk/wp-content/uploads/motivatingscfinal_000.pdf

Jennings, G.R. (2018). Reflections on research paradigms, In Liburd, J. and Edwards, D. (2018) *Collaborations for Sustainable Tourism Development*. Goodfellow Publishers, Oxford, UK.

Klöckner, C. A. & Blöbaum, A. (2010). A comprehensive action determination model: toward a broader understanding of ecological behaviour using the example of travel mode choice. *Journal of Environmental Psychology*, **30**(4), 574-586.

Kollmuss, A. & Agyeman, J. (2002). Mind the gap: why do people act environmentally and what are the barriers to pro-environmental behavior? *Environmental Education Research*, **8**(3), 239-260.

Liburd, J. & Becken, S. (2017). Values in nature conservation, tourism and UNESCO World Heritage Site stewardship. *Journal of Sustainable Tourism*, **25**(12), 1719-1735.

Metz, B., Davidson, O. R., Bosch, P. R., Dave, R. & Meyer, L. A. (Eds.). (2007). *Mitigation of climate change - contribution of working group III to the fourth assessment report of the Intergovernmental Panel on Climate Change*. Cambridge: Cambridge University Press.

Miller, D., Merrilees, B. & Coghlan, A. (2015). Sustainable urban tourism: understanding and developing visitor pro-environmental behaviours. *Journal of Sustainable Tourism*, **23**(1), 26-46. doi:10.1080/09669582.2014.912219

Miller, G., Rathouse, K., Scarles, C., Holmes, K. & Tribe, J. (2010). Public understanding of sustainable tourism. *Annals of Tourism Research*, **37**(3), 627-645.

Nordin, S. (2005). *Tourism of tomorrow - travel trends and forces of change*. Retrieved from www.miun.se/upload/Etour/Publikationer/Utredningsserien/U200527.pdf

Persson, I. & Savulescu, J. (2012). *Unfit for the Future: The need for moral enhancement*. Oxford: OUP.

Randles, S. & Mander, S. (2009). Aviation, consumption and the climate change debate: 'Are you going to tell me off for flying?' *Technology Analysis & Strategic Management*, **21**(1), 93-113.

Redmond, J., Wolfram Cox, J., Curtis, J., Kirk-Brown, A. & Walker, B. (2016). Beyond business as usual: how (and why) the habit discontinuity hypothesis can inform SME engagement in environmental sustainability practices. *Australasian Journal of Environmental Management*, **23**(4), 426-442.

Steg, L., Perlaviciute, G., Van der Werff, E. & Lurvink, J. (2012). The significance of hedonic values for environmentally relevant attitudes, preferences, and actions. *Environment and Behavior*, **46**(2), 163-192.

Stern, P. C. (2000). Toward a coherent theory of environmentally significant behavior. *Journal of Social Issues*, **56**(3), 407-424.

Stern, P. C., Dietz, T. & Kalof, L. (1993). Value orientations, gender, and environmental concern. *Environment and Behavior*, **25**(5), 322-348.

Stoll-Kleemann, S., O'Riordan, T. & Jaeger, C. C. (2001). The psychology of denial concerning climate mitigation measures: evidence from Swiss focus groups. *Global Environmental Change*, **11**, 107-117.

Thøgersen, J. (2004). A cognitive dissonance interpretation of consistencies and inconsistencies in environmentally responsible behavior. *Journal of Environmental Psychology*, **24**, 94-103.

Thøgersen, J. & Crompton, T. (2009). Simple and painless? The limitations of spillover in environmental campaigning. *Journal of Consumer Policy*, **32**(2), 141-163.

Verplanken, B., Aarts, H., & Van Knippenberg, A. (1997). Habit, information acquisition, and the process of making travel mode choices. *European Journal of Social Psychology*, **27**, 539-560.

Whitmarsh, L. (2009). Behavioural responses to climate change: asymmetry of intentions and impacts. *Journal of Environmental Psychology*, **29**, 13-23.

Whitmarsh, L. & O'Neill, S. (2010). Green identity, green living? The role of pro-environmental self-identity in determining consistency across diverse pro-environmental behaviours. *Journal of Environmental Psychology*, **30**(3), 305-314.

6 Voluntourism and the Sustainable Development Goals

Peter Devereux and Kirsten Holmes

Introduction

Volunteer tourism or voluntourism has become an extremely popular form of tourism as well as attracting significant and growing academic attention (Wearing & McGehee, 2013). In 2001 Wearing defined volunteer tourism (drawing on his own research in community based ecotourism and volunteer tourism in Costa Rica) as: "those tourists who, for various reasons, volunteer in an organized way to undertake holidays that might involve aiding or alleviating the material poverty of some groups in society, the restoration of certain environments, or research into aspects of society or environment" (Wearing, 2001:1). The significant growth in academic interest in the topic is reflected in a web of science search for volunteer tourism peer reviewed literature which counts 1 for 2001, 4 for 2008, 15 for 2013 and 41 for 2016 and the publication of a review paper in the leading journal *Tourism Management* (Wearing & McGehee, 2013) and several journal special issues.

As research on this topic has matured, there has been a conceptual shift from early studies, which have focused on the experience of the individual volunteer to a more critical approach, which questions the impact of the tourists' activities on the host community (Loiseau et al., 2016b; Lupoli et al., 2014). The vast majority of studies have examined international volunteering, with predominantly white western tourists travelling to low income countries, however there has been some interest in domestic voluntourism. The maturing of research on this topic, which has reconceptualised volunteer tourism as "taking many forms, occurring on an increasingly broad continuum" (McGehee, 2014: 206) and as a part of a tourist's overall trip, has mirrored the growing market for volunteer tourism holidays.

While significant and growing, the global market for voluntourism is hard to quantify, in part due to the diversity of not-for-profit and commercial providers and projects. Tomazos and Butler (2009) tracked a nearly 500% growth from

2003 to 2007 in projects and countries where these projects were available and provide some evidence of the enormous expansion in this niche area, alongside the publication of a Lonely Planet guide which has run to three editions (Holmes, 2014b). A 2008 report suggested there were at least 1.6 million volunteer tourists who contributed more than $1.76 billion toward the global economy (European Association for Tourism and Leisure Education & Tourism Research and Marketing, 2008).

There is a significant division in the academic literature on this phenomenon between tourism researchers, who focus on volunteer tourism as a form of tourism and not-for-profit studies that examine this as a form of volunteering (Holmes, 2014). Both approaches are rarely brought together, with each favouring different research questions, methods and outlets for dissemination. In contrast to the increasing attention that tourism academics have given to volunteer tourism, there has been substantially less interest from not-for-profit researchers on 'international voluntary service', as it is frequently termed. International voluntary service has generally had a stronger focus on development outcomes and hence has also been termed 'volunteering for development' to capture this focus as well as open up space for the consideration of the interface and synergies between international and national volunteers. Research in this area has increased significantly in the last 10 years but still nothing to the extent of growth of volunteer tourism research. Such 'different research worlds' with much common ground were discussed in some detail in a 2017 paper (Devereux et al., 2017a) that encouraged the promotion of a global research agenda and utilising the United Nations Plan of Action for integrating volunteerism into the implementation of Agenda 2030 (United Nations General Assembly, 2015a).

This chapter begins by reviewing how voluntourism practice and research has evolved over the past nearly two decades. Next, it identifies the potential relationships between voluntourism and the Sustainable Development Goals (SDGs). Following on from this analysis, the chapter considers how voluntourism can contribute to achieving the SDGs, identifying collaborative opportunities for voluntourism practice to support long term sustainable development both in low, middle and high income countries.

The evolution of voluntourism practice and research

The contribution of international volunteers to 'making a difference' has become increasingly controversial over the last 15-20 years. Initial positive commentary from participants and commentators, and in academic publications (Davis Smith et al., 2005; Devereux, 2008) were gradually overwhelmed by more mixed and negative views (Handy et al., 2010; Loiseau et al., 2016a; Perold et al., 2013) regarding the potential effects of mostly white western tourists visiting low income countries often for short periods of time. These studies rarely differentiated between different types of volunteer placements from short term to long term, skilled or unskilled or any attention to who facilitated the volunteer experience, whether this was an NGO, university, government or commercial enterprise (Holmes, 2014a).

Over 15 years ago the book *Volunteer Tourism: Experiences that make a difference* (Wearing, 2001) provided an early theoretical – and positive - rationale for the phenomenon, which focused on the experience for the volunteers. In contrast, Simpson (2004) highlighted the importance of a pedagogy of social justice in volunteer tourism to avoid or mitigate the negative consequences of unprepared or inappropriate international volunteer contributions in fragile development contexts. She suggested such a pedagogy would require explicit attention to why global differences, including injustice, exist and how the lives of people in different places intersect positively or negatively. These would form the basis of critical thinking and engagement beyond simplistic stereotypes. Since the early 2000s a less common treatment of international volunteering gained ground as a form of long term development rather than form of tourism. On the basis of field research findings this highlighted the distinctive contribution of skilled volunteers who live under local conditions for extended periods (Devereux, 2008, 2010; Howard & Burns, 2015; Lough et al., 2016). This latter approach suggested that skilled long term volunteering provides a collaborative and relational approach to international development. This was seen as a distinctive approach compared to conventional approaches to aid and development. Conventional development approaches had mixed success because they relied more on technical and financial solutions and less on the essential soft skills and cross cultural understanding and relationships of development workers with local communities (Liburd & Edwards, 2018; Morgan, 2002; Wilson, 2007).

The critique of voluntourism has identified problems with both the practice and organisation of this phenomenon (Guttentag, 2009). This critical discourse has led to the establishment of various industry codes of conduct as well as campaigns to eradicate particularly problematic forms of voluntourism such as orphanage tourism (Holmes, 2014a) and has led to the development of frameworks within both development and tourism contexts for evaluating impacts of this practice (Sherraden et al. 2008; Taplin et al., 2014; Zahra & McGehee, 2013). For instance, in Australia, a 'Smart Volunteering Campaign' aims to discourage Australians from doing short term, unskilled volunteering within orphanages overseas, with guidelines for being a 'child safe volunteer'. These emphasise three elements: 1. Avoid short-term, unskilled volunteering in orphanages; 2. Avoid activities where children are promoted as tourist attractions; and 3. Do your homework to ensure your local community impact is positive (Bishop & Birmingham, 2018).

Wearing et al. (2017) reflect on the debates and practices that have emerged since Wearing's initial theoretical exploration of volunteer tourism over 15 years ago. The paper asked how the vision of international volunteering 'making a difference' might be renewed despite the many ethical dilemmas surrounding voluntourism. Wearing et al. concluded there was a need to review the dominant Western aid model of voluntourism, which has promoted "unrealistic neo-colonial outcomes" and to seek to facilitate meaningful intercultural exchange and collaboration where volunteer tourists work together and alongside local people (Wearing et al., 2017: 1). Wearing at al's argument has been similarly advocated by other researchers working in both tourism and development studies, with Everingham (2015) emphasising the interdependent relationship between the volunteer and the local community and the need for the community also to own and advocate for change if it is to create long term change, using a bottom up and inside out approach.

The recognition of the problems associated with voluntourism and the efforts taken by both industry and academic commentators to improve practice have led to a reaction against the negative discourse with a call to find ways to achieve the potential positive outcomes associated with the activity (McGehee, 2012). Indeed the negative views are important reminders of what can go wrong particularly when tackling structural inequality is ignored in favour of individual volunteer action. However, it is also now seen that criticism can unwittingly deny agency to volunteers who may take collective action and use relationships to make a difference at practical as well as policy levels through affect (Griffiths, 2015a). Both tourism studies and not-for-profit research have generated models for evaluating the impacts of volunteer tourism programs. These models suggest a process which includes assessing the outcomes for the volunteers, the host community and the sending community (Sherraden et al., 2008; Taplin et al., 2014) noting that a successful voluntourism project should not only build relationships between the volunteer and the host community but also to the volunteer's home community and the destination. Nevertheless there is still considerable need for research that focuses on how host community impacts can provide evidence based recommendations that consolidate good practices and tackle negative ones (Schellhorn, 2010; Sherraden et al., 2008; Taplin et al., 2014).

While the study of voluntourism has followed a critical journey over the past nearly two decades, there remain geographical and contextual limitations to this body of research which has narrowed the focus of researchers' attention. Research to date has been primarily about volunteers from OECD countries completing projects in low income countries. This excludes both international volunteers travelling to other OECD countries – particularly for environmental projects – and domestic volunteer tourists (Leonard & Onyx, 2009). Voluntourists have tended to be a younger cohort and this is reflected in studies of voluntourism, especially those examining the role of voluntourism in personal development such as Wearing's original study. Yet there are diverse programs targeted at career breakers, retirees and families (Holmes, 2014a). The focus of research has been particularly on the experience of the individual volunteer as a tourist (Sin, 2009). Program impacts on the community or the needs and experiences of the hosts have only more recently receiving attention. Research on this phenomenon has overwhelmingly been in-depth, qualitative analyses of individual programs with few macro level studies. Many of these limitations have been exacerbated by the lack of cross-fertilisation between the tourism and not-for-profit approaches to examining this phenomenon. We will address these limitations later in this chapter.

From the outset voluntourism projects have involved direct action towards sustainable development whether building new wells, monitoring fragile environments or teaching much needed skills (Tomazos & Butler, 2009). As such, there would seem to be a symbiotic relationship between voluntourism and the United Nations Sustainable Development Goals (SDGs).

Relationships between SDGs and voluntourism

How do the SDGs and Agenda 2030 relate to volunteering and voluntourism in particular? There are at least five rationales for linking them. The rationales highlight potential synergies to mitigate negative trade-offs between voluntourism experiences and their impacts on communities and environments. These potential negative trade-offs are exemplified in the reports from the High Level Panel on Sustainable Development and others that the planet is in jeopardy and business as usual responses in tourism or other areas of the economy will not solve the deep seated problems (Global Compact & Unilever, 2011; Liburd & Edwards, 2018; United Nations, 2013; United Nations General Assembly, 2014).

First, in the development of Agenda 2030, volunteering was explicitly recognised for its cross-cutting role and ability to facilitate new interactions between governments, institutions and citizens in implementing sustainable development (UN General Assembly, 2014). This provides a very strong justification for voluntourism's role in encouraging mutually beneficial collaboration for sustainable development. This resonates with studies demonstrating the role voluntourism can play in facilitating cross-cultural understanding (Raymond & Hall, 2008). However, as highlighted earlier, this does require a pedagogy of social justice to counter the reproduction of cultural and other stereotypes (Devereux, 2008; Griffiths, 2015b; McBride et al., 2007; Simpson, 2004)

Second, the SDGs are universal, so voluntourism is just as pertinent nationally as internationally, and this can assist it to tackle the claims of neo-colonial approaches overseas by reminding people of the need for transitioning towards sustainable livelihoods, ecosystems and communities at home and abroad. Indeed voluntourism can help people to see the interconnections locally, nationally and internationally between issues of common concern, like climate change, sustainable cities and wellbeing (Devereux et al., 2017a; Devereux et al., 2017b).

Third, SDG target 4.7 explicitly aims for achieving education, cross-cultural learning and global citizenship, and fostering a culture of peace, as do many examples of best practice in voluntourism. SDG 4.7 states:

"By 2030, ensure that all learners acquire the knowledge and skills needed to promote sustainable development, including, among others, through education for sustainable development and sustainable lifestyles, human rights, gender equality, promotion of a culture of peace and non-violence, global citizenship and appreciation of cultural diversity and of culture's contribution to sustainable development" (United Nations General Assembly, 2015b).

Voluntourism is an apt vehicle to bring these educational elements together, and many of these subthemes are the specific subject of much academic writing on voluntourism (Everingham, 2015; Knollenberg et al., 2014; McAllum & Zahra, 2017)

Fourth, the SDGs explicitly talk about tourism as a tool for sustainable economies and ecosystems. Agenda 2030 is: "determined to promote sustainable tourism"…that under SDG 8 "creates jobs and promotes local culture and products". SDG 12 calls for monitoring "sustainable development impacts for sustainable tourism". SDG 14 aims to "increase the economic benefits to Small Island developing States and least developed countries from the sustainable use of marine resources, including through sustainable management of fisheries, aquaculture and tourism" (United Nations General Assembly, 2015b). Voluntourism through citizen science and other forms provides good examples of these opportunities (McGehee, 2014; McKinley et al., 2017). Citizen science includes Community Based Monitoring (CBM), "a process where concerned citizens, government agencies, industry, academia, community groups, and local institutions collaborate to monitor, track and respond to issues of common community [environmental] concern" (Whitelaw et al., 2003: 410).

Last, SDG 17 is about partnerships for sustainable development and, given the opportunities voluntourism provides for collaboration by connecting people within and between nations, this is an obvious and important area that can encourage an enabling environment for voluntourism and transformative partnerships (Devereux & Learmonth, 2017; Devereux et al., 2017b). It is also a new opportunity to tackle the potential negative effects of tourism, where the focus is only on an experience for the tourist and not an equal benefit beyond 'trickle down' effects for the local community's wellbeing, livelihoods and economies. Partnerships for sustainable development through voluntourism can thus contribute to "an integrated approach to sustainable community based tourism", that is community-driven and bridges local and global concerns based on principles of good governance, justice, community empowerment, and capacity building along with stewardship of natural, cultural and social goods (Dangi & Jamal, 2016).

The next section identifies opportunities for advancing positive voluntourism and avoiding the negative effects that researchers and commentators have previously identified.

Opportunities for voluntourism to contribute to the SDGs

The previous section proposes five rationales to link volunteering and the SDGs. The urgency of seeking collaborative modes for transitioning towards sustainability is still not recognised by many citizens and governments as important, because they do not recognise the dire situation the world is in, so this requires some reinforcing rather than to be treated as a given. Slow progress on decisive collective action to tackle climate change is one obvious example of this (Norgaard, 2009).

There have been many reports highlighting the need for global transformations, in the current and recent years, from business, NGOs and the United Nations (Global Compact & Unilever, 2011; United Nations, 2013). While there is great diversity in the players and their core focus, there is also much common agreement that we need a transformation of attitudes, lifestyles, business and action to transition towards global sustainability. This transformation will help shape views of how to achieve sustainable development through Agenda 2030, and particularly how we can achieve the SDGs through collaborative and transformative partnerships in voluntourism. The 2030 agenda is about people and planet and their interdependence. It highlights that not only can societies not survive without a livelihood or economy, but also that people's livelihood, health and wellbeing are inextricably linked to that of the planet. For many people and institutions, environmental concerns have not been a significant and systematic focus and are not well integrated with the rest of their lives and work, though there have been some significant and constructive individual programs and projects.

In other words tourism is a great example of mainstreaming and integrating environmental concerns with the everyday experience including recreation. It also reminds us of the increasing emphasis on volunteering beyond the common perception of service to include other elements like mutual aid and self help, participation, advocacy and even serious leisure (Rochester, 2013; United Nations Volunteers, 2011).

The World Economic Forum 2017 Global Risks Report

... the potential of persistent, **long-term trends such as inequality and deepening social and political polarization** to exacerbate risks associated with, for example, the weakness of the economic recovery and the speed of technological change. These trends came into sharp focus during 2016, with **rising political discontent and disaffection** evident in countries across the world.

... the next challenge: facing up to the importance of **identity and community**. Rapid changes of attitudes in areas such as gender, sexual orientation, race, multiculturalism, environmental protection and international cooperation have led many voters – particularly the older and less-educated ones – to feel left behind in their own countries. The resulting **cultural schisms** are testing social and political cohesion and may amplify many other risks if not resolved.

... Further challenges requiring global cooperation are found in the environmental category, which this year stands out in the GRPS. Over the course of the past decade, a cluster of **environment-related risks** – notably extreme weather events and failure of climate change mitigation and adaptation as well as water crises – has emerged as a consistently central feature of the GRPS risk landscape, strongly interconnected with many other risks, such as conflict and migration.

Figure 6.1: The World Economic Forum 2017 Global Risks Report. (World Economic Forum, 2017, : 6)

The World Economic Forum (WEF) (Figure 6.1) reports that the planet is increasingly making its pains more visible and undeniable, as a major feature of global risks and perceptions of these. In concrete terms, a 2017 International Institute for Sustainable Development (IISD) update highlighted information from the World Meteorological Organisation and the United Nations Office for Disaster Risk Reduction (UNISDR), which highlighted alarming temperatures around the world (Kosolapova, 2017). This was only reinforced by the WEF latest global risks report in January 2018. "…We have been pushing our planet to the brink and the damage is becoming increasingly clear. Biodiversity is being lost at mass-extinction rates, agricultural systems are under strain and pollution of the air and sea has become an increasingly pressing threat to human health." (WEF, 2018: 6). The WEF emphasises that growing nationalism and protectionism is a particular threat to solving wicked problems such as global warming.

Despite the need for new responses, business as usual approaches are hard to shift and this is also true in the tourism sector. A report by NGOs in 2017 evidenced the often negative effects of tourism (including voluntourism) on local communities and livelihoods. It highlighted in the context of Agenda 2030, the need for greater attention to meaningful local community participation in tourism and attention to vulnerable groups to uphold the SDG theme of 'leave no one behind'. It suggested measurement approaches for tourism to capture its broad, and potentially transformative sustainable development, not just the economic benefits (Canada et al., 2017). The report's authors emphasised the potential for transformative tourism. Transformative tourism is a relatively new concept that refers to forms of tourism that can improve the lives and environments of the destinations and respond to the risks of deepening social and political polarization, disaffection and environmental problems that require greater attention to the importance of identity and community. Voluntourism on organic farms is given as a positive example of transformative tourism that benefits the farmers, their community and the environment. In contrast, voluntourism programs at lion farms in Africa is presented as deeply problematic, when wildlife is essentially domesticated to foster economic benefits from voluntourism and hunting, despite potential trade-offs for deeper biodiversity concerns reflected within SDG target 15.5 to protect biodiversity and habitats (Canada et al., 2017: 87; Mysterud, 2010; Peterson et al., 2005). This requires relational approaches with an underlying pedagogy of social justice that can transform attitudes and practices through a more holistic approach that maximises synergies and minimises trade-offs between people and planet.

Voluntourism offers opportunities for individuals to connect and work together to solve long-term problems related to communities and the environment, with Bamber concluding from his research with student volunteers in international service learning (ISL) that "Transformative pedagogy, such as ISL, has the potential to nurture local, national and global aspects of citizenship" (Bamber, 2014:41). This resonates strongly with Göpel's (2014) findings on paradigm shifts and transformational change which emphasised the importance of applying a complex systems view to highlight relationships, not just 'technological-economic facts' in order to describe the foundations of negative behaviours and trends across systems. Göpel states that "intentional transformational change depends on soft factors like worldviews, beliefs, knowledge and vision." (2014:6)

Bamber and Göpel both speak clearly of the territory of volunteers and volunteer tourists through their volunteer work in relational development. This work can contribute to the mind shifts (of themselves and others) required to relatively quickly change course to tackle the multiple crises like political discontent and disaffection, climate change, biodiversity loss, conflict and inequality outlined in section one (Göpel, 2016; Messner & Weinlich, 2015). SDG target 4.7, as mentioned earlier, provides an appropriate framework for this mindset change that can bring cross-cultural understanding as well as other benefits. Research in Israel found that volunteer tourists who had intense social relationship with their hosts had the most positive attitude shift towards them and the location (Pizam et al., 2000). Griffiths highlighted the profound impact on him of his participation, along with a group of university students, in the first leg of the 300km Jan Satyagraha march for justice by courageous poor rural Indians. He said it was an example of the way "the practice of volunteering ties together the always present injustices with the bodily and intersubjective connections inherent to development work" (Griffiths, 2014: 90). Such an emotion charged collaborative experience, walking in solidarity alongside desperately poor people determined for justice, caught him in the moment so that he felt he was observing 'somehow from within' which infused him with a politics of hope and collective action. It brought a prospect for justice through an authentic and intense collaboration and human connection between people. These are the substantial transformational shifts possible through relational volunteer encounters founded on a pedagogy of social justice (Brondo, 2015; Simpson, 2004).

Voluntourism needs to respond to the system wide nature of global issues that the 2030 Agenda highlights. A complex systems understanding suggests the unpredictable nature of future events require mindshifts to respond appropriately in order to facilitate synergies rather than trade-offs in sustainable development and in the face of disruptive innovations. To achieve the transformation required at global, national and local levels, voluntourism is well placed to respond because of its work across boundaries, cultures and geographies (Wearing et al, 2017). Voluntourism research has demonstrated both good and bad experiences with partnerships, mostly in low income countries, but with some examples of cross-border translation of these possibilities also in high income countries (Wearing & McGehee, 2013). Most extant research is through the vehicle of volunteers, but the individual transformations in volunteer behaviour and understanding have yet to be harnessed to contribute to broader scale system wide change (Luh Sin et al., 2015; Tiessen, 2017). This change is considered crucial when volunteers work in low income countries, but has yet to be fully rolled out as a transformative tool in high income countries to build the necessary, but currently lacking, engagement and understanding of the 2030 Agenda. Yet, there are many opportunities for domestic volunteer tourism and high income to high income country exchanges (Leonard & Onyx, 2009), particularly in environmental programs, which align with citizen science (Cousins, 2007).

McGehee's (2014) review of volunteer tourism as a phenomenon, industry and field of research highlights the way some green groups that formerly shunned the term 'voluntourism' now embrace it. She highlights how voluntourism is now seen as an opportunity to draw in volunteers to contribute to citizen science in groups like Earthwatch, that has mobilised over 100,000 volunteers since it started in 1971 (Earthwatch Institute, 2016). Earthwatch demonstrates that volunteer tourists can and do much more than their stereotyped and negative orphanage engagements, and thus make a real difference to sustainable development. The engagement of volunteers through groups makes important contributions into biodiversity monitoring and conservation, but volunteers also have important roles to play when they come home and can then advocate for change in policy structures and the attitudes of friends, colleagues and family (Grabowski et al., 2017). This in fact might be seen as another important and transformative role for voluntourists under the SDG umbrella.

The SDGs remain under promoted and lacking ownership globally, particularly in high income countries. Perhaps, this is because governments and other key stakeholders perceive that, like the MDGs, the SDGs and their goals do not apply to high income countries. However, there is tentative evidence that this is beginning to be recognised, with positive examples in Finland, Holland and Germany. In Australia, the Government has recently established a national Returned Australian Volunteers Network for skilled long-term volunteers who have participated in its international volunteer program. It is not yet clear what the network will offer for community engagement in Australia. It would be interesting to see whether a similar network could be established for returned volunteer tourists to share experiences and apply their overseas learnings and insights at home – this would be an appropriate complement to the Smart Volunteering Campaign mentioned earlier.

Conclusions: the way forward

The discussion presented in this chapter demonstrates that while voluntourism has been the subject of substantial criticism, there are also considerable opportunities for the practice to contribute to the achievement of the SDGs in both low and high-income countries. Returning to the five connections between the SDGs and volunteerism highlighted earlier provides a framework for these opportunities going forward.

First, volunteering in a range of contexts is recognised for its cross-cutting contribution that can facilitate new forms of collaboration between governments, institutions and citizens in implementing sustainable development (United Nations General Assembly, 2014). Voluntourism opens new opportunities to enhance global citizenship by connecting citizens and facilitating the education and learning of citizens across country, region, religious or ethnic divides

(Comhlamh, 2015; Griffiths, 2015b; Howard & Wheeler, 2015). This interaction is not limited to the frequently researched – and critiqued – volunteering by young, Western tourists travelling to low income countries. Also, high income to high income country voluntourism can equally facilitate cross-cultural collaboration and mutual understanding. Volunteers in emerging economies like China also make significant but under-reported contributions through citizen action (Matsuzawa, 2012). Volunteer assignments involving older tourists or family groups are also well known in practice, but receive little attention from researchers (Holmes, 2014b; Leonard & Onyx, 2009).

Second, the SDGs are universal and so voluntourism is just as pertinent nationally as internationally. There are now opportunities for travel between and within a wider range of countries, particularly with emerging economies like China (Ong et al., 2014; Xu, 2016) and a growing recognition of voluntourism opportunities at home (De Lima, 2015; Webber, 2017). There are different possible scenarios as have been laid out for the Asia Pacific region by Ong et al. with not all so optimistic between 'Stable and principled', to 'vanguard' or 'discredited and superseded' volunteer tourism (Ong et al., 2014). However, voluntourism done well, and with an eye on the guiding SDG framework, can help people to see the potential positive or negative interconnections locally, nationally and internationally between issues of common concern including climate change, sustainable cities and wellbeing. Returned volunteer tourists can bring their newly learnt skills and broader cultural and political understanding to deepen understandings and benefits for their home community.

Voluntourism can also highlight and discourage potential negative 'international spillovers' where action by one country or its citizens may negatively affect the sustainability in another country or region (Sachs et al., 2017). People may initially become engaged with issues in their own countries, then take the opportunity to pursue them while travelling overseas. An example is people travelling to support and learn about organic agriculture at home and abroad through the Willing Workers on Organic Farms scheme (Yamamoto & Engelsted, 2014) or via local and global citizen science initiatives (Ballard et al., 2017).

Third, SDG target 4.7 explicitly aims for achieving education through cross-cultural learning, global citizenship, sustainable lifestyles and fostering a culture of peace that respects human rights and fosters gender equality (United Nations General Assembly, 2015b). Voluntourism can highlight the cross-cultural, social justice and collaborative elements so integral to sustainable development, but also so often hidden or neglected when the focus is more narrowly on cost effectiveness, development outcomes or impact. Griffith has emphasised the human side of transformation through volunteer tourism where affect intervenes despite neoliberal or other structural impediments. He says these "Affective moments give rise to love, solidarity and hope" (Griffiths, 2014: 89; 2016) and this is an opportunity for engagement and collaboration over cynicism, by volunteers demonstrating their agency alongside local communities and up to policy makers. This is also a call for people to see the SDGs as a transformative people-centred vision and process to build ownership and practical engagement, not just a technical blueprint to roll out top down.

Fourth, the SDGs explicitly talk about tourism as a tool for sustainable economies and ecosystems. This requires promoting transformative forms of tourism (Canada et al, 2017) by creating livelihoods and promoting local culture and products that do not create polluting waste but instead cultivate sensitivities to the impact of overconsumption. Equally important is developing tools that can monitor the impacts of sustainable tourism (Steele et al., 2017; Taplin et al., 2014) so that problems can be monitored and tackled and best practices promoted more widely. Voluntourism research plays an important role here and the importance of responding to community needs not just voluntourist wishes was highlighted earlier.

Voluntourism through citizen science helps capture useful data and sensitised citizens, as well as create economic opportunities by contributing to what one paper described as a "mutually beneficial triumvirate of ecotourism, conservation biology, and volunteer tourism" (Brightsmith et al., 2008; McGehee, 2014; McKinley et al., 2017). SDG 14 is focused on conserving and sustainably using "the oceans, seas and marine resources for sustainable development" including through "sustainable management of fisheries, aquaculture and tourism" (United Nations General Assembly, 2015b). Here again voluntourism can make a difference by creating new opportunities, for example through the conservation of handfishes (Edgar et al., 2017).

Finally, SDG 17 is about partnerships for sustainable development which provides opportunities for collaboration by connecting people within and between nations to encourage an enabling environment for voluntourism and transformative partnerships (Devereux & Learmonth, 2017). Such partnerships between voluntourism operators, volunteers and local communities can provide experiences that the tourists would not otherwise have been exposed to. Such partnerships, if developed in the context of respectful and trusting relationships, can give voluntourists and community's new understandings and opportunities that can move brief encounters to deeper understandings that challenge stereotypes and lifestyles over longer periods.

Voluntourism as a practice – and focus of research – is maturing. The early, almost euphoric studies, which were accompanied by phenomenal market growth, slowly gave way to a more critical consideration of the risks that poorly planned, often short term projects where the focus was on the tourists and not the community or the broader outcomes, could generate. Longer term collaborative initiatives, with tourists and locals – either internationally or domestically – working together in collaboration can support tourism and sustainable development at large.

References

Ballard, H. L., Dixon, C. G. H. & Harris, E. M. (2017). Youth-focused citizen science: Examining the role of environmental science learning and agency for conservation. *Biological Conservation*, **208**, 65-75. doi:https://doi.org/10.1016/j.biocon.2016.05.024

Bamber, P. M. (2014). Becoming Other-wise. *Journal of Transformative Education*, **13**(1), 26-45. doi:10.1177/1541344614551636

Bishop, J. & Birmingham, S. (2018). New campaign to tackle orphanage tourism [Press release].

Brightsmith, D. J., Stronza, A. & Holle, K. (2008). Ecotourism, conservation biology, and volunteer tourism: A mutually beneficial triumvirate. *Biological Conservation*, **141**(11), 2832-2842. doi:https://doi.org/10.1016/j.biocon.2008.08.020

Brondo, K. V. (2015). The spectacle of saving: conservation voluntourism and the new neoliberal economy on Utila, Honduras. *Journal of Sustainable Tourism*, **23**(10), 1405-1425. doi:10.1080/09669582.2015.1047377

Canada, E., Karschat, K., Jager, L., Kamp, C., de Man, F., Mangalas-Seri, S. Maurer, M., Monshausen, A., Plüss, C., Rutherford, A. & Tremel, C. (2017). *Transforming Tourism: Tourism in the 2030 Agenda*. Berlin: ECPAT Deutschland e.V.

Comhlamh (2015). *From Volunteers to Active Citizens*. Retrieved from https://comhlamh.org/2015/06/have-a-read-of-our-new-resource-on-active-citizenship/

Cousins, J. (2007). The role of UK-based conservation tourism operators. *Tourism Management*, **28**, 1020-1030.

Dangi, T. B. & Jamal, T. (2016). An integrated approach to "sustainable community-based tourism". *Sustainability*, **8**(5), 475. doi:http://dx.doi.org/10.3390/su8050475

Davis Smith, J., Ellis Paine, A. & Brewis, G. (2005). Cross national volunteering: a developing movement? In J. L. Brudney (Ed.), *Emerging Areas of Volunteering. Vol. 1*. Indianapolis: ARNOVA.

De Lima, I. B. (2015). International volunteer tourism and landscape restoration in New Zealand: The steering and emabling conservationist role of inbound operators. *Journal of Tourism Challenges and Trends*, **8**(2), 79-104.

Devereux, P. (2008). International volunteering for development and sustainability: outdated paternalism or a radical response to globalisation? *Development in Practice*, **18**(3), 357-370.

Devereux, P. & Learmonth, B. (2017). *Implementation of the SDGs through transformative partnerships in volunteering*. IVCO 2017 Framing Paper. Retrieved from https://forum-ids.org/2017/08/ivco-2017-framing-paper/

Devereux, P., Paull, M., Hawkes, M. & Georgeou, N. (2017a). Volunteering and the UN Sustainable Development Goals: Finding common ground between national and international volunteering agendas? *Third Sector Review*, **23**(1).

Devereux, P., Stocker, L. & Holmes, K. (2017b). Volunteerism: A crosscutting and relational method to achieve the Sustainable Development Goals. In D. Marinova & J. Hartz-Karp (Eds.), *Methods for Sustainability* (pp. 242-258): Edward Elgar.

Earthwatch Institute. (2016). *Earthwatch: From our Founding to our Future. 2015 Annual Report.* Retrieved from http://earthwatch.org/Portals/0/Downloads/About/2016-earthwatch-annual-report-US.pdf

Edgar, G. J., Stuart-Smith, R. D., Cooper, A., Jacques, M. & Valentine, J. (2017). New opportunities for conservation of handfishes (Family *Brachionichthyidae*) and other inconspicuous and threatened marine species through citizen science. *Biological Conservation, 208*, 174-182. doi:https://doi.org/10.1016/j.biocon.2016.07.028

European Association for Tourism and Leisure Education & Tourism Research and Marketing. (2008). *VolunteerTourism: A global analysis: a report.* Arnhem, The Netherlands: ATLAS.

Everingham, P. (2015). Intercultural exchange and mutuality in volunteer tourism: The case of Intercambio in Ecuador. *Tourist Studies, 15*(2), 175-190. doi:10.1177/1468797614563435

Global Compact & Unilever. (2011). *Catalyzing transformational partnerships between the United Nations and Business.* Retrieved from www.unglobalcompact.org/library/200

Gopel, M. (2016). *The Great Mindshift: How a New Economic Paradigm and Sustainability Transformations go Hand in Hand (Vol. 2).* Berlin: Springer.

Göpel, M. (2014). *Navigating a New Agenda Questions and Answers on Paradigm Shifts & Transformational Change.* Retrieved from www.giz.de/expertise/downloads/giz2014-en-climate-finance-navigating-new-agenda.pdf

Grabowski, S., Wearing, S., Lyons, K., Tarrant, M. & Landon, A. (2017). A rite of passage? Exploring youth transformation and global citizenry in the study abroad experience. *Tourism Recreation Research, 42*(2), 139-149. doi:10.1080/02508281.2017.1292177

Griffiths, M. (2014). The affective spaces of global civil society and why they matter. *Emotion, Space and Society, 11*, 89-95.

Griffiths, M. (2015a). I've got goose bumps just talking about it!: Affective life on neoliberalized volunteering programmes. *Tourist Studies, 15*(2), 205-221. doi:10.1177/1468797614563437

Griffiths, M. (2015b). Research towards a better future: Neoliberalism, global citizenship and international volunteering. (PhD), Kings College London, London. Retrieved from https://kclpure.kcl.ac.uk/portal/files/45170631/2015_Griffiths_Mark_1115881_ethesis.pdf

Guttentag, D. (2009). Possible Negative Impacts of Volunteer Tourism. International Journal of Tourism Research, 11, 537-551.

Handy, F., Cnaan, R. A., Hustinx, L., Kang, C., Brudney, J. L., Haski-Leventhal, D., Holmes, K., Meijs, L.C.P.M., Pessi,A.B., Ranade, B., Yamauchi, N. & Zrinscak, S. (2010). A cross-cultural examination of student volunteering: is it all about résumé building? *Nonprofit and Voluntary Sector Quarterly, 39*(3), 498-523.

Holmes, K. (2014a). 'It fitted with our lifestyle': an investigation into episodic volunteering in the tourism sector. *Annals of Leisure Research, 17*(4), 433-459.

Holmes, K. (2014b). Volunteer tourism and international contexts. In M. Oppenheimer & J. Warburton (Eds.), *Volunteering in Australia* (pp. 117-130), Federation Press.

Howard, J. & Burns, D. (2015). Volunteering for Development within the New Ecosystem of International Development. *IDS Bulletin*, **46**(5), 5-16.

Howard, J. & Wheeler, J. (2015). What community development and citizen participation should contribute to the new global framework for sustainable development. *Community Development Journal*, **50**(4), 552-570.

Knollenberg, W., McGehee, N. G., Boley, B. B. & Clemmons, D. (2014). Motivation-based transformative learning and potential volunteer tourists: facilitating more sustainable outcomes. *Journal of Sustainable Tourism*, **22**(6), 922-941. doi:10.1080/09669582.2014.902065

Kosolapova, E. (2017). Adaptation and loss and damage update: DRR efforts increased amid record high temperatures. Retrieved from sdg.iisd.org/news/adaptation-and-loss-and-damage-update-drr-efforts-increased-amid-record-high-temperatures/

Leonard, R. & Onyx, J. (2009). Volunteer tourism: the interests and motivations of grey nomads. *Annals of Leisure Research*, **12**, 315-332.

Liburd, J. & Edwards, D. (Eds.). (2018). *Collaboration for Sustainable Tourism Development*, Oxford: Goodfellow Publishers.

Loiseau, B., Sibbald, R., Raman, S. A., Benedict, D., Dimaras, H. & Loh, L. C. (2016a). 'Don't make my people beggars': a developing world house of cards. *Community Development Journal*, **51**(4), 571-584. doi:10.1093/cdj/bsv047

Loiseau, B., Sibbald, R., Raman, S. A., Darren, B., Loh, L. C. & Dimaras, H. (2016b). Perceptions of the role of short-term volunteerism in international development: views from volunteers, local hosts, and community members. *Journal of Tropical Medicine*, **12**. doi:10.1155/2016/2569732

Lough, B. J., Devereux, P., Perold, H. & Uhereczky, A. (2016). Stipended transnational volunteering. In D. H. Smith, R. A. Stebbins & J. Grotz (Eds.), *The Palgrave Handbook of Volunteering, Civic Participation, and Nonprofit Associations* (pp. 242-258). London: Palgrave Macmillan UK.

Luh Sin, H., Oakes, T. & Mostafanezhad, M. (2015). Traveling for a cause: Critical examinations of volunteer tourism and social justice. *Tourist Studies*, **15**(2), 119-131. doi:10.1177/1468797614563380

Lupoli, C. A., Morse, W. C., Bailey, C. & Schelhas, J. (2014). Assessing the impacts of international volunteer tourism in host communities: a new approach to organizing and prioritizing indicators. *Journal of Sustainable Tourism*, **22**(6), 898-921. doi:10.1080/09669582.2013.879310

Matsuzawa, S. (2012). Citizen environmental activism in China: Legitimacy, alliances and rights-based discourses. *AsiaNetwork Exchange*, **19**(2), 81-91.

McAllum, K. & Zahra, A. (2017). The positive impact of othering in voluntourism: The role of the relational other in becoming another self. Journal of International and *Intercultural Communication*, **10**(4), 291-308. doi:10.1080/17513057.2017.1280179

McBride, A. M., Sherraden, M. & Lough, B. J. (2007). *Inclusion and Effectiveness in International Volunteering and Service*. Retrieved from St Louis: https://csd.wustl.edu/Publications/Documents/P07-13.pdf

McGehee, N.G. (2012). Oppression, emancipation, and volunteer tourism: Research propositions. *Annals of Tourism Research*, **39**(1), 84-107. doi.org/10.1016/j.annals.2011.05.001

McGehee, N.G. (2014). Volunteer tourism: evolution, issues and futures. Journal of Sustainable Tourism, 22(6), 847-854. doi:10.1080/09669582.2014.907299

McKinley, D.C., Miller-Rushing, A.J., Ballard, H.L., Bonney, R., Brown, H., Cook-Patton, S.C., Evans, D.M., French, R.A., Parrish, J., Phillips,T.B., Ryan, S.F., Shanley, L.A., Shirk, J.L., Stepenuck, K.F., Weltzin, J.F., Wiggins, A., Boyle, O.D., Briggs, R.D., Chapin, S.F., Hewitt, D.A., Preuss, P.W. & Soukup, M.A. (2017). Citizen science can improve conservation science, natural resource management, and environmental protection. *Biological Conservation*, **208**, 15-28. doi:https://doi.org/10.1016/j.biocon.2016.05.015

Messner, D. & Weinlich, S. (Eds.). (2015). *Global Cooperation and the Human Factor in International Relations*. London: Routledge.

Morgan, P. (2002). Technical assistance: Correcting the precedents. *Development Policy Journal*, **2**.

Mysterud, A. (2010). Still walking on the wild side? Management actions as steps towards 'semi-domestication' of hunted ungulates. *Journal of Applied Ecology*, **47**(4), 920-925.

Norgaard, K. M. (2009). *Cognitive and Behavioural Challenges in Responding to Climate Change*. Retrieved from https://openknowledge.worldbank.org/handle/10986/9066

Ong, F., Lockstone-Binney, L., King, B. & Smith, K. A. (2014). The future of volunteer tourism in the Asia-Pacific Region: Alternative prospects. *Journal of Travel Research*, 53(6), 680-692. doi:10.1177/0047287514532365

Perold, H., Graham, L. A., Mavungu, E. M., Cronin, K., Muchemwa, L. & Lough, B. J. (2013). The colonial legacy of international voluntary service. *Community Development Journal*, **48**(2), 179-196. doi:10.1093/cdj/bss037

Peterson, M. N., Lopez, R. R., Laurent, E. J., Frank, P. A., Silvy, N. J. & Liu, J. (2005). Wildlife loss through domestication: the case of endangered key deer. *Conservation Biology*, 19(3), 939-944.

Pizam, A., Uriely, N. & Reichel, A. (2000). The intensity of tourist–host social relationship and its effects on satisfaction and change of attitudes: the case of working tourists in Israel. *Tourism Management*, **21**(4), 395-406. doi.org/10.1016/S0261-5177(99)00085-0

Raymond, E. M. & Hall, C. M. (2008). The development of cross-cultural (mis)understanding through volunteer tourism. *Journal of Sustainable Tourism*, **16**(5), 530-543. doi:10.1080/09669580802159610

Rochester, C. (2013). *Rediscovering Voluntary Action The Beat of a Different Drum*. Basingstoke U.K.: Palgrave Macmillan.

Sachs, J., Schmidt-Traub, G., Kroll, C., Durand-Delacre, D. & Teksoz, K. (2017). *SDG Index and Dashboards Report 2017. Global Responsibilities: International spillovers in achieving the goals.* Retrieved from http://www.sdgindex.org/

Schellhorn, M. (2010). Development for whom? Social justice and the business of ecotourism. *Journal of Sustainable Tourism*, **18**(1), 115-135. doi:10.1080/09669580903367229

Sherraden, M.S., Lough, B.J. & McBride, A.M. (2008). Effects of international volunteering and service: individual and institutional predictors. *Voluntas: International Journal of Voluntary and Nonprofit Organizations*, **19**, 395-421.

Simpson, K. (2004). 'Doing development': the gap year, volunteer-tourists and a popular practice of development. *Journal of International Development*, 16, 681-692.

Sin, H. L. (2009). Volunteer tourism—"involve me and I will learn"? *Annals of Tourism Research*, **36**(3), 480-501. doi:https://doi.org/10.1016/j.annals.2009.03.001

Steele, J., Dredge, D. & Scherrer, P. (2017). Monitoring and evaluation practices of volunteer tourism organisations. *Journal of Sustainable Tourism*, **25**(11), 1674-1690. doi:10.1080/09669582.2017.1306067

Taplin, J., Dredge, D. & Scherrer, P. (2014). Monitoring and evaluating volunteer tourism: a review and analytical framework. *Journal of Sustainable Tourism*, **22**(6), 874-897.

Tiessen, R. (2017). *Learning and Volunteering Abroad for Development: Unpacking Host organisation and volunteer perspectives*. Routledge.

Tomazos, K. & Butler, R. (2009). Volunteer Tourism: The New Ecotourism? *Anatolia*, **20**(1), 196-211. doi:10.1080/13032917.2009.10518904

United Nations. (2013). *A New Global Partnership: Eradicate Poverty and Transform Economies through Sustainable Development*. The Report of the High-Level Panel of Eminent Persons on the Post-2015 Development Agenda. Retrieved from New York: http://www.un.org/sg/management/pdf/HLP_P2015_Report.pdf

United Nations General Assembly. (2014). *The Road to Dignity by 2030: ending poverty, transforming all lives and protecting the planet*. Synthesis report of the Secretary General on the post-2015 sustainable development agenda. Retrieved from New York: https://sustainabledevelopment.un.org/majorgroups/post2015/synthesisreport

United Nations General Assembly. (2015a). *Integrating volunteering in the next decade:* Report of the Secretary General. Retrieved from www.unv.org/fileadmin/docdb/pdf/A_C.3_70_L.15_Rev.1.pdf

United Nations General Assembly. (2015b). *Transforming our world: the 2030 Agenda for Sustainable Development*. Retrieved from New York: www.un.org/ga/search/view_doc.asp?symbol=A/RES/70/1&Lang=E

United Nations Volunteers. (2011). *State of the World's Volunteerism Report: Universal values for Global Well-being*. Retrieved from www.unv.org/publications/2011-state-world%E2%80%99s-volunteerism-report-universal-values-global-well-being.

Wearing, S. (2001). *Volunteer Tourism: Experiences that make a difference*. New York: CABI Publications.

Wearing, S. & McGehee, N.G. (2013). Volunteer Tourism: A review. *Tourism Management*, **38**, 120-130.

Wearing, S., Young, T. & Everingham, P. (2017). Evaluating volunteer tourism: has it made a difference? *Tourism Recreation Research*, **42**(4), 512-521. doi:10.1080/02508281.2017.1345470

Webber, C. (2017). Behind the scenery: Voluntourism in Tasmania. *Third Sector Review*, **23**(1), 51-76.

Whitelaw, G., Vaughan, H., Craig, B. & Atkinson, D. (2003). Establishing the Canadian Community Monitoring Network. *Environmental Monitoring and Assessment*, **88**(1), 409-418. doi:10.1023/a:1025545813057

Wilson, G. (2007). Knowledge, innovation and re-inventing technical assistance for development. *Progress in Development Studies*, **7**(3), 183-199.

World Economic Forum. (2018). *The Global Risks Report 2018*. Retrieved from Geneva: http://www3.weforum.org/docs/GRR17_Report_web.pdf

Xu, Y. (2016). Volunteerism and the state: Understanding the development of volunteering in China. In J. Butcher & C. J. Einolf (Eds.), *Perspectives on Volunteering* (pp. 213-226): Springer.

Yamamoto, D. & Engelsted, A. K. (2014). World Wide Opportunities on Organic Farms in the United States: locations and motivations of volunteer tourism host farms. *Journal of Sustainable Tourism*, **22**(6), 964-982. doi:10.1080/09669582.2014.894519

Zahra, A. & McGehee, N.G. (2013). Volunteer Tourism: A Host Community Capital Perspective. *Annals of Tourism Research*, **42**, 22-45.

7 Whose Needs and What is to be Sustained?

Michael Hughes and Angus Morrison-Saunders

Introduction

This chapter explores sustainable tourism development and collaboration in relation to the needs of tourists and of host communities. It is a collaboration of two academics operating in parallel, although occasionally intersecting, fields of study: tourism, and sustainability assessment. Through combining our knowledge and pursuits in each field, we work towards a shared goal that hopefully transcends what could be accomplished alone.

Our approach is to explore the notion of human needs as it is expressed in the World Commission on Environment and Development (WCED) (1987) definition of sustainable development and the UN World Tourism Organisation (WTO) appropriation of the definition for sustainable tourism development. Our starting point is thus to unpack the key terms employed in these definitions prior to drilling down more specifically into analysing needs in the context of sustainable tourism development and collaboration. In so doing, many inter-related facets of sustainability thinking and of tourism understanding are revealed. Our method is principally a literature review amounting to a theoretical exploration of concepts, illustrated with published examples from practice. Our analysis leads us to propose an alternative definition of sustainable tourism development that emphasises the priority of 'host community' needs that better aligns with the spirit of the WCED definition.

On sustainable development and sustainable tourism development

Ultimately, the definition of sustainable development, in its various guises, rests on the core idea of meeting human needs for enduring wellbeing (Morrison-Saunders & Hughes, 2018; World Commission on Environment and Development, 1987).

The World Health Organization (1995) referred to wellbeing in the context of individual and community health. Drawing on the principles of this definition, wellbeing can be defined as a holistic concept that includes a state of positive physical health, mental health and social function, not just the absence of disease or social dysfunction. Enduring wellbeing means that this positive state persists potentially forever. But as the World Commission on Environment and Development (1987) definition of sustainable development makes clear, the notion of meeting human needs is the precursor to realising well-being. In the context of tourists, this begs the question as to whose needs and exactly what is to be sustained?

This World Tourism Organisation (1998) defined sustainable tourism development as development which meets the *needs* of present tourists and host regions while protecting and enhancing opportunities for the future (adapted from WTO, 1998). The United Nations World Tourism Organisation updated this definition to read:

> *"Tourism that takes full account of its current and future economic, social and environmental impacts, addressing the needs of visitors, the industry, the environment and host communities"* (World Tourism Organisation, 2018).

This definition invites collaboration between the three human stakeholder groups identified within it, along with the representatives of the environment. In this chapter we especially focus on exploring the needs of visitors and of tourism host communities. We take it as a given that needs of the tourism industry (e.g. economic viability) and that of the provisioning environment (e.g. conservation of natural and cultural heritage values) are relatively easily understood concepts.

The WCED definition of sustainable development and the WTO definition of sustainable tourism correspond in the main to a sustainability discourse of "pragmatic integration of development and environmental goals" (Pope, et al., 2017: 210). Dryzek equates this conception to "having it all" (1997:121) whereby the development and environmental goals are addressed in tandem with the aim of realising positive outcomes in both simultaneously "not just locally and immediately, but globally and in perpetuity" (p.121). It is often represented as three intersecting circles representing separate environmental, social and economic pillars with 'sustainability' being denoted as the 'sweet spot' in the centre where all three circles overlap. In practice achieving this 'win-win-win' within each of the sustainability pillars simultaneously is extremely unlikely and difficult to accomplish. Rather what tends to ensue is a balancing act which focuses on compromises and trade-offs (Gibson, 2006) seeking to deliver merely a "positive balance of benefits over sacrifices" (Gibson, 2013: 3). We return to the matter of trade-offs later on.

The WCED (1987) specifically identified and sought to address disparities and inequalities in the world wide distribution of wealth. It was recognised that there is pressing need for development that will bring millions of people out of abject poverty; a condition which is a key determinant of unsustainability. In this regard the definition of sustainable development and of sustainable tourism development arising from it also draws upon a discourse of sustainability as a process of directed change or transition (Pope et al., 2017). The starting point is thus that current global conditions are undesirable and consequently the goal is not to sustain 'business as usual' but to seek positive change. In this context, the pursuit of sustainable tourism development intended to meet the needs of tourists and host communities will deliver positive advancements or gains for each.

Collaboration is defined in this book as being more than simply cooperation, but the joint (integrated) effort of individuals to achieve a common objective. However, Liburd and Edwards (2010) noted that sustainable tourism development does not have a static or achievable goal, seemingly creating a conundrum. While sustainability is often framed as something that is uncertain and to be achieved at some point permanently in the future (Morrison-Saunders & Hughes, 2018), the common broad goal arguably is to meet human needs. How these needs are defined, and by whom, is fundamental to the process of sustainable development. In the remainder of this chapter we focus on the notion of 'needs' as central to the definition of sustainable development and how this relates to the notion of achieving a common objective in the context of tourism.

Tourism = Leisure time + voluntary travel

We are well aware that any tourism definition adopted here could spark a reaction by anyone who happens to read this text. Further, it is beyond the scope of this chapter to explore the complex academic discourse on tourism, tourists and the identities and meanings attributed to these concepts (see McCabe, 2005). Given that caveat, our argument in this chapter requires a general understanding of tourism as it relates to meeting human needs. As a starting point, we draw on the wisdom of tourism scholars to note that tourism is often defined to include people undertaking voluntary travel that includes temporarily leaving home and staying overnight somewhere other than at home for one or more of a variety of reasons (Gunn & Var, 2002; Hall & Lew, 2009; Leiper, 2004). Consideration of needs in the context of the tourist relates to the physical resources and infrastructure (for example, accommodation, transportation etc.) available to them and the kind of care (for example, services) that they will receive at their host destinations – both of which can contribute to their overall wellbeing. We return to this point below.

While scholars have dissected tourism, Hall and Lew (2009) note a difference in scholarly versus common understandings of tourism, where the common understanding focusses on leisure travel. With this in mind, Butler (2015) rather more stridently insists that any conceptualisation of tourism (scholarly or not) is by far and away dominated by the assumption it is travel involving leisure. Leisure includes any activity conducted for pleasure, without remuneration, undertaken in time left after conducting essential activities needed to maintain a living (Dillard & Bates, 2011; Tinsley & Kass, 1978). Tourism is also described as voluntary travel. The term 'voluntary' refers to an action undertaken of one's own free will, without coercion or legal obligation and without payment for the action (Anon, 2017). Voluntary travel is thus travel that a person may or may not choose to do without fear of recrimination or loss. There are obviously forms of voluntary travel that may contain a combination of work and leisure, but leisure is a commonly inferred part of tourism travel (Leiper, 2004). If tourism is an activity based on voluntary travel undertaken by tourists for leisure purposes it therefore does not serve to meet essential needs of people as tourists.

It is important to note that the UNWTO definition of sustainable tourism refers to needs of visitors, that is, tourists. This raises the notion of human needs as it is used in the sustainable development definition. The World Commission on Environment and Development (WCED) (1987) frames needs in terms of basic human rights necessary for enduring wellbeing (Morrison-Saunders & Hughes, 2018). The WCED (1987) definition refers to needs as "the essential needs of the world's poor, to which overwhelming priority should be given" (p.41). The report specifies essential needs as those required for basic survival, namely access to: jobs, food, energy, water and sanitation. The WCED (1987) differentiates between 'essential' and 'perceived' needs (p.42), where perceived needs, or wants, are socially determined and by inference, not directly essential for survival. The report also notes that excessive pursuit of wants can inhibit the progress of sustainable development. UNWTO adapted the original definition of sustainable development by tweaking the wording to include meeting the needs of both tourists and host communities. The appropriation of the WCED definition by the UNWTO appears to place needs of voluntary, leisure seeking tourists and needs of local community residents as being equal. This raises the question, are all needs equal, how and by whom are needs determined?

Are some needs are more equal than others?

Abraham Maslow (Maslow, 1943, 1962, 1970) theorised that people are motivated to act according to a set of universal human needs which he classified as lower needs and higher needs. As an aside, a need is not the thing itself (e.g. water) but is defined by the deficiency of the thing that subsequently motivates behaviour to meet that need. For example, a lack of water results in a need for water that motivates action to seek water (Taormina & Gao, 2013). According to Maslow, lower needs are those essential for individual survival, such as the need for food, shelter and safety. Beyond these physical needs are the lower psychological and social needs, such as social belonging and being loved. Building on meeting lower physical and psychological needs, people may address the need to know, understand, and aesthetically appreciate the wider environment through inquiry and exploration. Maslow's needs hierarchy is capped by concepts of emotional self-fulfilment and helping others to achieve self-actualisation. According to this theory, lower needs must be met before higher needs can be addressed suggesting some needs are more fundamental (or important) than others (Hughes, 2004).

This theory has been thoroughly critiqued by many authors over the decades. Criticisms point to the small, biased sample of people Maslow originally based his theory on, and the lack of scientific rigour in the research method among other criticisms (McCleod, 2014; Taormina & Gao, 2013). A comprehensive study by Tay and Diener (2011) analysed the relationship between Maslow's needs and subjective personal wellbeing. Subjective personal wellbeing is a person's own evaluation of the extent to which their needs and wants are met, based on self-imposed criteria and relative to social expectations (Diener et al., 1985; Diener, Inglehart & Tay, 2013). This brings to mind the important distinction between absolute and relative poverty. Absolute poverty is defined by the extremely limited ability to meet essential needs. The importance of eradicating absolute poverty in the name of sustainable development, as WCED (1987) advocates, is unequivocal. Relative poverty is defined as lacking the resources required to meet the average needs and wants enjoyed by others in the community (Senate Community Affairs References Committee, 2004). That is, relative poverty is influenced by the distribution of wealth in a community. A person may meet their essential needs but may live in relative poverty owing to the comparative wealth and wants of the community in which they live (e.g. Jackson, 2009; Wilkinson & Pickett, 2010). The wealthier a community is, the greater the resource consumption required to avoid relative poverty and achieve subjective personal wellbeing (Frank, 2007). Subjective personal wellbeing is thus determined by the extent to which needs and wants are met relative to the expectations of wellbeing within the community.

With regards to meeting needs for personal wellbeing, Tay and Diener (2011) analysed data from an international survey of more than 60,000 people across 123 countries. They found that different types of need make separate contributions to wellbeing, but that fulfilment of specific needs was independent of whether other needs were met. This suggests Maslow's idea of universal human needs has merit but that the sequential hierarchy does not. What Tay and Diener (2011) did find was that meeting survival needs (food, shelter, safety) took precedence, but this did not prevent attainment of other types of need as a contribution to wellbeing. For example, a person living in absolute poverty may meet the need for social belonging. While needs may be realised independently and contribute to subjective personal wellbeing in any particular order, the authors note that meeting essential needs (defined by the WCED) will take precedence when required for survival.

Meeting the needs of tourists ...

As noted by Butler (2015) and Leiper (2004), tourism is predominantly a voluntary, leisure based activity, and thus, is undertaken by people to meet needs other than essential needs. Authors such as MacCannell (1976) postulated that tourists may be motivated to explore and understand the wider society and give meaning to their lives, or at least put their lives in context. Similarly, Gunn and Var (2002), Moscardo et al.(2014), among others, later described tourism as a means for exploration of 'the other', achieving self-fulfilment, respecting the identity of others and other ideals, reminiscent of Maslow's higher needs, or wants. However, McKercher (1993) and Sharpley (2009) more critically noted that tourism is often characterised by hedonistic behaviour and excessive consumption of resources by tourists. There is ample evidence demonstrating that the vast majority of tourists generally consume more resources than they do during their routine daily lives, and significantly more than the residents of many host communities (Nepal et al., 2015). This extends to ecotourists, responsible tourists and other forms of 'sustainable tourist' because all at least involve travel related resource consumption over and above a person's usual daily requirements (Sharpley, 2009).

The needs of tourists align with the WCED's definition of 'perceived needs' that are socially and culturally determined. That is, perceived needs (wants) are determined by expectations communicated by a community between its members. This may include behaviours that function to maintain or enhance social status or conform to community expectations. For example, travelling internationally for leisure may be a socially determined means of achieving higher social status within a community. Meeting perceived needs (wants) may enhance subjective wellbeing but are not essential for survival as defined by the WCED (1987).

In this light, Moscardo et al. (2014) comment that associating tourism with fulfilment of essential needs is misguided. Butler (2015) more bluntly takes issue with the notion that the wants associated with a voluntary, leisure based activity conducted by people with surplus resources and time may be considered in the same context as essential human needs. He states,

> *To argue that tourism is a need is a viewpoint which, in this writer's opinion, borders on the obscene. To include tourism or travel as a human right … alongside such essential aspects of life as security, the right to life, freedom of religion, freedom from discrimination, freedom from hunger and illness and freedom for education … is ridiculous* (Butler, 2015: 69)

Butler's view is a criticism of the UNWTO definition of sustainable tourism development. His point rests on the notion that some needs are more important in the context of both survival and enduring human wellbeing. In this sense, failure to meet the wants motivating tourists (e.g. exploring the other, aesthetic appreciation, hedonism) will not threaten survival or even wellbeing. Failure to meet the essential needs listed by the WCED (1987) and Butler (2015) may well negatively impact on human wellbeing and survival. Ultimately, if a need is defined by the lack of something (Taormina & Gao, 2013), a lack of food, water, sanitation, shelter or employment arguably drives a need requiring attention as a matter of survival. A lack of experiencing the 'other', or a lack of excessive consumption may have little serious consequence, or could even be beneficial to enduring wellbeing.

… and host communities…

It is well documented that tourism as a sector can contribute to the provision of community needs and wants, such as employment, standards of living and social status as well as community sense of identity and community pride (Ap, 1990; Besculides et al., 2002; Dwyer et al., 2004; King et al., 1993; Newsome & Hughes, 2016). Thus it stands to reason that host communities, especially those strongly reliant on tourism as an economic sector, must cater to the wants of tourists in order to generate tourism activity to meet their own needs and wants. Much literature also points to the negative side of meeting tourists' wants, such as for luxury and excessive consumption, or low cost experiences, authenticity or commodified experiences (Hughes & Carlsen, 2010; Kim et al., 2013; McCool & Martin, 1994; Milman & Pizam, 1988; Pizam, 1978). For example, tourists' want for spa baths in hotel guest rooms and green lawn areas at caravan parks in a remote, arid region of Western Australia with a limited fresh water supply raised concerns about meeting the host community need for drinking water (Wood et al., 2008). Similar issues with tourist water consumption limiting supply for local communities have been noted for small island destinations (Nepal et al., 2015). As another example, Liu (2003) suggested employing experienced expatriate managers rather than less experienced locals to meet the tourists' want for a certain standard of service. However, such an action may reduce the ability of local communities to meet their need for employment or perhaps want for a higher status of employment position (e.g. hotel manager rather than reception-ist). Catering to tourists' wants can both hinder and facilitate the ability of host communities to meet their own needs and wants; a well-established understand-ing in the tourism literature (Weaver et al., 2015).

At this point, we acknowledge the complexity of sustainable development and tourism. These indicative and simplified examples consider the direct comparison of wants of tourists relative to host community needs and wants in a specific location. However, contributions to sustainability can be under-stood at different temporal and spatial scales (a theme we return to later). For example, tourists visiting and fulfilling wants in a protected area can help foster their support for the protected natural area. In such cases, tourist activity can potentially translate to advocacy and broader community support for nature conservation (Moore et al., 2013; Moyle & Weiler, 2016). Improved support for nature conservation can lead to better resourcing for maintaining or improving ecosystem services, as part of the sustainable development pathway, benefiting the community, including current and future generations (Dudley, 2010; Watson et al., 2014). However, the more remote the benefits are (in time and space), the more intangible and complex they become as demonstrative benefits of tourism for local communities versus realising tourist wants.

In terms of meeting needs and wants, The WCED (1987) sustainable develop-ment definition emphasises that priority should be given to meeting essential needs. The report clearly states that a key concept of sustainable development is… the concept of 'needs', in particular the essential needs of the world's poor, to which overriding priority should be given; … (World Commission on Envi-ronment and Development, 1987: 41). In other words, the WCED definition highlights that meeting human needs should take priority over addressing human wants.

In contrast, the UNWTO definition of sustainable tourism development appears to equate the wants of tourists with the needs of host communities. At worst, host community needs appear like an addendum in the UNWTO sustain-able tourism definition (World Tourism Organisation, 2018). If the true spirit of sustainable development is adopted by sustainable tourism, it is reasonable that the wants of a voluntary, leisure based activity take second place to meeting the needs of host communities. We acknowledge the reality is not clear cut, because needs and wants may be determined relative to social and cultural context and trade-offs can be unavoidable in many cases. Even so, perhaps the current UNWTO sustainable tourism develop definition should be modified to read:

Tourism that meets the needs of host communities and takes full account of its current and future economic, social and environmental impacts, while addressing wants of tourists and the tourism industry. (adapted from World Tourism Organisation, 2018)

Highlighting that host community needs come before tourist wants places tourism as one component of a broader systemic move toward sustainability, rather than being the focal point. Given the theme of this book is about collaboration and working toward a common goal, the emphasis in terms of 'whose needs, and wants?' inevitably influences what the goal is and how it is to be realised.

The decisions about whose needs and wants link with two key aspects of sustainability assessment thinking and practice. First, sustainability is a pluralistic concept (e.g. Bond et al., 2012; 2013) meaning that collaboration in sustainable tourism development must usefully commence with shared, or at least agreed, understandings of the concept itself. Second, identifying the desired outcome in the form of a shared goal is one of the early and key steps in a generic sustainability assessment approach (Morrison-Saunders & Pope, 2013). This includes establishing sustainability goals and criteria for making decisions. The latter may include thresholds of acceptability, that is, minimum standards or 'needs' that must be met as well as identification of unacceptable outcomes that must be avoided. Thresholds of acceptability come into play when making trade-off decisions. Collaboration thus can be seen as a pre-condition for sustainable tourism development.

... to achieve sustainable tourism development objectives

This book notes that collaboration means an integrated effort that works toward common objectives. An objective may be defined in terms of achieving a result to meet an identified need. In the context of sustainable development that common goal broadly relates to achievement of sustainability, raising the question of 'what is to be sustained?' (Morrison-Saunders & Hughes, 2018). The literature frames the concept of sustainable development and what it seeks to achieve as a journey involving multiple pathways toward objectives that are difficult to define or even determine if they have been realised (Hacking & Guthrie, 2006; O'Riordan, 2000). Other authors have highlighted the difficulty of articulating clear sustainable development objectives, especially at a local development level (Glasson et al., 2012; Ortolano & Shepherd, 1995). Gibson (2006) notes that sustainable development is not about making one project after another sustainable, but requires consideration of the broader context, a systems approach. Thus, while sustainable tourism development has merit as a global ideal, applying it in terms of working towards measurable objectives that addresses a defined need at the host community level is problematic (Butler, 2015; Nepal et al., 2015).

Collaborations to meet needs and wants

In view of the challenge in defining clear objectives, some authors suggest that sustainable development is about collective consideration of preferred development alternatives (Gibson, 2006; Newsome & Hughes, 2016). Preferred alternatives are identified according to achieving the greatest overall benefits while avoiding undesirable trade-offs as development proceeds (Gibson, 2006). In other words, Gibson's proposed preferred alternatives approach requires collaboration to identify which alternative best meets a set of agreed upon needs and wants. These decisions depend on who is involved in the journey, and whose needs and wants are given priority, and are strongly influenced by the power relations between those taking part in the decision making process (Morrison-Saunders & Hughes, 2018). Authors such as Aas, Ladkin and Fletcher (2005), Gaventa (2007) and Hughes, Jones and Phau (2016) discuss the influence of power relations on decision making and subsequently, whose needs and wants take priority. It is important to acknowledge and understand who influences decisions and for what purpose, as part of a transparent decision making process. This is because benefits and undesirable trade-offs are partly determined by judgements about what is negotiable and what is non-negotiable and the establishment of associated thresholds as part of the sustainable development journey.

Morrison-Saunders and Pope (2013) put forward a conceptual model of critical thresholds for use when making trade-off decisions in sustainability assessment practice. Each pillar is depicted in terms of negotiable and non-negotiable parameters. To achieve a sustainable outcome it is necessary to maintain (or ideally to grow) capital within each pillar but not to permit any loss or erosion of the non-negotiable attributes. Trade-offs between the sustainability pillars are only acceptable for the negotiable attributes and even where such acceptable losses occur, offsets are advocated to mitigate or restore what is lost. This model is transferrable to the negotiation of sustainable tourism development and specifically the consideration of needs. Thus, the priority of needs in sustainable tourism development is important, especially in terms of needs versus tourist wants. For example, the WCED (1987) definition of sustainable development makes it clear that meeting essential needs is non-negotiable. The UNWTO (2018) definition appears to place the wants of tourists and the tourism industry before host community needs or at least of the same importance. This is reflected in practice more generally whereby development alternatives tend to align with the needs of the developers who usually have preferred ways of conducting business and are reluctant to change (Morrison-Saunders & Hughes, 2018).

One key difficulty with identifying preferred development alternatives is knowing which alternative presents the 'most sustainable' option. Comparing alternatives can encourage the notion that a negative impact can be offset by balancing it with some other benefit, either now or at some point in the future, resulting in an overall net benefit (Morrison-Saunders & Hughes, 2018). The risk is that preferred alternatives may prioritise the wants of tourists over the needs of local communities. This balancing of alternatives often takes the form of trade-offs between the three pillars of environmental, economic and social concerns. A common example of this balance approach is the 'jobs versus the environment' argument, where creation of employment opportunities is a benefit that counters the environmental degradation associated with a development alternative (Glasson et al., 2012). The balance approach may also occur within pillars, for example, loss of access to lands for traditional activities in exchange for access to facilities associated with tourism development. The problem with the pillar oriented balance approach is that it potentially results in loss of a sustainability resource and the associated essential needs the resources support; for example a tourism development that creates jobs but results in ecological degradation and the associated loss of ecosystem services required to meet community needs. Gibson (2006) argued that viewing sustainable development in terms of balancing, focusses on compromises and trade-offs between aspects and associated needs that may not be substitutable. The trade-off conceptualization and management model of Morrison-Saunders and Pope (2013) outlined previously is intended to establish a transparent process and in particular agreed thresholds of acceptability that can be utilized in such circumstances. Ultimately, avoiding a trade-off decision-making situation is preferable. In this regard, Gibson (2006) suggested that sustainable development is about identifying alternatives that result in multiple reinforcing gains rather than tradeoffs and compromises.

An example of multiple reinforcing gains is provided by Newsome and Hughes (2016) in the context of nature-based tourism focused on wildlife in Uganda. The authors describe how nature-based tourists visiting a forested region of Uganda justifies conservation of the forest and its wildlife. In this case, nature-based tourism generates significant economic activity and creates local employment that drives action for forest conservation. Forest conservation maintains regional biodiversity and ecosystem services that benefit communities. In this case, carefully managed tourism development to meet tourist wants associated with the nature-based experience enables the needs and wants of local communities to be met. In the absence of nature-based tourists, alternative developments would no doubt occur in the forest area such as agriculture or logging. These alternatives could have short term gains but undesirable tradeoffs in the longer term affecting the continuing existence of the forest and wildlife and the ability of local communities to meet their own needs and wants.

Achieving multiple reinforcing gains in sustainable development requires a holistic, systems approach in order to best meet needs and contribute to enduring community wellbeing (Grace & Pope, 2015). In this regard, Liburd (2013) noted that tourism should not be considered in isolation but in the broader systems context of which tourism is a part. A significant body of literature discusses alternatives in relation to what constitutes the ideal approach to sustainable tourism development with examples of various alternatives and the resulting consequences (Hughes et al., 2015; Inskeep, 1991; Pigram & Wahab, 2005; Sharpley, 2009). From this perspective, while sustainable tourism development is considered within the regional context, the decision regarding preferred alternatives is often about what form tourism development should take. Authors such as Cochrane (2010), Farrell and Twining-Ward (2005), Hall (2011), and McCool et al. (2013) and Strickland-Munro et al. (2010) have all flagged the need for a broader systems approach to tourism development. A true systems approach to tourism development means that alternatives are not just about what form of tourism should be developed, but what is the best pathway for development that meets community needs, given that tourism may be one of a range of possible development options. This reiterates the transition sustainability discourse (Pope et al., 2017) and the notion of a collaborative journey or direction of travel rather than an end state or definitive goal that will be realised. It is about finding the most influential levers that will have the greatest (desired) effect on the system.

The 'Ecocean' whale shark tourism case study described by Hughes (2013) presents an innovative example of collaboration involving tourists' wants as a lever, combined with an identified need for conservation of a species. In this case, there was a need to better understand whale shark life cycle and migratory patterns and contribute to protecting this vulnerable species. Whale sharks are migratory and can travel widely, tending to aggregate where annual food pulses associated with coral spawning events occur. Protection of the species was haphazard with no coordinated approach to habitat protection or other actions to protect the species. At the same time, a significant tourist want to view and swim with whale sharks formed the basis for lucrative ecotourism operations in key locations where whale sharks regularly aggregate.

The case study describes a complex collaboration between an organisation, Ecoocean, concerned with understanding and conserving whale sharks, tourists wanting to swim with and photograph whale sharks and an astrophysicist with knowledge and skills that enabled analysis of whale shark images to facilitate with understanding whale shark biology and behaviour. Tourists were encouraged to collaborate by uploading their whale shark images to an online repository managed by Ecocean. Analysis of the images was enabled by resources provided by the astrophysicist collaborating with Ecocoean. This collaboration in turn revealed insights into the migratory patterns, life cycle and biology of whale sharks to better inform conservation efforts. Tourists were able to access the repository and results of the data analysis enabling them to view the results of their collaborative efforts. The collaboration was driven by a shared interest in whale sharks that enabled both tourist wants and a conservation need to be met (Hughes, 2013).

A starting point for collaboration for sustainable tourism development

A needs-based approach to collaboration for sustainable tourism development could draw on the framework proposed by Morrison-Saunders and Hughes (2018) that expresses sustainable development in spatial and temporal dimensions of human wellbeing (Figure 7.1). The matrix represents both a needs-based and systems thinking approach that avoids the focus of trade-offs within and between sustainability pillars. Rather, it considers development as a whole in the context of the here and now as well as there and then. This matrix presents a fundamental conceptualisation of sustainable development as a starting point for discussion in terms of needs and collaboration.

	HERE *(Host community)*	THERE *(wider community)*
NOW (present generation)	A sustainable development will directly and indirectly contribute to meeting the needs and enhance the wellbeing of the current host community.	A sustainable development will directly or indirectly contribute to the needs and enhance the wellbeing of the wider community.
THEN (future generations)	A sustainable development will ensure that the host community in the future will have an equal or better wellbeing relative to the present time.	A sustainable development will directly or indirectly continue to contribute to the needs and enhance wellbeing of the wider community.

Figure 7.1: A community needs based framework for sustainable development adapted from Morrison-Saunders and Hughes (2018).

The host community refers to the community of locale, that is, residents living within the geographically defined boundaries of the tourism destination. The wider community refers to the community of interest, that is, those people living outside the geographical area of the destination who have an interest in and/or value the destination, including tourists. Each of the matrix cells provides the basis for discussion between stakeholders in tourism development. This accommodates the pluralistic nature of sustainable development whilst working towards shared objectives. In short it forms a framing device for collaboration for sustainable tourism development.

Conclusion

In this chapter we set out to explore the notion of human needs as it is expressed in the WCED (1987) definition of sustainable development and the UNWTO appropriation of the definition for sustainable tourism development. We discussed the underpinnings of sustainable development and sustainable tourism development being founded on the ideas of positive change, social equity and working towards meeting needs for enduring human wellbeing. We discussed conceptual differences between essential needs and perceived needs (wants) as defined by WCED (1987). We suggested an alternative definition of sustainable tourism development that emphasises the priority of 'host community' needs that better aligns with the spirit of the WCED definition. Drawing on the field of sustainability assessment, we addressed the issue of preferred alternatives as part of the sustainable development journey (keeping in mind power relationships that may influence identification of preferred alternatives), rather than a process of negotiating balance and trade-offs.

We understand that sustainable development is a highly complex issue. We also point to the importance of fundamental principles that underlie that complexity. These principles include recognising that tourist wants are secondary to the needs of host communities, the importance of understanding power relations in decision making and the notion that meeting essential needs should take precedence over the wants of tourists. This journey is about promoting multiple reinforcing gains as part of a community needs-based, systems approach where tourism development is one amongst a range of development alternatives. From this foundation, collaboration in sustainable tourism development ideally works toward a common objective focussed on promoting enduring human wellbeing for the host community (first) as well as for tourists.

References

Aas, C., Ladkin, A. & Fletcher, J. (2005). Stakeholder collaboration and heritage management. *Annals of Tourism Research, 32*, 28–48.

Anon. (Ed.) (2017) *Oxford Dictionary*. Oxford, UK: Oxford University Press.

Ap, J. (1990). Residents' perceptions research on the social impacts of tourism. *Annals of Tourism Research,* **17**(4), 610-616.

Besculides, A., Lee, M. E., & McCormick, P. J. (2002). Residents' perceptions of the cultural benefits of tourism. *Annals of Tourism Research,* **29**(2), 303-319.

Bond A., Morrison-Saunders, A. & Howitt, R. (eds) (2013). *Sustainability Assessment Pluralism, Practice and Progress.* Abingdon: Routledge.

Bond A., Morrison-Saunders, A. & Pope, J. (2012). Sustainability assessment: The state of the art, *Impact Assessment and Project Appraisal,* **30**(1): 56–66.

Butler, R. (2015). Sustainable tourism: Paradoxes, inconsistencies and a way forward. In M. Hughes, D. Weaver & C. Pforr (Eds.), *The Practice of Sustainable Tourism: Resolving the paradox* (pp. 66-79). London: Routledge.

Cochrane, J. (2010). The sphere of tourism resilience. *Tourism Recreation Research,* **35**(2), 173-185.

Diener, E., Emmons, R. A., Larsen, R. J. & Griffin, S. (1985). The satisfaction with life scale. *Journal of personality assessment,* **49**(1), 71-75.

Diener, E., Inglehart, R. & Tay, L. (2013). Theory and validity of life satisfaction scales. *Social Indicators Research,* **112**(3), 497-527.

Dillard, J. E. & Bates, D. L. (2011). Leisure motivation revisited: why people recreate. *Managing Leisure,* **16**(4), 253-268.

Dryzek, J.S. (1997). *The Politics of the Earth: Environmental discourses,* Oxford: Oxford University Press.

Dudley, N. (2010). *Arguments for Protected Areas: Multiple benefits for conservation and use.* UK: Routledge.

Dwyer, L., Forsyth, P. & Spurr, R. (2004). Evaluating tourism's economic effects: new and old approaches. *Tourism Management,* **25**(3), 307-317.

Farrell, B. & Twining-Ward, L. (2005). Seven steps towards sustainability: Tourism in the context of new knowledge. *Journal of Sustainable Tourism,* **13**(2), 109-122.

Frank, R (2007). *Falling Behind: How Rising Inequality Harms the Middle Class.* Berkley: University of California Press.

Gaventa, J. (2007). Towards participatory governance: assessing the transformative possibilities. In Hickey, S. & Mohan, G. (Eds.) *Participation. From tyranny to transformation?* Zed Books Ltd., London, UK.

Gibson, R. (2006). Sustainability assessment: basic components of a practical approach. *Impact Assessment and Project Appraisal,* **24**(3), 170-182.

Gibson, R. (2013). Avoiding sustainability trade-offs in environmental assessment, *Impact Assessment and Project Appraisal,* **31**(1), 2-12.

Glasson, J., Therivel, R. & Chadwick, A. (2012). *Introduction to Environmental Impact Assessment.* London: Routledge.

Grace, W. & Pope, J. (2015). A systems approach to sustainability assessment. In A. Morrison-Saunders, J. Pope & A. Bond (Eds.), *Handbook of Sustainability Assessment* (pp. 285-320). Cheltenham: Edward Elgar.

Gunn, C. A. & Var, T. (2002). *Tourism Planning.* New York: Routledge.

Hacking, T., & Guthrie, P. (2006). Sustainable development objectives in impact assessment: why are they needed and where do they come from? *Journal of Environmental Assessment Policy and Management,* **8**(03), 341-371.

Hall, C. M. (2011). Policy learning and policy failure in sustainable tourism governance: From first-and second-order to third-order change? *Journal of Sustainable Tourism,* **19**(4-5), 649-671.

Hall, C. M. & Lew, A. (2009). *Understanding and Managing Tourism Impacts: An integrated approach.* London: Routledge.

Hughes, M. (2004). *Influence of varying intensities of natural area on-site interpretation on attitudes and knowledge.* (PhD), University of Notre Dame, Australia, Perth, Western Australia.

Hughes, M. (2013) *Ecocean*: conservation through technological innovation. In J. Liburd, J. Carlsen & D. Edwards (Eds.) *Networks for Sustainable Tourism Innovation: Case studies and cross-case analysis.* Tilde University Press, Australia, pp 25-32

Hughes, M. & Carlsen, J. (2010). The business of cultural heritage tourism: critical success factors. *Journal of Heritage Tourism,* **5**(1), 17-32.

Hughes, M., Jones, T. & Phua, I. (2016) Local community perceptions of the World Heritage nomination process for the Ningaloo Coast region of Western Australia. *Coastal Management,* 44(2), 139-155.

Hughes, M., Weaver, D. & Pforr, C. (2015). *The Practice of Sustainable Tourism: Resolving the Paradox.* UK: Routledge.

Inskeep, E. (1991). *Tourism Planning: An Integrated and Sustainable Development Approach*: Van Nostrand Reinhold.

Jackson, T. (2009). *Prosperity Without Growth: Economics for a Finite Planet,* London: Earthscan.

Kim, K., Uysal, M. & Sirgy, M. J. (2013). How does tourism in a community impact the quality of life of community residents? *Tourism Management,* **36**, 527-540.

King, B., Pizam, A. & Milman, A. (1993). Social impacts of tourism: Host perceptions. *Annals of Tourism Research,* **20**(4), 650-665.

Leiper, N. (2004). *Tourism Management.* Sydney, Australia: Pearson Education Australia.

Liburd, J. (2013). *Towards the Collaborative University: lessons from tourism education and research.* (Professorial Dissertation), University of Southern Denmark, Denmark.

Liburd, J. , & Edwards, D. (Eds.). (2010). *Understanding the Sustainable Development of Tourism.* Oxford: Goodfellows.

Liu, Z. (2003). Sustainable tourism development: A critique. *Journal of Sustainable Tourism,* **11**(6), 459-475.

MacCannell, D. (1976). *The Tourist. A new theory of the leisure class.* Berkley, USA: University of California Press.

Maslow, A. (1943). A theory of human motivation. *Psychological review,* **50**(4), 370.

Maslow, A. (1962). *Toward a Psychology of Being.* New York: Van Nostrand Reinold.

Maslow, A. (1970). *Motivation and Personality* (3rd ed.). New York: Addison Wesley Longman.

McCabe, S. (2005). Who's a tourist? A critical review. *Tourist Studies,* **5**(1), 85-106.

McCleod, S. (2014). Maslow's heirarchy of needs. Retrieved 5 December, 2017, from www.simplypsychology.org/maslow.html

McCool, S., Butler, R., Buckley, R., Weaver, D. & Wheeller, B. (2013). Is concept of sustainability utopian: ideally perfect but impracticable? *Tourism Recreation Research,* **38**(2), 213-242.

McCool, S. F. & Martin, S. R. (1994). Community attachment and attitudes toward tourism development. *Journal of Travel Research,* **32**(3), 29-34.

McKercher, B. (1993). Some fundamental truths about tourism: understanding tourism's social and environmental impacts. *Journal of Sustainable Tourism,* **1**(1), 6-15.

Milman, A. & Pizam, A. (1988). Social impacts of tourism on central Florida. *Annals of Tourism Research,* **15**(2), 191-204.

Moore S.A., Weiler, B., Moyle, B. & Eagles, P. (2013). Our national parks need visitors to survive. *The Conversation,* Retrieved 27 March, 2018, from http://theconversation.com/our-national-parks-need-visitors-to-survive-15867.

Morrison-Saunders, A. & Hughes, M. (2018). Overcoming sustainability displacement – The challenge of making sustainability accessible in the here and now. In M. Brueckner, R. Spencer & M. Paul (Eds.), *Disciplining the Undisciplined: Perspectives on responsible citizenship, corporate social responsibility and sustainability,* Springer.

Morrison-Saunders A., & Pope J. (2013). Conceptualising and managing trade-offs in sustainability assessment, *Environmental Impact Assessment Review,* **38**, 54–63.

Moscardo, G., Dann, G. & McKercher, B. (2014). Do tourists travel for the discovery of 'self' or search for the 'other'? *Tourism Recreation Research,* **39**(1), 81-106. doi: 10.1080/02508281.2014.11081328

Moyle, B. D. & Weiler, B. (2017). Revisiting the importance of visitation: Public perceptions of park benefits. *Tourism and Hospitality Research,* **17**(1), 91-105.

Nepal, S. K., Verkoeyen, S. & Karrow, T. (2015). The end of sustainable tourism? Re-orienting the debate. In M. Hughes, D. Weaver & C. Pforr (Eds.), *The Practice of Sustainable Tourism: Resolving the paradox* (pp. 52-65): Routledge, UK.

Newsome, D. & Hughes, M. (2016). Understanding the impacts of ecotourism on biodiversity: a multiscale, cumulative issue influenced by perceptions and politics. In D. Geneletti (Ed.), *Handbook on Biodiversity and Ecosystem Services in Impact Assessment* (pp. 276-298). Cheltenham, UK: Edward Elgar.

O'Riordan, T. (2000). The sustainability debate. In T. O'Riordan (Ed.), *Environmental Science for Environmental Management* (pp. 29-62). Routledge.

Ortolano, L. & Shepherd, A. (1995). Environmental impact assessment: challenges and opportunities. *Impact assessment,* **13**(1), 3-30.

Pigram, J. J. & Wahab, S. (2005). *Tourism, development and growth: the challenge of sustainability.* Routledge.

Pizam, A. (1978). Tourism's impacts: The social costs to the destination community as perceived by its residents. *Journal of Travel Research,* **16**(4), 8-12.

Pope J., Bond, A., Hugé, J. & Morrison-Saunders, A. (2017). Reconceptualising Sustainability Assessment, *Environmental Impact Assessment Review,* **62**, 205–215

Senate Community Affairs References Committee (2004) *A hand up not a hand out: renewing the fight against poverty (report on poverty and financial hardship).* Parliamentary Report, Commonwealth of Australia, Canberra.

Sharpley, R. (2009). *Tourism Development and the Environment: Beyond sustainability?* Milton Park, UK: Earthscan.

Strickland-Munro, J. K., Allison, H. E. & Moore, S. A. (2010). Using resilience concepts to investigate the impacts of protected area tourism on communities. *Annals of Tourism Research,* **37**(2), 499-519.

Taormina, R. J. & Gao, J. H. (2013). Maslow and the motivation hierarchy: Measuring satisfaction of the needs. *The American Journal of Psychology,* **126**(2), 155-177.

Tay, L. & Diener, E. (2011). Needs and subjective well-being around the world. *Journal of Personality and Social Psychology,* **101**(2), 354.

Tinsley, H. E., & Kass, R. A. (1978). Leisure activities and need satisfaction: A replication and extension. *Journal of Leisure Research,* **10**(3), 191.

Watson, J. E. M., Dudley, N., Segan, D. B. & Hockings, M. (2014). The performance and potential of protected areas. *Nature,* **515**, 67-73.

Weaver, D., Hughes, M. & Pforr, C. (2015). Paradox as a pervasive characteristic of sustainable tourism: Challenges, opportunities and trade-offs. In M. Hughes, D. Weaver & C. Pforr (Eds.), *The Practice of Sustainable Tourism: Resolving the paradox* (pp. 281-290): Routledge, UK.

Wilkinson R. & Pickett, K. (2010). *The Spirit Level: Why equality is better for everyone.* London: Penguin

Wood, D., Jones, T., Hughes, M., Lewis, A., Chandler, P., Schianetz, K., Scherrer, P., Horwitz, P., Northcote, J., Newsome, D. & Morrison-Saunders, A. (2008). *Ningaloo Cluster Project 3: the Ningaloo Destination and Data Modelling project.* http://researchrepository.murdoch.edu.au/id/eprint/7912/

World Commission on Environment and Development. (1987). *Our Common Future.* Oxford: Oxford University Press.

World Health Organisation (1995) *Constitution of the World Health Organisation* (Amended July 1994). World Heath Orgasniation, Geneva. Retrieved 20 February, 2018, from www.who.int/about/mission/en/.

World Tourism Organisation. (2018). Sustainable development of tourism: definition. Retrieved 20 February, 2018, from http://sdt.unwto.org/content/about-us-5.

8 The Responsibility of Corporations for Sustainable Tourism Development

Larry Dwyer and Dagmar Lund-Durlacher

The purpose of this chapter is to provide an understanding of the principles and practices of Corporate Social Responsibility (CSR) and to discuss how the concept of collaboration can facilitate the implementation of CSR strategies and operations. Increasing numbers of tourism companies are incorporating the concept of CSR in their business models, to improve the environment, the quality of life of local communities and the welfare of their employees. The chapter first illustrates and discusses the principles of CSR, and identifies the key benefits of incorporating CSR such as efficiencies, improved stakeholder relationships and enhanced profitability. Next, the chapter highlights the necessary changes in organisational attitudes and behaviour needed to underpin the implementation of CSR. Finally, it identifies the roles of internal and external stakeholders and suggests how collaboration among stakeholders can contribute to positive societal change.

Understanding corporate social responsiblity

The tourism industry shares with local residents, governments, and community the obligation to protect and maintain the natural and cultural heritage resources of our planet, both to sustain economies and to be passed on unimpaired to future generations. On 1 January 2016, the United Nations General Assembly adopted the 2030 Agenda for Sustainable Development with the 17 Global Sustainable Development Goals (SDGs) to be the plan of action for global sustainable development. The 2030 Agenda for Sustainable Development does not only call for all stakeholders to act in collaborative partnership to implementing the SDGs, but also explicitly addresses businesses "to apply their creativity and innovation to solving sustainable development challenges." (United Nations General Assembly, 2015: 29).

The most comprehensive approach to achieving sustainable operations of businesses (i.e., to integrate economic, environmental, and social thinking into core business activities) is Corporate Social Responsibility (CSR).

Research on CSR concepts started in the 1950s when Howard Bowen defined CSR, in his book *Responsibilities of a Businessman*, as the obligations of companies to reflect the expectations and values of the society in their performance, and thus to envision the total benefit to society as the most important factor for their operations (Bowen, 1953). Despite criticism of this social value approach (Friedman, 1970), businesses' were increasingly seen as members of the society which serve the needs of society by fostering social morality in business behavior (Lund-Durlacher, 2015). Several definitions of CSR have emerged and the CSR concept became more specific (Frederick, 1960: 60; McGuire, 1963: 144; Davis, 1967:46; Walton, 1967:18; Carroll, 1979 & 1991; Dahlsrud, 2008; Sheldon and Park 2011:398). In particular, Stakeholder Theory, introduced by R. Edward Freeman (1984), had great influence on contemporary CSR concepts as it states that corporations have relationships with many groups in society (stakeholders) and that responsible corporations must consider the interests of all stakeholders in their operations.

Today, although there are many deviating definitions and numerous terms used to describe CSR, it is the economic, social and environmental performance, combined with the voluntary nature and the consideration of stakeholder relations, which describe the comprehensive scope of CSR. This gives CSR an explicitly strategic character. It is a management approach based on moral commitment, which aims to create shared values for the shareholders, stakeholders and society as a whole (European Commission, 2011 in Fifka, 2017).

Simple explanations of the terms, however, belie the deep philosophical change required of business and the expanded role, responsibility and accountability that change will embody (Dwyer, 2017). The dilemma that businesses face in adopting the new philosophy is one of identifying, in the first instance, the accountable areas in the environmental and social pillars, and then to develop adequate indicators of performance. Recognising that a single, universally-agreed definition of CSR is elusive, our understanding of the concept can be advanced by identifying the principal elements of a responsible approach to business operations and management (Crane, Matten and Spence, 2008; McElhanye, 2009; Porter and Kramer, 2011; Visser, 2011):

Voluntary approach

CSR is typically seen as related to voluntary activities that go beyond those prescribed by the law. This does not of course preclude a role for legally mandated accountability where the government deems this to be appropriate.

Beyond philanthropy – strategic CSR

'Real' CSR is more than just philanthropy and community giving, but about how the entire operations of the firm – i.e. its core business functions – engage with society. CSR is considered a philosophy or set of values that underpins these practices. This debate rests on the assumption that CSR as a management philosophy needs to be integrated into corporate strategy and core business practice rather than being left to discretionary activity (McElhanye, 2009). The attempt to consider how CSR might be 'built in' to the core business of firms as opposed to 'bolted on' as an added extra has become a major theme in the CSR practitioner world (Grayson and Hodges, 2004).

Commitment to CSR by senior management

Social responsibility lies with senior management and not within the company as an organization, since only natural persons are able to have a conscience and sense of responsibility (Bowen, 1953). Since CSR is a morally grounded concept, such conviction of executives is even more important. This includes the recognition and commitment of the social responsibility and a vision of which path the company wants to take in the future. It is therefore about the fundamental management philosophy and is reflected in the central question: "Who are we and what do we want to achieve?" A vision which integrates a CSR perspective thereby reflects the values of the company.

Multiple stakeholder orientation

Companies are part of society and communicate continuously with members of the society, the so-called stakeholders. It is this society that enables economic activities in providing not only the necessary resources such as well-educated employees, infrastructure and legal frameworks but also sales markets. Stakeholders have expectations of responsible corporate governance and addressing their interests and impacts is central to credible CSR management. Major stakeholder groups include consumers, employees, suppliers, and local communities.

Organisational cultural change

Organisational cultural change is inevitable when implementing sustainability practices within an organisation. The role of senior management in driving and leading a strategy, fitting the strategy within the organisation's operations and strategic planning and communicating the strategy to employees are important considerations. With the positive encouragement of government, firms are attempting to develop ways to cultivate an organisational culture of compliance, including an awareness of the possibility of illegality, a personal ethic of care and an assumption of responsibility in the event that improper practices occur (Sarre, Doig, and Fiedler, 2001).

Empowerment and participation of employees

Corporate responsibility is only possible if the employees are willing to support the vision and the corporate policy. For this reason, CSR management requires first and foremost dialogue, empowerment and participation of all employees.

CSR as a learning and improvement process

CSR is linked to a continuous learning process. The corporations' environments and frameworks are constantly changing, and companies have to adapt their strategies and actions to these changed conditions. Therefore, it is important to understand the implementation of CSR strategies and programs as a process of continuous improvement which seeks to take advantage of new opportunities.

Alignment of social and economic responsibilities

No universal, global sustainability standard exists and there are often conflicting goals based on conflicting stakeholder interests. The balancing of different stakeholder interests requires judgements as to appropriate trade-offs, which may in some cases imply reduced profitability, though many believe that it should not conflict with profitability (Stark, 1993).

Internalizing or managing externalities

Externalities are the positive and negative side-effects of economic behaviour that are borne by others but are not taken into account in a firm's decision-making process, and are not included in the set market price for goods and services. Proponents of CSR argue that businesses have a much greater obligation to account for their actions to a much broader audience than is presently acknowledged (Visser, 2011). CSR activity to reduce negative externalities could include managing human rights violations in the workforce, minimizing carbon emissions, investing in clean technology or reducing the health impacts of toxic or otherwise dangerous products, etc. The size and type of externalities vary from sector to sector and from company to company. The voluntary activity of firms to address externalities can also be reinforced by government regulations that force firms to internalise the costs.

These core principles, we would suggest, capture the main thrust of CSR. We next discuss the benefits of CSR approaches to hospitality and tourism management.

Benefits of CSR in hospitality and tourism management

CSR represents an argument for a company's economic self-interest in that satisfying stakeholders' needs is central to retaining societal legitimacy (and therefore financial viability) over the long term (Werther and Chandler, 2011). A company that can meet the needs of the present in terms of social and environmental impact, without compromising the needs of the future, is more likely to appeal to investors and customers alike, and thus be financially successful (Sauvante, 2001). This may be of particular relevance for firms in the tourism industry which depend crucially on unique features of the natural and social environments to maintain competitive advantage (Dwyer & Kim, 2003, Lund-Durlacher, 2013). The business case for CSR can be found in several interlocking aspects of performance.

Cost and risk reduction

Integrating CSR into an existing business plan will likely lead to a review of various internal company policies and procedures, which may result in the identification of opportunities to both improve efficiencies and save costs.

Reduced operating costs

These can be achieved through the detection of wasteful activities, eg. reducing use of materials such as chemicals, reducing water and energy use, increasing operational and design efficiencies, reduce – reuse – recycle wastes, reduced transportation, storage, and packaging costs. Intangible benefits beyond the balance sheet have involved potential cost savings from recycling, energy saving, waste reduction and a variety of other environmental measures (Kasim, 2010). According to a study among European hoteliers concerning their attitudes towards the environment, "nearly 85% of the hoteliers stated that they were involved in some type of environment-oriented activities" and that the main areas of engagement were energy and water conservation and responsible waste management, all leading to significant cost reductions (Bohdanowicz, 2005:198).

Potentially lower compliance costs

Regulatory processes will run more smoothly if regulators have greater understanding of a company's performance. The same as for other business, tourism and hospitality firms are responsible for compliance with operational development plans, planning conditions, standards and targets for sustainable tourism (Suggett and Goodsir, 2002; Kasim, 2010). Being proactive with certain social and environmental activities will lower the costs of complying with present and future regulations.

Attracting and retaining competent staff

By demonstrating that an organisation is focused on values and engages in CSR in the form of equal employment opportunity policies and practices to illustrate an inclusive policy, CSR can have positive effects on employee motivation, recruitment and retention. The tourism industry is notorious for its high turnover, anti-social working hours, low pay, seasonal employment, instability and low job status (Hinkin and Tracey, 2000; Deery et al., 2018). A healthier working environment for employees results in reduced turnover of staff, fewer sick days, reduced penalties, lower insurance, and workers' compensation costs, higher levels of worker satisfaction, and the ability to attract good quality staff. There is evidence that CSR attracts and retains high calibre employees, improves employee morale, productivity and creativity (Sauvante, 2001). Bohdanowicz and Zientara (2009) note that well-designed CSR programmes can benefit human resources management in the hotel industry, in particular in the area of recruitment, retention and productivity.

Improved access to capital from potential shareholders and institutions

The proliferation of so-called 'green' and 'ethical' investment funds is making it more attractive for listed companies to meet the investment criteria of such funds. Tourism firms typically face strong impediments to investment due to lack of expertise in assessing high risk tourism investments with variable cash flows, coupled with a reluctance to invest heavily or in the long term in the tourism industry (Dwyer, 2017).

Increased profit, more competitive advantage and higher reputation

Evidence is mounting that businesses implementing CSR practices enjoy higher brand equity and profitability than those focused primarily on profit (Sisodia et al., 2003; Mackay and Sisodia, 2014). Porter and Kramer (2011) acknowledge trade-offs between short-term profitability and social or environmental goals, while emphasising the opportunities for competitive advantage from building a social value proposition into corporate strategy. CSR increases customer satisfaction, which in turn leads to positive financial returns and enhanced market value of the firm (Luo and Bhattacharya, 2006). Also, in the tourism context, studies identify a positive relationship between hotel company CSR actions, revenue increases from higher sales and market share due to consumer preferences (Garcia and Armas, 2007; Nicolau, 2008; Lee and Park, 2009; Inoue and Lee, 2010). Kang, Lee and Huh (2010) examined the positive (proactive) and negative (reactive) effects of CSR activities on the performance of tourism-related industries (airlines, casinos, hotels and restaurants) and found that in hotels and restaurants there was an improvement in the value of the company.

· There is a growing understanding that social responsibility implies risk minimization, and that customers perceive the operator's 'duty of care' to extend to the environment and the global community. Good organisational performance in relation to environmental and social issues can build the reputation of firms in the industry (Coles et al., 2013). CSR can also have positive impacts on the branding of the organisation's products or services, thereby creating value through enhanced reputation and positive customer response (Suggett and Goodsir, 2002).

CSR can help the firm to appeal to new and growing markets and encourage existing customers to return. In today's tourism industry, travelers are typically more sophisticated, have more disposable income and are more confident about their expectations. As such, these consumers are attracted to businesses that are showing responsibility and awareness for the environment and the communities in which they operate (McWilliams et al., 2006).

While such findings are welcome, it must be noted however, that the relationship between CSR and corporate financial performance "has not yet been unequivocally verified through empirical studies", with measurement errors, model misspecifications, incomplete data sets, and organisational culture cited as possible reasons for the lack of clarity (Lee, 2008: 64).

Improved business practices

A CSR approach can influence a company's business practices and many companies have begun to define social or sustainability goals in their strategies or business plans (Coles et al., 2013; Lund-Durlacher, 2017).

☐ CSR systematises and institutionalises best practice and provides the ability to benchmark CSR best practice both within and across sectors. CSR can foster innovation – addressing environmental and social impacts can lead to innovations that result in new markets and value creation (Suggett and Goodsir, 2002).

☐ CSR can result in improved management of risk through stakeholder engagement, enhanced management systems and performance monitoring (Gray and Bebbington, 2000). This may also lead to more robust resource allocation decisions and business planning, as risks are better understood and factored into decision making.

☐ CSR also supports the development of communication tools that enable internal information to be shared more effectively, facilitating company learning (Gray and Bebbington, 2000). Formalising and enhancing communication with key stakeholders allows an organisation to develop a more proactive approach to addressing future needs and concerns.

☐ CSR is a means of promoting integrated decision-making within businesses and other organisations – a way of embedding sound corporate governance and ethics systems throughout all levels of an organisation.

CSR helps ensure a values-driven culture is integrated at all levels of an organisation. The importance of organisational culture in tourism firm performance is well recognised (Dwyer et al., 1998/99; Dwyer et al., 2000; Maon et al., 2009). There is growing evidence to suggest that over time these benefits do contribute to the increased market value of an organization, generating substantial competitive advantages (Sadri and Lees, 2001). Hence, CSR thinking is not a short-lived marketing ploy but a strategy that is designed to enhance long-term competitiveness.

Synergistic value creation through stakeholder relationships

As mentioned earlier, CSR is best described as a multi-stakeholder concept where a consideration of the interests of different stakeholders and the dialogue between them plays a major role. According to Freeman, *"a stakeholder in an organization is any group or individual who can affect or is affected by the achievement of the organizations objective"* (Freeman, 1984; Frederick et al., 1992). Important stakeholders for tourism businesses are employees, tourists, businesses in the supply chain, shareholders, investors, local communities, government authorities, NGOs and the media. In this context, stakeholders are not only beneficiaries, but also partners for realizing and implementing CSR strategies and projects (Lund-Durlacher, 2015).Therefore, the development of CSR strategies, activities and indicators involves collaboration with stakeholders. Firms must understand:

☐ The various processes to integrate and engage different stakeholders in participatory planning and consensus building in the planning process;

☐ The role of different stakeholders in strategy implementation, including industry, government and community roles in the establishment of codes of practice; and

☐ How their activity affects stakeholders, what the main concerns/issues of stakeholders are, and how they are being addressed, and need to ensure that their positive initiatives are being recognized.

Formalised, collaborative and meaningful stakeholder engagement, rather than an ad hoc approach, is an essential component to integrating CSR into business strategies and operations. Competitive advantages can be derived from strong and meaningful relations between a company and its key stakeholders (especially those at the local community level). Effective stakeholder engagement can produce significant corporate value in the form of: reputation/brand strengthening and assurance, enhanced operational certainty through achievement of social license to operate, reduced/minimized pressure on government to implement restrictive regulatory frameworks, and enterprise agility through a strong understanding of external issues and trends (Dwyer and Kemp, 2004). By engaging in stakeholder dialogue, the company may also find new business opportunities which may lead to innovation (Hjalager, 2018) increased profits and which have the consent and support of the stakeholders (Carroll and Shabana, 2010).

Attitudes and behaviour for CSR implementation

CSR therefore needs to be perceived as good business practice for today, as well as contributing to sustainable development over time, and not merely as adding to regulatory burdens on business. There are several essential behaviours and attitudes that are required in those firms that seek to adopt CSR for sustainable tourism development (Suggett and Goodsir, 2002) including accountability, transparency, organisational culture, stakeholder engagement, shared value, working with Non-Governmental Organizations (NGOs) and reporting practice.

Accountability

The globalisation of many corporations has increased their power and the impact they have on the social, political and ecological environment of the countries in which they operate, and subsequently there has been an increasing expectation from society for companies to act responsibly and be accountable for those impacts (Adams and Zutshi, 2004). CSR is founded on the assumption that firms are accountable not only to shareholders for generating returns but also to stakeholders for contributing, within their context and capabilities, to sustainable development. This notion of accountability is most often expressed in the 'vision' or mission statement of the firm and is inculcated in its 'organisational culture' (Dwyer et al., 2000).

There is no doubt that adopting CSR means that companies are becoming more accountable to stakeholders by reporting on social and environmental performances as well as economic performance. Increased demand for accountability will deliver three clear benefits (Beckett and Jonker, 2002):

☐ **Improved transparency:** The life of organisations will be made more visible and the effects both within the organisation and in society around it, will achieve greater transparency.

☐ **Quality of decisions:** Greater quantities and quality of information will tend to provide better capacity to make decisions, both within the organisation itself and society as a whole.

☐ **Clear responsibility:** Through the development of greater transparency, the organisation brings closer the connection between its actions and their results, thereby leading to greater responsibility.

Transparency

CSR reporting increases the transparency of company performance to stakeholders. There is a growing trend and demand from stakeholders for the operations of a company to become more transparent both internally and externally as well as at a domestic and international level. Factors that have led to the trend of increasing transparency of companies include:

☐ The rapid developments in information technology and ease of means of communication,

☐ The powerful role of the media, and

☐ The increasing demands by investors and stakeholders.

Companies also have an obligation, within commercial limits, to be transparent about their activities and impacts beyond financial performance. Recognising the legitimacy of the stakeholders' 'right to know', disclosing multi-dimensional results and impacts is a powerful idea embodied in the triple bottom line which can be included in the company 'vision' or mission statement, its communication with stakeholders and in the actual content of its public reporting. That transparency needs to be embedded into the organisational culture, allowing the process to be viewed openly by all (Dwyer et al., 1998/99; Dwyer et al., 2000; Maon et al., 2010).

Organisational culture

Changes of the type required for CSR need to be well integrated into core management systems including planning, operations, employee relations, community involvement, information management, environmental management and management appraisal and reward systems. Taking the holistic approach demanded by CSR requires significant internal cultural change in an organisation, with detailed attention paid to values, ethos, mission and long term corporate reputation, stakeholder inclusiveness, employee engagement and so on. Organisations committed to integrating CSR as a philosophy have developed and implemented training and processes to support management and staff.

Stakeholder engagement

CSR involves a strategic, whole-business view of responsibility that is expected to permeate all areas of operations, across the entire value chain, with due consideration of distinctive stakeholders. Research on stakeholders internal to a business or organisation has been largely absent. This is somewhat curious in so far as research in the mainstream suggests that it is vital to the success of CSR programmes or initiatives to have their buy-in and active participation (Porter and Kramer, 2006). Effective stakeholder engagement is something that tourism firms can easily relate to. Recognition of the importance of broad community participation, of effective coordination and support between all involved parties is crucial to the achievement of sustainable tourism (Timothy, 2002; Lund-Durlacher et al., 2013).

An internal environment that encourages employees to share their ideas and opinions on business and workplace practices is considered by many businesses to be both ideal and effective. One of the most effective ways to encourage input from employees is open and respectful exchange, and collaboration between employees and owners/managers, which should underpin work-life balance (Deery et al., 2018).

Focus on societal needs through shared value

Developing CSR further and focusing on societal needs, Michael Porter and Mark Kramer developed the concept of Shared Value (CSV), which shifts the emphasis from the perceptions of stakeholders to focus on addressing the prevailing needs of society. Porter and Kramer argue that every "firm should look at decisions and opportunities through the lens of shared value" (Porter and Kramer 2011:5). The concept of shared value can be defined as policies and operating practices that enhance the competitiveness of a company while simultaneously advancing the economies and social conditions in the communities in which it operates (Porter and Kramer 2011). According to Porter and Kramer (2011) there are three ways to create shared value opportunities:

1 By reconceiving products and markets,

2 By redefining productivity in the value chain, and

3 By enabling local cluster development.

Reconceiving products and markets addresses the question if products and services meet societal needs. A good example can be found in Chapter 12, in which Foley, Edwards and Harrison present the case of the International Convention Centre (ICC) in Sydney, New South Wales (NSW), Australia. ICC Sydney's collaborative partnership with suppliers ensures that ICC Sydney clients receive fresh produce, paddock to plate, while contributing to the livelihoods of local and regional small food suppliers in NSW. Examining suppliers regarding energy use, logistics, resource use, procurement, distribution and employer productivity can reimage value chains offering "new ways to innovate and unlock new economic value that most businesses have missed" (Porter and Kramer, 2011:11), which is addressed more detail by Hjalager (2018).

The most successful cluster development programs are ones that involve collaboration within the private sector, as well as trade associations, government agencies, and NGOs (Porter and Kramer, 2011). Utilising clusters to promote and diffuse CSR practices across industries and multi-sectors can address problems that cannot be solved by individual companies alone. Collaborations then transform clusters "into durable alliances that address real societal concerns" (Maon, Lindgreen and Swaen, 2010:23).

Collaboration with NGOs

To meet their social responsibility, companies increasingly enter into partnerships with NGOs, e.g. World Wildlife Fund and Royal Caribbean Cruises Ltd. or TUI Group with The Code and the Travel Foundation (www.tuigroup.com/en-en/ sustainability/sus_business/partnerships-cooperations).Considering the needs of corporations, NGOs build professional structures to facilitate the collaboration with corporations (for example, www.worldwildlife.org/partnership categories/ corporate-partnerships).

Another example is the joint project of TUI Care Foundation and World Animal Protection in Tarangire National Park in Tanzania "Using chilies to save elephants' lives". Because elephants frequently trample crops outside the park, World Animal Protection has come up with a simple and animal friendly solution to this problem: chili peppers and bees, with support from the TUI Care Foundation (www.tuicarefoundation.com/en/projects/using-chillies-to-save-elephants-lives).

Multi-dimensional measurement and reporting

CSR reporting is a vehicle for organisations to render account of their activities towards a wide group of stakeholders and thereby respond to society's growing expectations of transparency. A more complete picture of the company will be communicated through the disclosing of environmental, social and financial information. As a powerful corporate communication tool, this information will allow stakeholders to obtain a more detailed understanding of the company, allowing them to make more informed decisions.

In many cases CSR reporting is often very simplistic and superficial thereby casting doubt on the level of action and the likely outcomes associated with CSR activity (de Grosbois, 2012; Blichfeldt, 2018). Multi-dimensional indicators are required as part of a CSR framework to accurately measure the company's economic, social and environmental performance and report on their triple bottom line (TBL).

There is a substantial research literature on environmental and social indicators for tourism (Bossel, 1999; Manning, 1999; McCool et al., 2001). Indicators are critical to the success of environmental monitoring and reporting as they provide the basis for objective performance assessment. Indicators function as a 'measuring stick', by which companies can evaluate how they are accomplishing explicit goals (Suggett and Goodsir, 2002).

Hawkins and Bohdanowicz (2012) discuss the relevance of many international CSR reporting schemes, raising the possibility of the potential application of the Global Reporting Initiative (GRI), AA100 (an accounting standard), SA 8000 (a social accountability standard) and guidelines produced by FTSE-4-Good, the Dow Jones Sustainability Index and Business in the Community programmes.

CSR measurements must be based on solid information of better quality than is generally available now. The required information can be generated through the use of environmental management systems (EMS) and updated accounting practices. Since CSR at its broadest level is an integral decision making process based upon outcomes rather than outputs, reporting needs to reflect this activity and not only place measurements into three separate bottom lines. Until (if ever) a common measurement is created and achieves broad acceptance, the accounting and reporting of the three sectors of the "triple bottom line" will continue to be measured and reported separately and against a variety of criteria (Dwyer, 2005). The exciting challenge for researchers is to discover new ways to join more than just the economic, environmental and social bottom lines together.

CSR and small business

Arguably, the language of *corporate* social responsibility indicates that CSR is predominantly a concept that applies to large corporations, typically owned by shareholders and run by employed managers. Small and medium-sized enterprises (SMEs) tend not to communicate externally about their CSR activities (Ellerup Nielsen and Thomsen, 2009; Schlenker et al., 2018). All business systems in SMEs, including CSR, are rather informal and ad hoc in nature as opposed to the structured, formalized and codified approach of large corporations.

Whilst the CSR literature has paid disproportionate attention to larger organizations (Morsing and Perrini, 2009) this is changing (Schlenker et al., 2018). Various limitations of SMEs in implementing and communicating CSR have been discussed (Lepoutre and Heene, 2006; Schlenker et al., 2018). Larger businesses and multi-national corporations have more developed infrastructure and capacity to develop programmes of CSR activity and to report on them. In many SMEs, the owners face a lack of knowledge about management systems and communication of CSR, and do not understand CSR as a source of competitive advantage. It is therefore not a business priority for them (Spence, 2007). CSR can also be a problem for SMEs if they follow the same processes set for large companies, given the bureaucratic demands of standards and reporting procedures.

However, SMEs possess several characteristics that can help them to minimise limitations and realise opportunities from CSR (Jenkins, 2009), especially in tourism (Schlenker et al., 2018). The common owner-managed nature of the small firm means that there is no separation of ownership and control, unlike in publicly traded large firms. Responsibility is often embedded in the personal values of the owners and operators (Kasim, 2006) and owner-managers typically enjoy the autonomy of running their own firm and are not seeking to maximize profit as their reward (Spence and Rutherford, 2001). This frees them to invest time and resources according to their, and importantly their employees' (seen as key stakeholders) values and beliefs (Schlenker et al., 2018). Jenkins (2006, 2009) shows how SMEs can take advantage of the opportunities presented by CSR.

SMEs can be very adaptive, swiftly adjusting their trading capacities according to changing market opportunities. This flexibility means that they can respond quickly to changing circumstances. SMEs may be able to rapidly take advantage of new niche markets for products and services that incorporate social and/or environmental benefits in their value. Given his/her closeness to the day-to-day operations of the company, the owner-manager is closer to the organisation and so can more easily influence the values and culture of the company and champion CSR throughout the company (Schlenker et al., 2018).

The role of codes of conduct in CSR

Self-management practices may be expected to increase through the adoption of codes of practice and certification schemes. Globally, many tourism industry sectors have responded to sustainable development through the establishment of voluntary initiatives. Chief among these are codes of conduct, that are "a set of expectations, behaviours or rules written by industry members, (often interchangeably) with an emphasis on accreditation of operators" (Newsome et al., 2002:223–230). Examples in the tourism industry include: Code of Ethics and Guidelines for Sustainable Tourism (Tourism Industry Association of Canada); Environmental Codes of Conduct for Tourism (United Nations Environment Program); Sustainable Tourism Principles (Worldwide Fund for Nature and Tourism Concern); Code for Sustainable Tourism (Pacific Asia Travel Association); Responsible Traveller Guidelines (Africa Travel Association); Declaration of Earth Friendly Travelers (Japanese Travel Association); Agenda 21 for the Tourist and Travel Industry (promoted by the World Tourism Organization, the Earth Council and the World Travel and Tourism Council).

Introducing professional codes of conduct in support of CSR would mean that corporate policies and behaviour would need to reflect a more ethical approach in relation to the economic, environmental and social performance of their firm. This would form part of the integration process of a CSR framework within an organisation and the overall corporate social responsibility strategy. It is also making firms more accountable for the manner in which they go about doing business. Input from stakeholders (internal and external) should be considered when drafting codes of conduct and if monitored and enforced properly, will hold credibility with stakeholders.

A case study analysis of Dutch tour operators (Van de Mosselaer et al., 2012:87) demonstrates that there has been a shift from CSR as a more defensive mode of thinking, to a more positive, proactive position related to the 'institutionalisation of moral responsibility'. Central to this reorientation has been the advocacy of trade associations in promoting CSR in the industry itself. Another study (Whitfield and Dioko, 2012) suggests discretionary CSR to be more effective in promoting environmentally sound practices than formal accreditation or eco-label schemes.

The role of government in supporting CSR

Economic, environmental and socio-cultural pressures resulting increasingly stringent legislation and taxation designed to encourage people to act more responsibly. Some form of government support may be needed (and justified in terms of the wider destination benefit) to promote CSR measurement, reporting and auditing. Governments at all levels can act as catalysts for the development of CSR.

Inter alia, governments can do the following:

☐ Provide support for and facilitate CSR to allow collaborative partnerships to develop and experiences to be shared;

☐ Develop and promote collaborations that encourage sharing of experiences among government agencies including the implementation of a CSR procurement policy for state government agencies;

☐ Develop improved strategies and measurements of accountability and transparency in public sector decision making.

☐ Governments can support research into CSR reporting, providing financial incentives (eg. tax concessions) for firms collaborating to improve their triple bottom line performance (Allen Consulting Group, 2002).

Government pressure on business to adopt CSR reporting will only be credible, however, if government bodies are subjected to the same discipline. For the government to demonstrate a commitment to CSR, opportunities need to be created for stakeholders to genuinely engage with the public sector in its decision making and reporting. The best businesses will anticipate such action and minimize their impacts, well in advance (Lindgreen and Swaen, 2010)

Conclusion

The tourism industry operates throughout the world; in developing and developed economies; in countries with cultural diverse backgrounds; with entities from large multi-national companies to very small owner-operated businesses; and, in remote locations as well as cities and towns. This diversity, not reflected in most other commercial sectors, presents tourism entities with an opportunity to provide leadership in the conduct of business and particularly in the adoption of the new philosophy that reflects not only the ideals of the societies in which they operate but also the international community. Part of the leadership role is the active engagement and reporting by the tourism sector of CSR performance.

Collaboration between corporations and their stakeholders can act as catalysts for sustainable tourism development. There are numerous unresolved theoretical and empirical issues relating to the strategic and collaborative implications of CSR. These include: defining CSR in the 21st century as challenged by the collaborative economy (Dredge, 2018); identifying institutional, strategic and collaborative differences in CSR across countries; determining the motivations for CSR; modelling the effects of CSR on the firm and stakeholder groups; determining the effects of leadership and corporate culture on CSR activity; assessing the effects of CSR on the firm and stakeholder groups; measuring the demand for CSR in the sharing economy; measuring the costs of CSR; understanding the role of CRS leaders; developing mixed-method approaches to blend and triangulate data (Coles et al., 2013); and co-design *with* internal and external stakeholders (Heape and Liburd, 2018). For CSR to underpin sustainable businesses, "organisations must progressively become sites for dialogue and collaboration" (Maon et al., 2010:26).

References

Adams, C. & Zutshi, A. (2004). Corporate social responsibility: Why business should act responsibly and be accountable. *Australian Accounting Review*. **14**(3), 31-39. Accessed 21 March 2006 at www.mei.monash.edu.au/gs_present/pdf/IntroCSR.pdf.

Allen Consulting Group (2002). *The 'Triple Bottom line' in the Australian Public Sector; a collaborative exploration*, Public Sector Collaborative Research Project, Canberra.

Beckett, R. & Jonker, J. (2002). AccountAbility 1000: a new social standard for building sustainability. *Managerial Auditing Journal*, **17**(1/2), 36-42.

Blichfeldt, B.S. (2018). Co-branding and strategic communication. In J. Liburd and D. Edwards (Eds.) *Collaboration for Sustainable Tourism Development* (pp. 35-54). Oxford: Goodfellow Publishers

Bohdanowicz, P. (2005). European Hotelier's Environmental Attitudes: Greening the Business. *Cornell Hotel and Restaurant Administration Quarterly, 46*, 188-204

Bohdanowicz, P. & Zientara, P. (2009). Hotel companies' contribution to improving the quality of life of local communities and the well-being of their employees. *Tourism and Hospitality Research, 9*(2), 147-158.

Bossel, H. (1999). *Indicators for sustainable development: Theory, Methods, Applications. Winnipeg, Manitoba.* Canada: International Institute for Sustainable Development.

Bowen, H. R. (1953). *Social Responsibilities of the Businessman.* Harper & Brothers, New York

Carroll, A. B. (1979). A three-dimensional conceptual model of corporate social performance. *Academy of Management Review, 4*(1), 497-505

Carroll, A.B. (1991). The pyramid of corporate social responsibility: toward the moral management of organizational stakeholders. *Business Horizons,* July - August, 39-48.

Carroll, A.B. & Shabana, K.M. (2010). The business case for corporate social responsibility: a review of concepts, research and practice. *International Journal of Management Reviews.* doi: 10.1111/j.1468-2370.2009.00275.x.

Coles, T., Fenclova, E. and Dinan, C. (2013). Tourism and corporate social responsibility: A critical review and research agenda. *Tourism Management Perspectives, 6,* pp.122-141.

Crane A., Matten, D. & Spence, L. (2008). Corporate social responsibility: in a global context. In A. Crane, D. Matten & L. Spence: *Corporate Social Responsibility: Readings and Cases in a Global Context,* Routledge: Abingdon, UK. 3-20.

Dahlsrud, A. (2008). How corporate social responsibility is defined: an analysis of 37 definitions. *Corporate Social Responsibility and Environmental Management, 15*: 1-13.

Davis, K. (1960). Can business afford to ignore social responsibilities? *California Management Review, 2,* 70-76.

Deery. M., Jago, L., Harris, C. & Liburd, J. (2018). Work-life balance for sustainable tourism development. In J. Liburd and D. Edwards (Eds.) *Collaboration for Sustainable Tourism Development* (pp.151-166). Oxford: Goodfellow Publishers.

de Grosbois, D. (2012). Corporate social responsibility reporting by the global hotel industry: Commitment, initiatives and performance. *International Journal of Hospitality Management, 31*(3), pp.896-905.

Dredge, D., & Meehan, E. (2018). The collaborative economy, tourism and sustainable development. In Liburd, J. and Edwards, D. (2018) *Collaboration for Sustainable Tourism Development.* Oxford: Goodfellow Publishers.

Dwyer L. (2005). Relevance of triple bottom line reporting to achievement of sustainable tourism: a scoping study. *Tourism Review International, 9* (1), 79-94.

Dwyer L. (2017) Saluting while the s hip sinks: the necessity for tourism paradigm change. *Journal of Sustainable Tourism, 26*(1)29-48. dx.doi.org/10.1080/09669582.2017 .1308372

Dwyer L. & Kim, C.W. (2003). Destination competitiveness: a model and indicators. *Current Issues in Tourism,* **6**(5), 369-413

Dwyer L., Teal, G. & Kemp, S. (1998/99). Organisational culture & strategic management in a resort hotel. *Asia Pacific Journal of Tourism Research,* **3**(1), 27-36

Dwyer L., Teal, G., Kemp, S. &. Wah, C.Y (2000). Organisational culture and human resource management in an Indonesian resort hotel, *Tourism Culture and Communication,* **2** (1), 1-11.

Dwyer L. &. Kemp, S. (2004) Closure of an ecolodge: a failure of strategic management? *Journal of Pacific Studies,* **26**(1 & 2), 51-75.

Eichhorn, M. & Pleuser, K. (2015). Kooperationen zwischen Unternehmen und NGOs im CSR Kontext. In R. Schneider A.; Schmidpeter (Ed.), *Corporate Social Responsibility: Verantwortungsvolle Unternehmensführung in Theorie und Praxis.* 2. Auflage (pp. 1139-1153). Berlin: Springer.

Ellerup Nielsen, A. & Thomsen, C. (2009) CSR communication in small and medium-sized enterprises: A study of the attitudes and beliefs of middle managers. *Corporate Communications: An International Journal* **14**(2), 176-189.

Fifka, M.S. (2017). Strategisches CSR-Management im Tourismus. In: Lund-Durlacher, D., Fifka. M.S., Reiser, D. (Hrsg.). *CSR und Tourismus - Handlungs- und branchenspezifische Felder.* Berlin: Springer-Gabler

Frederick, W.C. (1960). The growing concern over social responsibility. *California Management Review,* **2**, 54-61.

Freeman, R.E. (1984). *Strategic Management: A Stakeholder Approach.* Mansfield, MA: Pitman.

Friedman, M (1970). The social responsibility of business is to increase its profits. *The New York Magazine.*

Garcia, F. & Y. Armas. (2007). Relationship between social-environmental responsibility and performance in hotel firms. *International Journal of Hospitality Management,* **26** (4): 824-39.

Gray, R. and Bebbington, J. (2000). Environmental Accounting, Managerialism and Sustainability, *Advances in Environmental Accounting and Management,* **1**: 1-44.

Grayson, D. & Hodges, A.(2004) *Corporate Social Opportunity! Seven steps to make CSR work for your business.* Sheffield: Greenleaf.

Hawkins, R. & Bohdanowicz, P. (2012) *Responsible Hospitality. Theory and Practice.* Oxford: Goodfellow Publishers.

Heape, C., & Liburd, J. (2018). Collaborative learning for sustainable tourism development. In Liburd, J. and Edwards, D. (2018) *Collaboration for Sustainable Tourism Development.* Oxford: Goodfellow Publishers.

Hinkin, T.R. & Tracey, J.B. (2000).The cost of turnover, *Cornell Hotel And Restaurant Administration Quarterly,* **41**(3): 14-21.

Hjalager, A. (2018). Suppliers as key collaborators for sustainable tourism development. In Liburd, J. and Edwards, D. (2018) *Collaboration for Sustainable Tourism Development.* Goodfellow Publishers, Oxford, UK.

Inoue, Y. & Lee, S.(2011) Effects of different dimensions of corporate social responsibility on corporate financial performance in tourism-related industries. *Tourism Management*, **32**(4), 790-804.

Jenkins, H. (2006). Small business champions for corporate social responsibility. *Journal of Business Ethics*, **67**(3), 241-256.

Jenkins, H. (2009). A 'business opportunity'model of corporate social responsibility for small-and medium-sized enterprises. *Business Ethics: A European review*, **18**(1), 21-36.

Kang, K.H., Lee, S. & Huh, C. (2010). Impacts of positive and negative corporate social responsibility activities on company performance in the hospitality industry. *International Journal of Hospitality Management*, **29**(1), 72-82.

Kasim, A. (2010) The need for business environmental and social responsibility in the tourism industry. *International Journal of Hospitality and Tourism Administration*, **7**(1): 1-22.

Lepoutre, J. & Heene, A. (2006). Investigating the impact of firm size on small business social responsibility: A critical review. *Journal of business ethics*, **67**(3), 257-273.

Lee, M-D. P. (2008). A review of the theories of corporate social responsibility: its evolutionary path and the road ahead. *International Journal of Management Reviews*, **10**(1), 53-73.

Lee, S. & S. Park. (2009). Do socially responsible activities help hotels and casinos achieve their financial goals? *International Journal of Hospitality Management*, **28**(1), 105-12.

Lindgreen, A. & Swaen, V. (2010). Corporate social responsibility. *International Journal of Management Reviews* **12** (1), 1-7.

Lund-Durlacher, D. (2013). Corporate social responsibility in tourism. In S. Idowu, N. Capaldi, L. Zu, and A. Das Gupta, *Encyclopedia of Corporate Social Responsibility.* Berlin Heidelberg: Springer-Verlag.

Lund-Durlacher, D., Hergesell, A., & Mentil, K. (2013). Alpine Pearls – stakeholder management for sustainable tourism. In P. Benckendorff, & D. Lund-Durlacher (Eds.), *International Cases in Sustainable Travel and Tourism.* (pp. 9-23). Oxford: Goodfellow Publishers Limited.

Lund-Durlacher, D. (2015). Corporate social responsibility and tourism. In P. Moscardo, & G. Benckendorff (Eds.), *Education for Sustainability in Tourism - A Handbook of Processes, Resources, and Strategies.* (pp. 59-73). Berlin: Springer.

Lund-Durlacher, D. (2017). Unternehmensverantwortung für nachhaltigen Tourismus. *Tourismus Wissen - quarterly*, **7**, 21-26.

Luo, X. & Bhattacharya, C.B. (2006). Corporate social responsibility, customer satisfaction, and market value. *Journal of marketing*, **70**(4), pp.1-18.

Mackay, J. & Sisodia, R. (2014). Conscious capitalism. *Harvard Business School Publishing Co, Boston, MA.*

Manning T (1999). Indicators of Tourism Sustainability *Tourism Management*, **20**, 179-181.

Maon, F., Lindgreen, A. & Swaen, V. (2009). Designing and implementing corporate social responsibility: an integrative framework grounded in theory and practice. *Journal of Business Ethics*, **7**(1), 71-89.

Maon, F., Lindgreen, A. & Swaen, V. (2010). Organizational stages and cultural phases: A critical review and a consolidative model of corporate social responsibility development. *International Journal of Management Reviews, 12*(1), 20-38.

McCool, S., Moisey, N. & Nickerson, N. (2001). What should tourism sustain? the disconnect with industry perceptions of useful indicators. *Journal of Travel Research.* **40**, (2), 124-131.

McElhanye, K. (2009). *A Strategic Approach to Corporate Social Responsibility. Executive Forum – Leader to Leader.* http://responsiblebusiness.haas.berkeley.edu/documents/Strategic%20CSR%20%28Leader%20to%20Leader,%20McElhaney%29.pdf. Accessed 4 September 2013.

McGuire, J. (1963). *Business and Society.* New York: McGraw-Hill

McWilliams, A., Siegel, D.S. & Wright, P.M. (2006). Corporate social responsibility: Strategic implications. *Journal of Management Studies,* **43**(1), 1-18.

Morsing, M. & Perrini, F. (2009). CSR in SMEs: do SMEs matter for the CSR agenda?. *Business Ethics: A European Review,* **18**(1), pp.1-6.

Newsome, D., Moore,S. A. & Dowling, R. K. (2002). *Natural Area Tourism: Ecology, impacts and management.* Mona Vale, NSW: Footprint Books.

Nicolau, J. L. (2008). Corporate social responsibility worth-creating activities. *Annals of Tourism Research,* **35** (4): 990-1006

Porter, M.E. & Kramer, M. (2006). Strategy and society: the link between competitive advantage and corporate social responsibility. *Harvard Business Review,* Dec, 78–92.

Porter, M.F. & Kramer, M.R. (2011). Creating shared value. *Harvard Business Review.* Jan-Feb.

Sadri, G. & Lees, B. (2001). Developing corporate culture as a competitive advantage. *Journal of Management Development,* **20**(10), 853-859, doi.org/10.1108/02621710110410851

Sarre, R. Doig, M. & Fiedler, B. (2001). Reducing the risk of corporate irresponsibility: the trend to corporate social responsibility, *Accounting Forum,* **25**(3).

Sauvante, M. (2001) The 'Triple Bottom Line': a boardroom guide, *Directors Monthly,* **25**, (11), 1-6.

Schlenker, K., Edwards, D. & Barton, C. (2018). Modelling engagement in corporate social responsibility in small and medium tourism enterprises (SMTEs), In: Lund-Durlacher, D., Dinica, V., Reiser, D. & Fifka, M.S. (2018). *Corporate Sustainability and Responsibility in Tourism.* Berlin-Heidelberg: Springer, in press.

Sheldon, P. & Park, S-Y. (2011). An exploratory study of corporate social responsibility in the US travel industry. *Journal of Travel Research,* **50**(4): 392-407.

Sisodia, R., Wolfe, D. & Sheth, J.N. (2003). *Firms of Endearment: How world-class companies profit from passion and purpose.* Pearson Prentice Hall.

Spence, L.J. (2007). CSR and small business in a European policy context: the five 'C's of CSR and small business research agenda. *Business and Society Review,* **112**(4), 533-552.

Spence, L J. & Rutherfoord, R. (2001). Social responsibility, profit maximisation and the small firm owner-manager. *Journal of Small Business and Enterprise Development* **8**(2), 126-139.

Stark, A. (1993). What's the matter with business ethics? *Harvard Business Review*. May – June. Accessed hbr.org/1993/05/whats-the-matter-with-business-ethics. 23/4/2018.

Suggett, D. & Goodsir, B. (2002). *Triple Bottom Line Measurement and Reporting in Australia: Making it Tangible*, the Allen Consulting Group, Canberra.

Timothy D.J. (2002). Tourism and community development issues, in R. Sharpley and D. Telfer, *Tourism and Development: Concepts and Issues*, Channel View Publications, Clevedon, UK

United Nations General Assembly (2015). Transforming our world: the 2030 Agenda for Sustainable Development. Resolution adopted by the General Assembly on 25 September 2015 - A/RES/70/1. http://www.un.org/ga/search/view_doc.asp?symbol=A/RES/70/1&Lang=E. Accessed 2.1.2017.

Van de Mosselaer, F., van der Duim, R. & van Wijk, J. (2012) Corporate social responsibility in the tour operating industry: the case of Dutch outbound tour operators. In D. Leslie (Ed.) *Tourism Enterprises and the Sustainability Agenda across Europe* (pp.71-92). Farnham: Ashgate.

Visser, W. (2011). CSR 2.0: Transforming the role of business in society. *Social Space*, 26-35. http://ink.library.smu.edu.sg/lien_research/87/. Accessed 30.9.2017

Walton, C.C. (1967). *Corporate Social Responsibilities*. Belmont, CA: Wadsworth.

Werther, W.B., Chandler, D. (2011). *Strategic Corporate Social Responsibility: Stakeholders in a Global Environment*, 2nd ed. Los Angeles: Sage Publications.

Whitfield, J. & Dioko, L.A.(2012) Measuring and examining the relevance of discretionary corporate social responsibility in tourism: Some preliminary evidence from the UK conference sector. *Journal of Travel Research*, **51**(3), 289-302.

Websites

Accor Hotels. https://www.accorhotels.com/gb/sustainable-development/index.shtml. Accessed 17 April 2018.

Alpine Pearls. https://www.alpine-pearls.com/en/. Accessed 17 April 2018.

Global Reporting Initiative. www.globalreporting.org/guidlines/2002/c52.asp.

Tui Care Foundation. https://www.tuicarefoundation.com/en/projects/using-chillies-to-save-elephants-lives). Accessed 17 April 2018

World Tourism Organisation. Agenda 21 for the Travel and Tourism Industry. www.world-tourism.org/frameset/ frame_sustainable.html

World Wildlife Fund (WWF). https://www.worldwildlife.org/partnership-categories/corporate-partnerships. Accessed 17 April 2018.

Work-Life Balance for Sustainable Tourism Development

Margaret Deery, Leo Jago, Candice Harris and Janne Liburd

The tourism and hospitality industry is very much a 'people industry', which requires a stable and talented workforce as a fundamental component. However, there are some aspects of the industry that make it unattractive to potential employees. These aspects include the long and unsocial hours of work, the low pay and often stressful working environment (Deery and Jago, 2015: Karatepe, 2013). These aspects contribute to the industry's reputation for not providing staff with an acceptable work-life balance. The question then becomes how the tourism and hospitality industry can contribute to a better balance and thus underpin the socio-cultural aspects of sustainability. This study examines the sustainability of the industry across three countries, Australia, the United Kingdom (UK) and New Zealand, by focusing on whether tourism employees in hospitality organisations consider they have a balance between their personal and work lives. Hospitality is chosen as the focus for this study since it plays a fundamentally important role in underpinning the viability of the broader tourism industry. Current practices are confronted by larger societal changes in the labour market, where lifelong careers within the same firm (or industry) are challenged by rapid employee turnover, demands for greater flexibility, new technologies, and alternative work schedules. We discuss how collaboration between industry, employees and wider community may help underpin sustainable tourism development.

Literature review

There is debate as to whether work-life balance (WLB) refers to: an objective state of affairs or a subjective experience, perception or feeling; an actuality or an aspiration; a discourse or a practice; a metaphor for flexible working; a metaphor for the gendered division of labour; or a metaphor for some other political agenda (Fleetwood, 2007). Although many definitions exist, WLB can be defined in general terms as "an individual's ability to meet both their work and family commitments, as well as other non-work responsibilities and activities" (Parkes and Langford, 2008: 267). However, WLB is influenced by a range of factors operating at micro (individual), meso (organisational) and macro (national) levels (Gregory and Milner, 2009). As a multifaceted concept, WLB is shaped by unique life paths encompassing differences in culture, income, gender, age, occupation, personality, class, health needs, personal goals and choices, responsibilities for families and other life stakeholders, migration experiences, workplace relationships, hobbies, critical life events and other factors.

WLB policies are typically promoted as win-win for both individuals and organisations with the often espoused benefits including improved recruitment and retention rates, reductions in worker stress and increased productivity (Harris et al., 2005; Zhao et al., 2011; Deery and Jago, 2015). Work-life balance programs by hotels can assist through the use of flexible working hours, compressed work weeks and leave for child care (Lee et al., 2015). In the first broadly representative study of why New Zealanders move between employers and why they stay, conducted by Boxall, Macky and Rasmussen (2003) with 549 New Zealand employees, it was found that nearly half of the sample, the 'movers' (48.8%, n = 268) had changed employers over the past five years. Furthermore, over half (52%) of the 'movers' listed their desire to improve work–life balance as a reason for moving.

An assessment of the issues overlooked in the WLB debate highlight that what is needed is a more nuanced appreciation, and research agenda, of the complex relationship between work and life (Eikhof et al., 2007). A review by Chang et al. (2010) of methodological choices in 245 empirical WLB papers published in a range of journals between 1987 and 2006 found that sampling choice in previous studies is somewhat constrained, and may be enhanced by targeting areas such as the hospitality industry, single people, manual and lower skilled service workers, and through cross-national studies. They explain that samples of organizations employing relatively larger proportions of professional employees were over-represented in study samples at the expense of organizations employing a low-skilled or semi-skilled workforce. Hence, they posit that "organizations sampled in much work-life balance research are not representative of the population of organizations to which they purport to generalize" (p. 2395). The omission of casual and/or low skilled workers is problematic as these workers often hold positions that lack strong conditions such as tenure, power and income.

According to Todd and Binns (2011), the widespread assumption that individuals freely make choices and negotiate their preferred working arrangements allows managers to ignore the need to transform workplace structures, cultures and practices that may be impeding the implementation of WLB. They stress that the WLB literature has increasingly highlighted the critical role played by managers in implementing WLB practices. Despite the robustness of the policies, where managers are ambivalent about flexible policies or apply them inconsistently, their usability and meaningfulness is undermined (Eaton, 2003; Todd & Binns, 2011). If "the bottom-line of WLB research is whether we can improve working conditions and subsequent levels of work-life satisfaction in employees in order to attract, motivate and retain personnel" (Poelmans et al., 2008: 228), then managers and organisations have a critical role to play.

The literature suggests that lack of balance between work and non-work activities is related to reduced psychological and physical well-being (Sparks et al., 1997; Felstead et al., 2002; Hughes and Bozionelos, 2007). Where their needs are not met, employees experience work–life stress (Gregory and Milner, 2009). While complaints about WLB may be common in all occupations, there is variance by occupation in the WLB issues faced, as well as unequal access to coping strategies (Roberts, 2007). Across various organisational studies, a commonly reported finding is that managers and professionals have greater flexibility and autonomy in their roles, hence WLB initiatives are more available to managers and professionals (Harris and Pringle, 2008). As an example of the disparity in access to WLB solutions, unlike managers and professionals, food service employees tend to enjoy less flexibility and autonomy in their work schedules (Rowley and Purcell, 2001).

While issues relating to obtaining a WLB have received substantial attention over recent years, less attention has been given to researching the impact of WLB in the hospitality area (Deery and Jago, 2009). Hospitality is a rich area for the study of WLB issues given the workforce is often characterised by its youth, feminisation, high proportion of immigrants, non-standard employment patterns, low coverage of collective agreements, low pay and high level of labour turnover. A culture of long working hours in the hospitality industry is so typical that many workers see their long working hours as normal (Cullen & McLaughlin 2006; Wong and Ko, 2009; O'Neill, 2011; Karatepe, 2013). In an Indian study, Kandasamy & Ancheri (2009) found imbalance in work and social life is pervasive among employees in the hospitality industry. However, as Ghazi (2003:xiii) states, "it is not necessarily about working less, rather about having personal control and flexibility over when, where and how we work".

A great deal of the literature in the hospitality and tourism fields shows a strong relationship between job satisfaction and organizational commitment (Yang, 2010). How workers feel about their work environments can vary due to individual characteristics, and these differences may determine the level of satisfaction with work environments and workers' intentions to remain in their positions (Franek and Vecera, 2008 in Lee and Way, 2010). Blomme, Rheede and Tromp (2010) found in a study of the hospitality industry that work-family conflict and organizational support can explain a substantial amount of variance among highly educated employees regarding their intention to leave an organization. WLB practices are believed to moderate the relationship between job demands and stress outcomes (Chiang et al., 2010).

Co-worker emotional support may also help employees who struggle to balance work and family needs, and to maintain a positive attitude (Warner et al., 2009). In a study on WLB of employees in a Swiss hotel, Lewis (2010) found that variables which positively affected employee well-being included increased schedule flexibility and mutually beneficial relationships with line managers. He also found that WLB issues perceived by employees can be mitigated through organisational support and the recognition of informal feedback. The importance of co-worker relationships is also supported by O'Neill and Davis (2011) who found that hotel employees reporting relatively more interpersonal tensions at work were significantly less satisfied with their jobs and significantly more likely to be considering leaving their jobs.

Age and WLB

There is not a clear relationship in the literature between WLB and age. Many studies use generational cohorts (Baby boomers, Gen X, Gen Y and Millennials) to examine the desires for, and perceptions of, WLB. According to Cennamo and Garnder (2008), generational differences in work values have been linked to changes in the meaning of work, to increasing numbers of dual-career and single parent families' expectations for work/life balance and to the increased use of electronic media and continuous learning of new skills. However, there is not clear consensus about which cohort reports WLB as the most important factor, or have achieved what they consider to be a good WLB. Some authors claim that Generation Y is known to place high importance on autonomy and WLB (Smola and Sutton, 2002; Zemke et al., 2000 from Cennamo & Gardner, 2008).

> *"Empirical evidence has suggested that the expectations of Gen Y worker in the hospitality industry are often in disagreement with the view of their employers and the reality of the industry (Barron et al., 2007; Cairncross and Buultjens, 2007) and this misalignment subsequently impacts upon organisational outcomes such as turnover and productivity"* (Davidson et al., 2010:453).

In contrast, data from Statistics New Zealand's *Survey of Working Life* (2008) reflects that older employees were more satisfied with both their main job and their WLB than prime-aged and young employees, and satisfaction with their main job and WLB increased with age among older employees (Boyd & Dickson,

2009). Parkes and Langford (2008) from their study utilising an Australian sample of over 16,000 employees to assess whether employees are satisfied with their ability to balance work and other life commitments found that age was a positive predictor of WLB; that WLB generally increases with age, except for a drop between the ages 30–49 due to the impact of dependents. A study conducted by Chen and Choi (2008) to explore the structure of hospitality management work values and the perceived differences among three generations of managers and supervisors in the hospitality industry found that members of all three generations expected a balance between professional and private lives.

Education and WLB

Parkes and Langford (2008) in an Australian sample of over 16,000 employees assessing whether employees are satisfied with their ability to balance work and other life commitments found that number of hours worked, overtime hours worked, salary, seniority and education level were all negatively correlated with WLB. WLB is more at risk among the higher classes of employees (professionals and managers) than among middle and lower classes (Pichler, 2009).

Karatepe and Uludag (2008) found that more educated employees and those with longer tenure experience higher family–work conflict, while older employees have less family–work conflict. They explain that it seems that better educated employees and those with longer tenure are unable to allocate the required amount of time to work responsibilities due to a number of prescribed family responsibilities. These findings also suggest that older employees might have learnt how to manage various problems emanating from conflicts between family and work domains.

A changed relationship between working hours and education is highlighted by Roberts (2007: 342) who explains that "in 1961 the best-educated men worked for fewer hours than less educated males; by 2001 the best-educated people were working the longest. Among women in 1961 there was little difference in hours worked by educational level; by 2001 the best-educated women were working on average for 40 minutes per day longer than other female employees."

In their study on work stress and well-being in the hotel industry, O'Neill and Davis (2011) found that hotel managers had significantly more education, worked significantly more hours per week and had been in the hotel industry longer on average than hourly employees. They also found that hotel managers reported significantly more stressors than hourly employees, with the most frequent types of stressors being interpersonal tensions and then work overloads.

Gender, marital status, children and WLB

Women, particularly mothers and those in traditionally female occupations such as nursing and education, remain over-sampled in multi-disciplinary WLB research. A review of the literature reveals that work and family issues, which are increasingly popular topics in contemporary organizational research, have received little attention in hospitality and tourism journals (Mulvaney et al., 2007). This is a puzzling gap, as Mulvaney et al. (2007) highlight; turnover in the hotel industry that stems from problems associated with work and family issues appears to be very costly.

The discourse has moved from family-friendly to WLB, and in doing so, becomes quite deliberately gender neutral (Lewis et al., 2007). WLB has the advantage of presenting a more holistic approach to the challenge of integrating paid work into employees' lives and the fact that this then encompasses the whole of the workforce may increase pressure for change (Todd & Binns, 2011). Irrespective of the change in discourse, what has not changed is that responsibility for the family remains solely with the individual; "co-workers and society are not expected to be interested in their colleagues' needs in the private sphere and the provision of affordable quality childcare and elder care is an economic rather than a social issue"(Todd & Binns, 2011:4). In a departure from the problematisation of the family, Haddon et al. (2009) draw attention to the growing body of research to suggest that work and family can positively influence one another and that participation in multiple roles can be stimulating and can enhance the well-being of individuals (Thompson & Werner, 1997; Barnett & Hyde, 2001; Greenhaus & Powell, 2006).

Clarke et al. (2004) argue that structural factors such as working hours and the household division of labour tend to influence other constructs such as work-family fit, which may be more relevant to the low skilled labour force. For families with children where both spouses work full time, finding balance may be a challenge, which could be exacerbated by shift work (Williams, 2008). Although, when workers have some control over the scheduling of their shifts, and/or when work schedules are regular, it is much easier to reduce the conflicts relating to family and work (Halpern, 2005).

Shift work is significantly related to greater marital disagreements and child-related problems (Presser, 2004; Staines & Pleck, 1983), and work schedules that involve weekends and holidays (Almeida, 2004), common in hotel work, pose challenges for people trying to negotiate the work–family interface (Cleveland, et al, 2007). O'Leary and Deegan (2005) highlight barriers to career progression in tourism and hospitality as including long unsociable hours, poor pay, and the physical and stressful nature of the work and explain that female graduates are more likely to drop out due to WLB issues. In a similar vein, female managers in the hospitality industry often fail reach top management positions due to inflexible working practices and the long hours work culture (Doherty, 2004; Mooney, 2009).

In a study by Cleveland et al., (2007) examining what work factors hotel managers identify as positive and instrumental in shaping the extent to which the hotel is perceived as family supportive, factors such as the general manager, co-worker support and friendship networks, and opportunities for flexibility were most often discussed. They found that in addition to the influence the general manager has on the hotel environment, approximately 70% of hotel managers described the influence of their co-workers in creating a positive workplace climate and that in supportive hotels, people are encouraged to talk about their families. A supportive work environment provides resources that can buffer the impact of high job demands and low job control on employees' job stress (Grandey et al., 2007). While it is accepted that hotels should provide a supportive work environment, 'how' this is done is not well known.

> "Due to the lack of rigorous research and a guiding framework, the effectiveness of hotel companies' work–family practices, and relationships between their work–family practices, organizational culture, and strategic management processes are not well-understood" (Xiao and O'Neill, 2011:416).

In short, long, unsocial working hours, lack of personal control, flexibility and co-worker support, coupled with a division between the work and private spheres result in an   unsustainable WLB, and subsequent lack of retention in the hospitality industry. Hospitality workers with young dependants seem to be particularly vulnerable. Extant research shows that supportive work environments may mitigate some of the work life imbalances, but the role of collaboration in furthering WLB, and the larger contribution to sustainable tourism development, has hitherto escaped critical attention.

Method

This study, which was undertaken in 2010 was part of a larger study examining employee attitudes and behaviour in the hospitality industry, used a quantitative approach to the data collection. First, we used a survey to collect data from hospitality employees across three nations. The research instrument used in the study adapted that used by Wong and Ko (2009) with many of the statements based on a 5-point Likert scale. The questionnaire included questions on (a) demographics; (b) working patterns such as the number of hours worked; (c) perceptions of the balance between work and family/social activities, work commitment and relationships, work stress and culture; (d) job turnover intentions and work satisfaction.

Given the operational difficulties of collecting data across three nations, data were collected through a research company using respondent panels. Criteria for selection of respondents were provided to Research Now, an international fieldwork and panel specialist company and these included that the respondents (a) be over 18 years of age; (b) have worked in the hotel industry within the last two years or were still working in it; (c) reside in the UK, NZ or Australia. The research team requested 100 - 200 respondents from each country with the final sample containing 513 respondents comprising 204 Australian respondents, 208 NZ respondents and 101 UK respondents (who were mainly from London).

Results and analysis

For the purpose of this study, the sample is considered only as a whole and relationships between the sub-samples collected across the three countries are not considered.

Profile of the total sample

Of the total sample, 75% were currently employed within the hospitality industry, the rest having worked in the industry within the last two years. Table 9.1 provides further details of the sample profile.

Table 9.1: Sample profile (total sample n=513)

Age (mean)	35.8	Department %	
Gender (%)		Food and Beverage	48.3
Male	46	Front desk	14.2
Female	54	Housekeeping	8.8
		Other	28.7
Education (%)		**Current position %**	
Primary	0	Frontline staff	34.7
Secondary	35.3	Supervisor	16.2
Vocational	29.4	Manager	23.6
Undergraduate	21.6	Director	2.5
Postgraduate	13.7	Other	23.0
		No. of years in hotel industry %	
Marital status %		Less than 6 months	4.9
Single	26.3	6-12 months	6.6
Married	36.1	1-3 years	22.6
Long term partner	29.6	3-5 years	14.4
Divorced	5.1	5-7 years	11.5
Other	2.9	More than 7 years	40.0

Independent means t-test were conducted to explore statistical differences in the sample. No statistically significant differences in perceived WLB were found across age categories. Whilst females in the sample perceived their WLB to be higher than males, the difference was not statistically significant. Those with a lower level of education in the sample perceived their WLB to be higher than those who were more highly educated, which is consistent with Parkes and Langford (2008) but the difference was not statistically significant. Singles in the sample perceived their WLB to be higher than those with partners, although the difference was not statistically significant. There were moderate statistically significant correlations between perceived WLB and 'having an understanding supervisor' (.410) and 'having supportive co-workers' (.380).

There were moderate to strong statistically significant correlations between perceived WLB and 'having enough time for my family' (.521), 'having enough time for my friends' (.461), 'having enough time after work to carry out personal matters' (.477) and 'having enough time for sleeping' (.463). These were the items that showed the strongest correlations with WLB. Those who intended to leave their current position had a statistically significantly lower perception of their WLB than did those who were intending to stay. This supports the importance of WLB as an indicator of potential intention to leave an organisation.

To identify key differences between those having a higher WLB with those with a lower WLB a median split was used to divide respondents into two groups on WLB. An analysis was then undertaken to identify the key differences between the two groups. The main characteristics of the group with the lower WLB compared to the higher WLB group were:

☐ Older age

☐ Had less sleep

☐ Were in fulltime positions

☐ Were in managerial positions

☐ Had a higher intention to leave their current position.

Discussion

It is clear that those who have a lower WLB demonstrate a much higher intention to leave their position, so there is a substantial incentive for employers to take steps to improve the WLB of their staff. The analysis suggests that if employees have energy and time for private life – with family and friends, less stress at work, less stress at home (because of work) and time to fulfil aspirations/interests, their WLB will be more acceptable. This implies a need for alignment in work design that allows employee's control over managing family and work demands (Batt and Valcour, 2003). This could be addressed through monitoring hours and scheduling of work, providing time out for managers and providing professional development for all staff so that 'burn out' does not occur.

However, if industry is to address sustainabilit,y not only as an external communication and branding tool, we argue that they must consider a broad range of collaborative human resource practices which internally shape employees' motivation and capacity to meet work and family demands in an integrated fashion that underpins sustainability. For example, employees will often share responsibilities, both personal and work related, in order to meet the demands on their time. Alfonso et al. (2016) in their examination of workplace citizenship behaviors found a direct link between 'good' citizenship behaviours and a high work life balance score. It was seen in the analysis that those who had supportive supervisors and co-workers had higher WLB.

The development of corporate social responsibility (CSR) in hospitality and tourism, and the commitment to sustainability (Dwyer and Lund-Durlacher, 2018) involves strategic communication and collaboration with others. Blichfeldt (2018) argues that this is not about transmitting carefully crafted messages about sustainability to passive, external audiences, which is simply done for marketing purposes. Strategic communication with staff on WLB is inherently an internal, collaborative endeavour. Collaboration between industry and employees in hospitality and tourism is indicative of mutual commitments to interrelations where shared responsibilities and accountability for success are based on principles of sustainable development. Collaborative interrelationships are based on aligning sustainability missions and pursuing corporate responsibility with staff, management and directors, as well as external stakeholders and ultimately society at large (Dwyer and Lund-Durlacher, 2018).

Already in 2001, Sauvante argued that CSR attracts and retains high calibre employees, improves employee morale, productivity and creativity. Still, current tourism and hospitality practices are challenged by larger societal changes and with staff shortages in various sections of the hospitality industry. This implies that new methods for attracting and retaining employees are required (Bolger, 2015). Especially as rapid employee turnover, demands for greater flexibility, new technologies and alternative work schedules enabled by the sharing economy (Dredge, 2018) have become the norm rather than the exception.

In many countries, the 21st century labour market, technologies and demographic changes require examination. For example, Millennials are known to change jobs more frequently than previous generations by moving, on average, every 2.5 years in their first ten years in the workforce (Holmes, 2016). They are influenced, more than ever before by employer brand and reputation, often through social media (Popescu and Avram, 2012). Employers need to attract these potential employees through employment which is both comfortable and interesting; they seek an active work environment, and professional development opportunities (Starineca, 2015). Collaboration between these employees and employers in designing such jobs will make for greater job satisfaction and improved performance. Nørmark and Jensen (2018) provokingly refer to current work life practices as "pseudo-work" dominated by presenteeism, endlessly passive meetings and PowerPoint presentations, paperless documentation and bureaucracy, and lack of individual decision making capacity. They argue that work life should be radically reconsidered. It should be based on a higher degree of trust and workplace collaboration in order to avoid burn out, and where employees engage in meaningful activities while at work, with family, friends and the local community. In tourism and hospitality this would shift attention towards the social, empathetic and emotional skills required to support sustainability, and successful experience development *with* others.

In addition, the use of Artificial Intelligence and robots have already started to disrupt traditional hospitality functions, such as concierge and front desk tasks as has occurred in some Japanese hotels. Since 2015, customers have been able to choose between assistance from robots (in the shape of a dinosaur or doll-like female) or a real human being at the Henn na Hotel. Facial recognition technology enables a range of services by use of robotics, not as a gimmick or cost saving device, but as a serious effort to use technology, achieve efficiency and to ultimately underpin meaningful, human interactions and more sustainable WLB for those engaged in tourism and hospitality operations.

Conclusion

The results of this study support findings of earlier studies that showed that low levels of WLB lead to higher intention to leave. Respondents to the study indicated that their WLB was enhance when they felt that they had sufficient time with family, friends and to attend to personal matters. It was also found that having sufficient sleep was an important indicator of WLB. Support from supervisors and co-workers also played important roles in enhancing WLB, which highlights the importance of collaboration in the workforce and with society at large.

As a stable workforce appears fundamental to underpinning sustainability in the tourism and hospitality industries and WLB is so important to reducing intention to leave, it is critical that substantial effort is put into crafting more WLB-friendly job designs and developing more extensive collaborative practices, such as job sharing, even in an unofficial capacity. Ensuring work task (rather than workforce) stability and trust in sharing jobs should be subject to further, collaborative experimentation and research.

Transitional changes based on collaboration are needed, not just by individual organisations improving the employer brand for employees, such as Millennials, but also by the industry working with individual organisations to enhance WLB overall. Neetu and Prachi argue:

"If organisations truly want to attract talented people, then management needs to bring about the necessary organisational support and infrastructure at the early and middle stages of an employee's career, which are most often the stages where important choices (career and life) are made" (2015: 645).

References

Alfonso, L., Zenasni, F., Hodzic, S., & Ripoll, P. (2016). Understanding the mediating role of quality of work life on te relationship between emotional intelligence and organizational citizenship behaviors. *Psychological Reports,* **118**(1), 107-127.

Almeida, D. (2004) Using daily diaries to assess temporal friction between work and family in Crouter, A. C., & Booth, A. (Eds.). (2004). *Work-Family Challenges for Low-Income Parents and their Children.* Lawrence Erlbaum Associates, Inc.pp 127-141.

Barnett, R.C. & Hyde, J.S. (2001). Women, men, work, and family: An expansionist theory. *American Psychologist,* **56**(10), 781-796.

Barron, P., Maxwell, G., Broadbridge, A. & Ogden, S. (2007). Careers in hospitality management: Generation Y's experiences and perceptions. *Journal of Hospitality and Tourism Management,* **14**(2), 119-128.

Batt, R. & Valcour, P.M. (2003). Human resource practices as predictors of work-family outcomes and employee turnover. *Industrial Relations,* **42**(2), 189-220.

Boyd, S. & Dickson, S. (2009). *The Working Patterns of Older Workers.* Wellington: Department of Labour.

Bolger, J. (2015) Boiling Point: Ross Lewis on Ireland's chef shortage, *Irish Independent.*

Blichfeldt, B.S. (2018). Co-branding and strategic communication. In J. Liburd and D. Edwards (Eds.) *Collaboration for Sustainable Tourism Development* (pp. 35-54). Oxford: Goodfellow Publishers

Blomme, R., Rheede, A. & Tromp, D. (2010). Work-family conflict as a cause for turnover intentions in the hospitality industry. *Tourism and Hospitality Research,* **10**(4), 269-285.

Boxall, P., Macky, K., & Rasmussen, E. (2003). Labour turnover and retention in New Zealand: The causes and consequences of leaving and staying with employers. *Asia Pacific Journal of Human Resources,* **41**(2), 196-214.

Cairncross, G. & Buultjens, J. (2007). *Generation Y and work in the tourism and hospitality industry. Problem? What problem?* Occasional paper 9, Centre for Enterprise Development and Research, Southern Cross University, Tweed Heads, Australia

Cennamo, L. & Gardner, D. (2008). Generational differences in work values, outcomes and person organisation values fit. *Journal of Managerial Psychology,* **23**(8), 981-906.

Chang, A., McDonald, P. & Burton, P. (2010). Methodological choices in work-life balance research 1987 to 2006: a critical review. *The International Journal of Human Resource Management,* **21**(13), 2381–2413.

Chen, P. & Choi, Y. (2008). Generational differences in work values: a study of hospitality management. *International Journal of Contemporary Hospitality Management,* **20**(6), 595-615.

Chiang, F.F.T., Birtch, T.A. & Kwan, H.K. (2010). The moderating roles of job control and work–life balance practices on employee stress in hotel and catering industry. *International Journal of Hospitality Management,* **29**, 25–32.

Clarke, M.C., Koch, L.C. and Hill, E.J. (2004). The work-family interface: Differentiating balance and fit. *Family and Consumer Sciences Research Journal,* **33**(2), 121–140.

Cleveland, J. N., O'Neill, J. W., Himelright, J. L., Harrison, M. M., Crouter, A. C. & Drago, R. (2007). Work and family issues in the hospitality industry: Perspectives of entrants, managers and spouses. *Journal of Hospitality and Tourism Research,* **31**, 275-298.

Cullen, J. & McLaughlin, A. (2006). What drives the persistence of presenteeism as a managerial value in hotels? Observations noted during an Irish work-life balance research project. *Hospitality Management,* **25**, 510-516.

Davidson, M., Timo, N. & Wang, Y. (2010). How much does labour turnover cost?: A case study of Australian four- and five-star hotels. *International Journal of Contemporary Hospitality Management,* **22**(4), 451-466.

Deery, M. & Jago, L. (2009). A framework for work-life balance practices: Addressing the needs of the tourism industry. *Tourism and Hospitality Research,* **9**, 97–108.

Deery, M. & Jago, L. (2015) Revisiting talent management, work-life balance and retention strategies, *International Journal of Contemporary Hospitality Management,* **27**(3), 453-472.

Dredge, D., & Meehan, E. (2018). The collaborative economy, tourism and sustainable development. In Liburd, J. and Edwards, D. (2018) *Collaboration for Sustainable Tourism Development.* Oxford: Goodfellow Publishers.

Doherty, L. (2004). Work-life balance initiatives: Implications for women. *Employee Relations, 26*(4), 433-452.

Dwyer, L. and Lund-Durlacher, D. (2018). The responsibility of corporations for sustainable tourism development. In J. Liburd and D. Edwards (Eds.) *Collaboration for Sustainable Tourism Development.* Oxford: Goodfellow Publishers.

Eaton, S. C. (2003). If you can use them: Flexibility policies, organizational commitment, and perceived performance. *Industrial Relations: A Journal of Economy and Society,* **42**(2), 145-167.

Eikhof, D., Warhurst, C. & Haunschild, A. (2007). Introduction: What work? What life? What balance?: Critical reflections on the work-life balance debate. *Employee Relations,* **29***(4), 325-333.*

Felstead, A., Jewson, N., Phizacklea, A. & Walters, S. (2002). Opportunities to work at home in the context of work-life balance. *Human Resource Management Journal,* **12**(1), 54-76.

Fleetwood, S. (2007). Re-thinking work-life balance: Editor's introduction. *The International Journal of Human Resource Management,* **18**(3), 351-359.

Franek, M., Vecera, J. (2008). Personal characteristics and job satisfaction. *Ekonomie A Management,* 4, 63–75.

Ghazi, P. (2003). *The 24 Hour Family: A Parents Guide to Work-Life Balance.* London: The Women's Press Ltd.

Grandey, A. A., Kern, J. H., & Frone, M. R. (2007). Verbal abuse from outsiders versus insiders: Comparing frequency, impact on emotional exhaustion, and the role of emotional labor. *Journal of Occupational Health Psychology,* **12**(1), 63.

Greenhaus, J.H. & Powell, G.N. (2006). When work and family are allies: a theory of work-family enrichment. *Academy of Management Review,* **31**, 72-92.

Gregory, A. & Milner, S. (2009). Editorial: Work–life balance: A matter of choice? *Gender, Work & Organization,* **16**(1), 1-13.

Haddon, B., Hede, A. & Whiteoak, J. (2009). Work-life balance: Towards an integrated conceptual framework. *New Zealand Journal of Human Resource Management,* **9**(3), 174-186

Halpern, D. F. (2005). How time-flexible work policies can reduce stress, improve health, and save money. *Stress and Health,* **21**(3), 157-168.

Harris, C., Lewis, K. & Massey, C. (2005). Nice rhetoric, but it's not quite us: Work-life balance and NZ SME owners. In P. Dickson, (Ed). *Proceedings of the 50th ICSB World Conference.* (CD-ROM). Washington, D.C: ICSB, 15-18 June 2005.

Harris, C. & Pringle J. (2008) Work-Life Balance: Who is the Target for this Silver Bullet? Paper presented at the ACREW Work-Life Workshop. http://www.buseco.monash.edu.au/mgt/research/acrew/worklife/work-life-manuscripts.html

Holmes, R. (2016) *An Unexpected Way to Stop People from Quitting*: LinkedIn. Available at: www.linkedin.com (Accessed: 13th April 2018)

Hughes, J. & Bozionelos, N. (2007). Work-life balance as source of job dissatisfaction and withdrawal attitudes. *Personnel Review,* **36**(1), 145-154.

Kandasamy, I. & Ancheri, S. (2009). Hotel employees' expectations of QWL: A qualitative study. *International Journal of Hospitality Management,* **28**, 328-337.

Karatepe, O. M. (2013) The effects of work overload and work-family conflict on job embeddedness and job performance: The mediation of emotional exhaustion, *International Journal of Contemporary Hospitality Management,* **25**(4), pp. 614-634.

Karatepe, O. M., & Uludag, O. (2008). Role stress, burnout and their effects on frontline hotel employees' job performance: evidence from Northern Cyprus. *International Journal of Tourism Research,* **10**(2), 111-126.

Lee, C. & Way, K. (2010). Individual employment characteristics of hotel employees that play a role in employee satisfaction and work retention. *International Journal of Hospitality Management,* **29**, 344-353.

Lee, J.-S., Back, K.-J. and S. W. Chan, E. (2015) Quality of work life and job satisfaction among frontline hotel employees: A self-determination and need satisfaction theory approach, *International Journal of Contemporary Hospitality Management*, **27**(5), 768-789.

Lewis, R. (2010) Work-life balance in hospitality: Experiences from a Geneva-Based hotel. *International Journal of Management & Information Systems*, **14**(5), 99-106.

Lewis, S., Gambles, R., & Rapoport, R. (2007). The constraints of a 'work–life balance'approach: An international perspective. *The International Journal of Human Resource Management*, **18**(3), 360-373.

Mooney, S. (2009) Children and a career: Yeah right! Barriers to women managers' career progression in hotels. *New Zealand Journal of Human Resource Management*, **9**(3), 151-161.

Mulvaney, R., O'Neill, J., Cleveland, J. & Crouter, A. (2007). A model of work-family dynamics of hotel managers. *Annals of Tourism Research*, **34**, 66-86.

Neetu, J. & Prachi, B. (2015). Employment preferences of job applicants: unfolding employer branding determinants, *Journal of Management Development*, **34**(6), 634-652.

Nørmark, D. & Jensen, A.F. (2018). *Pseudoarbejde*. Copenhagen: Gyldendal Business.

O'Leary, S. & Deegan, J. (2005). Career progression of Irish tourism and hospitality management graduates. *International Journal of Contemporary Hospitality Management*, **17**(5), 421-432.

O'Neill, J. (2011). Face time in the hotel industry: An exploration of what it is and why it happens. *Journal of Hospitality & Tourism Research*, **36**(4), 478-494. DOI: 10.1177/1096348011407489.

O'Neill, J. & Davis, K. (2011). Work stress and well-being in the hotel industry. *International Journal of Hospitality Management*, **30**(2), 385-390.

Parkes, L. & Langford, P. (2008). Work-life balance or work- life alignment?: A test of the importance of work-life balance for employee engagement and intention to stay in organisations. *Journal of Management & Organization*, **14**(3), 267-284.

Pichler, F. (2009). Determinants of work-life balance: Shortcomings in the contemporary Measurement of WLB in large-scale surveys. *Social Indicators Research*, **92**(3), 449-469.

Poelmans, S., Kallaith, T. & Brough, P. (2008). Achieving work-life balance: Current theoretical and practice issues. *Journal of Management & Organization*, **14**(3), 267-284.

Popescu, C. and Avram, D. M. New Trends in Human Resource Management in the Hospitality Industry, *International Conference of Scientific Papers AFASES 2012*, Brasov, Romania.

Presser, H. B. (2004). The economy that never sleeps. *Contexts*, **3**(2), 42-49.

Roberts, K. (2007). Work-life balance – the sources of the contemporary problem and the probable outcomes: A review and interpretation of the evidence. *Employee Relations*, **29**(4), 334-351.

Rowley, G. & Purcell, K. (2001). As cooks go, she went: is labour churn inevitable? *Hospitality Management*, **20**, 163-85.

Smola, K.W., & Sutton, C. D. (2002). Generational differences: Revisiting generational work values for the new millennium. *Journal of Organizational Behavior*, **23**(4), 363-382.

Sparks, K., Cooper, C., Fried, Y. & Shirom, A. (1997). The effects of hours of work on health: A meta-analytic review. *Journal of Occupational and Organizational Psychology,* **70**, 391-408.

Staines, G. L., & Pleck, J. H. (1983). *Impact of Work Schedules on the Family.* Institute for Social Research, University of Michigan, Survey Research Center.Starineca, O. (2015) Employer brand role in HR recruitment and selection, *Economics & Business,* **27**, 58-63

Statistics New Zealand's *Survey of Working Life* (2008) http://archive.stats.govt.nz/browse_for_stats/income-and-work/employment_and_unemployment/SurveyOf-WorkingLife_HOTPMar08qtr/Commentary.aspx

Todd, P. & Binns, J. (2011). Work–life Balance: Is it now a problem for management? *Gender, Work and Organization,* DOI: 10.1111/j.1468-0432.2011.00564.x

Thompson, H.B. & Werner, J.M. (1997) The impact of role conflict/faciliation on core and discretionary behaviors: Testing a mediated model. *Journal of Management,* **23**(4), 583-602.

Warner, M., Slan-Jerusalim, R. & Korabik, K., (2009). Backlash and support: co-worker responses to work–family policies and practices. In: Sweet, S., Casey, J. (Eds.), *The Work–Family Encyclopaedia.* http://wfnetwork.bc.edu/encyclopedia.php?mode = nav. Accessed 25.12.2009.

Williams, C. (2008). Work-life balance of shift workers. *Perspectives on Labour and Income,* **20**(3), 15-15-26. Retrieved from: http://ezproxy.aut.ac.nz/login?url=http://search.proquest.com/docview/61686417?accountid=8440

Wong, S.C. & Ko, A., (2009). Exploratory study of understanding hotel employees' perceptions on work–life balance issues. *International Journal of Hospitality Management* **28**, 195–203.

Xiao, Q, & O'Neill, J. (2010). Work-family balance as a potential strategic advantage: A hotel general manager perspective. *Journal of Hospitality and Tourism Research,* **34**(4), 415-439.

Yang, J. (2010). Antecedents and consequences of job satisfaction in the hotel industry. *International Journal of Hospitality Management,* **29**, 609-619.

Zhao, X., Qu, H. and Ghiselli, R. (2011) Examining the relationship of work–family conflict to job and life satisfaction: A case of hotel sales managers, *International Journal of Hospitality Management,* **30**(1), pp. 46-54.

10 The Collaborative Economy, Tourism and Sustainable Development

Dianne Dredge and Eóin Meehan

Introduction

This chapter explores the collaborative economy, tourism and sustainability. The emergence of the digital collaborative economy has had profound transformative effects on the structure, organisation and business logics underpinning contemporary tourism (Dredge & Gyimóthy, 2017). It is opening up new business opportunities and livelihoods traditionally inaccessible to many individuals, and is driving deep transformation within existing industry practices. It is, however, not as new as many advocates claim, and can be best understood as an old economic model that has been transformed by the digitalisation processes associated with Industry 4.0 (Gilchrist, 2016; Smit et al., 2016). The collaborative economy has been claimed to be more sustainable than traditional business practices by lowering consumption and using existing resources more effectively (Botsman & Rogers, 2010). However, there is little evidence to support these claims, and for a variety of reasons, it has been difficult to undertake research to verify such assertions (Dredge & Gyimóthy, 2015). What is clear however, is that the collaborative economy is responsible for wide-ranging social and economic impacts and has proven to be very difficult to regulate. Despite these potential concerns, all indications are that it will continue to expand unabated. The impact and effects of the growth of the collaborative economy on sustainability is, therefore, a major issue that warrants further investigation.

Our departure point for this chapter is to explore the collaborative economy as a form of collaborative exchange through which tourism products, services and experiences are produced and consumed. We explore historical antecedents, arguing that the collaborative economy can be traced back through the millennia, and that the recent, and highly transformative iterations emerging as a result of Industry 4.0, must be understood within this broader landscape. However, before we can start to discuss the effects and consequences of the collaborative economy and tourism on sustainability, we first need to define key terms and outline our own understanding of the sustainability challenge.

Scope of the collaborative economy

Definitions and concepts

In its contemporary framing, and the one that most readers will be familiar with, the collaborative economy is framed as a digital peer-to-peer global marketplace that facilitates real-time transactions enabling anyone with an internet connection and smartphone to engage in buying, trading, sharing or gaining access to goods and services (Dredge and Gyimóthy, 2017). Terms such as 'collaborative economy', 'gig economy', 'sharing economy', and the 'we-conomy' are often used to capture these innovations. Various authors have drawn attention to the difficulty of defining the sharing/collaborative economy phenomena, arguing that the concept is much older and more diverse than this present framing. It is important therefore, that any discussion of the collaborative economy takes into account the diversity and depth of alternative collaborative economic forms irrespective of digitalisation (Dredge & Gyimóthy, 2017; Frenken & Schor, 2017).

Taking a step backwards from this contemporary definition, it is important to understand that our economic organisation is socially embedded, and is anchored within social, cultural and political conditions and practices (Polanyi, 1944; 1978). Collaboration is the cornerstone of economic organisation regardless of the particular economic system in question, with Benkler (2004) drawing attention to modes of social sharing that range from utterly impersonal, loose affiliations to very personal transactions. Anthropologists and ethnographers have also been arguing that sharing, gift and barter economies have existed for millennia in various formats (e.g. Mauss, 1922/1990; Rehn, 2014). These forms of exchange usually focus their explanatory power on the social, cultural and moral value of transactions, regardless of whether the commodity that is traded changes ownership permanently or temporarily. In contemporary tourism settings, Germann Molz (2012) draws attention to this in her explorations of couchsurfing, and the collaborative, networked and technologized enactments of travel through which mobile sociality is practiced:

In detailing the way togetherness and intimacy are performed in these online social media spaces, and though the mediatized tourist gaze, I have aimed to uncover some of the nuanced qualities of mobile sociality. One of the things that analysis indicates is that most travellers do not see their journeys as a solitary endeavour, but rather and collective experience. In this sense, the mediated tourist gaze is a collaborative project (Germann Molz, 2012: 78).

Germann Molz's (2012) contributions, drawing attention to the intangible but often world-making role of collaborative sociality, rarely enter into these public discourses about tourism because they are often seen as too intangible or 'fluffy' for economists and policy makers to grasp and incorporate in their work. As a result, the economic value of collaborative transactions dominate discussions.

In literature, the first mention of the collaborative economy can be traced back to Felson and Speth (1978), who were interested in understanding social and economic entanglements when, for example, a group buys a pitcher of beer because it is cheaper than the purchase of individual glasses. The contribution of these early discussions was to recognise that the social and economic values produced in the exchange process become entangled and hybridized, where the sum value is greater than the economic value alone. In this process, collaboration between the giver and the receiver is shaped by relational parameters, such as trust, reciprocity, proximity, and care (Dredge & Gyimóthy, 2017). Contemporary forms of the digitised collaborative economy build upon these older ideas about collaborative exchange, however their increasing prominence in public discourses are most often linked to economic growth afforded by digitalisation, new jobs and employment growth, economic innovation, and workforce flexibility. Additionally, the collaborative economy is characterised by digitally mediated exchanges between parties that are often unknown to each other, by real-time transactions often across international borders, and by the incorporation of trust mechanisms such as reviews and feedback.

Investigations of the various business logics, motivations, emphases, transaction characteristics and values have led to a wide variety of terms and concepts that try to capture collaborative economy in the literature. Table 10.1 summarises alternative conceptualisations of the collaborative economy. The table is by no means a complete list of all the terms appearing in the literature, but provides an overview of the diversity in the way it has been conceptualised and the underpinning values and metaphors that have shaped its description. Examining these various terms and definitions in Table 10.1, four key aspects of collaborative economy cut across these conceptualisations, and which can be used to understand and characterise any particular model of type:

☐ The nature of the transaction itself (e.g. characteristics of the collaborative exchange, motivations for the transaction, the resources, assets, services exchanged, tools/techniques of mediation, and so on).

Table 10.1: Alternative conceptualisations of collaborative economy. Adapted from Gyimóthy & Dredge (2017).

Term	Description	Key author/ Reference
Human ecology	Social and economic organisation as a coordinated ecological system	Hawley (1950)
Collaborative consumption	Involves joint consumption of goods and services	Felson & Spaeth (1978)
Access economy	Access to use property temporarily	Rifkin (2000)
Moral economy	Moral commitment to caring for a community, neighbour-hood, friendship groups, and in making a shared life	Bauman (2000; 2014)
Social sharing	Nonreciprocal pro-social behaviour	Benkler (2004)
Post-capitalist economies	Envisions, politicizes and enacts social-economic transformation by empowering placed-based community approaches	Gibson-Graham (2006; 2008)
Collaborative consumption v. 2.0	A system activating the untapped value of assets through models and marketplaces that enable greater efficiency and access (Botsman 2014)	Botsman & Rogers (2010)
Collaborative lifestyles	People with similar interests share and exchange less tangible assets such as time, space, skills, and money	Botsman & Rogers (ibid.)
The mesh/the sharing society	Digital technologies of Web 2.0 provide full interconnectedness between people and things in real time	Gansky (2010)
Circuits of commerce	Transactions take place in social circuits which are dynamic, negotiated interactions among individuals, households, and organizations, and incorporating monetized and non-monetised transactions	Zelizer (2010)
Access-based consumption	Transactions based on access to goods and services but where no change of ownership takes place	Bardhi & Eckhardt (2012) Rifkin (2000)
Peer-to-peer economy	Direct exchanges among peers and entail a variety of platforms on which citizens rent, sell and share things without the involvement of shops, banks, agencies and other intermediaries	P2Pfoundation.net (2012)
Moral economy of alternative tourism	Non-monetized exchange of goods and services (outside the market economy) based on an ethos of cooperation and generosity	Molz (2013)
Sharing vs. Pseudo-sharing	Coordinated acquisition and distribution of a resource for a fee or other compensation	Belk (2007; 2010; 2014ab)
Connected consumption	Based on a culture of access, use, and re-circulation of used goods as alternatives to traditional private ownership.	Schor & Fitzmaurice (2015)
Collaborative commerce/ Sharing economy	An exchange/sharing economy whereby customers become producers/suppliers and sellers of their own goods by negotiating and bartering exchanges for trading, without the use of money. Sharing and collaboration is ethos of exchange.	Huang & Benyucef's (2013) Lessig (2008)
Collaborative commons / Pro-commons	Alternative to capitalism where social capital is as important as financial capital, access promoted over ownership, sustainability supersedes consumerism, cooperation ousts competition.	Rifkin (2015)

☐ The relational characteristics of the actors involved in the exchange (e.g. trust, empathy, reciprocity, mutuality, responsibility, solidarity, reputation, ties; and the ethical undercurrents within the exchange (e.g. public good, profit, justice, etc.).

☐ The contextual factors that influence the exchange (e.g. social, economic, environmental, political conditions).

☐ The impacts and consequences of the collaborative economy over time and space, and to whom benefits/disadvantages accrue (Dredge & Gyimóthy, 2017).

Our interest in excavating this broad landscape of collaborative economy is to draw attention to the breadth of models, overlapping conceptualisations, and ultimately, the importance of keeping an open mind to the diversity of the collaborative economy as it is translated into tourism. Moreover, the field is so dynamic that new models and ideas are being generated regularly. The present focus on the digital collaborative economy is quite narrow and may create blind spots in understanding the social and economic transformations taking place. A wider view of the collaborative economy in digital and non-digital forms; from pro-social to economic models; and on diverse monetised and non-monetised types of collaboration can provide greater insights into the transformative effects of collaborative economy on the tourism industry, and its effects and consequences for sustainability.

Collaborative economy and tourism

From the above discussion, it becomes clear that the size and impact of the collaborative economy is difficult to define if we take into account all the different models and framings. That is, due to the monetised/non-monetised, formal/informal, access over ownership dimensions, the collaborative economy blurs the boundaries between the economy and everyday life, making it difficult to measure in economic terms through, for example, GDP, value of new investment, jobs or economic value (WEF, 2016). This kind of obsession about defining it in economic terms is also misleading, and does not take into account the wider social, cultural, economic, environmental and political valuing of collaborative transactions that take place in travelling.

The collaborative economy uses digital technologies to connect producers/hosts and consumers/guests who otherwise may never have connected. Any individual with an apartment or a room can now rent it in the global marketplace. No, or minimal, barriers to entry, greater diversity of accommodation products, greater demand for temporary accommodation capacity, increased efficiency of transactions, reduced costs and global reach are some of the reasons why the collaborative economy peer-to-peer accommodation sector has grown so rapidly. In the process, supply chains have been re-configured, producer-consumer relations are being transformed, existing markets have expanded and new markets created. The European Commission, in its recently adopted Communication on the collaborative economy has noted that the collaborative economy has potential to open up new opportunities for consumers and service providers, it has the potential to create employment and, by using existing resources more efficiently, it can contribute to the objectives of the circular economy (European Commission, 2016).

In relation to tourism, the growth of the collaborative economy peer-to-peer accommodation sector has significant impacts for traditional tourism industry structures, practices, and relationships. The growth of the collaborative economy peer-to-peer accommodation market has received considerable attention due to the extent of disruption it has unleashed. It has led to the diversification of accommodation stock, it has led to increased competition, and it has stimulated a range of ancillary services offered by small and micro-entrepreneurs. However, incumbent industry actors (such as hotels, apartment hotels, bed and breakfasts, hostels and vacation rentals) are concerned about the uneven regulatory landscape and the unfair competition this may create (HOTREC, 2015). Municipal governments and host communities are also raising concerns over the impact of unregulated tourist accommodation within residential neighbourhoods and the conflicts that are emerging due to the changing commercial nature of traditional residential areas close to city centres. In many cities across Europe, there have also been considerable concerns raised over the conversion of residential stock, and particularly social housing, into commercially oriented peer-to-peer tourist accommodation.

Figure 10.1 shows the potential extent of collaborative opportunities in tourism, and identifies examples in food, travel services, health and wellness, currency exchange, travel companions and support, accommodation and work space, transport and education:

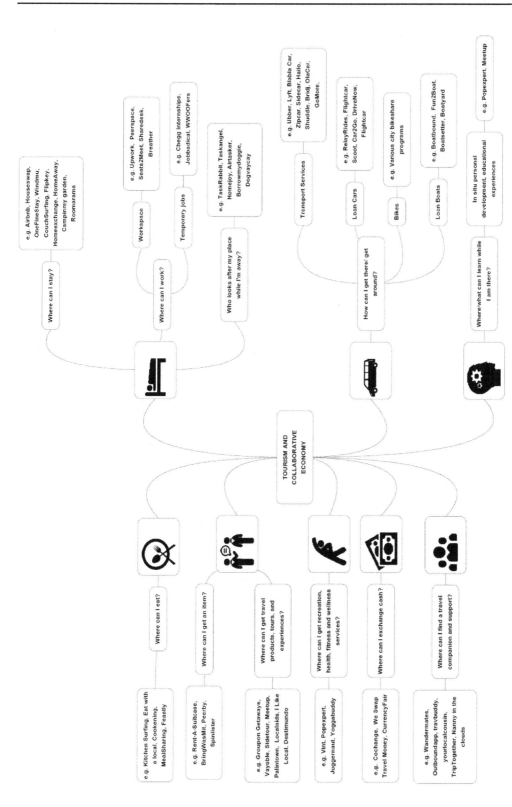

Figure 10.1: The collaborative economy and tourism (Dredge & Gyimóthy, 2017)

Sustainability, the collaborative economy and tourism

The collaborative economy has been widely mooted as a more sustainable form of living that has the potential to address several of the sustainable development goals (SDGs). The collaborative economy reduces consumption through more efficient use of resources (SDG 12 - Responsible consumption and production); it facilitates more authentic relationship building (SDG11- Sustainability cities and communities); and it has also been mooted as a means of increasing local livelihoods by allowing individuals and micro-entrepreneurs to access markets that they may not have had access to (SDG 8 – Decent work and economic growth). However, sustainability, framed in such a way, does not adequately cover the short-sightedness of a framework built on the expansion of economic consumption. Our argument here is that any consideration of sustainability must engage with what sustainability means, and it is here that we open up discussion of alternative ways of thinking about sustainability in the world.

The particular point we seek to explore is that sustainability is a particularly problematic concept that has been criticised as being too human-focused and has been co-opted to reinforce capitalism (Benson & Craig, 2014; Foster, 2015). Claims that the collaborative economy might be more sustainable and less damaging to the planet than other forms of tourism consumption usually focus their attention on exploring only the motivations and behaviours of visitors (Tussyadiah & Sigala, 2018). Not only do these studies have a very narrow understanding of what sustainability entails, which centres around consumption, but they also ignore the broader systemic impacts of the growth of travel that the collaborative economy contributes to. So, before we discuss the effects and consequences of collaborative economy on sustainability, we take a short detour to consider sustainability under late modern capitalism, which underpins how sustainability is generally (and perhaps, unthinkingly) framed.

Sustainability under late modern capitalism

Under late modern capitalism, tourism has enjoyed a long boom. Late modern capitalism describes the period from the 1980s (commencing with Reaganism and Thatcherism), where we see a period of sustained growth and accelerated neoliberalism. Picketty (2014) argues that under late modern capitalism, ideologically-driven neoliberal governments have become handmaidens of the private sector, and have begun to focus more heavily on capital accumulation amongst the wealthiest. There has been a reassignment in the value of both nature and labour as being of service to capitalism (Moore, 2015). This cheapening of nature, where planetary resources are simply the fuel on which to base growth, has significantly benefitted tourism. For example, growth in low cost airline passenger capacity has been facilitated by increased investment in airport infrastructure which has opened up new markets, by a reduction in environmental barriers, and by a situation where the full environmental cost of travel is not factored into the market (Higham et al., 2013). The impacts of this travel at a planetary level are unsustainable but outside the responsibility of any one actor, organisation or agency to address. Into this discourse, advocates of the digital or platform collaborative economy have promised that sharing is less resource consumptive, more authentic, and sustainable (Botsman & Rogers, 2010), a claim that is highly questionable within a broader systemic perspective that includes taking into account increased air travel and its environmental impacts.

The cheapening of labour can also be illustrated in the rise of collaborative economy, and the effects and consequences of this on the availability of decent work directly affects the sustainability of local communities. The rise of the collaborative economy is a new form of capitalism empowered by information and communication technologies, that enables easy entry for micro-entrepreneurs, immediate and seamless financial transactions, and it allows global platform companies to access and profit from assets they do not own (Slee, 2016). The cost of labour is subsumed into the cost price of accessing the asset (an apartment, a car, a boat, etc.) and the digital platform uses algorithms to optimize its pricing which, in the process, removes control from the owner of the asset and the labour to set their price. Global collaborative economy platforms often operate outside local laws and, as a result, have been able to expand at the fringes of planning and regulation. Historically, these planning and regulation systems were designed through democratic processes to protect public interests, including labour and nature. However, the peer-to-peer (p2p) format of collaborative economy, and the increasing individualisation of the marketplace, has reduced the power and influence of regulatory bodies to protect these interests (Moral-Espín & Fernández-García, 2018).

From these above discussions, two key observations can be devised. First, the diverse types of collaborative economy described above, and their different rationales and underlying modalities, make any holistic assessment of the effects and consequences of collaborative economy impossible to assess (Böcker & Meelen, 2017). That is, given that the collaborative economy is unable to be clearly defined and is highly heterogeneous, assessments of the impacts of collaborative economy on sustainability can only ever be partial. Second, any discussion of the effects of the collaborative economy on sustainability must necessarily take into account the wider socio-political influences of late modern capitalism. We carry forward these observations into the next section where we review claims about the effects and consequences of the collaborative economy on sustainability.

Effects and consequences of the collaborative economy on sustainability

The collaborative economy is notoriously difficult to research due to definitional challenges, the difficulty of accessing producers, consumers and other actors to collect data, the opaqueness of data released by platform companies, and the asymmetries of information that result from platforms undertaking their own advocacy research but not making the data available to independent researchers (e.g. Dredge & Gyimóthy, 2015; Slee, 2016). Here we rehearse and critically assess the arguments about sustainability, with the aim of assisting readers understand the complexity of the issues and to conceptualise their own future investigations.

Reducing hyper-consumption

Advocates of the collaborative economy claim that is more sustainable than traditional forms of consumption because it reduces demand for new products, and makes more efficient use of existing resources via collaborative access. Botsman and Rodgers (2010) presented the sharing economy as a possible disruption to hyper-consumption, a form of over-consumption stemming from the capitalist ideology that consumerism is a path to happiness and fulfilment. Sharing can also make us happy, Botsman argues (2014). Similarly, others have also praised the sharing economy as the sustainable alternative to more traditional unsustainable commercial practices and economic models (Palgan et al., 2017; Martin, 2016). We cannot dismiss the sharing economy's ability to reduce over-consumption by putting idle resources to use because, at least in isolation, this argument makes sense. The ambiguity of the collaborative economy emerges, however, when we examine the impacts in a wider system where the collaborative economy has reduced prices, made accommodation cheaper and more accessible to the masses, and simultaneously contributes to the growth in air travel and consumption of a range of other travel products (Martin, 2016). As a result, it might also be argued that collaborative consumption has contributed (in ways not yet quantified or analysed) to the hyper-consumption of mass air travel, and to the overcrowding, environmental degradation and community impacts associated with over-tourism. Similarly, research into car-sharing has not uncovered any substantial reduction in CO2 emissions (e.g. see Frenken & Schor, 2017).

Attracting consumers more interested in sustainability

The uptake of the collaborative economy has also been linked to consumers interested in, and motivated by, sustainability concerns. Böcker & Meelen

(2017) examine a number of collaborative economy sectors including car, ride, accommodation, tool and meal sharing, finding that motivations to participate in these sectors are diverse and not necessarily strongly correlated to environmental concerns, finding that:

> *"Younger and low-income groups are more economically motivated to use and provide shared assets; younger, higher-income and higher-educated groups are less socially motivated; and women are more environmentally motivated."* (Böcker & Meelen, 2017)

These authors further compound the challenge by pointing out that the slow diffusion and uptake of sustainability innovations is at odds with the rapid growth of the accommodation sector in recent years. This rapid scaling up of collaborative economy accommodation has not been driven by sustainability arguments, and is more likely the result of the economic motivations of mass markets.

Reshaping demand

The collaborative economy is said to reshape demand by increasing resource efficiency and decreasing waste generation. However, as we have noted above, these practices do not exist in a vacuum but are part of broader interconnected system, and macro-economic impacts are rarely taken into account in these arguments (Frenken & Schor, 2017). Demand does not simply dissipate but is re-purposed or re-directed as economic-driven consumption continues to be a key feature of late modern capitalism. For instance, in high-demand, high-growth destinations (e.g. Barcelona, New York, Venice, etc.), the offering of accommodation on collaborative platforms has reinforced the ability of some asset owners to accumulate capital, which allows them to purchase more rental properties. In the process, local inhabitants may be displaced. Framing the collaborative economy only in terms of the first transaction (i.e. asset owners generate an income from an idle asset) and linking this to sustainability minimises the impact on the system as whole, and is what economists refer to as 'partial-equilibrium analysis' (Frenken & Schor, 2017). Case studies of the impact of collaborative economy accommodation suggest that incumbent accommodation providers such as hotels have been greatly impacted by the rise of online accommodation suppliers such as Airbnb. Some traditional accommodation incumbents (generally lower grade establishments) become less attractive to consumers and these providers are thus caught up in constant processes of product renewal and renovation, which in turn generates demand for a range of other building and consumer products. As a result, demand for products is shifted elsewhere (e.g. anything from construction to interior decoration supplies) and does not necessarily disappear.

Democratising the economy

The collaborative economy has been claimed to re-democratise the economy by increasing its accessibility to a range of people, especially individuals, micro-entrepreneurs. Not only can the collaborative economy increase the access of lower and middles socio-economic groups to resources and assets that they cannot ordinarily afford (e.g. a second home or holiday house), but individuals with an asset can also access an economic opportunity by listing it on a digital platform. In this way, it potentially contributes to sustainability by promoting economic inclusivity and growth, invoking a "trickle-up" economic argument.

Jiang (2016) found that the sharing economy distributes assets through four systems—sharing, giving, access and exchange—identifying the access-based approach as a rising force in the sharing economy marketplace. The sharing economy is portrayed as less competitive, and less orientated towards maximising returns on investment, with the marketplace characterised by inclusivity and wide spread accessibility (Gansky, 2010). Examining the digital collaborative economy and the increasing reliance on and uptake of technology in society would suggest that accessibility to online sharing marketplaces has never been greater (Krueger, 2002). Participation and accessibility however must be viewed as different dimensions in this discourse and not conflated. Accessibility does not necessarily require extensive resources at one's disposal from a consumer perspective. However, from the supplier side, those with accumulated capital and who own desirable resources hold positions of power in the marketplace (Andreotti et al., 2017). Access therefore does not equate to equitable participation, as those with the resources will always be in an advantageous position. In this perspective, the collaborative economy is little more than digital platform capitalism, where those with resources, and in positions of power, remain powerful (Belk, 2014b). So, while ease of accessibility to the collaborative economy grows, it is not ubiquitous across all of society and can be seen to further increase the chasm between those included and those not. Schor (2017) further found such gaps were heightened where highly educated individuals dominate provider-scapes, crowding-out the potential for more equitable participation and gains.

Problematizing the issue further places the prominent collaborative economy players at a crossroads where a continuation of the current trajectory will see less emphasis placed on sharing and more on profit maximisation (Schor & Fitzmaurice, 2015; Belk, 2014a). Alternatively, market trailblazers could incorporate more holistic approaches to sharing which de-emphasise (but do not disregard) economic considerations in favour of environmental and societal concerns. We are starting to see this with ethical platforms such as Fairbnb and the urban commoning movement emerging (Bauwens & Niaros, 2017; Scholz, 2016). As the growth of the collaborative economy accelerates, issues and opportunities will continue to appear and affect the future engagement and composition of the marketplace. While finding clearly defined solutions has proved to be challenging at this stage, it has become clearer that what is needed is an open dialogue to identify collaborative models and practices that create social, economic, environmental and cultural value for a multitude of stakeholders (Dredge & Gyímothy, 2017). As the collaborative economy continues to have an impact upon sustainable tourism, this process must first be addressed by establishing who and what is being accounted for, and what values are being produced in collaborative exchange processes. The World Economic Forum (WEF, 2016) has raised a similar concern in declaring the benefits of the platform economy must extend to all corners of society and include those who remain without access.

Contributing to sustainability by promoting social connectivity

The collaborative economy is mooted as a mechanism to promote economic activity and social cohesion and, in the process, contribute to social sustainability (Grimes, 2003; Manniche et al., 2017). This sustainability claim is often focused around the role that the collaborative economy plays in re-establishing local connections, in increasing community wellbeing, and in building social capital. While there is much research on the unfolding impacts of tourism on major destinations subject to high growth, and where the collaborative economy has played a contributing role, there is very little research that we are aware of that has examined the effects and consequences of the digital collaborative economy in rural, coastal and peripheral areas. As a result, we now discuss these landscapes separately.

In many urban destinations, concerns about overtourism and issues of social and environmental sustainability are linked to the rapid scaling of these destinations beyond their social, political and environmental capacities. The pace of growth has been so great that destinations have not had time to plan for growth, nor have they had the opportunity to anticipate and devise ways of addressing impacts. While the factors contributing to overtourism are complex and might be likened to a perfect storm created by a confluence of housing, investment, economic, tourism and other policies (Dredge et al, 2016), there is little doubt that the collaborative economy has been an important contributing factor and that many destinations have significant sustainability concerns as a result (Quaglieri Domínguez & Russo, 2010). In peripheral localities (e.g. Iceland and Rovaniemi), collaborative economy accommodation has provided much needed capacity allowing these destinations to scale up more quickly than traditional investment and construction of hotels would normally allow. However, and similar to larger destinations commonly associated with overtourism, there are indications that social, political and environmental capacities have also been reached.

Many digital platforms, from Airbnb to Vayable and Dinner Sharing, leverage romantic notions of authentic encounters between hosts and guests, which suggest social bonding and a sense of wellbeing is possible. In her research on couchsurfing, Molz (2012:12) argues that these encounters "can lead to emotionally intense, but ultimately brief and potentially commodified face-to-face interactions". Her research suggests that any positive social benefits are performative, enacted in relations between collaborators, and not necessarily spatially grounded. Hence, the contribution of the digital collaborative economy to the sustainability of places/destinations might be questioned. That said, there is ample evidence showing how the collaborative economy plays out in city centres, and upsets the lives of inhabitants. The Distortion street festival in Copenhagen, is a collaborative event comprising up to 40 street parties with an estimated 100,000 participants per day. It has brought about intolerable noise levels, littering, hooliganism and petty crime and has angered residents (Brunstedt, 2017). While this is a week-long event, the upsurge of Airbnb accommodation in residential areas in cities such as Barcelona and Amsterdam has longer-term and sustained negative effects including the displacement of local residents, negative impacts on community cohesion, the closure of local services as a result of declining permanent populations (Dredge et al., 2016). Both cases illustrate the difficulty that local authorities have in managing the effects of the collaborative economy, and raise serious questions over blanket claims that the it is more sustainable than traditional forms of exchange in tourism.

The effects on labour

The collaborative economy has been linked to the generation of new kinds of jobs, greater flexibility in work conditions and low entry barriers, that in turn increase opportunities for micro- and small entrepreneurs. Gig economy and crowd-sourced work models such as TaskRabbit, Freelancer and Amazon Mechanical Turk have come under much criticism because this work has cheapened labour, and has contributed to the removal of hard won labour rights, to the de-localisation of work, and to the blurring of work-life boundaries. Negative impacts on the wellbeing, quality of life and power of workers have been noted in this human-cloud, although with no reliable estimates of the number of workers in the collaborative economy, it makes it difficult to assess the impacts (De Groen & Maselli, 2016). In the tourism sector however, the characteristics of labour are different and work is often location-bound, which means that these broader discussions about the gig economy and delocalised mobile workers must be assessed in context and may not be transferable.

Beyond these structural changes in the workforce, the rise of the collaborative economy has also been linked to an expanding ecosystem of micro-entrepreneurial activities, ranging from apartment cleaning to key deposit services. These emergent forms of non-routine, low-skilled, on-call work, are dependent upon new technologies, and are negating traditional hourly-based work practices in favour of itinerant work that is neither regulated or predictable (Degryse, 2016). Rarely do these activities account for the real time a worker spends on the task, so it becomes necessary for a worker in the collaborative economy to hold down several jobs to make a living wage. At the other end of the spectrum, the collaborative economy can facilitate the mobile dwelling of high-skilled, non-routine, middle-skilled jobs whose work comprises complex problem-solving activities (Goos, Manning & Salomons, 2009). These workers can work in the cloud from almost anywhere, their jobs are not at risk from automation, so destinations that offer vibrant, exotic, cheap locations can benefit from medium longer-term mobile dwelling of these workers (Pupillo et al., 2018). This blurring of work-lifestyle is evident in the increasing number of digital nomads congregating in exotic locations such as Ubud (Bali), Goa (India) and Ho Chi Minh City (Vietnam) among others.

In sum, the effects and consequences of the collaborative economy on labour in tourism are difficult to characterise and the implications for sustainability can only be understood through closer investigations into the skills in demand, and the location and quality of work. On one hand the collaborative economy and digitalisation has opened up opportunities for more flexible micro-entrepreneurial work, and there are arguments that it has improved economic accessibility and inclusiveness. On the other hand, the quality of work also needs to be considered, and here there are indications that a polarisation of work is occurring. The collaborative economy has cheapened labour, subsuming it into the cost price of the asset being shared, and resulting in low paid collaborative economy workers having to respond to multiple workflows on different digital platforms. Alternatively, high paid cloud workers can become digital nomads colonising cheap and exotic destinations. Moreover, there are gender and diversity implications of this changing work environment. Women and ethnic workers tend to take on lower status jobs, are more likely to take on menial roles in the collaborative economy. Gender has an influence on rewards and achievement in this digital workplace, especially where women are responsible for household and family obligations, and are not as free to accept all tasks. There are, as a result, corresponding implications for job security and social mobility (Baum 2007; 2015; OECD, 2011; UNWTO, 2010). It is therefore likely that transitioning to the collaborative economy, where labour is often subsumed in the cost price, where time is often not adequately accounted for, and where hard-won labour rights and employer obligations disappear within fluid, mobile, global transactions, there are significant but little understood gender and diversity implications emerging from tourism related work in the collaborative economy.

Conclusions

The aim of this chapter was to explore the collaborative economy, tourism and sustainability, and in doing so illustrate the complexities and ambiguities that characterise debates about its effects on, and consequences for, sustainability. The nature of collaborative transactions, the relational characteristics of the actors involved, the contextual factors that influence the exchange, and the impacts and consequences of the collaborative economy over time and space all influence how we might assess its effects on sustainability. Thus, due to the heterogeneity of the collaborative economy, not only in tourism but more broadly, an overall assessment is not possible. The chapter has also explored the extent of the collaborative economy in tourism. Its presence in accommodation, transport, personal services, education, recreation and leisure services, and dining/catering services also suggests that the effects on sustainability cannot be easily nor universally discussed.

The chapter discussed that the collaborative economy has been widely mooted as a more sustainable form of living, with the potential to address several of the sustainable development goals (SDGs). The collaborative economy reduces consumption through the more efficient use of resources (SDG 12 - Responsible consumption and production); it facilitates more authentic relationship building (SDG11- Sustainability cities and communities); and it has also been mooted as a means of increasing local livelihoods by allowing individuals and micro-entrepreneurs to access markets that they may not have had access to (SDG 8 – Decent work and economic growth). However, our discussion explored these sustainability claims, and found that there were many ambiguities in the emergent literature that meant these claims are often nothing more than rhetoric.

The digital collaborative economy is a relatively new research area in tourism despite that the concept of collaborative exchange has been around for millennia. As a novelty, insufficient time may have passed to allow full development of the subfield. As in other cases of novel and emergent research, there is a tendency for early movers to jump on a term, to colonise it, and to argue for its utility, significance and contribution. Later waves of research usually offer more balanced and critical perspectives and evaluations. This chapter is positioned as a contribution within this secondary wave of critical thinking, although we recognise that significantly more theoretical and empirical research is required before we can form any evidence-based insights into the effects and consequences of collaborative economy in tourism on sustainability. In other words, the field requires substantial unpacking, a critical lens to the various types of collaborative economy models and logics, and greater criticality to the above discussed claims.

Our final thoughts on the matter of the collaborative economy, tourism and sustainability require a step back from the operational intricacies and effects of collaborative economy in tourism. We have acknowledged that the collaborative economy is diverse, difficult to define, and that digitalisation has led to a new landscape of digitally mediated collaborative relations. They might produce intense moments of intimate collaboration, but platform capitalism ensures that these fleeting relations are highly commoditised. The current platform capitalism can be read as digitally enabled sharing practices that are no more than a re-shaping and re-organisation of traditional business logics under late modern capitalism. There are however other models of the collaborative economy that we have identified here that have a stronger social, environmental and moral ethos (e.g. collaborative commons, circular economy models) than the platform capitalism models that dominate current thinking. Looking towards the future, the ability of the collaborative economy to address sustainability will depend on deeper engagement with these kinds of models, and by addressing the ambiguities that we have excavated in this chapter in explicit and meaningful ways.

References

Andreotti, A., Anselmi, G., Eichhorn, T., Hoffmann, C. P. & Micheli, M. (2017). Participation in the sharing economy. *SSRN Electronic Journal*. doi:10.2139/ssrn.2961745

Bardhi, F. & Eckhardt, G. M. (2012). Access-based consumption: the case of car sharing. *Journal of Consumer Research*, **39**(4), 881-898. doi:10.1086/666376

Baum, T. (2007). Human resources in tourism: Still waiting for change. *Tourism Management*, **28**(6), 1383-1399. doi:10.1016/j.tourman.2007.04.005

Baum, T. (2015). Human resources in tourism: Still waiting for change? – A 2015 reprise. *Tourism Management*, **50**, 204-212. doi:10.1016/j.tourman.2015.02.001

Bauman, Z. (2000) *Liquid Modernity*. Cambridge: Polity.

Bauman, Z. (2014). *Liquid Love: On the frailty of human bonds*. Cambridge: Polity Press.

Bauwens, M. & Niaros, V. (2017). *Changing societies though urban commons transitions*. https://commonstransition.org/wp-content/uploads/2017/12/Bauwens-Niaros-Changing_societies.pdf

Belk, R. (2007). Why not share rather than own? *The ANNALS of the American Academy of Political and Social Science*, **611**(1), 126-140. doi:10.1177/0002716206298483

Belk, R. (2010). Sharing. *Journal of Consumer Research*, **36**, 715–734

Belk, R. (2014a). You are what you can access: Sharing and collaborative consumption online. *Journal of Business Research*, **67**(8), 1595-1600. doi:10.1016/j.jbusres.2013.10.001

Belk, R. (2014b). Sharing versus pseudo-sharing in Web 2.0. *The Anthropologist*, **18**(1), 7-23. doi:10.1080/09720073.2014.11891518

Benkler, Y. (2004). Sharing nicely: on shareable goods and the emergence of sharing as a modality of economic production. *The Yale Law Journal*, **114**(2), 273. doi:10.2307/4135731

Benson, M. H. & Craig, R. K. (2014). *The end of sustainability*. doi:10.2307/j.ctt1x07zhx.

Botsman, R. & Rogers, R. (2010). *Whats Mine is Yours: The rise of collaborative consumption*. New York: Harper Business.

Botsman, R. (2014). Sharing is not just for startups. *Harvard Business Review, 92*(3), 23-26.

Böcker, L., & Meelen, T. (2017). Sharing for people, planet or profit? Analysing motivations for intended sharing economy participation. *Environmental Innovation and Societal Transitions, 23*, 28-39. doi:10.1016/j.eist.2016.09.004

Brunstedt, H. (2017). Desperat beboer: Distortion er en syg ideologi - sponsoreret af Royal Bryggeri. *Politiken*, 29 May. politiken.dk/debat/art5968154/Distortion -er-en-syg-ideologi-sponsoreret-af-Royal-Bryggeri

De Groen, W.P. & Maselli, I. (2016). *The Impact of the Collaborative Economy on the Labour Market*. Brussels: Centre for European Policy Studies.

Degryse, C. (2016). *Digitalisation of the economy and its impact on labour markets.* European Trade Union Institute. Available at: www.etui.org/Publications2/Working-Papers/ Digitalisation-of-the-economy-and-its-impact-on-labour-markets.

Dredge, D. & Gyimóthy, S. (2015). Collaborative economy and tourism: critical perspectives, questionable claims and silenced voices. *SSRN Electronic Journal*. doi:10.2139/ ssrn.2739091

Dredge, D., Gyimóthy, S., Birkbak, A., Jensen, T. E. & Madsen, A. K. (2016). *The impact of regulatory approaches targeting collaborative economy in the tourism accommodation sector: Barcelona, Berlin, Amsterdam and Paris*. Brussels: European Commission.

Dredge, D. & Gyimóthy, S. (2017). *Tourism and Collaborative Economy: Perspectives, Politics, Policies and Prospects*. Springer.

European Commission. (2016). *A European Agenda for the Collaborative Economy*. Brussels, 2.6.2016 COM(2016) 356 final.

Felson, M. & Spaeth, J. L. (1978). Community structure and collaborative consumption: a routine activity approach. *American Behavioral Scientist, 21*(4), 614-624. doi:10.1177/000276427802100411.

Foster, J. (2015). *After Sustainability: Denial, hope, retrieval*. London: Earthscan.

Frenken, K. & Schor, J. (2017). Putting the sharing economy into perspective. *Environmental Innovation and Societal Transitions, 23*, 3-10. doi:10.1016/j.eist.2017.01.003

Gansky, L. (2010). *The Mesh: Why the future of business is sharing*. New York, NY: Portfolio/ Penguin.

Gibson-Graham, J. K. (2006). *A Postcapitalist Politics*. Minneapolis: University of Minnesota Press.

Gibson-Graham, J.K. (2008). Diverse economies: Performative practices for 'Other Worlds' *Progress in Human Geography, 32* (5), 613-632.

Gilchrist, A. (2016). Introducing Industry 4.0, in *Industry 4.0: The Industrial Internet of Things*. Berkley: APress.

Goos, M., Manning, A. & Salomons, A. (2009). Job polarization in Europe, *American Economic Review, 99* (2), 58-63.

Grimes, S. (2003). The digital economy challenge facing peripheral rural areas, *Progress in Human Geography, 27* (2), 174-193.

Hawley, A. H. (1950). *Human Ecology: A theory of community structure*. New York: Ronald Press.

Higham, J., Cohen, S.A., Peeters, P. & Gössling, S. (2013). Psychological and behavioural approaches to understanding and governing sustainable mobility. *Journal of Sustainable Tourism*, **21** (7), 949-967.

HOTREC (2015) *Levelling the Playing Field*. Policy paper on the sharing economy. http://www.hotrec.eu/policy-issues/sharing- economy.aspx

Huang, Z. & Benyoucef, M. (2013). From e-commerce to social commerce: A close look at design features. *Electronic Commerce Research and Applications*, **12**(4), 246-259. doi:10.1016/j.elerap.2012.12.003

Jiang, J. (2016) The challenges and opportunities of sharing economy – a new wrapping for doing business online? PACIS 2016 Proceedings. 111. http://aisel.aisnet.org/pacis2016/111

Krueger, B.S. (2002). Assessing the potential of internet political participation in the United States. *American Politics Research*, **30**(5), 476-498. doi:10.1177/1532673x02030005002

Lessig, L. (2008). *Remix: Making art and commerce thrive in the hybrid economy*. New York: Penguin Books.

Martin, C. J. (2016). The sharing economy: A pathway to sustainability or a nightmarish form of neoliberal capitalism? *Ecological Economics*, **121**, 149-159. doi:10.1016/j.ecolecon.2015.11.027

Mauss, M. (1922/1990). *The Gift: forms and functions of exchange in archaic societies*. London: Routledge

Manniche, J., Topsø Larsen, K., Brandt Broegaard, R. & Holland, E. (2017). *Destination: A circular tourism economy. A handbook for transitioning toward a circular economy within the tourism and hospitality sectors in the South Baltic Region*. Nexoe: Centre for Regional & Tourism Research.

Molz, J.G. (2012). *Travel Connections: Tourism, technology and togetherness in a mobile world*. Abingdon: Routledge.

Molz, J. G. (2013). Social networking technologies and the moral economy of alternative tourism: the case of couchsurfing.org. *Annals of Tourism Research*, **43**, 210-230. doi:10.1016/j.annals.2013.08.001

Moore, J. W. (2015). *Capitalism in the Web of Life: Ecology and the Accumulation of Capital*. Verso.

Moral-Espín, L. D. & Fernández-García, M. (2018). Moving beyond dichotomies? The collaborative economy scene in Andalusia and the role of public actors in shaping it. *The Sociological Review*, **66**(2), 401-424. doi:10.1177/0038026118758539

OECD. (2011). *Education and training for competitiveness and growth in tourism: Final report*. OECD: Paris.

P2pfoundation.net. (2012). Retrieved from https://p2pfoundation.net/

Palgan, Y. V., Zvolska, L. & Mont, O. (2017). Sustainability framings of accommodation sharing. *Environmental Innovation and Societal Transitions*, **23**, 70-83. doi:10.1016/j.eist.2016.12.002

Piketty, T. (2014). *Capital in the Twenty-First Century*. Cambridge MA: Belknap Press/ Harvard University Press.

Polanyi, K. (1944) *The Great Transformation: The Political and Economic Origins of Our Time,* New York: Rinehart.

Polanyi, K. (1968) *Primitive, Archaic and Modern Economies: Essays of Karl Polanyi,* New York: Anchor Books.

Pupillo, L., Noam, E., & Waverman, L. (2018). *The Internet and Jobs: Opportunities and ambiguous trends.* Brussels: Centre for European Policy Studies. No.2018/06.

Quaglieri Domínguez, A. & Russo, A.P. (2010). Paisajes urbanos en la época post-turística. Propuesta de un marco analítico. *Scripta Nova,* **XIV**(323) Available at: http://www.ub.es/geocrit/sn/sn-323.htm

Rehn, A. (2014). Gifts, gifting and gift economies: On challenging capitalism with blood, plunder and necklaces. In M. Parker, G. Cheney, V. Fournier, and C. Land (eds.), *The Routledge Companion to Alternative Organization* (pp. 195–209). London: Routledge.

Rifkin, J. (2000). *The Age of Access: How the shift from ownership to access is transforming capitalism.* New York: Penguin Books.

Rifkin, J. (2015). *The Zero Marginal Cost Society: The internet of things, the collaborative commons, and the eclipse of capitalism.* New York: Palgrave Macmillan.

Scholz, T. (2016) *Platform Cooperativism: Challenging the Corporate Sharing Economy.* Rosa Luxemburg Stiftung New York Office. Available at: http://www.rosalux-nyc.org/wp-content/files_mf/scholz_platformcoop_5.9.2016.pdf

Schor, J. B. & Fitzmaurice, C. J. (2015). Collaborating and connecting: The emergence of the sharing economy. *Handbook of Research on Sustainable Consumption,* 410-425. doi:10.4337/9781783471270.00039

Schor, J. B. (2017). Does the sharing economy increase inequality within the eighty percent?: Findings from a qualitative study of platform providers. *Cambridge Journal of Regions, Economy and Society,* **10**(2), 263-279. doi:10.1093/cjres/rsw047

Slee, T. (2016). What's yours is mine: against the sharing economy. *Working USA,* **19**(2), 286-289. doi:10.1111/wusa.12241.

Smit, J. K., S. Moeller, C. & Carlberg, M. (2016) *Industry 4.0.* European Parliament. Directorate General for Internal Policies. IP/A/ITRE/2015-02.

Tussyadiah, I. P. & Sigala, M. (2018). Shareable tourism: Tourism marketing in the sharing economy. *Journal of Travel & Tourism Marketing,* **35**(1), 1-4. doi:10.1080/10548408.2018.1410938

UNWTO (2010) *Global Report on Women in Tourism 2010.* World Tourism Organization (UNWTO) and the United Nations Entity for Gender Equality and the Employment of Women (UN Women).

WEF (2016). How much is the sharing economy worth to GDP? Available: https://www.weforum.org/agenda/2016/10/what-s-the-sharing-economy-doing-to-gdp-numbers/ Accessed 26th October, 2016.

Zelizer, V. A. (2010). *Economic Lives: How culture shapes the economy.* Princeton: Princeton University Press.

11 Suppliers as Key Collaborators for Sustainable Tourism Development

Anne-Mette Hjalager

Rationale

The purpose of this chapter is to introduce a conceptual approach to under-standing driving forces for innovation in sustainable tourism development. The model underpins the fact that innovation in tourism is not solely the effect of a strategic and wilful internal action in tourism firms and organisations, but also the consequences of external driving forces. Further, the article offers a more detailed review of the importance of suppliers as (one of several) push factors for sustainable tourism development. Examples are provided, and possibilities and limitations in terms of a rapid development of more sustainable practices in tourism are discussed. A four-field model aims at stimulating the search for new forms of collaboration between tourism firms and their suppliers in the upstream supply chain, and it adds dimensions to the traditional perspectives on value chains in tourism.

The context of innovation in tourism

There are many definitions of the term '*innovation*'. At the broad level, innovation implies the materializing of something new and the successful exploitation of ideas. Joseph Schumpeter (1934) distinguished between the introduction of new goods, new methods of production, the opening of new markets, the conquest of new sources of supply, and the carrying out of a new organization.

Innovation takes place in all sectors of the economy, including the public and voluntary sectors. Some organizations renew their products and services continuously, others only occasionally. Some depend for their survival on being sprinters, while others operate feasible businesses without introducing much change. Investigations of innovations in tourism firms often come up with very bleak results. The observation is that, understood as individual entities, tourism firms are not particularly innovative (Camison & Monfort-Mir, 2012: Martinez-Roman et al., 2015; Hjalager, 2010a), although attractions and travel services are found to be more innovative than accommodation facilities and restaurants (Sundbo et al., 2013). Even the largest tourism corporations seldom employ people in research and development departments (R&D). At best, innovations consist of incremental changes, mostly aimed at obtaining higher productivity and cost savings. Supplementary studies of management attitudes and practices reveal a distinct conservatism and risk aversion that is likely to counteract the inclination to innovate or hinder the implementation of new product and services (Orfila-Sintes et al., 2005; Jacob & Groizard, 2007; Pikkemat et al., 2016). In small and medium-size firms, changes often do not take place until the facilities are closed and restarted by new proprietors with novel concepts or ideas.

Nevertheless, tourism, as it is experienced by the customer, is undergoing quite dramatic changes. Specifically, in the field of sustainable tourism, green labelling and auditing started more than two decades ago and represent major steps forward both for protection of the environment and for the image of tourism products (Hallet al., 2015). With varying success, national and international programs have attempted to achieve a dissemination of sustainable practices in the tourism sector, as illustrated by Jia & Wahnschafft (2015) in the case of China. Likewise, the conceptualization and re-launching of destinations as eco-friendly embody innovations in the larger geographical scale. Such initiatives require inclusive and collaborative attitudes in their local settings to harvest the benefits of the being advanced in terms of sustainability. Destinations in all parts of the world, in rural and urban and in coastal and inland zones compete for consumer attention through green and responsible profiles. However, both distinctiveness and trustworthiness may suffer, if obtained consumer attention is mismanaged (Hanna et al., 2017).

Unlike other sectors – for example, the automobile or pharmaceutical industries – innovations in tourism are not noticeably embedded inside existing corporative structures. Rather, innovations in tourism are to a greater extent associated with external collaboration and with entrepreneurship (Hall & Williams, 2008). Commonly, the search for, the discovery and creativity, the experimentation and the development of products and services take place in association with recently started firms or through networks for which the tourism aspect represents a new business strategy (McLeod & Vaughan, 2014; Komppula, 2014). The tourism sector is highly volatile with many start-ups and closures, and this dynamic partly explains the ongoing restructuring of tourism and the emergence of new products and services (Kozak, 2014). Knowledge needed for the innovative processes is shared with many actors and flows across sectors, and, as shown in this chapter, not the least upstream to and from suppliers.

In *Innovation and Entrepreneurship*, Peter Drucker (1985) elaborates on the various sources of innovation. Drucker finds that during an innovation process, actors search consistently and purposefully and are organized for changes in the surrounding environment. Innovations exploit changes. His approach and examples demonstrate the existence of a range of external factors that may promote an innovative activity, and which open new profitable niches.

☐ **The unexpected:** For example, a success or a failure that can be enhanced. The first Icehotel in Sweden was based on the unexpectedly positive feedback of guests who happened to spend a night in an igloo, which was – reluctantly – provided for them.

☐ **Incongruence:** Misunderstandings about the customers' needs and preferences. For example, tour operators believed that travelers invariably want extensive service packages, luxury and relaxation. That made room for contrasts to luxury: 'back to basics' and 'rough adventure trips'.

☐ **Process need:** Sometimes it becomes necessary to break routines and invent new modes of operation. For example, congestion on roads and in festivals has led to electronic traffic control and crowd management systems, and (potentially) the saving of energy, as well as higher customer satisfaction.

☐ **Industry and market structure:** Refocused political agendas lead to changes in industry and market structures. Future climate agendas will continually influence the operations of fuel-intensive airlines and cruise ships and challenge the business models in these and other subsectors of tourism.

☐ **Demographics:** It is recognized that demographic changes affect the nature of tourism. For example, an increase in the average age of tourists shifts the demand patterns. But demographics that are important for sustainability issues also include changes in education, employment status, income distribution etc.

☐ **Changes in perceptions:** Changing consumer perceptions require industries to adapt. Tourists are influenced by public and peer opinion in terms of what tourism destinations are worthwhile to visit. For example, the perception of destinations such as Bangladesh and the Arctic/Antarctic are shifting from 'no-go' places towards an image as destinations to visit as a last chance before they sink into the sea.

☐ **New knowledge:** Technical and scientific knowledge is often regarded as a prime source of innovation, and indeed is essential in many respects. Achievements from hardcore scientific research will, however, often only indirectly affect tourism, as they will be embedded in supplies and machinery.

A concise understanding of what drives the development of tourism will have to take into account not one of these factors, but all of them. Drucker's point is that existing and well-established firms will only reluctantly observe new developments, and that opens up opportunities for new entrepreneurs in the field. As observed by Ateljevic and Doorne (2000) and Komppula (2014), entrepreneurs play a key role in the renewal of the sustainable tourism product as they bring in inspiration and knowledge from other categories of economic activity.

Driving forces – a systematic overview

Classic academic authors such as Rogers (1995) and Rosenberg (1976) emphasize R&D as drivers for innovation. They include the firm's own R&D as well as R&D mediated through universities and public research units. Increasingly, research in innovation takes other driving forces into account. Ideas and inspiration for innovation are fostered in diverse ways, and studies progressively recognize that many firms are innovative even though they do not invest in formal R&D. It is helpful to distinguish between the following driving forces:

- ☐ **Technology** in tourism which is the result of technical progress, e.g. new types of sustainable guiding practices due to digitalization (Gössling, 2017).

- ☐ **Research**: Innovations that would not have been possible without integration with academic research efforts. An example is Ecocean, which combines whale-shark habitat and migration research with tourism experiences (Hughes, 2008).

- ☐ **Price:** Tourism businesses are often cost-constrained, and innovations are occurring to maintain acceptable yields under aggressive competition. It is an ongoing discussion whether customers are willing to pay a price premium for sustainable products (Hultman et al., 2015).

- ☐ **Employees**: Innovation frequently depends on the knowledge and creativity of the staff, particularly under circumstances where they are encouraged through appropriate management systems and incentives (Zarim et al., 2017).

- ☐ **Users:** Some niche tourists are 'lead users' in the sense that they are months or years ahead of what will eventually become products in high demand (Sigala, 2014). Learning from these users is becoming a method that is applicable in sustainable tourism, for example in the formats of focus groups, observations, anthropological experimentation etc.

- ☐ **Legislation**: Regulation is often considered negative for business development. However, regulation and taxing can urge the industry to look for new modes of organization and operation, for example in terms of radical energy savings. Authors in Hall et al. (2015) discuss the case of an environmentally critical sector, namely aviation and the handling by national and transnational governance bodies of issues as for example taxes on fuel.

☐ **Suppliers:** Tourism firms are directly or indirectly dependent on a broad range of services and sectors: information technology, food services, mechanics, building materials etc. Some suppliers are advanced innovators. When tourism firms are purchasing a product or a service, the innovation is embedded therein (Hjalager, 2015). In this understanding, the acquisition of a product/service represents a shortcut to innovations for the tourism firm.

All seven driving forces deserve separate analytical attention. Quite overwhelmingly, the tourism debate focuses on the market-related driving forces for innovations – what do the customers want and what are their attitudes? In this chapter only the last-mentioned – supplier-driven innovation – will be unfolded and discussed. There is a need to bring suppliers out of anonymity in order to use their full capacity in the drive for a more sustainable tourism. A higher level of transparency throughout the value chain is essential.

Suppliers' roles in sustainable tourism: a brief review

It is a commonplace in the literature that a tourism experience is a collection of many components delivered by a variety of providers, and consumed in a continuous process (Song et al., 2013). There is less research attention paid to those suppliers who have an earlier position in the value chain, i.e. those who deliver goods or services to core tourism firms (transportation, accommodation, catering and attractions). Following a review of value chains in tourism, Zhang et al. (2009) identify some examples of studies of value chains in tourism and emphasize that the strategic role of suppliers and the collaboration between tourism firms and suppliers is an upcoming research theme. The discipline of Supply Chain Management (SCM), which is well known in other sectors of the economy, is gradually receiving more attention in the case of tourism (Song, 2012). The financial and operational benefits of a distinctive supply chain management endeavor remain to be addressed in most categories of tourism firms.

The potential of collaboration with suppliers for innovative product and process developments has also received considerable attention in the general business literature and research. In manufacturing, for example, firms are often dependent on suppliers who feel a responsibility not only to deliver required qualities, but also to be visionary on behalf of their customers and their customers' customers. Such upstream suppliers may be the origin of an innovative 'push' and contribute with knowledge that leads to a comprehensive competitive capability for both suppliers and buyers (Arlbjørn et al., 2010).

Weidenfeldt et al. (2010) suggest that tourism firms lack awareness of the possibilities of learning from suppliers. Orfila-Sintes et al. (2005) observe that when hotels purchase technical equipment, only 6% develop equipment jointly with their supplier, while nearly 80% just buy and install equipment. Radical innovations are mostly seen in connection with ICT investments. Environmental quality management is found to be affected very modestly in an innovative direction by suppliers (Orfila-Sintes et al., 2005).

Some research addresses specifically the sustainability issues of supply chains. Quite uniformly, however, they accentuate the 'trend to use purchasing policies and practices to facilitate sustainable development at the tourist destination' (Font et al., 2008: 260). Sigala (2008) investigates the influence of tour operators on suppliers, the rationale being that tour operators' contribution to sustainable tourism will be more effective, as they are able to set (new and enhanced) standards for the suppliers. Tour operators are concerned with the sustainability performance of hotels, transportation companies, local guides and attractions, while stepping back in the value chain to suppliers is less common.

It is interesting to observe that suppliers are mainly seen as passive providers who must comply with standards set by the buyers in the tourism industry (Zhang et al., 2009). That is hardly the full picture, as suggested by Font et al. (2016) who point to underlying interrelationships which are far more complex. To understand how suppliers in tourism can act as driving forces for innovation, it is essential to address the form that these interrelationships may take.

A model of suppliers' roles and capacities in sustainable tourism

The following model (first introduced by Hjalager, 2010b) is applied in order to spell out the complexities of the interrelationships between tourism firms and their suppliers. The model attempts to stimulate a deeper understanding of why and how relationships between tourism firms and their suppliers emerge, and to recognize the rationale of the density and frequency of interaction. The model follows alleys of conceptual issues of the supply chain strategy discipline, which focuses for example on not operational and economic logics, relationship building, interpersonal trust etc. (Simchi-Levi et al.,1999). The horizontal axis in this model (Figure 11.1) is developed to ensure critical features for tourism and describes a continuum of interaction distance between suppliers and tourism actors – from a greater distance (culturally, geographically and in terms of communication) on the left side, where cooperation is in rigid format to a closer collaboration on the right side, where relationships are more fluid. The vertical axis demonstrates the nature of suppliers' business strategy – from the lower situation where suppliers are only passively responding to the demands from tourism firms to the situation at the top of the figure where they aim at affecting the behavior of tourism firms, and interact in the total value chain.

The four fields in Figure 11.1 represent different supplier-driven innovation situations: the passive suppliers, the proactive suppliers, the co-branding suppliers and the co-creating suppliers. The following section examines these four fields with examples from sustainable tourism.

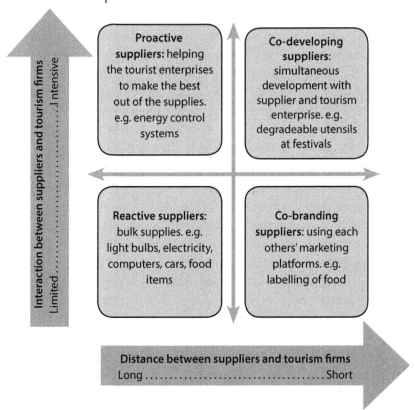

Figure 11.1: Model of suppliers' roles in sustainable tourism development

The reactive suppliers

By definition, reactive suppliers distribute products and services to the tourism sector with a minimum of formal or informal collaboration and without significant attempts to adapt to the particular needs of purchasing firms in (sustainable) tourism. To judge from the literature on purchasing practices in tourism, the majority of supplies seem to be repetitive standard purchases, where the price is a decisive determining factor (Jayawardena et al., 2013; Becken, 2013).

Much supply to tourism consists of indistinguishable bulk products that are shipped off to a broad variety of consumers, for example electricity and food supplies. Several categories of products are highly standardized, for example light bulbs, paper, gardening equipment, cars etc. For producers of such supplies, tourism is one of many customer groups, and there is limited capacity or motivation to differentiate products or marketing methods in order to reach tourism in special ways or to adapt to individual needs of tourism firms. As noted in Warren & Becken (2017), purchasing and management traditions, which have been built over long periods of time, may be complicated to revolutionize.

Manufacturers of machinery, information and communication technology (ICT), and food are, on average, found to be in closer contact with the needs of their customers than, for example, transport companies, sellers of materials and wholesale companies (Pulles et al., 2014). Tourism firms do not often hold strong links to their primary producers in agriculture and manufacturing, but find it more feasible to purchase through intermediaries, such as wholesalers and retailers. This stifles communication is as it has to go through filtering layers. If individual tourism firms have comments and suggestions that could lead to improvements and adaptations by the manufacturer, such communications are unlikely to reach the producer at all.

As previously mentioned, the sustainable tourism literature has focused on setting environmental standards as part of a sustainable business strategy. The standards are translated into requirements throughout the supply chain. Processes towards consistent strategies and sustainability programs include the gathering of information about and monitoring, via the internet, of suppliers' environmental compliance status. E-trade platforms often allow an efficient comparison of standardized products' environmental performances. Further, tourism firms may influence their suppliers through systematic supplier meetings and workshops, and offer suppliers' staff training in the tourism firms' standards. These strategies can assist the supplier to better respond to the tourism firms' environmental requests (Sigala, 2008). Tourism firms with significant purchasing power have better opportunities to influence suppliers in a backward supplier chain.

The proactive suppliers

Proactive suppliers have an opposite profile to reactive suppliers, mainly because they deliver other categories of products and services. When a tourism firm, such as a large hotel or attraction, purchases a new heating or air-conditioning system, it is likely to engage in dialogue with the provider of the equipment in order to ensure an adaptation to the firm's particular needs. The supplier may then be in a position to affect the choice of solutions, for example by promoting systems with higher energy-saving potential. Construction work is also in this category, where design measures include a broad variety of issues that can be adapted to the tourism firm. Suppliers will then be in a position to provide relevant advice.

An expanding number of suppliers are offering packaged solutions of equipment that simultaneously give promises of CO_2 reductions and cost savings. As suggested by Wang et al. (2014), suppliers are a key influencer with the ability to argue for combined cost and resource efficiency that initiate efficient supplier-driven influences on tourism firms.

Suppliers' creativity has increased over recent years, and there are quite a number of sustainability compliant offers available. Examples range from thinner towels that will help save water and washing detergent, use to the insistence on the use of degradable or recyclable materials in stationary. Not surprisingly, we also see a variety of waste and wastewater handling systems and bio-fuel provisions for heating purposes, which can economize with resources in tourism enterprises. The upcycling wave has hit the tourism sector, and a consistent design effort tends to ensure that the use of scrap building materials, for example in constructions and furnishing, will not compromise an image of luxury, rather contrarily, as shown by Adebayo & Iweka (2014), who underline that upcycling is becoming a fashionable trend. From "waste to value" is a slogan for producers of, for example, mattresses, wall decoration, and furniture, and the ideas transform well into the products that declared eco-lodges want to present for their guests (Sempels & Hoffmann, 2013). Consulting firms offer environmental audits and staff training. Green advisory programs, many with public support, have emerged in numerous countries, ensuring stronger transparency of the market for sustainable supplies (OECD, 2012).

Trade fairs and exhibitions are intermediary events and locations where suppliers can indirectly affect innovations in tourism. Judging from exhibitor lists, the suppliers with distinct sustainability profiles continue to show strongly at traditional hospitality fairs.

Proactive suppliers are most likely to be successful if there is a direct interface and, possibly, also a personal contact. That is most evidently the case in non-standard, incidental and non-routine purchases. If a tourism firm has a distinct environmental agenda and if it is known to be actively in search of innovative supplies, there is scope for suppliers to come up with solutions. Interaction of a proactive nature has been found to lead to improved financial performance in the restaurant sector (Kim, 2006; Iraldo et al., 2017), and this is a strong argument for tourism firms to become more involved with their suppliers.

In recent years, the gastronomy field has become an important driver in sustainable tourism (Richards, 2015). Suppliers are essential in achieving local employment, low waste, few food miles etc. However, an integrated image of a sustainable tourism destination requires proactivity among small scale producers and a stronger practice of not only purchase, but also collaboration for mutual innovation outcomes. Font et al. (2008) stress that while small local food producers have the potential to operate as both reactive and proactive suppliers, working with them requires constant supervision and commitment from purchasing tourism firms. Crucial in this context, suppliers must address key operational issues such as lead times, delivery reliability and costs, which are often given a higher priority than sustainable ingredients or production methods in the restaurant sector (Gössling & Hall, 2013).

Co-branding suppliers

The third field in the model suggests a closer collaboration between suppliers and tourism firms, but based on well-recognized and accepted products and services. Co-branding is when two companies form an alliance to work together, thereby creating a marketing synergy. In this situation, a tourism firm will enhance its image by using respected and, preferably, already well-branded products, while the supplier can achieve an extra marketing platform for its products. Most simply, hotels or restaurants may add environmentally labeled food items on the menu, and tourists can also find the same products in the hotel shop to bring back as souvenirs. Co-branding can also take place on the websites of firms, sometimes even including e-shopping opportunities, as illustrated by Hjalager and Konu (2011) in the case of cosmeceutical products and spa destinations.

Co-branding initiatives may be wider in scope and 'sponge' image elements from more general reputations of a nation or a region. Scandinavian hotels and conference centers, for example, are often consciously furnished with trendy designer items. In this sense, they are 'showrooms' vis-a-vis a large audience of visitors. Sometimes there are explicit alliances between hotels and the producers of the furniture to promote an image of Scandinavian design.

The brand equity literature elaborates on the many dimensions of effective co-branding. Aaker (1996) demonstrates that companies in collaboration must have a deep understanding of their customers' motivations in order to create and enhance loyalty for more products in a co-branding group. Furthermore, the quality levels must be comparable, and the product character stable and untouchable, as compromising will harm collaborating partners. In cases of successful co-branding, mutual respect and trust have been built over time. Suppliers are likely to be more willing to launch into risky partnerships if they have the prospect of lasting contracts that guarantee a return on their innovation and other investment.

In tourism, much co-branding is embedded in destination management initiatives, where the main activity is joint marketing. We also see co-branding as part of, for example, an airline's loyalty program where miles can be spent on hotels, rental cars, and many other services, most of which enjoy beneficial exposure in inflight magazines. Ranasinghe et al. (2017) analyze how Ceylon tea forms the core of strong relationship marketing and branding, which also includes and affects the tea grower communities with rural tourism opportunities. When exhibited on the supermarket shelves all over the globe, there is a supplementary opportunity to ensure the attention on Sri Lanka as a tourism destination. Sports and popular music events are prominent examples of the opportunities of branding alliances with suppliers of for example beverages, sports equipment, electronic gadgets etc. With busy social media behavior at such events, the alliances may provide further marketing benefits for partners, such as found in festivals (Hjalager & Kwiatkowski, 2018). In branding collaborations, sustainability features tend to be weak, if existent at all, due to the fact that most brands are large and international and feature no sustainability issues, with CocaCola as a powerful example. That demonstrates the struggle for suppliers of sustainable products and services to obtain a place on the most influential tourism providers' marketing platforms.

Co-branding in the sustainable tourism sector is still quite limited, but tends to be emerging as both tourism firms and their suppliers see the wider perspectives of achieving an image as climate conscious and ethical players on the market. Examples are seen in terms of 'fair' tourism in developing countries and economically challenged regions, which may mean, for example, that food comes from the local area rather than being flown in (Mangi & Urassa, 2017), and that furniture is local and authentic. Slow food alliances are supporting the notion of alliances and relationships of the totality of the foodways (Marletto et al., 2016). Fair trade and fair tourism are increasingly intermingling, and branding alliances can be one of the ways to break the strong co-marketing dominance of international airlines, hotels and similar tourism corporations.

Co-developing suppliers

Co-development represents the most integrated manner for supplier-driven innovation in the tourism sector. According to our definition, a supplier will collaborate with one or more tourism firms to develop new products specifically for those tourism firms. The argument behind co-development is that value is generated by a firm and its customer, rather than being created entirely by a closed organization An open process leads to cross-fertilization of knowledge. It opens extra dimensions of reflexivity. During co-development, the intention for the supplier is to gain new ideas and insights, which may eventually lead to new products for a wider market (Batran et al., 2017; Möller & Törröne, 2003). Accordingly, tourism firms and suppliers are partners in an innovation process, and as 'lead users' (von Hippel, 2005) progressive tourism firms are responsive test opportunities for new supplies with higher quality and better specifications in terms of environmental sustainability. Cooperative relationships are typically present in enduring alliances, where trust has been built, and where both sides in the relationship have a readiness to adapt to ensure a satisfactory aggregate performance. The objective is to ensure a marketable product in the hands of the supplier. However, this objective should not overshadow the need to create solutions that fit the immediate needs and objectives of the tourism firm, both as a 'first-mover' in a new field and in a longer perspective. Co-developing partnerships are risky, as the outcomes may be unpredictable, as collaborative relationships can fail, and as money can run out. A continual mitigation of the risk, the related costs and benefits must be part of the process. The obvious asymmetries must not be forgotten as a hampering factor – some actors in collaboration may be more influential than others. Suppliers and tourism firms must be at about the same level in terms of values and organizational culture and possibly in much the same financial league to proceed quickly, to achieve the agreed outcomes.

A practical example of the difficulties is provided by Murphy and Smith (2009). In a study of the relationship between upscale restaurants and suppliers, they found that some suppliers lacked the ability to be alert and proactive, while others during a period of collaboration began to see themselves in new and more active roles of alliances with groups in the high-end market. Thus, suppliers developed their businesses simultaneously with restaurants towards a higher degree of authenticity.

Sustainable tourism strategies in the developing world often include the establishment of durable partnerships with local producers as part of building a development capacity and to ensure induced employment impacts. The experience in both the developed and the developing world is that non-governmental organizations (NGOs) take a leadership role to release any innovative abilities of local actors (Liburd et al., 2017), and to stimulate entrepreneurial aptitude into directions complying with general sustainability measures. The development of a comprehensive biking destination with many stakeholders on Funen, Denmark, includes collaboration with a producer of a 'signature bike'.

Co-creation in tourism is often connected with events, festivals, sports, games etc. Here, boundaries between the various actors from production to consumption in the value chain tend to be rather fluid, a feature that facilitates innovation. In these situations, leadership roles are also momentarily made flexible, which is an invitation to creativity and non-standard employee behavior. Finally, events provide excellent opportunities to create media attention and exposure, which can benefit producers of novel products and services. This was the case when the Lillehammer Winter Games were launched as the first Green Games in 1994. One innovative practice in Lillehammer was that disposable plates and utensils were made of potato-based starch, allowing them to be recycled and used as animal feed and compost.

Increasingly, the annual Climate Change Conferences are regarded as excellent opportunities by suppliers to become a distinct part of a tourist experience, which also attracts considerable media interest. Every year, side events are flourishing, and suppliers show their creativity, often in close collaboration with the tourism firms that host delegates and media. A competitive race between zero-pollution electrical motorcycles was organized for the experience of a soundless event and to demonstrate new technology in Copenhagen. Similarly, the Doha event made food security in dry areas a topic of unmistakable real-life demonstration. These and many other examples reveal that climate activism and business progress are not incompatible.

The annual Roskilde Festival in Denmark makes a special effort to invite into the festival program young entrepreneurs, who, for example, offer new forms of environmental control, waste management etc. Meeting a large festival audience can provide entrepreneurs with relevant feedback. The festival achieves early access to new technologies/products/services, and the audience witnesses new services that could enhance the festival experience and/or quality (Haugbølle & Forman, 2014).

Future challenges and issues

This chapter focused on the functions of suppliers in sustainable tourism. It investigated the early and upstream steps in the sometimes long and often complex tourism supply chain. It must be concluded that the many suppliers to tourism firms of products, concepts and services represent considerable innovative capacity. The inclusion of the suppliers into the full picture of what makes tourism sustainable is still weak, and their position as proactive agents on the wider sustainable tourism agenda is lagging behind.

In order to achieve comprehensive joint innovations, it is necessary to develop a new and more balanced mode of sustainable supply chain management for tourism. Sigala (2008) argues that beneficial management processes include:

☐ Better information sharing, including early warnings of problems that need to be solved, specifications of requirements etc. Information sharing also includes performance parameters for new supplies. External certification bodies have an important complementary role in ensuring reliability in information flows.

☐ Decision synchronization which comes out of closer collaboration where both the suppliers and the purchaser are able to schedule and plan their strategies. It is important for actors to meet at various events and in an ambiance of honesty and mutuality.

☐ Incentive alignment, where the risk and the benefits of innovation processes are properly balanced. New business models have to be created.

Additionally, leadership is required. It could be either the tourism enterprise or the supplier, depending on the nature of collaboration or sustainable development aspirations.

There is a need for more efficient intermediaries and 'translators'. Research points towards a requirement for institutional measures to improve the links between tourism firms that foster partnerships throughout the value chain at a destination or in a wider context. Destination Management Organizations (DMOs) sometimes line up to undertake this task by introducing cluster models to regional collaboration (Gursoy et al., 2015; Pechlaner et al., 2009). However, DMOs need to serve all tourism firms and organizations in an area. Consequently, sustainability objectives are often given a lower priority.

There is also a challenge for those tourism firms who are already in the forefront of sustainable management. They have the potential to enhance their functions as role models for others in terms of collaborating in new ways and more extensively with suppliers. Sigala (2008; 2014) accentuates the responsibility of tour operators as powerful initiators, but when examining their codes of conduct it becomes clear that they typically do not exercise their purchasing power throughout the supply chain, and their certification procedures tend to be rather superficial. A good example of this is the tour operator TUI, which has established a foundation that supports and stimulates innovative practices in the supply chains. Another example is the French resort Village Nature, part of the Center Parcs group, with a 'deep green' procurement practice. Saarinen and Rogerson (2014) explain how a supplying strategy which involves collaboration with locals enhances the positive reputation and can catalyze the local bonds, but also align with international agendas, such as the UN Millennium development and environmental goals with potentially more wide-ranging effects.

Many festivals and events are publicly supported. Public funds can be regarded as more than just a way to help to create tourism activity and help organizers; they can be mechanisms to stimulate innovations in the value chain and in experience economy clusters. Eco-certification of festivals may have self-augmenting effects, a target objective of many initiatives and agencies (Zeppel & Beaumont, 2011).

Supplier relations and sustainable supply chain management are not quick fix solutions to innovation in sustainable tourism. There is still a lack of genuine, research-based observation and interpretation of 'supplier power' compared to other driving forces in innovation. Motivational aspects and institutional structures require closer inspection. There is a lack of attention on both sides – the supplier and the tourism firm – which is a key barrier for integrated sustainability measures and innovations. However, there are also structural barriers, as many suppliers may regard the many small tourism firms as less attractive customers and partners as they lack a qualified supply chain management capacity. After many years of debate about sustainable tourism, tourism firms are frequently only in their initial phases of environmental management, and comprehensive strategic approaches still appear to be glaringly infrequent (Gössling, 2017).

Some alliances between suppliers and tourism firms may be innovative in controversial ways. 'Greenwashing' – when firms disingenuously spin their products and policies as environmentally friendly – is sometimes carried out instead of action with deeper impacts (Holden, 2016). Suppliers might help tourism enterprises to give the impression of being green and environmentally conscious. The ethical dimensions of sustainable tourism development remain to be comprehensively addressed, even when professional segments of suppliers are invited into innovation strategies.

Moving towards sustainability is a complex political and practical mission, which is at risk of being compromised at any time and during many stages. On behalf of the UN Environment program, Simpson et al. (2008) work systematically through a large of number of mitigation tools for industries and destinations. They claim that reducing, eliminating and substituting emissions that threaten the climate and the environment are a key responsibility to address. In this perspective, suppliers to the tourism sector are indispensable allies for tourism leaders who want to commit themselves to work towards the sustainable development of tourism.

References

Aaker, D.A. (1996). *Building Strong Brands,* New York: Free Press.

Adebayo, A. K. & Iweka, A. C. (2014). Optimizing the sustainability of tourism infrastructure in Nigeria through design for deconstruction framework. *American Journal of Tourism Management,* **3**(1A), 13-19.

Arlbjørn, J. S., de Haas, H., Mikkelsen, O.S. & Zachariassen, F. (2010). *Supply Chain Management.* Aarhus: Academica.

Ateljevic, I. & Doorne, S. (2000). 'Staying within the fence": lifestyle entrepreneurship in tourism, *Journal of Sustainable Tourism,* **8** (5), 378-392.

Batran, A., Erben, A., Schulz, R. & Sperl, F. (2017). *Procurement 4.0: A survival guide in a digital, disruptive world.* Frankfurt: Campus Verlag.

Becken, S. (2013). *Operators' perceptions of energy use and actual saving opportunities for Danish firms.* Danish Centre for Studies in Research and Research Policy, University of Aarhus. http://www.cfa.au.dk/fileadmin/site_files/filer_forskningsanalyse/dokumenter/Diverse/Innovation_indicators_Ignored.pdf

Camisón, C. & Monfort-Mir, V. M. (2012). Measuring innovation in tourism from the Schumpeterian and the dynamic-capabilities perspectives. *Tourism Management*, **33**(4), 776-789.

Drucker, P. (1985) *Innovation and Entrepreneurship: Practice and Principles*, London: Heinemann.

Font, X., Tapper, R., Schwartz, K. & Kornilaki, M. (2008). Sustainable supply management in tourism, *Business Strategy and the Environment*, **17**, 260-271.

Font, X., Garay, L. & Jones, S. (2016). Sustainability motivations and practices in small tourism enterprises in European protected areas. *Journal of Cleaner Production*, **137**, 1439-1448.

Gössling, S. (2017). Tourism, information technologies and sustainability: An exploratory review. *Journal of Sustainable Tourism*, **25**(7), 1024-1041.

Gössling, S. & Hall, C. M. (2013). Sustainable culinary systems. In Gössling, S. & Hall, C.M. (eds). *Sustainable Culinary Systems: Local foods, innovation, tourism and hospitality*, Abingdon: Routledge, 3-44.

Gursoy, D., Saayman, M. & Sotiriadis, M. (Eds.). (2015). *Collaboration in Tourism Businesses and Destinations: A handbook*. Bingley: Emerald Group Publishing.

Hall, C. M., Gossling, S. & Scott, D. (Eds.). (2015). *The Routledge Handbook of Tourism and Sustainability*. Abingdon: Routledge.

Hall, C. M. & Williams, A.M. (2008). *Tourism and Innovation*, London: Routledge.

Hanna, P., Font, X., Scarles, C., Weeden, C. & Harrison, C. (2017). Tourist destination marketing: from sustainability myopia to memorable experiences. *Journal of Destination Marketing & Management*. (Available ahead-of-print).

Haugbølle, K. & Forman, M. (2014). Festivals as laboratories: Developing new temporary housing. In *World SB14 Barcelona* (pp. 1-8).

Hjalager, A. M. (2015). 100 innovations that transformed tourism. *Journal of Travel Research*, **54**(1), 3-21.

Hjalager, A.-M. (2010a). A review of the innovation research in tourism, *Tourism Management*, **31** (1), 1-12.

Hjalager, A-M. (2010b). Supplier-driven innovations for sustainable tourism. In Liburd, J. & Edwards, D. (eds). *Understanding the Sustainable Development of Tourism*, Oxford: Goodfellows. 148-162.

Hjalager, A. M. & Konu, H. (2011). Co-branding and co-creation in wellness tourism: the role of cosmeceuticals. *Journal of Hospitality Marketing & Management*, **20**(8), 879-901.

Hjalager, A. M. & Kwiatkowski, G. (2018). Entrepreneurial implications, prospects and dilemmas in rural festivals. *Journal of Rural Studies*. (Available ahead-of-print)

Holden, A. (2016). *Environment and Tourism*. Routledge.

Hughes, M. (2008). Ecocean, Western Australia, in Carlsen, J., Liburd, J., Edwards, D. & Forde, P. (eds), *Innovation for Sustainable Tourism*, International Case Studies BEST Education Network.

Hultman, M., Kazeminia, A. & Ghasemi, V. (2015). Intention to visit and willingness to pay premium for ecotourism: The impact of attitude, materialism, and motivation. *Journal of Business Research*, **68**(9), 1854-1861.

Iraldo, F., Testa, F., Lanzini, P. & Battaglia, M. (2017). Greening competitiveness for hotels and restaurants. *Journal of Small Business and Enterprise Development*, **24**(3), 607-628.

Jacob, M. & Groizard, J.L. (2007). Technology transfer and multinationals: the case of Balearic hotel chains' investments in two developing economies, *Tourism Management*, **28**(4), 976-992.

Jayawardena, C., Pollard, A., Chort, V., Choi, C. & Kibicho, W. (2013). Trends and sustainability in the Canadian tourism and hospitality industry. *Worldwide Hospitality and Tourism Themes*, **5**(2), 132-150.

Jia, F. & Wahnschafft, R. (2015). Eco-certification and labeling programmes of hotels in China. In Reddy, M.V. & Wilkes, K. (eds). *Tourism in the Green Economy*, Abingdon: Routledge. 176-191.

Kim, B.-Y. (2006). The impact of supplier development on financial performance in the restaurant industry, *International Journal of Hospitality and Tourism Administration*, **7**(4), 81-103.

Komppula, R. (2014). The role of individual entrepreneurs in the development of competitiveness for a rural tourism destination - A case study. *Tourism Management*, **40**, 361-371.

Kozak, M. W. (2014). Innovation, tourism and destination development: Dolnośląskie case study. *European Planning Studies*, **22**(8), 1604-1624.

Liburd, J. , Nielsen, T. K. & Heape, C. (2017). Co-designing smart tourism. *European Journal of Tourism Research*, **17**, 28-42.

McLeod, M. & Vaughan, R. (Eds.). (2014). *Knowledge Networks and Tourism*. Abingdon: Routledge.

Mangi, H. O., & Urassa, J. K. (2017). Local versus imported food: opportunities and constraints for Tanzanian hotels. *Journal of Gastronomy and Tourism*, **2**(4), 247-258.

Marletto, G., Franceschini, S., Ortolani, C. & Sillig, C. (2016). Towards sustainable food: a contested transition. In Marletto, G., Franceschini, S., Ortolani, C. & Sillig, C. (eds). *Mapping Sustainability Transitions* (pp. 23-38). Springer.

Martínez-Román, J. A., Tamayo, J. A., Gamero, J. & Romero, J. E. (2015). Innovativeness and business performances in tourism SMEs. *Annals of Tourism Research*, **54**, 118-135.

Möller, K.E. & Törrönen, P. (2003). Business suppliers' value creation potential: a capacity-based analysis, *Industrial Marketing Management*, **32** (2), 109-118.

Murphy, J. & Smith, S. (2009). Chefs and suppliers: an exploratory look at supply chain issues in an upscale restaurant alliance, *International Journal of Hospitality Management*, **28** (2), 212-220.

OECD (2013). *Green Innovation in Tourism Services*. Paris: OECD.

Orfila-Sintes, F., Crespi-Cladera & Martinez-Ros, E. (2005). Innovation activity in the hotel industry: Evidence from Balearic hotels, *Tourism Management*, **26** (6), 851-865.

Pechlaner, H., Raich, F. & Fisher, E. (2009). The role of tourism organizations in location management: the case of beer tourism in Bavaria, *Turis Review*, **64** (2), 28-40.

Pikkemaat, B., Pikkemaat, B., Zehrer, A. & Zehrer, A. (2016). Innovation and service experiences in small tourism family firms. *International Journal of Culture, Tourism and Hospitality Research*, **10**(4), 343-360.

Pulles, N. J., Veldman, J. & Schiele, H. (2014). Identifying innovative suppliers in business networks: An empirical study. *Industrial Marketing Management*, **43**(3), 409-418.

Richards, G. (2015). Evolving gastronomic experiences: From food to foodies to foodscapes. *Journal of Gastronomy and Tourism*, **1**(1), 5-17.

Ranasinghe, W. T., Ranasinghe, W. T., Thaichon, P., Thaichon, P., Ranasinghe, M. & Ranasinghe, M. (2017). An analysis of product-place co-branding: the case of Ceylon Tea. *Asia Pacific Journal of Marketing and Logistics*, **29**(1), 200-214.

Rogers, E.M., (1995). *Diffusion of Innovations,* New York: Free Press.

Rosenberg, N. (1976). *Perspectives on Technology,* Cambridge: Cambridge University Press.

Saarinen, J. & Rogerson, C. M. (2014). Tourism and the millennium development goals: perspectives beyond 2015. *Tourism Geographies*, **16**(1), 23-30.

Schumpeter, J.A. (1934). *The Theory of Economic Development: An Inquiry into Profits, Capital, Credit, Interest and the Business Cycle,* Cambridge, Mass: Harvard University Press.

Sempels, C. & Hoffmann, J. (2013). Circular economy: transforming a 'waste' into a productive resource. In Sempels, C., & Hoffmann, J. (eds). *Sustainable Innovation Strategy* (pp. 103-138). Palgrave Macmillan.

Sigala, M. (2008). A supply chain management approach for investigating the role of tour operators on sustainable tourism: the case of TUI, *Journal of Cleaner Production*, **16**, 1589-1599.

Sigala, M. (2014). Customer involvement in sustainable supply chain management: A research framework and implications in tourism. *Cornell Hospitality Quarterly*, **55**(1), 76-88.

Simchi-Levi, D., Simchi-Levi, E. & Kaminsky, P. (1999). *Designing and Managing the Supply Chain: Concepts, strategies, and cases*. New York: McGraw-Hill.

Simpson, M.C., Gössling, S., Scott, D., Hall, C.M. & Gladin, E. (2008) *Climate Change Adaptation and Mitigation in the Tourism Sector: Frameworks, Tools and Practices*, Oxford: UNEP, University of Oxford.

Song, H. (2012). *Tourism Supply Chain Management*. Abingdon: Routledge.

Song, H., Liu, J. & Chen, G. (2013). Tourism value chain governance: Review and prospects. *Journal of Travel Research*, **52**(1), 15-28.

Sundbo, J., Sørensen, F. & Fuglsang, L. (2013). 12. Innovation in the experience sector. *Handbook on the Experience Economy*, **228**.

von Hippel, E. (2005). *Democratizing Innovation.* Boston: Massachusetts Institute of Technology.

Wang, Y. F., Chen, S. P., Lee, Y. C. & Tsai, C. T. S. (2013). Developing green management standards for restaurants: An application of green supply chain management. *International Journal of Hospitality Management*, **34**, 263-273.

Warren, C. & Becken, S. (2017). Saving energy and water in tourist accommodation: A systematic literature review (1987–2015). *International Journal of Tourism Research*, **19**(3), 289-303.

Weidenfeld, A., Williams, A. M. & Butler, R. W. (2010). Knowledge transfer and innovation among attractions. *Annals of Tourism Research*, **37**(3), 604-626.

Zarim, Z. A., Mohamad, O., Rahman, M. S., Zaki, H. O., Sergio, R. P. & Haladay, D. J. (2017). The role of organisational commitment, leadership style, strategic human resources practices and job satisfaction towards sustainable tourism industry. In Benlamri, R. & Sparer, M. (eds). *Leadership, Innovation and Entrepreneurship as Driving Forces of the Global Economy* (pp. 255-268). Springer.

Zeppel, H. & Beaumont, N. (2011). *Green Tourism Futures: Climate change responses by Australian government tourism agencies*. University of Southern Queensland.

Zhang, X., Song, H. & Huang, G.Q. (2009). Tourism supply chain management: a new research agenda, *Tourism Management*, **30**, 345-358.

12 A Case Study in Collaborative Supplier Partnerships

Carmel Foley, Deborah Edwards and Bronwen Harrison

Introduction

Globally there are hundreds of convention centres, which host more than 24,000 different association meetings each year (International Congress and Convention Association, 2016). Unlike the hotel sector (Bohdanowicz-Godfrey, 2013) and tourism operations sector (Carlsen & Edwards, 2013a) which have documented "practices towards more sustainable modes of operation" (Carlsen & Edwards, 2013a: 33), little has been documented in the research literature about the collaborative potentials of a convention centre to deliver benefits beyond tourist visitation (Edwards et al., 2014; Mair & Jago, 2010).

This case study makes a contribution to this research gap by examining a convention centre, International Convention Centre Sydney (ICC Sydney), with significant purchasing power to work with and influence suppliers in a backward supply chain. ICC Sydney's Feeding Your Performance (FYP) initiative encourages environmentally sustainable behaviour as part of its organisational practices and supports and collaborates with a range of suppliers who are working to improve the agricultural ecosystems in their farming areas. *Ecosystem* is defined as "the minimum aggregated set of processes (including biochemical, biophysical and biological ones) that ensure the biological productivity, organisational integrity and perpetuation of the ecosystem" (Swift et al., 2004:115).

ICC Sydney is the largest integrated convention, exhibition and entertainment venue in Australia. It is situated in Sydney, New South Wales, Australia in the active leisure precinct of Darling Harbour, and is flanked by the Sydney Central Business District and a university precinct. Opened for business in December 2016, it employs 1,300 staff (300 full time and 1,000 casuals) and replaces the previous structure of the Sydney Convention & Exhibition Centre.

The United Nations' 70th General Assembly designated 2017 as the International Year of Sustainable Tourism for Development (UNWTO, 2015). The goals include making tourism a catalyst for positive change by promoting socially inclusive and sustainable economic growth including employment as well as resource efficiency and environmental protection (UNWTO, 2017). Through collaborative partnerships with New South Wales (NSW) suppliers ICC Sydney is making a contribution to these goals in four key areas: environmental sustainability, knowledge sharing, economic development, and social contributions. The case study will show how these contributions provide benefits for multiple stakeholders (Figure 12.1) and highlights the role of collaborative partnerships in enhancing firms' sustainable practices.

Environmental practices are concerned with reducing negative human impact and supporting healthy ecosystems necessary for the survival of humans and other organisms (Liburd & Edwards, 2010). Key initiatives for environmental practices in the agricultural sector in Australia are reducing the use of agri-chemicals, managing water scarcity, and maintaining biodiversity (Australian Government, 2009). Resource efficiency and waste reduction are important goals for the whole community (NSW Government, 2014).

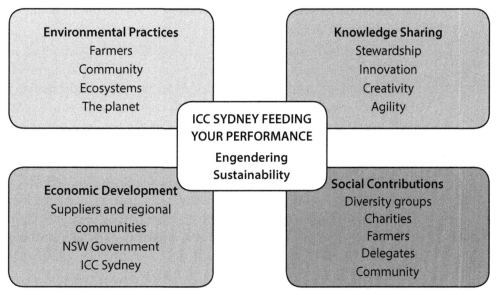

Figure 12.1: Key areas of contribution and beneficiaries

Economic development depends on inclusive economic growth, including employment in vulnerable communities (UNWTO, 2017). The agricultural industry is a significant employer in Australia, supporting employment for 1.68 million people, particularly small producers in rural and regional areas (Spencer & Kneebone, 2012). The industry contributed $130.4 billion in food and beverage retail turnover in 2010-11 (Spencer & Kneebone, 2012). Australian food and beverage is highly regarded in terms of quality and food safety, and gastronomic tourism is becoming increasingly important to the tourism industry (Tourism Australia, 2017). However, many NSW growers and suppliers in rural and regional areas struggle to compete with low cost imports, and unemployment is significantly higher than the state average in regional and rural NSW (Australian Bureau of Statistics, 2017). Research has shown that local food supply chains can regenerate rural development (King et al., 2015; Ilbery & Maye, 2005), but this requires tourism and associated hospitality sector to recognise the importance of sourcing locally, to support small business and community livelihoods.

Over the past 20 years, local food has received renewed attention in the western world for a number of reasons. A growing awareness of the origin of food, food safety and standards, animal welfare issues, and unfair trade could be noted among buyers (Ilbery & Maye, 2005; Renting et al., 2003). Moreover, the environmental impacts associated with industrial mass food production and global supply chains have been increasingly criticized (Dunne et al., 2011; Ilbery & Maye, 2005; Renting et al., 2003; Engelseth & Hogset, 2016) with many non-governmental organizations and researchers recommending to reduce "the fraction of animal-sourced foods in our diets" (Springmann, Godfray, Rayner & Scarborough, 2016: 4146).

To source fresh and healthy local produce, ICC Sydney identified and partnered with New South Wales (NSW) farmers, co-operatives and providers who shared a similar focus for sustainability. Objectives of the collaborative partnership were to ensure that ICC Sydney clients receive fresh produce, 'paddock to plate', and through direct purchasing contribute to the livelihoods of local and regional small food suppliers in NSW. In Chapter 11, Hjalager (2018) presented a model of suppliers' roles and capacities in sustainable tourism. In many respects, the ICC case study demonstrates the benefits highlighted in Hjalager's model, which arise when a firm takes a proactive, co-developing and/or co-branding role with their suppliers. According to Hjalager (2018) "proactive suppliers are most likely to be successful if there is a direct interface and, possibly, also a personal contact" (p. 196).

This case study provides an overview of the development of such partnerships, looks at the ways in which the FYP program is permeating the culture of the ICC Sydney operations, and documents some of the outcomes for external stakeholders. Data are drawn from fourteen interviews conducted with NSW suppliers (6), ICC Sydney staff (7) and a consultant nutritionist (1). A detailed methodology is set out below.

Methodology

This is a qualitative study, the purpose of which is to provide an overview of the outcomes that arise from the FYP program. Interviews were conducted with six NSW suppliers at their workplaces in January 2017 and with seven executive staff from ICC Sydney between December 2016 and February 2017 on the premises of ICC Sydney (Table 12.1). Suppliers were identified by ICC Sydney. The final interview was conducted by telephone with ICC Sydney's consultant nutritionist, Dr Joanna McMillan in February 2017. The interviews, ranging in length from 38 minutes to 182 minutes, were recorded with the permission of participants and subsequently transcribed. For purposes of confidentiality, the names of participants have not been used in this case study. Suppliers are referred to by pseudonyms that represent their area of supply (e.g., potato farmer).

Table 12.1: Interview participants

ICC Sydney Staff	Suppliers
Chief Executive Officer (CEO)	Potato farmer from Crookwell
Director of Human Resources	Cheese maker from Lisdale
Director of Finance and Administration	Lime grower from Kempsey
Director of Communications	Wine maker from Molong
Director of Culinary Services	Butter maker from Tempe
Procurement Manager	Seafood supplier from Taren Point
Executive Chef	Dr Joanna McMillan – consultant nutrionist

In addition to the interviews, further evidence was collected in the form of relevant media reports, website material and managerial documents. This data and the interview transcripts were analysed using a qualitative data analysis software package (NVIVO). The key themes identified included environmental sustainability, economic development and social impacts. The next section provides an overview of the program and practices underpinning the FYP.

About Feeding Your Performance

ICC Sydney implements a sustainability strategy that incorporates energy, waste, water and social targets. Energy resource efficiencies are delivered through smart design strategies integrated with cost efficient and renewable technologies, collaboration with OzHarvest to enable useable food from events to be redistributed to communities in need, and all recovered non-reusable organic waste being composted into fertilizer pellets. They also have the first community-funded solar energy project in Australia – Sydney Renewable Power Company. A project which allows members of the public to buy shares in a social venture that will own the building's solar array.

As part of their strategy, FYP was initially developed as a point of difference to promote the convention centre and its offerings but has since become a cornerstone of their strategy (ICC Sydney, 2016) as well as using the program for marketing purposes (Blichfeldt, 2018; ICC Sydney, 2018). The FYP program underpins many aspects of ICC Sydney's service delivery. According to the Director of Culinary Services, the FYP program is manifest most notably in the organisation's food and beverage service areas where the aim is for restaurant quality meals to be made from fresh, seasonal and ethically sourced local produce, that are nutritionally balanced to energise the physical and mental performance of conference and trade show participants. Supporting the energy levels of delegates has implications for a much broader range of conference outcomes that bring benefits to delegates, communities and economies (see Edwards et al., 2017; Edwards et al., 2016; Foley et al., 2014; Foley et al., 2014a; Foley et al., 2014b; Foley et al., 2013).

Having worked in the industry for decades, the CEO believes that food and beverage (F&B) is one of the areas of convention centres that attracts the most criticism and complaints. Thus, it was a strategic decision to address F&B from the beginning. "We wanted to have a greater economic impact than just room nights and coffee cups" (CEO, ICC Sydney). To this end the CEO tasked the new teams to apply an innovative approach to everything they did. Indeed "the philosophy came before the slogan" (CEO, ICC Sydney), because he feels that "people are now seeking health and vitality and good living". However ICC Sydney soon realised that the slogan and the philosophy had a much broader application as it would be "feeding delegates' professional performance as well" (CEO, ICC Sydney). Thus, FYP is a program that aims to encourage the performance of delegates, regional economy, and ICC Sydney.

ICC Sydney designed menus that incorporate "seasonal, fresh, nutritious, and healthy food" to provide "the best opportunity for minds to think clearly, engage fully, best ideas, and for bodies to remain light and energised" (Executive Chef). To achieve these goals ICC Sydney engaged a nutritionist who provided advice on menu ingredients that would improve concentration, such as the use of grains that deliver slow-release energy throughout the day.

> *Feeding Your Performance is all about healthier eating or healthier meal options particularly for our conference guests who might be here for a lunch and then they've got to go back and sit down and still continue to listen and learn ... nutritionally balanced options enable people to still concentrate and take in information.* (Executive Chef)

Another FYP goal is supporting regional economies by "buying fresh seasonal food from small regional producers in New South Wales" (Procurement Manager). Direct access also means improved efficiencies and produce that arrives "fresher" since it has not been transported via additional warehouses or distributors. To progress this philosophy, the Executive Chef identified and visited a range of farmers and small food supplier producers to "establish a direct relationship with the people who produced the produce and to share the FYP approach" (Executive Chef). Collaborations were established with over 65 locally sourced suppliers providing ICC Sydney with a specialist in every major food area.

By offering nutritious, energising food to delegates, through a new menu while supporting NSW industries, ICC Sydney found:

> They [clients] were really excited about what we're doing, and the quality and the standard of the food as well as its presentation is making a powerful impact on their perception of convention centre dining and their guests' experience. (Director of Culinary Services)

The CEO did not want FYP to be "just another … F&B slogan. [It is] an underpinning philosophy for everything that we want to do". The opening of the convention centre provided ideal conditions for the FYP program to develop and become embedded in ICC Sydney's operations. They believe it would be difficult to introduce such a philosophy to an established convention centre. "I think we've been lucky that we did it from day one, so it's just been embedded in ICC Sydney."

Information about FYP is part of both recruitment and induction processes for all staff members, something that was established by the CEO, "one of the mantras we have here is we're only in business to make our clients successful, that's all. There's no such thing as a successful convention centre." The passion of ICC Sydney staff for the FYP program is palpable; they were clearly very proud that they were able to implement strategies that improved their sustainable practices. According to the Director of Finance and Administration "because our Director of Culinary Services and our Executive Chef were part of developing the program from the outset, every new culinary recruit has had to adopt this approach".

A major stakeholder in the establishment of ICC Sydney is the NSW Government. An unexpected outcome is the FYP program supporting government ministers to deliver on their goals for the state, in terms of regional development (NSW Government, 2015). The ICC Sydney CEO found that the ministers are appreciative of the support given to suppliers in regional NSW. In one example, Stuart Ayres, the NSW Minister for Trade, Tourism and Major Events (at the time) assisted the ICC Sydney to launch their wine list. At the launch, Stuart Ayers stated "I know that this facility is going to sell over 200,000 bottles of wine every year. That's a huge boost to the local wine industry… a massive endorsement of NSW wine… and a fantastic way to showcase the high quality and world-class wines that we have available" (News.com.au, 2016). It is an unsurprising response as the ICC Sydney is delivering goals for government.

In summary, a philosophy aimed at sustainability and menu innovation (by delivering food to sustain delegate performance), became a strategic program supporting delegates and venue patrons, as well as local and regional suppliers in NSW.

Engendering sustainability

This section draws upon the interview data and discusses how the FYP program/philosophy engenders sustainability through environmental practices, knowledge sharing, economic development, and social contributions; each is discussed in turn.

Environmental practices

ICC Sydney sources much of its food and wine from local (NSW) suppliers. An important component of the FYP philosophy is that their suppliers hold the same sustainability focus as ICC Sydney and are vetted for sustainability through a comprehensive questionnaire process and, in many cases, through face-to-face interviews and tours of farms and facilities. According to the Director of Finance and Administration the request for proposal (RFP) pack and procurement plan is a check that the suppliers they adopt or contract share their philosophy. "If they are not on-board, they won't reply to our tender".

There is general agreement in the literature that a local food supply chain is beneficial for the environment in terms of reduced 'food miles' (Shukla & Jharkharia, 2013) and a smaller carbon footprint (King et al, 2015; Kneafsey et al., 2013). Additionally, because of a shorter transportation distance there is generally less need for packaging, processing and refrigeration when compared with long haul industrial food (Kneafsey et al., 2013). The lime grower from Kempsey said that he can "throw the fruit in the back of the truck, leave at two o'clock in the morning … [be] down there by 6-7 o'clock in the morning at his (ICC Executive Chef's) doorstep – drop them off and turn around and come back again home by lunch time" and because he is driving at night he does not need a refrigerated truck. By choosing NSW suppliers ahead of interstate and international alternatives, ICC Sydney is reducing its carbon footprint.

ICC Sydney's consultant nutritionist made the point that there are exceptions to the food miles argument taking rice as an example: "rice is a very water intensive crop, and therefore lots of people have ideas [that] we shouldn't be growing rice in most parts of Australia, because it takes too much water". Dissent for the food miles argument was also voiced by the butter supplier who felt that in a country as large as Australia, dictating food miles can stifle business, particularly in a niche area such as cultured butter (butter made with a starter culture bacteria which ferments the cream resulting in a richer flavour).

In addition to geographical location, ICC Sydney chose suppliers based on the quality of their produce and their sustainable practices. "The best farming practices protect the ecosystem by recycling to reduce waste and reducing the use of agrochemicals" (potato farmer). Suppliers expressed a range of views when it came to sustainability. A second generation wine maker stated:

If you are using bad practice, whether it's from in your vineyard, in your winery ... it gives you an inferior product. So we recycle everything we can, we compost, we do everything we can, in a manner that just makes sense. Why spray for pesticides if they're not a problem and you've got balance in your vineyard? Why use other chemicals if they're not necessary? It's just common sense... I wouldn't want to drink it if I was lacing it with chemicals, so why would anybody else?

As well as growing their own grapes their sustainability principles extends to their grape suppliers. The wine maker noted that they only take fruit from local vineyards who adopt similar approaches to their own.

The potato farmer had both a pragmatic and an ideological stance believing in the importance of balancing farming with the ecosystem. Thirty-two per cent of his farmland has been converted to conservation areas at the time of interview, including wetlands that support waterfowl habitats. He promotes his practices within the local community to encourage other farmers to adopt similar approaches and hopes to "create better outcomes for the whole community and the whole area".

The potato farmer also made the point that potato farms in his area, Crookwell, NSW, have less reliance on the addition of water, nutrients and insecticides than commercially produced crops grown through hydroponics, in sand using applied nutrients and water. He argued that because their potatoes are grown in the "actual organic matter in the soil" they take on a richer flavour and have a better texture.

Our soils are very sustainable because they're very old soils and they're rich in organic matter. With the high altitude that we're at which is 1,000 metres above sea level, we have cool nights ... and less insect problems. So we have less reliance on insecticides and fungicides. (Potato farmer)

The cheese maker noted "we're pretty much sustainable farmers; he [husband] did a diploma in sustainable agriculture after he did his rural degree". Many suppliers were chosen by the Executive Chef for their attention to sustainable practices. The Director of Culinary Services gave an overview of her first impression of the lime grower.

He's been in the industry for many years and he's [evolved] his farming practic-
es… when you meet him, his hands are covered in dirt and he's this very passion-
ate grower of chillies and Tahitian limes. The limes … he can grow for 12 months
of the year … he stopped growing beans because he was having to water them from
the top which meant he was having to use all these sprays to keep the mould off.

The lime grower has minimised the use of chemicals for the last 7-8 years. His philosophy is "if the grubs want to eat the chillies they can have them … (laughing) – there is enough to go around". He no longer uses white oil on his limes "because with the flowers – the ants eat the aphids" and black mould on the leaves can be brushed off with a machine. The Director of Culinary Services was impressed that the lime grower focuses on hiring locals and buying Australian. On meeting him, she thought he was special and explained how "he's in a really tough industry so listening to him talk about what he's doing with regards to his farming practices and his whole attitude towards Australian produce makes it easy to add him to our supplier list".

Effective waste management systems are integral to sustainability for organisations and communities (Shrivastava, 1995). ICC Sydney's contributions to sustainable practice in terms of waste management are numerous. The chefs at ICC Sydney are keen to reduce waste wherever possible incorporating a number of strategies. They have a whole of produce policy for example; for broccoli they use the stem, the stalks and the broccoli florets so waste is minimal (Executive Chef).

ICC Sydney is innovative in their approach to the handling of food waste by donating surplus food to OzHarvest and working with Clean Away to make better use of the recycling system. OzHarvest is a food rescue charity that collects and distributes surplus food to people in need. Clean Away composts unusable food to make organic fertiliser. Some of this fertiliser is returned to ICC Sydney for its own rooftop herb gardens.

In summary, ICC Sydney has adopted sustainable practices within its own organisation, around reducing waste and recycling as well as supporting farmers and small businesses who take sustainability seriously by adopting stewardship roles in their areas of expertise.

Knowledge sharing

Stewardship

Stewardship implies service to a community, the responsibility to care for something, including for the benefit of future generations, and the accountability to exercise responsibility (Liburd & Edwards, 2010). Indeed, this caring leads to an informal governance that is exercised by stewards who care, display loyal devotion, and identify with conservation practices beyond their own and state interests (Liburd and Becken, 2017). This section looks at the contribution that ICC Sydney is making in its stewardship role (beyond their own interests) as well as the contribution it makes to other industry areas by supporting suppliers who also take their stewardship roles seriously.

Many of the suppliers understood their role as stewards. The potato farmer explained that his interest in sustainability developed as he became older and realised that his role as a farmer was less about ownership and profit and more about stewardship, being a responsible custodian of the land he farmed, and improving and protecting the natural ecosystems. Farming is a "part of his soul" and money has no interest in his life. He stated that he works because he loves being able to produce a good crop along with the luxury of being able to feed people and to take pride in this. He sees himself as just a custodian of the land and that he has "to care for it in a way that enhances it, ready for the next generation".

A similar narrative comes from the lime grower who constantly evolves his practices to be more sustainable and shares his experience and knowledge with others, speaking at events and running seminars on farming techniques.

The Director of Finance and Administration spoke of some of the long-term educational aspects of FYP for apprentice chefs:

> You don't come here to be a chef. You come here to be sustainable and work on Feeding Your Performance and it's like it's become its own education. You learn [that] we're using the whole carrot. So, the impact to apprentices is huge. They're going to learn those life lessons forever.

The Director of Finance and Administration also noted the motivational aspects of FYP on staff. During monthly team meetings pictures of the Executive Chef's visits to regional suppliers are shared "so, they see him there, and because he's just one of us, it's that connection too, like they feel like they're actually there picking the mussels". These pictures augment an understanding of the food "People don't necessarily know that these regions…that we regularly visit…also have wonderful produce". These practices enable the staff to say "well I work for a company that supports this business".

The Executive Chef spoke of the deep knowledge he had gained by liaising with suppliers, and his belief that this product knowledge enables them to educate their clients and staff to an extent that knowledge found in books could not.

Innovation, creativity, agility

FYP has outcomes in terms of innovation, creativity and agility. These attributes are considered vital for the long-term sustainability of organisations and industry sectors (Edwards et al., 2016). The Director of Finance and Administration believes ICC Sydney's approach is extremely innovative. "Not just for sustainability or CSR responsibility. It's innovative, there is no doubt about it, no one is doing this, particularly from a finance point of view". She commented that they added a component to their request for proposal document that asks the suppliers if they have any new ideas.

> It's amazing the stuff that they're putting in there. They're going, "as well as this service, we also offer this service", and that opened up a few ideas...So, it was putting the power back in the supplier's hands to tell us what they're good at, which in turn would help us...

Staff at ICC Sydney believes that FYP is an innovative approach in terms of serving restaurant quality food in a convention centre, which is nutritionally balanced and energising: "I don't know how many conventions I've sat in where you get the same stuff for morning tea, lunch, afternoon tea, and by about three-thirty, you just want to have a sleep under the table, because you've eaten far too much carbohydrate" (Director of Finance and Administration).

FYP is acting as a catalyst for further innovations through its close collaborative relationships with suppliers, creativity in menus and approaches to corporate social responsibility. For example, they are working with the potato farmer to develop an ancient potato variety that will turn orange and crisp without the use of oil. By committing to purchasing these potatoes, the ICC Sydney is enabling the potato farmer to invest in developing new product lines.

Economic development

Supporting local producers

> I love that the Executive Chef has embraced using local producers. He's really ... helping them improve their businesses, as well as them providing really great produce for him, so I think that's a real plus, and essentially that's what real food's all about...supporting our agricultural producers, as well as those who are [contributing] through making foods like cheeses, and pickles, and relishes, and popular butchers, great fishmongers. (Consultant nutritionist)

Local food supply chains exert positive economic influences on their local region, mainly in terms of economic growth and employment (Ilbery & Maye, 2005). Local food supply chains are seen as the new paradigm to regenerate rural development, globally. An exploratory study of seven European countries, representing 75-85 per cent of the farms in Europe, determined that the additional net value generated by local food supply chains on top of conventional agricultural production was positive in all cases (Renting et al., 2003). Similar outcomes have been identified by studies conducted in the US and the UK over the past decade (Otto and Varner, 2005; King et al., 2015; Kneafsey, et al., 2013;

Hughes et al., 2008) Local food strategies have been found to reverse the decline of rural services and the depletion in food and farming physical infrastructure (Kumar et al., 2013).

Further, there has been slow growth in the food market since 2008 (Spencer & Kneebone, 2012). Added to this is the issue of ongoing volatility of the operating environment for food producers caused by both climatic and economic conditions. The economic volatility comes from exposure to currency fluctuations that affect export sales, competition from imports, and price fluctuations within or between produce seasons (Spencer & Kneebone, 2012). In Australia the cost reduction strategies of the two biggest retailers in the fresh food market, Coles and Woolworths, have also contributed to the erosion of farmers' margins and many small growers have been forced to exit (IBISWorld, 2017). These reports are supported by the suppliers interviewed who noted that they have been 'squeezed' by large supermarket chains.

The volatility of the operating environment for food producers is not expected to decrease in the near future and, in this context, ICC Sydney's strategy to provide a level of stability for their food suppliers is very welcome. In addition to supporting individual suppliers ICC Sydney is contributing to a growing set of farmer and consumer-led initiatives which include: farmers' markets; marketing cooperatives; community supported agriculture; and direct and online sales hubs (Estrada-Flores & Larsen, 2010). The Department of Agriculture, Fisheries and Forestry has determined that such initiatives represent an opportunity for fresh food specialists. The seafood supplier has noted the growth of this movement:

> It has opened up people's eyes to what food is ... and maybe [future generations] will start demanding Australian produce ... the emergence of the little operators is coming back again. Retail for small operators has boomed because people, as time poor as they are, will go to a butcher... they'll go down to the fish markets ... it's better than where it was five years ago.

Patronage by a high quality-conscious customer such as ICC Sydney provides an opportunity for small food production enterprises to increase stability in a volatile market and to grow their customer base. It is also a leadership role that the ICC Sydney is proud to undertake.

While collaboration between suppliers and ICC Sydney are new, suppliers anticipate several benefits. Expected job growth may be small but suppliers felt the impact on regional towns would be meaningful. Other benefits include business expansion, promotion of their businesses and regions, and increased tourism opportunities. As the potato farmer stated "if it employs one more person in this little town well that's a bonus".

Supporting small business

A number of the suppliers are using their relationship with ICC Sydney to plan for their future growth. As noted previously the potato farmer is extending his business and that of others in his region by growing a specialty 'ware' potato just for ICC Sydney. The cheese maker is using the increase in sales to consolidate and improve their cash flow situation. Such activities are achievable as ICC Sydney allows suppliers to set their own payment terms choosing a quick turnaround of 15 days or the end of the month.

However, for the butter maker it is not just about the direct income but the indirect benefits such as the increased exposure that comes from the video produced by ICC Sydney which promotes the supplier partnerships. Also, being on the ICC tables' means that their butter is on the world stage. They are using their relationship with ICC Sydney to get to "that next level", particularly through world-wide exposure via international visitors to the convention centre.

It is a similar story for the sustainable seafood supplier because he is now able to say that his firm "doesn't just cater for small restaurants … or two chef hat restaurants, we also supply businesses like the ICC". From his perspective, if ICC Sydney is buying from them, then others can be confident that they can deliver. "I'm proud in telling them that we're doing ICC because … that these guys aren't your usual volume event space." This is supported by ICC Sydney promoting suppliers through ongoing marketing activities and during events. The suppliers become part of ICC Sydney's "messaging, and storytelling [which they feel] deeply personalises the whole process" (CEO ICC Sydney).

The artisan cheese makers have won numerous awards for their goat cheese products and have some high-end clients. However, they have been struggling to sell enough volume. As events at the ICC Sydney are booked well in advance the chef is able to order menu ingredients well in advance of service requirements. Thus, they are able to provide suppliers with advance notice of products required. Open communication between supplier and purchaser means that suppliers are able to advise on product availability for the requested period. Hence, the cheesemakers are pleased to partner with ICC Sydney as it means they can focus on making cheese products, which is their forte, and spend less time looking for new customers.

Partnering with ICC Sydney allows suppliers to focus on their core competencies of delivering high quality produce. The suppliers welcome the opportunity for not only the promotion of their own business but for their regions and communities. All suppliers highlighted the opportunity for regional development as a key benefit. Indeed, FYP could not have come at a better time for the Kempsey region. The Kempsey Council has plans to promote and develop the region as a food bowl. To this end the lime grower believes that the promotion that comes with supplying ICC Sydney can play a part in this new development.

The wine maker made the point that while 'paddock to plate' has become popular in terms of sustainable practice and promoting high quality restaurant food, the same cannot be said for beverages.

> We've seen farmers' markets pop up everywhere - paddock to plate, hundred mile this - and there are some fantastic restaurants in Sydney that will sit you down and they'll tell you about the food that, "comes out of the garden here and we've got our own farm at Windsor and we pick everything there, and then … would you like this French shiraz to have with that?"

His concern is that this rhetoric does not translate to their beverages and he hopes that a major convention centre like ICC Sydney will influence change and encourage greater local support. He went on to make the point that ICC Sydney is contributing to a newly emerging movement towards a well-deserved appreciation of NSW wines.

The Director of Culinary Services explained that they "were very aware from the outset the impact the ICC Sydney wine list could have for that winemaker" from a volume and sales perspective as well as for regional brand awareness. The sommelier was tasked with building an 80 per cent NSW wine list, which he is very passionate about. The Director of Culinary Services feels that there is not enough support and promotion of local regions "there's 14 regions now in New South Wales going from cooler climates right through to Hunter Valley … normally in big venues and in hotels your house wine or your house package is done on price… but we want to offer our guests quality wine, regional wine labels".

The wine list was built through a blind tasting of just over 1,300 NSW wines ensuring that every wine earned its place on the wine list for its quality and not its price. They believe this is an industry first. The strategy is paying off with positive feedback and an ability to promote "New South Wales and smaller wineries. Since opening, the Australian wine industry has held two events in the ICC Sydney aimed at sommeliers, wine buyers, critics and media, focussing on NSW labels. One event largely used the ICC Sydney wine list of labels for its master class tasting" (Director of Culinary Services).

Social contributions

Local food supply chains can strengthen relationships within food chain communities. A focus on local food arouses social concern for farmers. Studies have shown that people buy local food, to a large extent, because they feel sympathy for the farmers (Mundler & Laughrea, 2016; Corsten & Felde, 2005; Arsil et al., 2014)

As the Procurement Manager said: "I think it's a good story that we're supporting local communities like that, and they're doing it tough out there for whatever reason, and if it creates wealth and jobs and things like that for the families it's great". She is proud of the small difference that ICC Sydney could make.

Supporting farmers to grow high quality produce

ICC Sydney's Executive Chef is sourcing produce with high nutritional value and flavour. He explained: "Remember the way tomatoes used to taste before they were modified for long shelf life and to look good in supermarkets? I've found someone who grows heritage tomatoes. I don't even like to call them heritage, they are just real tomatoes, full of flavour".

The potato farmer provided a detailed explanation of a similar issue in the potato industry where intensive farming is now a problem when producing high quality produce. He stated that fruit and vegetables today do not have the same level of nutrients in them as they are grown in sand which is inert, and the vegetable does not take in the zinc and all the things that are in soil. Partnering with ICC Sydney enables him to "look at more sustainable land and smaller areas that will produce a much higher quality nutritional food".

A collaborative partnership with ICC Sydney means opportunities for new produce to be realised that would otherwise not be feasible. The potato farmer suggested that ICC Sydney consider niche potatoes such as the wild potatoes that come from the Andes as they are better nutritionally and will "ooze flavour".

"If you want to buy commodity potatoes you just go to the supermarket and buy whatever's cheap. But if you want to have a meal experience which is what we're talking about now, where you want to know the story of your food... it needs to be an all complete experience that takes a whole different strategy." (Potato farmer)

Supporting the local community

ICC Sydney supports the local community through recruitment of diverse groups including people with learning disabilities, the LGBTI community, youth from technical colleges and hospitality schools, working mothers and mature workers. They have achieved this by "partnering with diversity organisations that focus on specific demographics" (Director of Human Resources).

In addition, ICC Sydney's relationship with OzHarvest is important as "[they do] the collection of [surplus] food and then redistribute to people in need and the homeless". OzHarvest also work with young people to give them opportunities to find employment by connecting them with organisations like ICC Sydney (Director of Human Resources).

Overall, local food schemes have been shown to contribute to increased knowledge and behavioural change around healthy eating (Mundler &

Laughrea, 2016; Kneafsey et al., 2013). ICC Sydney's FYP program is contributing to a new level of nutritional awareness in three ways. First, they are supporting growers who are working towards producing food with improved nutritional value. Second, they can then provide delegates with nutritionally superior food. Finally, they are donating any excess of this high-quality food to an organisation that provides meals for people in Sydney who are experiencing disadvantage.

Nourishing performance

The benefit of nourishing food on delegate performance has been an important motivator. Engaging a consultant nutritionist was an important step in developing menus with the aim of "controlling energy levels for people [who are] there all day, for helping brain power throughout the day ... for concentration and to stop people having that struggle to keep your eyes open".

Increasing performance is founded on minimising carbohydrate portions and lowering the glycaemic index (GI). This would enable "energy to trickle into the bloodstream through the afternoon, helping to feed your brain, helping you to keep your brain power and concentration, and not allow you to have quite such a big slump in the afternoon" (Consultant Nutritionist). There is a stronger focus on the use of whole grains and legumes, quinoa, and a variety of newer grains. The nutritionist has reviewed every single recipe being used by the culinary team to assist them to ensure the meals are light, high in protein, and use low GI carbohydrates, wholegrain, minimally processed grains, and reducing the amount of sugar. "You know, the Executive Chef and I, are exactly on the same page with regards to using real food and using top quality produce, and ... well it's not rocket science ... to understand what the nature of your philosophies are, and once you can, generally you get a really nice balance" (Consultant Nutritionist).

Research has found a strong link between diet and sustainability. In particular, dietary changes that involve increased consumption of plant-based foods and reduced consumption of animal foods leads to a reduction in greenhouse gas emissions (Scarborough et al. 2014; Stoll-Kleemann & O'Riordan, 2015; Springmann et al., 2016). The Consultant Nutritionist does not believe that enough consumers understand this issue and feels that through the FYP program the message can "get out there" to eat more plant foods, sustainably sourced oysters, mussels, and seafood. Eating more plants, she argues, "will have a huge influence on the health of our planet".

Conclusions

Maintaining collaborative relationships and knowledge continuity when key people retire or move away is significant to ongoing collaborative programs (Carlsen & Edwards, 2013b). Whilst this case study highlights important benefits and outcomes from a program strategically designed to support a range of stakeholders, its future is unclear and a number of questions arise. A change in any of the key ICC Sydney employees may put the program in jeopardy should new employees not hold the same passion for driving a sustainability agenda (Carlsen & Edwards, 2013b; Gill & Williams, 2011). This could conceivably damage the collaborations with small suppliers who can be vulnerable to economic changes. Can a passion for sustainability be sustained? Fifteen months later and the ICC Sydney are again evaluating the FYP program; it remains to be seen if the FYP program will continue to translate into beneficial outcomes. A number of questions arise. Have collaborations deepened? What new collaborations have arisen and have the outcomes over the past 15 months met the expectations of suppliers? Have delegates noticed if their performance improved as a result of enjoying the food and beverage offerings at the ICC Sydney? It is hoped that further research will answer these questions.

This case study reports on the collaborative benefits and effects of the sustainable and inclusive practices adopted by a convention centre, ICC Sydney, as part of its FYP program. ICC Sydney is making contributions in four key areas: environmental sustainability, knowledge sharing, economic development, and social contributions. This case study presents strong evidence of how the direct interface plays out in practice. The case aligns with Hjalager's (2018) model in which ICC Sydney are formally collaborating with suppliers to achieve their sustainability agenda. Advancing their knowledge of each other because of an emphasis on people-to-people interactions, the gains are fruitful for both parties. The ICC Sydney FYP program is a clear example of a tourism firm with a distinct sustainability agenda, actively in search of collaborative suppliers and enabling those suppliers to come up with solutions (Hjalager, 2018). It demonstrates that in tourism, collaboration and partnerships *can* form a basis for resilient action. It remains to be seen how and whether such collaborations continue.

References

Arsil, P., Li, E., Bruwer, J. & Lyons, G. (2014), Exploring consumer motivations towards buying local fresh food products. *British Food Journal*, **116**(10), 1533-1549.

Australian Bureau of Statistics (2017), *New South Wales (S/T)*. viewed 20/03/17, stat.abs.gov. au/itt/r.jsp?RegionSummary&region=1&dataset=ABS_REGIONAL_ASGS&geoco ncept=REGION&measure=MEASURE&datasetASGS=ABS_REGIONAL_ASGS& datasetLGA=ABS_REGIONAL_LGA&regionLGA=REGION&regionASGS=REGION

Australian Government (2009) Feeding the future: sustainable agriculture. www. chiefscientist.gov.au/2009/10/feeding-the-future---sustainable-agriculture/ viewed 30 April 2017.

Blichfeldt , B.S. (2018). Co-branding and strategic communication. In Liburd and Edwards (2018) *Collaborations for Sustainable Tourism Development*. Goodfellow Publishers, Oxford, UK.

Bohdanowicz-Godfrey, P. (2013). Scandic Hotels: Embracing Omtanke - 'caring for each other'. In Liburd, J., Carlsen, J., & Edwards, D. (Eds.) *Networks for Innovation for Sustainable Tourism: Case Studies and Cross-Case Analysis* (pp.15-24). Tilde University Press: Melbourne.

Carlsen, J. & Edwards D. (2013a). Xanterra LLC: Networking for the[ir] future. In Liburd, J., Carlsen, J., & Edwards, D. (Eds.) *Networks for Innovation for Sustainable Tourism: Case Studies and Cross-Case Analysis* (pp. 33-40). Tilde University Press: Melbourne.

Carlsen, J. & Edwards D. (2013b). The Diablo Trust: Planning sustainable land use. In Liburd, J., Carlsen, J., & Edwards, D. (Eds.) *Networks for Innovation for Sustainable Tourism: Case Studies and Cross-Case Analysis* (pp. 41-48). Tilde University Press: Melbourne.

Corsten, D. & Felde, J. (2005). Exploring the performance effects of key-supplier collaboration: an empirical investigation into Swiss buyer-supplier relationships, *International Journal of Physical Distribution & Logistics Management*, **35**(6), 445-461.

Dunne, J. B., Chambers, K. J., Giombolini, K. J. & Schlegel, S. A. (2011). What does 'local' mean in the grocery store? Multiplicity in food retailers' perspectives on sourcing and marketing local foods. *Renewable Agriculture and Food Systems*, **26**(1), 46-59.

Edwards, D. C., Foley, C. T., Dwyer, L., Schlenker, K. & Hergesell, A. (2014). Evaluating the economic contribution of a large indoor entertainment venue: an inscope expenditure study. *Event Management: an International Journal*. **18**(4), 407-420. doi.org /10.3727/152599514X14143427352076

Edwards, D., Foley, C. T. & Hergesell, A. (2016). *Conferences: Catalysts for thriving economies*. Australia: UTS.

Edwards, D., Foley, C. & Malone, C. (2017). *The Power of Conferences: stories of serendipity, innovation and driving social change*. Sydney:UTS ePress. doi.org/10.5130/ 978-0-6481242-0-7

Engelseth, P. & Hogset, H. (2016). Adapting supply chain management for local foods logistics. *Proceedings in System Dynamics and Innovation in Food Networks*, Innsbruck, Austria: International Center for Food Chain and Network Research, University of Bonn, Germany, pp. 143-160.

Estrada-Flores, S. & Larsen, K. (2010). *Best Practice Food Distribution Systems*. Melbourne: Food Chain Intelligence and Victorian Eco-Innovation Lab.

Foley, C. T., Edwards, D. C. & Schlenker, K. (2014). Business events and friendship: leveraging the sociable legacies. *Event Management: an international journal*, **18**(1), 53-64. doi.org/10.3727/152599514X13883555341887

Foley, C. T., Edwards, D. C. Schlenker, K. & Hergesell, A. (2014a). *Beyond Tourism Benefits: Building an International Profile, Future Convention Cities Initiative*. Australia: UTS.

Foley, C. T., Edwards, D. C., Schlenker, K. & Hergesell, A. (2014b). *Estimating Inscope Expenditure Attributed to Business Events Held in New South Wales*. Business Events

Sydney. Australia: UTS.

Foley, C., Schlenker, K., Edwards, D. & Lewis-Smith, L. (2013). Determining business event legacies beyond the tourism spend: An Australian case study approach. *Event Management*, **17**(3), 311-322. www.cabdirect.org/cabdirect/abstract/20133350856

Gill, A.M. & Williams, P.W. (2011). Rethinking resort growth: understanding evolving governance strategies in Whistler. British Columbia. *Journal of Sustainable Tourism* **19**(4-5), 629-648.

Hjalager, A.M. (2018). Suppliers as key collaborators for sustainable tourism. In Liburd and Edwards (2018) *Collaborations for Sustainable Tourism Development*. Goodfellow Publishers, Oxford, UK

Hughes, D.W., Brown, C., Miller, S. & McConnell, T. (2008). Evaluating the economic impact of farmers' markets using an opportunity cost framework. *Journal of Agricultural and Applied Economics*, **40**(1): 253-265.

IBISWorld (2017). *Dairy Cattle Farming in Australia*. viewed 15 March 2017, www.ibisworld.com.au/industry-trends/market-research-reports/agriculture-forestry-fishing/agriculture/dairy-cattle-farming.html.

ICC Sydney (n.d.). *ICC Sydney Culinary Philosophy*. viewed 15 March 2017, www.iccsydney.com.au/~/media/ICC/Files/PDF/Culinary/ICC%20Sydney_CulinaryPhilosophy.ashx?la=en.

ICC Sydney (2016). ICC Sydney Feeding Your Performance. video file, viewed 15 March 2017, www.youtube.com/watch?v=EabNOVg0uiw.

ICC Sydney (2018). *News*. viewed 5 April 2018, www.iccsydney.com.au/news.

International Congress and Convention Association (2016). *2015 ICCA Statistics Report: Public Abstract*. ICCA: Netherlands. viewed 8 April 2018.

Ilbery, B. & Maye, D. (2005). Food supply chains and sustainability: Evidence from specialist food producers in the Scottish/English borders. *Land Use Policy*, **22**(4), 331-344.

King, R. P., Hand, M. S. & Gómez, M. I. (Eds.) (2015). *Growing Local: Case Studies on Local Food Supply Chains*. Lincoln: University of Nebraska Press.

Kneafsey, M., Venn, L., Schmutz, U., Balázs, B., Trenchard, L., Eyden-Wood, T., Bos, E., Sutton, G. & Blackett, M. (2013). *Short food supply chains and local food systems in the EU. A state of play of their socio-economic characteristics*. JRC Scientific and Policy Reports, Seville: Joint Research Centre, Institute for Prospective Technological Studies, European Commission.

Kumar, R., Agrawal, R. & Sharma, V. (2013). e-Applications in Indian Agri-Food Supply Chain: Relationship among Enablers. *Global Business Review*, **14**(4), 711-727.

Liburd, J. & Becken, S. (2017). Values in nature conservation, tourism and UNESCO World Heritage Site stewardship. *Journal of Sustainable Tourism* **25**(12), 1719-1735. DOI:10.1080/09669582.2017.1293067

Mair, J., & Jago, L. (2010). The development of a conceptual model of greening in the business events tourism sector. *Journal of Sustainable Tourism*, **18**(1), 77–94.

Mundler, P. & Laughrea, S. (2016). The contributions of short food supply chains to territorial development: A study of three Quebec territories. *Journal of Rural Studies*, **45**, 218-229.

News.com.au (2016). New ICC sommelier is up to the job choosing the 200,000 wines that will be poured each year. viewed 15 March 2017, www.news.com.au/national/nsw-act/new-icc-sommelier-is-up-to-the-job-choosing-the-200000-wines-that-will-be-poured-each-year/news-story/091e15c8e2cca84750e35a8821 4ea364.

NSW Government (2014). *NSW Waste Avoidance and Resource Recovery Strategy 2014-2021*. viewed 18 April 2017, www.epa.nsw.gov.au/resources/wastestrategy/140876-WARR-strategy-14-21.pdf.

NSW Government (2015). *Economic Development Stategy for Regional NSW*. viewed 18 April 2017, www.industry.nsw.gov.au/invest-in-nsw/news-and-events/news/new-economic-development-strategy-for-regional-nsw.

Otto, D. & Varner, T. (2005). Consumers, Vendors, and the Economic Importance of Iowa Farmers' Markets: An Economic Impact Survey Analysis. *Leopold Center Pubs and Papers*, Paper 145, viewed 15 April 2017. http://lib.dr.iastate.edu/cgi/viewcontent.cgi?article=1146&context=leopold_pubspapers.

Renting, H., Marsden, T. K. & Banks, J. (2003). Understanding alternative food networks: Exploring the role of short food supply chains in rural development. *Environment and Planning A*, **35**(3), 393-411.

Scarborough, P., Appleby, P. N., Mizdrak, A., Briggs, A. D., Travis, R. C., Bradbury, K. E. & Key, T. J. (2014). Dietary greenhouse gas emissions of meat-eaters, fish-eaters, vegetarians and vegans in the UK. *Climatic Change*, **125**(2), 179-192.

Shrivastava, P. (1995). The role of corporations in achieving ecological sustainability'. *Academy of Management Review*, **20**(4), 936-960.

Shukla, M. & Jharkharia, S. (2013). Agri-fresh produce supply chain management: a state-of-the-art literature review. *International Journal of Operations & Production Management*, **33**(2), 114-158.

Spencer, S & Kneebone, M (2012). *FOODmap: An analysis of the Australian food supply chain*. Canberra: Department of Agriculture, Fisheries and Forestry.

Springmann, M., Godfray, H. C. J., Rayner, M. & Scarborough, P. (2016). Analysis and valuation of the health and climate change cobenefits of dietary change. *Proceedings of the National Academy of Sciences*, **113**(15), 4146-4151.

Stoll-Kleemann, S. & O'Riordan, T. (2015). The sustainability challenges of our meat and dairy diets. *Environment: Science and Policy for Sustainable Development*, **57**(3), 34-48.

Swift, M. J., Izac, A. M., & van Noordwijk, M. (2004). Biodiversity and ecosystem services in agricultural landscapes—are we asking the right questions? *Agriculture, Ecosystems & Environment*, **104**(1), 113-134.

Tourism Australia (2017). *Food and Wine*. viewed 15 April 2017, www.tourism.australia.com/campaigns/Food-Wine.aspx.

UNWTO (2015). *United Nations declares 2017 as the International Year of Sustainable Tourism for Development*. viewed 7 April 2017, media.unwto.org/press-release/2015-12-07/united-nations-declares-2017-international-year-sustainable-tourism-develop.

UNWTO (2017), *2017 International Year of Sustainable Tourism for Development*, viewed 30 March 2017, /www2.unwto.org/tourism4development2017.

13 Collaborative Learning for Sustainable Tourism Development

Chris Heape and Janne Liburd

Introduction

Tourism is a global social and economic phenomenon, which calls for a holistic approach to tourism higher education, where the broader aims of the industry and society are explicitly addressed. The indispensable complexity of the tourism phenomenon demands professionals with a far-reaching and integrated understanding of the multiple disciplines and paradigms that are concerned with sustainable tourism development and adaptive management. Rather than resting on predefined learning outcomes, where students simply acquire knowledge about sustainable tourism development, this chapter unfolds the processes of how complex and critical understandings of sustainable tourism development are collaboratively designed with students, tutors and teachers.

At the University of Southern Denmark, the principal aim for the MA in International Tourism and Leisure Management and European Master in Tourism Management is to educate today's students to become philosophic practitioners of tomorrow. Therefore, it is important to create a learning environment that takes the challenges of unknown future practices into account. To advance higher education and learning cannot be a value-free process. Barnett laments how "the higher education community consistently evades its responsibility to declare the particular values that underpin its activities" (Barnett, 1990: 44). Bringing together the issues of unknown futures and values on epistemological terms, the knowledge collaboratively designed and disseminated will also reflect on the kind of human development we want to see (Barnett, 1990: 44; Liburd, 2013: 65).

This chapter will both trace the explorations and experiments we made and the processes we engendered over the past five years that enabled us to develop a genuinely unique and alternative approach to Sustainable Tourism

Development (STD) education, learning and inquiry, and map out what we see as the essential theoretical and practical elements of that concept of learning. The numerous projects the students have carried out have also enabled us to also better understand, from a research perspective, the nuances of process that make up STD. Aligned with Chapter 2, our point of departure is that STD is a process and not the development of a specific tourism product or outcome (Liburd, 2010; 2018). Our research has revealed that by further unfolding this notion, one can say that STD is a process that fosters new relationships and interactions between stakeholders and practitioners, and that through these interactions a range of perspectives are brought to bear on a tourism endeavour or situation that can reveal aspects that might otherwise be overlooked, and engender concepts, strategies and outcomes that shift what STD can achieve.

We have primarily worked with three interrelated theoretical approaches: Collaborative Design, Complex Processes of Relating and Educating Attention, which in turn have been interwoven as a concept we describe as Participatory Inquiry. In our interactions with the students we have striven to engage them with an understanding of skilled practice that enables them to develop the necessary skills, values, competencies and knowledge to become philosophical practitioners. This chapter will briefly introduce our three theoretical departure points, unpack them in more detail with examples of learning situations to finally, and on that basis, describe our concept of participatory inquiry and its relation to STD.

Whilst we acknowledge that Heron and Reason (1997) have used the term 'participatory inquiry', they do so by considering it as a paradigm in itself, which we choose not to do. Our understanding rests more in a complex relational and pragmatic understanding of doing inquiry where all participants are interdependent on each other within a field of inquiry. This differs from an understanding of action research and the idea of participatory inquiry as described by Reason and Bradbury (2008) that draws on systems thinking. As Stacey and Griffin (2005) notice about systems theory perspectives, researchers are sometimes understood as standing outside the system, the field of inquiry, and from that position observe, design or reflect, and sometimes as being part of the system. As will become clearer below, an emphasis on the interdependency of participatory inquiry informs our process of doing STD as a *designing with* and not a *designing for*!

We are for the most, two faculty: a professor and a design research consultant. We also invite two students from the previous year to act as tutors who can either independently supervise the student groups or act as assistants to the professor or consultant.

Collaborative design

Central to the development of our STD education has been the introduction of collaborative design (co-design). Co-design contributes a unique range of processes, methods, tools and an attitude of mind and perception that enables its practitioners, with others, to explore, reveal, encompass and address issues and nuances in an overall sustainable tourism development process. Co-design is a social practice where participants relate to the dynamic and iterative nature of the task in hand where outcomes emerge from the social interactions of those involved (Buur & Larsen, 2010; Heape, 2007; Minneman, 1991). This understanding deliberately challenges the notion that a development process can be planned and micro-managed with pre-determined outcomes.

Complex processes of relating

Our STD educational practice is highly influenced by a focus on complex responsive processes of relating as initiated by Stacey et al. (2000), Stacey (2001 & 2003) and Shaw and Stacey (2006). Based on theories of George Herbert Mead (1934) and Norbert Elias (1956), they understand social interaction as transformative. This perspective understands the sociality of people's collective actions and participatory practice by noticing the complex and processual nature of human knowing, doing, making, relating and organising. "For Mead, the source of variation lay in the gesture and response structure of interaction between organisms. Variation, with its potential for transformation, arises in the micro detail of interactions" between people (Stacey et al., 2000: 43). Sense-making, sense-giving and understanding emerge from the ongoing interactions between interdependent people involved in collective doings in specific situations (Heape et al., 2015), where "practices change in the emergent processes of negotiating new meaning, new opportunities, new insights, new thinking and new doing" (Larsen & Sproedt, 2013: 2).

Educating attention

The education of attention was a term originally introduced by James Gibson (1979) as a fine-tuning or sensitisation of the entire perceptual system to particular features of the environment (Gibson, 1979: 246-8). Tim Ingold (2017: 2-4) points out that "education is a practice of attention, not of transmission – that it is through attention that knowledge is both generated and carried on... We can – in a sense – travel the same paths and, in so doing, make meaning together. It is not that you end with a piece of knowledge implanted in your mind that once had belonged only to me; rather we come into a concordance that is new to both of us. Education is transformative." This closely relates to Lave and Wenger

(1991) who consider "learning and knowing as social participation, in which person, activity, and world are mutually constitutive, rather than on cognitive processes or conceptual structures. We do not learn about a practice, they say. Our learning, as the experience of engaging day-to-day as bodily persons in supporting and developing meaningful activity with others, is practice. Practice and personal identity emerge together as our experience of co-created patterns of meaning" (Shaw, 2002: 166). It also gives way for creative conceptualisations of STD as a space for transformation of the self; a space for receiving and contributing to critical knowledge about the past and present; and a space to engage in future world-making.

Embracing the unknown

Moving from the linear to the emergent

We are well aware that when we first meet the students, they come, for the most, from educations across the world that emphasise a notion of tourism as predominately marketing and business oriented. As discussed in Chapter 2, tourism is also seen as a vocational practice that leans to a linear and rational understanding of development that prescribes process and predetermines outcomes. We challenge this by emphasising that professional tourism practice can also be considered a skilled practice carried out with others, where understanding and meaning emerge through a practical engagement with the social and physical world, the outcome of which one cannot know beforehand; and where its practitioners, if they are to truly embrace that process, must engage the task with all its inherent and messy uncertainty. We are confident, and have become more so over the years, that by encouraging tourism students to work with their projects in a similar fashion, they engage in a transformative learning experience and practice that embraces and legitimises an alternative understanding of themselves as people, and as a result, develop the necessary skills, values, competencies and knowledge to become philosophical tourism practitioners.

Our challenge is how to quickly introduce the students to this transformative and socially oriented way of approaching their studies and help them grasp alternative understandings of what 'development' can be.

We ask a simple question. How do you explore a city? Do you just stride through according to a plan or do you wander through and improvise? Most students realise very quickly that they more often than not improvise as they explore or vice versa, explore through improvisation. This is followed by asking the students: Who do you meet on the way? How do they relate to each other? What are the dynamics of yours and their interactions?

Again they realise their city exploration has a social and material dimension and the interactions they have with others and how others interact with each other counters the notion that those interactions are fixed or symmetrical. This is deliberately designed to challenge the conventional mapping of tourism stakeholders as fixed and symmetrical, with either a low or high stake (e.g. Tribe, 2010: 37-40). Finally we ask: What mementos, objects and impressions did you collect along the way? Again, an effort on our part to indicate that what the students do as people as they explore a city by collecting images and impressions, taking photos and maybe buying a souvenir or keepsake is something they can also do in their projects. This initial, basic introduction, literally on day one, encapsulates our STD educational ethos from a process and experiential perspective.

So how can this basic pull on the students' experience help engender an alternative learning approach? The principal pedagogical thrust we have is that students have far greater resources than they realise. The question being: how can one bring those resources into play and more importantly how to legitimise that they may do so? When we say resources, we are thinking of basic human resources of empathy, imagination, association, metaphor, narrative and the ways in which we navigate the world. Tim Ingold (2001) describes the unfolding within a field of practice as a taskscape. We use the notion of a design space where the design process, in this case a STD process, is considered as the construction, exploration and expansion of a conceptual space (Heape, 2007). By referring back to their experience of exploring a city, we encourage the students to understand their learning process as emerging from the exploration and resolution of their STD projects as they navigate their design space, a process we consider a process of inquiry that is conducted *with* others (ibid: 7). By referring to the mementos and impressions they might collect on their way, this equates to the traces of activities and expressions of understanding the students generate and note as objects, visuals and text as they explore their task. In a sense these notations can be thought of as: we've been here, we've done this, we've understood some of this or that and we leave a way-marker to indicate what we understand for now (ibid: 126). These traces of a process of inquiry demarcate the places where their inquiry has taken them, their trajectories of curiosity and exploration, what they have experimented with in those places and how any emergent understanding, however vague, is articulated as an expression of those experiments or doings. In this sense, in order to tone down the design emphasis of our concept of participatory inquiry, which we will explain below, it is reasonable to call a design space a field of inquiry.

It is worth noting here that the STD course is, with the exception of a few students, carried out as secondary research. It is mostly desktop literature research, but over the years increasing numbers of students also use blogs and TripAdvisor, for example, to engender vignettes (Blichfeldt & Therkelsen, 2010) and imaginary scenarios, best case/worse case, for example, that act as a bridge between secondary and primary research. This process helps them introduce and engage what people actually think and experience, and to project their understanding into a shared, imagined space. Through this process, students are again able to pull on their own experience and bring their latent resources of imagination, association and metaphor and the co-construction of shared narratives into play. The reason for this initial STD focus is that when we started in 2013, we quickly discovered that to ask the students to both engage a new context, a new demanding learning process, and work with primary research was too great a task for them. So, for the sake of this chapter and to give as rich an insight into our STD educational process as possible, we choose to conflate our experience of running the STD course with the next semester course entitled "Tourism Co-Design." In the tourism co-design course the students must work, again in groups, with primary research by engaging stakeholders, organisations or businesses in the field. The development of the two courses has in many ways influenced each other, hence our conflating the two here.

Designing with

It is also worth noting that although we introduce this alternative process of doing an inquiry and resolving a task, we do not expect the students to just "get it." We are well aware that by introducing this collaborative approach the students feel very provoked and insecure, in particular as it is mandatory they work in groups. We reassure them however that as they proceed with their tasks they will better understand the complexity and nature of doing such an inquiry. This does in fact prove to be the case and demands on our part that we provide ongoing support for the students. According to their needs, they receive weekly personal supervision in their respective groups. All supervision takes its departure point in the state of their task. Additionally, as the task matures the students are referred to and independently seek additional literature that specifically relates to their task.

So, by drawing on the experiential thread of exploring a city, and the idea that the students' process is considered a process of inquiry that is conducted *with* others, we are also able to introduce another central tenet, in that STD is a *designing with* not a *designing for*. The distinction is crucial. It underscores the fact that if one is to truly shift tourism development, in particular if one considers sustainability as a process as opposed to a product or specific outcome (Liburd, 2010; 2018) and, to boot, a process that engenders other kinds of relationships, interactions and conversations between people, then designing with is the quintessential expression of an ethical, ongoing involvement of others through a respect for their ways of being in the world and their sense of values. This as opposed to acting as a designer or tourism developer who interacts with others as an expert who serves up ideas to be vetted!

Naturally one cannot predict how people will interact. One cannot begin to imagine, until one has engaged a range of stakeholders, how the dynamics of their relating will affect any understanding or resolution of an STD task. Each stakeholder has a different perspective on a situation or task. As such we emphasise that, apart from an overall time framework, the process is emergent and that the idea of imposing a rigorous plan of action before even knowing the nature of a task will suffocate that which could emerge. A classic example of the urge to plan and control we have witnessed was a group of students who predetermined the table of contents of their final written assignment and tried to use that as a means of resolving their task. Naturally we discouraged them to do so, but it took a while before they realised the impossibility of their approach. On the contrary the students are encouraged to engage the dynamic, contingent and fluid nature of an STD or tourism co-design process with others in all its messiness, with all its wickedness (Rittel & Webber, 1973); 'wicked' in as much as there is no one resolution to a task. Similarly we emphasise that working with their task is as much about, if not more so, identifying (latent) opportunities rather than solving problems.

This is a conscious attempt to counter the notion that designing is a problem solving process (Simon, 1981) that situates design in a rational and linear paradigm of thought. Simon sees design problems as "instrumental problems in which one selects from available alternatives the best means for achieving some set of purposes... The designer transforms an existing state of affairs, a problem, into a preferred state, a solution. When his process is rational, it takes the form of a series of rule-governed decisions... A design process is considered rational, in the strongest and simplest case, if and only if its problem-solving steps are fully programmable under a set of designer rules" (Schön, 1990: 111-112). As will become clear, for the students to know beforehand how they will resolve a STD task with others is impossible. They have neither the means nor the experience to do so, and as we've stressed above, nor should they.

Identifying with

In order to give the students the freedom to experiment and explore, it is essential they engage a task they can identify with (Heape, 2007: 7). From Chris Heape's earlier research into design students' learning process, it became abundantly clear that unless students find a way to identify with their task, it is very difficult for them to be both motivated and to sustain that motivation. More importantly, a lack of intrinsic identification with a task hinders students in bringing their resources of empathy, imagination, association and metaphor into play, lessens their ability to reflect on their process and inhibits their will to freely explore and experiment. Their ability to narrate their project to life (ibid: 287) and to imagine through the co-construction of narratives and scenarios just doesn't lift off the ground. They become mired in a confusion that centres around: why are we doing this? We also ask students to work with a high degree of risk, in as much as they are working in a learning environment that is new and engage tasks that are open ended and have no identifiable or correct outcome. It is clear in the courses we have held hitherto and in Heape's research elsewhere (Heape, 2015a & b), that if the students are unable to identify with their task, they are basically unwilling, or find it very difficult, to engage with the unknown that we ask of them. They become over cautious, they hedge the risk.

This was also the case when we made our first attempt at involving the tourism students in our new educational process in 2013. They were assigned tasks that represented issues from chapters in *Understanding the Sustainable Development of Tourism* (Liburd & Edwards, 2010). The students lacked an intrinsic and motivated reason for engaging the tasks. It took a while for us to realise the issue, but by not allowing the students to identify what they thought of as having value to work with, we were in fact disempowering them. We eventually resolved the conflict, but the experience forced us to realise, as noted above, that to ask students to work with both primary and secondary research, and a new learning process was too much for them. Added to that we saw how important it was for the students to identify, in both the STD course and the next semester's tourism co-design course, what it was they wanted to work with.

Having identified their STD project, much of the start-up for the course, and the reason for most of the initial group supervision, is focused on helping the students engender a research question that enables them to engage their task as an authentic process of inquiry, rather than identify a question that encapsulates a 'solution' from the outset. This process is exceedingly important. We recognise that their wish to explore an STD issue is, for the most, very intuitive, yet clearly reflects a sense of value in the group. The question is, 'what is that sense of value and motivation?', as in it lies the seeds of what can emerge. In the ensuing conversations between faculty, tutors and students it gradually becomes clear as to what the essence is they wish to explore.

This process signals a number of qualities to the students. We emphasise there is no need for them to initially be very articulate about what they want to do. Vague notions are acceptable. We do not tell them what to do. Through our interactions with and questions to the students, we signal they have the upper hand. We take our departure point in their learning experience, their confusion even. To tell them what to do is to rob them of their own initiative, curiosity and responsibility for their own learning and process of inquiry. Our questions are not designed to fault them. On the contrary, we emphasise the need to leave the notion of making a mistake on the shelf. Park it! They do experiments they learn from. Our questions are designed to encourage them to maybe look elsewhere or to unpack what they might know without realising it. Above all, our careful questions and gentle prodding signal our sincere wish to follow their process and not ours as faculty or tutors. Initially the students often feel confused, restless and uncertain. It really does take them a while to understand that what we say we do actually mean! So, the initial process of collaboration is clearly about building trust between us and establishing a safe zone for their STD project, their process of inquiry and their budding transformation to an altered sense of self.

Altogether, and born out by our experience with the STD and tourism co-design courses, one can say that an education of attention helps individual students develop both a heightened attention to and perception of the nuance of their process of inquiry, their relating to those others involved, both group members and stakeholders, and, not least, develop a greater understanding and empowerment of themselves. Barnett describes this in similar terms when he points to learning not only knowledge and skills but for "authentic being" (2004: 259). Learning to live over time with uncertainty involves the cultivation of certain qualities, or human dispositions, including carefulness, thoughtfulness, criticality, receptiveness, resilience, courage, and stillness so that students can act purposively and judiciously (Barnett, 2004: 258). Attention to the self entails critically seeing into oneself in ontological and epistemological terms, thus cultivating deeper self-awareness in order to open up for the possibility of seeing beyond the self. This is not to be mistaken for a self-indulgent process (Liburd, 2013). Rather, we contend it alludes to an emancipatory concept of higher education rooted in critical examination of what is being taught, learned and achieved (Barnett, 1990) with others.

Design and perception as...

As regards educating the tourism students to become philosophical practitioners by engaging skilled practice and not just attempting to think their way to a resolution of their projects, an ongoing goal of our approach is to have the students reflect on, actively describe and discuss the nature of their practice, on both reflective and reflexive levels. It is their understanding of their practice at a micro level, their ability to account for what works and what doesn't in relation to the context of the task and their interactions with others that they can take into other task contexts. Thus, their understanding of their practice is informed by reflections of that practice and by relating what they notice to a broad range of process, organisational, complex relational, perception, narrative and design research.

Design is considered "a reflective conversation with the materials of a design situation" (Schön & Wiggins, 1992), "the construction and negotiation of meaning (Heape, 2003), "intentional change in an unpredictable world" (Nelson & Stolterman, 2003), and "a social endeavour where design emerges from the interactions involved in this social activity" (Minneman, 1991). Indeed Scott Minneman emphasises even further the social nature of design when he says: "The moment-to-moment work of design activity is given meaning by interest-relative negotiation... Previous design activity is, at any moment, subject to re-negotiation and re-registration... Things are achieved in design activity by moment to moment negotiation... where designers are seen to be actively conserving ambiguity as a way to reach these negotiated understandings, as opposed to trying to eliminate it. Ambiguity is reduced not by the use of increasingly precise language, but by the design group's repeated negotiative interactions, that come to mean closer to the same thing" (Minneman, 1991: 139- 155). Janet McDonnell (2013) touches on the ethical and quintessential humanness of doing design when emphasising that by noticing ordinary, everyday design practice one can bring the overlooked aspects of lived experience and the dignity of ordinary behaviour into view.

From a complex relations perspective, Stacey, Griffin and Shaw (2000: 189) introduce the notion of variations of interpretation, where "...we want to think of the ever-present, ordinary, detailed differences of interpretation in communication between people as the generators of variety and, hence, the source of novelty... It is in these ongoing differences of interpretation that individual and collective identities are continually recreated and potentially transformed."

From a narrative, metaphor and association perspective, Ochs and Capps indicate: "We use narrative as a tool for probing and forging connections between our unstable, situated selves (1996: 29)." David Silverman (2000:130-131) introduces Morgan's (1986: 344) observation that: "Images and metaphors... are central to the process of imaginization through which people enact or 'write' the character of organizational life." Silverman goes on to describe how "organizational members themselves work with images and metaphors to establish the 'whatness' or 'quiddity' of organisations," a whatness that reflects a turn in organizational studies towards "exploring and representing the extraordinary qualities of the ordinary" (Jeffcutt 1993: 47).

As regards an STD co-design process, the students learn that in both their groups and their involvement with various stakeholders, it is to their advantage to leverage the variations of interpretation that naturally arise, as people see the same situation differently, and to embrace complexity and chaos, rather than strive for consensus. As Stacey et al. (2000) point out, variations of interpretation are generative. The students are also encouraged to engender and facilitate situations in the field where differences of understanding are actively pursued and built on. They learn to engage people in the co-construction of narratives, both so that those involved can draw on and share their experience, their metaphors and their associations, and so that the students can use those stakeholder narratives to understand how others appreciate a situation and their own narratives to probe and forge connections by projecting scenarios into the future; to rehearse the future if you will (Halse et al., 2010).

McDonnell's (2013) call to notice the dignity of ordinary human behaviour and Jeffcutts' (1993: 47) attention to "the extraordinary in the ordinary" touch on the essence of what we are doing here. We encourage the students to embrace a degree of humility in how they approach their tasks and in particular how they understand themselves and others. They learn that by engaging others. It is from the micro interactions of gesture and response (Mead, 1934) and the variations of interpretation that emerge between those involved that the way forward for their practice will reveal itself.

From an education of attention and perception perspective, Ingold (2000: 195) describes practice as embedded in the "current of sociality... because people, in the performance of their tasks, also attend to one another... By watching, listening, perhaps even touching, we continually feel each other's presence in the social environment, at every moment adjusting our movements in response to this ongoing perceptual monitoring... For the orchestral musician, playing an instrument, watching the conductor and listening to one's fellow players are all inseparable aspects of the same process of action: for this reason, the gestures of the performers may be said to resonate with each other... Or what Schutz (1951: 78) called a 'mutual tuning-in relationship' - is an absolute precondition for successful performance."

One characteristic of a design or STD task is that it is not fixed at the outset. It is unknown and those involved will have to familiarise themselves with it as the task unfolds and reveals itself as an emergent becoming. A revealing that is directly affected by how those involved perceive and carry out the task, how they shape its context. Ingold's orchestra players have a score, conductor and instruments they are accustomed to, but what if the situation were otherwise? How would the "mutual tuning-in relationship" develop?

So, what is guiding designers, or in our case tourism students, in this unfamiliar and emergent unfolding? How do they know that a potential solution that emerges is an adequate response to a design or STD task when they do indeed identify it? Or even more complex, how can they recognise parts they identify as of value when they have no real sense of the emergent whole? How do they "tune-in" together and what structures their endeavour?

What emerges from these various accounts of perception, action and sociality is the intimate relationship between an *appreciative awareness* of the unfolding of the task and its context as a whole and the *attuned perception* of its parts (Heape, 2015b) and their relation to the actions that arise, regardless of whether one is dealing with a tangible doing or the attending to of a social doing, or balancing certainty with uncertainty. A characteristic of co-design is that one is typically relating to all these aspects at the same time, the one affecting the other. We see this as an ethical aspect of collaboration for STD that is 'other-regarding' as one cannot expect oneself to be able to flourish without reciprocity and responsibility (Liburd, 2013; 2018).

Clearly, we as educators are asking the tourism students to explore notions of doing an STD inquiry that reach far beyond conventional student teaching and learning. This complex interweaving of philosophy, perception, practice, skill and learning, quite apart from STD theory and the vexing question of just what sustainability means, can, if we are not careful, overwhelm the students. However, we are of the firm conviction, which is born out by the students' own reflections after each STD course, is that they can and do grapple with the process and experience a truly transformative educational process.

One thing is to introduce piecemeal aspects of design, complex relations, perception, narrative and process theory. Another is how to weave these together to an understandable whole that is graspable. Precisely because our aim is aligned with the tourism students' wish to become philosophic tourism practitioners who can work in industry, the public sector, as university researchers, or to create jobs that don't even exist today, it has been one of our tasks to come up with a coherent concept that can accommodate those ambitions. It is also our responsibility to understand that tourism students identify with their future role as tourism practitioners and not to force them into considering themselves as designers. So, how can one take the richness of the above design and other related research and describe a process that tourism students can embrace? As such we have developed, and will continue to develop, a unique approach to learning and process that we choose to call Participatory Inquiry.

Participatory inquiry

When regarding STD from a research, educational or practitioner's perspective, the temptation can be to focus on formal outcomes: technology, concepts, products and services. As a result it can be deemed necessary to streamline such a process to achieve those outcomes. However this understanding can divert attention from how things and operations are actually achieved. Value may be lost in the process, because the resources of those involved, how they get things done on a day to day basis, are not identified as such (Sproedt & Heape, 2014; Liburd & Becken, 2017). By adopting a perspective that is based on complex processes of relating (Stacey et al., 2000; Stacey, 2001; Stacey, 2003; Shaw & Stacey, 2006) one can argue that an STD process can be otherwise seen as the emergence of new meaning (Buur & Larsen, 2010) that arises from the ongoing gesture and response interactions between those involved (Mead, 1934).

A traditional approach to an STD process is that it is the efficient predicting, planning, making and controlling of specific objects, concepts or services, a process that requires a significant degree of a priori knowledge about outcome and possibilities. An alternative approach is to consider STD as open ended; a process of inquiry where people are brought together in a space of possibilities; a participatory environment that is inherently variable and thus emergent, where the known often has to be reappraised as the unknown. As such, STD can be considered an unfolding rather than a foreclosure, where objects or concepts emerge from positionings engendered within these sets of relationships. It is a field of relationships thick with the sociality of complex responsive processes of relating. Tensions are engendered between these positionings through an interplay of the hopes, dreams and aspirations of those involved and the inherent constraints of the present. Variations of interpretation in the tensions leverage shifts in understanding, the emergent synthesis of which are ultimately expressed as STD proposals: concepts, strategies, services, products or new research understanding. In order to engage this dynamic flux, participants improvise to deploy a range of sensibilities, skills and methods that are continually adjusted in close relationship with the contingency of the task in hand. Participants respond to this variable complexity through ongoing improvisation and the deployment of flexibility, foresight and imagination that interweave with the unfolding situation.

Sense-making, sense-giving and understanding emerge from the interdependent interactions between those involved in a particular situation in a continually evolving present and as embedded in that situation. By drawing on this perspective one can infer that "practices also change in the emergent processes of negotiating new meaning, new opportunities, new insights, new thinking and new doing" (Larsen & Sproedt, 2013: 2), in this case new STD practice. So, instead of considering STD as solely related to the resolution or development of a specific solution, technology or product, one can also consider it as a continuous process of "becoming" (Thomas et al., 2011) that emerges from the local interactions of those involved (Stacey & Griffin, 2005). As such, one can understand the becoming of philosophic practitioners and their practice as inherently learning driven and as a process of participatory inquiry.

Participatory inquiry is an inquiry based learning process that interweaves *knowing, doing, making* and *relating*, and leverages the participatory nature of communicative interaction between people. *Learning* emerges as thematic patterns of meaning or *knowing* in the ongoing relating between those involved in such an inquiry: *relating*. Participatory inquiry brings co-design processes, methods, tools and interventions into play in order to explore and expand the inquiry. In this regard, learning is also considered as understanding in practice and as situated in that practice: *doing* and *making*.

Participatory inquiry is also a collaborative, project-oriented, task- and practice-based process of inquiry, driven by action research that engages both faculty and students in a co-generative and co-learning research and development endeavour. A process of inquiry that enables tourism students to bring theory acquired from their lectures or analysis-based learning into play with the theory and skills they discover through their own practice. Students are encouraged to identify tasks and opportunities that are open ended or 'wicked', in that a number of resolutions can apply. Students pursue their inquiry in an STD project by moving from experiment to experiment as they open up and explore a range of perspectives on that inquiry. In the process they engage, direct and critically reflect on their learning and on the social dimensions of working with others as they navigate the highly contingent, dynamic and emergent flux of their task.

Conclusion

By introducing tourism co-design to STD, we wish to engender a shift from an overt management orientation to that of a tourism co-design oriented, STD process that takes its departure point in the notion of designing with, rather than developing for. We wish to bring into play the latent potential that lies waiting to be nurtured if one considers STD as a social endeavour, the interrelated nature of which is continually evolving, rather than as a linear, rational process that attempts to control tourism development. We advocate a tourism co-design, STD learning process that leverages a "collective creativity as applied across the whole span of a design process" (Sanders & Stappers, 2008: 6).

As students choose tasks they identify with, the co-design framing of the STD curriculum gives room for a variety of learning opportunities that are not restricted to traditional lectures or short-term industry projects. On the contrary, by opening up the STD curriculum, the learning space engenders an ontological shift in higher education that can reach for "authentic being" (Barnett, 2004: 259). Authentic being can be described as a being-in-the-world engendered through dialogue with others. By defending our ideas and ideals in our interactions with others, we reproduce and reveal what we believe to be of importance (Taylor, 1992). This involves a degree of intervention in the lifeworld of students that is maybe greater than university teachers find feasible, or which they ideologically dispute on the grounds they do not have the mandate for such deep engagement with students (Feldt & Feldt, 2009). Intellectual considerations, such as teachers' concerns, chances of climbing the career ladder, maximising self-performance and gaining recognition may also impede the social ideals of collaboration (Walsh & Kahn, 2010: 41). Moreover, if the dialogue between partners in a collaborative endeavour is biased and unequal, some may find that an authentic identity with and ownership of the joint process is undermined.

Our experience is that a subjugation of the authentic self can be avoided if the shared goals and contributions necessary to achieve a fully collaborative process are explicitly recognised and acknowledged by those involved (Walsh & Kahn, 2010: 40). This infers that the learning generated in an STD process is collaboratively engendered, developed and disseminated through interpersonal exchange, rather than just stemming from individuals cooperating. This understanding is profoundly influenced by how each participant values that learning and the process that leads to it. In turn, this educational process has a transformative effect on how teachers and students experience this collaborative process of learning, knowledge creation and design for sustainable tourism development.

References

Barnett, R. (1990). *The Idea of Higher Education.* Buckingham: The Society for Research into Higher Education and Open University Press.

Barnett, R. (2004). Learning for an unknown future. *Higher Education Research & Development,* **23**(3), 247-260.

Barnett, R. (2011). *Being a University.* London and New York: Routledge.

Blichfeld, B.S. & Therkelsen A. (2010). *Food and Tourism: Michelin, Moussaka and McDonald's.* Aalborg: Aalborg University.

Buur, J. & Larsen, H. (2010). The quality of conversations in participatory innovation. *CoDesign,* **6**(3) 121–138.

Elias, N. (1978). *What is Sociology*: Columbia University Press.

Feldt, L.E. & Feldt, J.E. (2009). Culture and Cultural Analysis at the University. In M. Blasco and M. Zølner (Eds.) *Teaching Cultural Skills. Adding Culture in Higher Education.København pp.* 227-248. Nyt fra Samfundsvidenskaberne.

Gibson, J. (1986). *The Ecological Approach to Visual Perception.* Lawrence Erlbaum Associates, New Jersey.

Halse, J.,Brandt, E., Clark, B. & Binder, T. (Eds.) (2010). *Rehearsing the Future.* The Danish Design School Press.

Heape, C. (2003). *Design as the construction and negotiation of meaning.* ICSID 2nd Educational Conference Proceedings: Critical Motivations and New Dimensions,

Hannover.

Heape, C. (2007). *The Design Space: the design process as the construction, exploration and expansion of a conceptual space*. University of Southern Denmark, Sønderborg - Unpublished thesis.

Heape, C. (2015a). Doing design practice: design inquiry as an improvised temporal unfolding. *Conference Proceedings of Pin-C 2015*, The Hague, Netherlands

Heape, C. (2015b). Today's students, tomorrow's practitioners. In R. V. Zande, E. Bohemia, & I. Digranes (Eds.), LearnxDesign: *Proceedings of the 3rd International Conference for Design Education Researchers* (Vol. 4) Aalto University, pp. 1362-1380.

Heape, C., Larsen, H. & Revsbæk, L. (2015). Participation as taking part in an improvised temporal unfolding. *Conference Proceedings 5th Decennial Aarhus Conference*, Aarhus, Denmark.

Heron, J. & Reason, P. (1997). A Participatory Inquiry paradigm. *Qualitative Inquiry*, **3**(3), 274-294.

Ingold, T. (2001). From the transmission of representations to the education of attention, in: H. Whitehouse (Ed.) *The Debated Mind: Evolutionary Psychology versus Ethnography*. Berg, Oxford, pp. 113–153.

Ingold, T. (2000). *The Perception of The Environment: Essays in livelihood, dwelling and skill*. London and New York: Routledge.

Ingold, T. (2017). *Anthropology and/as Education*. London; New York:Routledge

Jeffcutt, P. (1993). From interpretation to representation. In J. Hassard & M. Parker (Eds.), *Postmodernism and Organizations*, pp. 25-24. London: Sage.

Larsen, H. & Sproedt, H. (2013). Researching and Teaching Innovation Practice. *Conference Proceedings 14th International CINet Conference, Business Development and Co-creation*, Nijmegen, Netherlands.

Lave, J. & Wenger, E. (2001). *Situated Learning - Legitimate Peripheral Participation*. Cambridge: Cambridge University Press.

Liburd, J. (2010). Sustainable tourism development In: J. Liburd and D. Edwards (Eds.) *Understanding the Sustainable Development of Tourism* pp. 1-18. Oxford: Goodfellow Publishers

Liburd, J. (2013). *Towards the Collaborative University. Lessons from Tourism Education and Research*. Odense: Print & Sign.

Liburd, J. (2018). Understanding collaboration and sustainable tourism development. In Liburd, J. and Edwards, D. (2018) *Collaboration for Sustainable Tourism Development*. Oxford: Goodfellow Publishers.

Liburd, J. & Becken, S. (2017). Values in nature conservation, tourism and UNESCO World Heritage Site stewardship. *Journal of Sustainable Tourism* DOI:10.1080/096695 82.2017.1293067

Liburd, J., & Edwards, D. (Eds.). (2010). *Understanding the Sustainable Development of Tourism*. Oxford: Goodfellows.

Liburd, J., Nielsen, T.K. & Heape, C. (2017) Co-designing smart tourism. *European Journal of Tourism Research* **17**, 28-42.

McDonnell, J. (2013). Keynote - Looking in the Right Place: What the study of micro-structures of design activities tells us about design expertise and collaboration skills. *Conference Proceedings Eksig*, Loughborough University, UK.

Mead, G. H. (1934). *The Philosophy of the Present*. Chicago: Chicago University Press.

Minneman, S. L. (1991). *The Social Construction of a Technical Reality: Empirical studies of group engineering design practice*. Stanford University.

Morgan, G. (1986). *Images of Organization*. Beverly Hills, CA: Sage.

Nelson H.G. & Stolterman, E. (2003). *The Design Way: Intentional Change in an Unpredictable World*. MIT Press, Boston MA.

Ochs, E. & Capps, L. (1996). Narrating the self. *Annual Review of Anthropology*, **25**(1), 19-43.

Reason, P. & Bradbury, H. (Eds.). (2008). *Sage Handbook of Action Research: Participative inquiry and practice* (2nd ed.). London : Sage Publications.

Rittel, H. W. J. & Webber, M. M. (1973). Dilemmas in a general theory of planning. *Policy Sciences*, **4**, 155-169.

Sanders, E. B.-N. & Stappers, P. J. (2008). Co-creation and the new landscapes of design. *CoDesign*, **4**(1), 5–18.

Shaw, P. (2002). *Changing Conversations in Organizations: a complexity approach to change*. London; New York: Routledge

Shaw P. & Stacey R. (Eds.). (2006). *Experiencing Risk, Spontaneity and Improvisation in Organizational Change*. London and New York: Routledge.

Schutz, A. (1951). Making music together - a study in social relationship. *Social Research*, **18**(1), 76-97.

Schön, D.A., 1990. The design process. In: Howard, V.A. (Ed.), *Varieties of Thinking : Essays from Harvard's Philosophy of Education Research Center*. Routledge, New York.

Schön, D. A. & Wiggins, G. (1992). Kinds of seeing and their functions in designing. *Design Studies*, **13**(2), 135-156.

Silverman, D. (2000). Routine pleasures: the aesthetics of the mundane. In S. Linstead & H. Höpfl (Eds.), *The Aesthetics of Organisation*. London and New Dehli: Sage Publications, pp. 130 – 153.

Simon, H.A., (1981). *The Sciences of the Artificial*, 2nd ed. MIT Press, Cambridge, Mass.

Sproedt, H. & Heape, C.R.A. (2014) Cultivating imagination across boundaries – How to create, capture and deliver learning value through participatory inquiry. *Conference Proceedings the 15th International CINet*.

Stacey, R., Griffin, D. & Shaw, P. (2000). *Complexity and Management: Fad or radical challenge to systems thinking*. London and New York: Routledge.

Stacey R. (2001). *Complex Responsive Processes in Organisations*. London and New York: Routledge.

Stacey, R. (2003). Learning as an activity of interdependent people. *The Learning Organization*, **10**(6), 325-331.

Stacey, R. & Griffin, D. (2005). *A Complexity Perspective on Researching in Organizations. Taking Experience Seriously*. London: Routledge.

Taylor, C. (1992). *The Ethics of Authenticity*. Cambridge, MA: Harward University Press.

Thomas, R., Sargent L.D. & Hardy C. (2011). Managing organizational change: negotiating meaning and power-resistance relations. *Organization Science*, **22**(1), 22-41.

Tribe, J. (2010). *Strategy for Tourism*. Oxford, UK: Goodfellow Publishers.

Walsh, L. and Kahn, P. (Eds) (2010). *Collaborative Working in Higher Education*. The Social Academy. New York and London: Routledge.

Reflections on Research Paradigms:
Their relationship to understanding and facilitating collaboration for sustainable tourism development

Gayle R. Jennings

"The future of humanity and of our planet lies in our hands."

(United Nations, Department of Economic and Social Affairs, 2015: 14)

Wicked problems of the world—poverty, health and wellbeing, equality, climate change, refugee crises, sustainability, … ; continue to challenge humankind. Despite decades of collaborations, partnerships, policies and research, these wicked problems remain primarily unresolved and manifold. This is not unexpected as this is inherent in the nature of wicked problems. As Horst Rittel (1967 in Churchman, 1967) and Rittel and Webber (1973) noted, wicked problems are marked by the inability to provide a universal solution and a universal research approach. Instead the problems are context specific and continually transmogrify – there is no end point. In addition, they can overlap, interrelate, interconnect and intersect. In framing the nature of a wicked problem, the knowledge sets and experiences, social situatedness, respective insider- or outsider-ness and worldviews of the various stakeholders involved play critical roles with regard to how the problem is addressed. They inform and shape what is given attention and why; what is included or excluded and why; as well as the methodologies and methods used. Every attempt to address a wicked problem leaves a legacy including repercussions and unintended consequences. There is no undoing of actions. As four of the manifold stakeholders concerned with wicked problems, researchers, planners, designers and practitioners have the task of "improv[ing] some [of the] characteristics of the world where people live …" (Rittel & Webber, 1973:167). These four stakeholders, like all stakeholders, are responsible for the consequences of their actions and ongoing ramifications associated with the redress of wicked problems. Unlike traditional "scientized" (Xiang, 2013: 2) linear approaches used to address solvable, or 'tame', problems; non-linear, social process-based problem-solving approaches are required for wicked problems. Rather than outcomes being supported/not supported or validated/not validated in the case of tame problems, strategies used to address wicked problems are usually evaluated using criteria, such as "better or worse", and are always influenced by stakeholder viewpoints (Rittel & Webber, 1973:163). As a consequence of the nature of wicked problems, there is no 'quick fix' or easy way to address these 'malignant', 'vicious', 'tricky', 'aggressive' – wicked problems (Rittel & Webber, 1973:160).

In the beginning decades of the 21st century, some wicked problems have been reclassified as 'super wicked problems'. Based on Rittel and Webber's (1973) description of wicked problems, super wicked problems are further denoted by four characteristics: "time is running out; those who cause the problem also seek to provide the solution; the central authority needed to address them is weak or non-existent; and irrational discounting occurs that pushes responses into the future" (Levin et al., 2012:124). The key super wicked problem that this book addresses is sustainable development, specifically, the related wicked problem of sustainable tourism development and the means by which collaboration can support resilient action towards facilitating tourism development that is inherently sustainable. The various chapters in this book present critical reflections on research actions undertaken in the spirit of fostering sustainable tourism development. As such, the chapters offer critical insights into the consequences and affect of those research actions.

This chapter, however, takes a step back from these exemplars. Rather than focus on completed research, this chapter reflects on the suite of research paradigms that can inform researchers, planners, designers, practitioners, indeed all stakeholders, with regard to engaging in resilient action founded on collaboration to facilitate sustainable tourism development. Knowledge of this suite of paradigms and their respective tenets, especially the paradigms that best serve action, collaboration and facilitation can then act as a tool to mitigate against the various social processes that generate, ratify, and reinforce practices that are counterproductive to overall global sustainability. For some, it may mean an upskilling in paradigmatic knowledge, experience and practice, for others, a need to extend the same, and for still others, it may be a (re)affirmation of their paradigmatic practices.

At the core of collaboration is stakeholder meaning-making engagement—essentially a dynamic, social process. Subsequently, all researchers, planners, designers and practitioners need to evaluate their intra-, interpersonal, cross-cultural, team, leadership and facilitation skills sets in order to effectively participate in such dynamism (Jennings, 2007a & b, 2009, 2018a; Brundiers et al., 2010). Again, for some, it may mean an upskilling in these skills sets, for others, a need to extend the same, and for still others, it may be a (re)affirmation of their practices. Moreover, such evaluation should be undertaken by all participants/ stakeholders. If skills are lacking, then time needs to be spent to skill or up-skill all participants/stakeholders in order that they are 'collaboratively ready'! Elsewhere, this may be referred to as 'capacity building'. But before address-ing paradigmatic knowledge, practice and skill sets and complementary social engagement skill sets; I want to return to the super wicked problem of sustain-ability, and the wicked problem of sustainable tourism development to provide some background for the arguments presented in this chapter. I also want to define the concepts collaboration, partnership, collaborative partnership, and resilience to contextualise their use or later lack of use in this chapter.

Sustainability, sustainable tourism development, related definitions and research issues

"meanings differ across time, across societies, cultures (Urry, 1990, 2002)*, nation states, ... as well as between individuals"* (Jennings, 2007b: 261)

Despite the fact that "[c]oncepts of stewardship of ... land, resources, and interconnectivity of all things—that is, sustainable practices—have informed indigenous peoples' ways of life for hundreds of years" (Jennings, 2007c:225), within the western English-speaking world, attention to such 'stewardship' only became more pronounced in the later decades of the 1900s. Meadows and her co-researchers (1972) provided one of the earliest research-based sustain-ability framings that highlighted the finite nature of resources and 'limits to growth'. Almost a decade later, the International Union for the Conservation of Nature and Natural Resources, the World Wildlife Fund, and the United Nations Environment Program (IUCN, WWF & UNEP, 1980) offered another framing, which focussed on the need for 'sustainable utilization' and 'sustain-able development'. In that same decade, one of the better-known and oft uti-lised sustainability framings, the 1987 Brundtland Report, also known as *Our Common Future*, was promulgated. This report defined sustainable development as "development that meets the needs of the present without compromising the ability of future generations to meet their own needs" (World Commission on Environment and Development, 1987). Despite the alerts that these framings identified, and World Summits held on sustainable development, for example, in Rio 1992, and Johannesburg in 2002; goals set failed to be achieved. And, of course, not only does this reflect the nature of (super) wicked problems but also the aspirational and broad parameters of goal setting/statements as well as their subsequent interpretations by stakeholders. Such interpretations have and continue to have specific and direct consequences for action and research, as discussed by Janne Liburd in Chapter 2.

More contemporaneously, fulfilment of sustainable development goals continues to vex stakeholders. Despite progress towards the aspirations of the United Nations, UN Millennium Development Goals, which focussed on developing worlds up until 2015; apart from "halving poverty", the other goals remained variously unfulfilled (Ki-Moon, 2013: iii). Building on the previous Millennium goals, the UN 2030 Agenda for Sustainable Development is broader in scope and aims at both developing and developed worlds. Within the goal-scape of the UN 2030 Agenda, there are 17 goals. Tourism is identified within three goals—specifically, Goal 8 ("decent work and economic growth"), Goal 12 ("responsible consumption and production"), and 14 ("life below water") (UN DESA, n.d. -a). The implementation of the 2030 Agenda is to be orchestrated by "all nations and all stakeholders, acting in collaborative partnership, … [to] implement this plan" (p. 3). Such a path is expected to yield "bold and transformative" (p. 3) changes predicated on sustainability and resiliency for the world and its future. While a definition of collaborative partnerships is not provided in Agenda 2030, elsewhere the UN DESA (n.d. -b), provides 'who' and 'when' insights with regard to "collaborative partnerships [being] between governments and non-State actors at all levels, and at all stages of the programmatic cycle-planning, consultations, implementation, monitoring and reviews".

Within extant tourism literature, usage of the concept of 'collaborative partnerships' is relatively recent (see for example Stone, 2015). The constituent terms of the concept—collaboration and partnerships have been disparately and interchangeably used in tourism planning and policy, and sustainable tourism development literature, see for example Bramwell and Lane's (2000) edited work. As a form of usage, partnership tends to associate with practitioner and public sector usage, and collaboration with academic discourses (Bramwell & Lane, 2000). Despite the use of the concept of collaborative partnerships by the United Nations in the 2030 Agenda, and the interchangeable usage of collaboration and partnerships within tourism literature, this book and the editors of this book along with this chapter distinguish between collaboration and partnerships. I leave it for others in this book to explain how they use the terms and/or distinguish between them.

Collaboration is a critical process for sustainable tourism development (Zhoa & Ritchie, 2007; Liburd & Edwards, 2010). From my perspective, collaboration is also a critical element for sustainable tourism development-oriented research. In 2013, Liburd wrote: "[c]ollaboration originates from Latin, *collaborare*, meaning to work together … more or less [as] equal partners [and wherein] the sum of the work is more than its individual parts" (p. 12-13). Relatedly, Rolling (2015) commented with respect to "creation of surplus" and "social swarms" that "our deepest and richest achievements are not the product of single individuals, but of the social systems proliferating our prosthetic capacity toward the transmission and spread of ideas and behaviors that aid our collective resilience, ensuring the survival of the patterns that sustain us" (p. 543). Bearing these in mind, for the purposes of this chapter, collaboration is deemed to mean engaging in dynamic, social processes of creative meaning-making predicated on democratic dialogue founded on mutual respect, trust and equality in order to achieve shared goals and learnings by working together. Dynamic, creative, social meaning-making processes engender flexibility so that people do not feel coerced or compromised from a consensus perspective (Jamal & Getz, 1999). Further, democractic dialogue is critical, for as Levin et. al., (2012) advise "[t]he challenge for ... multi-stakeholder processes in general, is to find ways to promote stakeholder learning that move away from an emphasis on achieving consensus, which militates against addressing super wicked problems" (p. 147).

With regard to learning and the address of wicked problems, amongst the myriad of learning frameworks, Bateson's (1972) Levels I, II, III model and Argyris and Schön's (1978) single and double loop learning model are useful. Bateson's Level 1 is characterised by rote learning. Argyris and Schön call this single loop learning, learning which works unquestioningly within given parameters for action. Level 2 learning requires more input and reflection by the learner, as it does in double loop learning wherein learners critically question existing parameters for action and subsequently, creatively change parameters and then actions. Level 3 is associated with disruption in order to make a significant change in practice. This level resonates in Argyris and Schön's double loop learning. To address wicked problems, Level II and III and/or double loop learning are required.

Turning now to *partnership*, "[a] partnership is an arrangement where parties, known as partners, agree to cooperate to advance their mutual interests" (Wikipedia, 2018). Wherein such cooperation tends to associate with "the division of labour" (Liburd, 2013:13), varying degrees of equality and power as well as echoes of a 'business' arrangement. The processes and outcomes associated with partnership and collaboration are different. Next, *resilience*: Evans and Reid (2015:156) in discussing "violence and insecurity", purport that resilience is a somewhat nihilistic term, which has generated a worldview that such "phenomena [herein super/wicked problems such as sustainability/sustainable tourism development can be read] ... are assumed as natural and contestable". For them, resilience depoliticises us as we try to learn from one catastrophic [sustainable tourism development] event to the next in order to be more prepared. As they say resilience "promotes adaptability so that life may go on living despite experiencing certain destruction" (Evans and Reid, 2015:156). While acknowledging the nihilism inherent in resiliency, this chapter embraces a more politicised and fecund view of resilience. Politicised because "resilient populations have the potential to "emerge as a ... referent of governance" (Zebrowski, 2013: 172). In this chapter, resiliency refers to "our shared capacity to behave together for the common good manifested as the production of a most generative differential space—that multitudinous theatre of possibilities wherein we 'create and open spaces into which existing knowledge can extend, interrelate, coexist, and where new ideas and relationships can emerge prosthetically' (Garoian, 2013: 6)" (Rollings, 2015, p. 543).

Penultimately, sustainable tourism manages "all resources in such a way that economic, social and aesthetic needs can be fulfilled while maintaining cultural integrity, essential ecological processes, biological diversity, and life support systems" (WTO, 1998:21). Finally, and obviously drawing on the Brundtland Report, sustainable tourism development refers to "meet[ing] the needs of present tourists and host regions while protecting and enhancing opportunity for the future" (WTO, 1998:21).

Given the preceding discourse and extant literature, inherent in the development of sustainable tourism research agendas founded on collaboration and resiliency is the need to consider the nature and role of:

1 Researcher values (Jennings, 2007c), and all stakeholder values, (Bramwell & Lane, 2011; Mowforth & Munt, 1998);

2 Researcher positionality – objectivity, subjectivity, intersubjectivity (Jennings, 2018b), and stakeholder relationships (Jennings, 2018b, Wall, 1997);

3 Collaboration with stakeholders in research design and implementation processes (Jennings, 2007c; 2018b);

4 Democratic dialogue rather than consensus (Levin et.al., 2012; Grybovych & Hafermann, 2010, see also Jamal & Getz, 1999; Weiler & Ham, 2002)

5 Partnerships (Bramwell and Lane, 1999; Pigram & Wahab, 1997);

6 Stakeholder participation (Akyeampong, 2011; Jennings, 2007c, 2018b; Mowforth & Munt, 1998; Moscardo, 2011);

7 Education/learning (Bramwell & Lane, 1999; Jennings, 2007c; Jamal & Watt, 2011; Koutsouris, 2009; Marien & Pizam, 1997; Wray, 2011), specifically:

   a Communication skills (intra- and interpersonal), cross-cultural understandings (Bramwell & Lane, 1999; Jennings, 2007a & b, 2009, 2018a);

   b Team, leadership and facilitation skills, (Jennings, 2007a & b, 2009, 2018a; Brundiers et. al., 2010);

    c Critical thinking (Jennings, 2018a; Liburd & Edwards, 2010);

    d Reflection and/or reflexivity (Bradbury & Reason, 2006; Jennings, 2007b);

    e Types of learning (Bramwell & Lane, 2011) and knowing (Bradbury & Reason, 2006);

    f Creativity, innovation and imaginivity (Bradbury & Reason, 2006; Bramwell & Lane, 1999; Garoian, 2013; Jennings, 2018a; Rittel & Webber, 1973; Rollings, 2015);

8 Power (Bradbury & Reason, 2006; Marien & Pizam, 1997; Dredge & Jenkins, 2007, Bramwell & Lane, 1999, 2011);

9 Agency (Matarrita-Cascante, Brennan & Luloff (2010)

10 Empowerment (Sofield, 2003; Schilcher, 2007)

11 Emanicipation (Reason & Bradbury, 2006);

12 Research action outcomes

    a Social action (Bevir, 2009; Bramwell & Lane, 2006; Healey, 2006)

    b Policy (Bramwell & Lane, 2011),

    c Practice (Bradbury & Reason, 2006; Wray, 2011)

    d Level of impact (Bramwell & Lane, 2011),

    e Adaptation (Bramwell & Pomfret, 2007; Jennings, 2018b; Evans & Reid, 2015)

    f Transformation (UN DESA, n.d.-a; 2015; Healey, 2006; Walker & Weiler, 2017).

How and if these considerations are incorporated depends on the nature of the paradigm selected for the sustainable tourism development research at hand. Additionally, regardless of research focus, every research project should consider sustainability, ethics, socio-cultural, environmental and aesthetic responsibility as well as accountability, and the integration of evaluative research processes. Researchers need to 'walk' the sustainability development 'talk' so to speak. And this directly associates with "first person research/practice" , wherein researchers, planners, designers, and practitioners inquire into their various life-worlds, including their professional practice, to bring about change. On the other hand, in second person research/practice, the researcher co-researches shared issues with others through 'interpersonal dialogue', 'communities of inquiry' and 'learning organizations'. Third person research/practice associates with community, organisational, and national projects predicated on 'communities of inquiry' interacting via communication networks to support transformational change (Reason & Torbert, 2001:1).

Research paradigms, collaboration and sustainable tourism development

"More attention may well be paid to the philosophical frameworks which define what we know and how we can come to know about it, and to the rules and procedures which indicate how research is conducted and how information can be collected and organised." (Bramwell & Lane, 1999: 2).

The range of paradigms available to tourism researchers and indeed any researcher includes post/positivism, pragmatism, critical realism, chaos and complexity theory, critical theory orientation, constructivist, and the participatory paradigm. Herein, for meaning-making purposes, the term 'paradigm' associates with Thomas Kuhn's (1962) discussion. Subsequently, a paradigm is deemed to represent a "locus of professional ... commit[ment] to the same rules and standards for scientific practice" (Kuhn, 2012: 11). This chapter aims to consider those paradigms with regard to their ability to support collaboration and resiliency for sustainable tourism development. As background, Table 14.1 has been included to provide an overview of the various paradigms with respect to their ontology (study of the nature of reality), epistemology (study of knowledge), methodology (guidelines for the conduct of research) and axiology (study of ethics and values) (Jennings, 2009: 672). A fuller discussion of these paradigms can be found in Jennings (2010).

Table 14.1 was developed from Denzin and Lincoln (2000), Guba (1990), Guba and Lincoln (1994), Jennings' (2001, 2007a, 2010), Lincoln and Guba (2000), Lincoln, Lynham, Guba (2011, 2018), Schwandt (2000), Tashakkori and Teddlie (1998, 2003), Teddlie and Tashakkori (2009), Powell (2001), Levy (2000).

Although Table 14.1 overviews nine paradigms from which researchers may choose—are they all suited to contributing to sustainable tourism development and the principles of collaboration, and resilient action? While all paradigms may variously contribute to the overall pursuit of sustainable tourism development, some are more supportive of the principles of collaboration, and resilient action than others. Why an emphasis on collaboration and resilient action? Because it resonates in Agenda 2030, but also because:

"Researchers need to be aware that the work that they do, no matter how applied in intent and how practical in orientation, is not likely to have major influence on the policy decision at which it is purportedly directed ... When competing with other powerful factors, such as officials' concern with political or bureaucratic advantage, one limited study (and all studies are limited in some way) is likely to have limited impact" (Carol Weiss, 1986:232).

Table 14.1: Paradigms that may inform sustainable tourism development research[i]

Paradigms	Paradigmatic guiding elements			
	Ontology	Epistemology	Methodology	Axiology
Positivism	Truths and laws are universal	Objective	Quantitative	Ethics important, externally regulated, and extrinsic to the pursuit of research[ii] Value free
Post-positivism	Truths are fallible and a product of historical and social contexts	Objective - acknowledges potential for researcher bias (subjective)	Quantitative	Ethics important, externally regulated, and extrinsic to the pursuit of research[ii] Recognition of potential role of values and the need for their subsequent management
Critical realism	Truths are fallible and a product of historical and social contexts	Objective - acknowledges potential for researcher bias (subjective)	Quantitative Inclusion of mixed methods	Ethics important, externally regulated, and extrinsic to the pursuit of research, Management of role of values Research may have an emancipatory purpose
Pragmatism (Mixed methods)	"What works" in the external reality	Ability to solve problems Objective and subjective	Mixed methods	Ethics important, externally regulated, and extrinsic to the pursuit of research Values influence interpretations
Chaos and Complexity theory orientation	Systems complex, non-linear dynamic, ever-changing and unpredictable Chaotic and disordered Self organizing	Objective and subjective Self referential	Open systems and descriptive algorithms Metaphors	Ethics important, externally regulated, and extrinsic to the pursuit of research Systems orientation essays to be value free Metaphoric orientation acknowledges values
Critical theory	Socio-historical realities Realities reflective of power relations	Subjective-objective unless post-positivist critical theory (objective)	Qualitative Some quantitative	Ethics important and while externally regulated, are intrinsic to the pursuit of research due to the embedded moral stance of researcher/s towards revelation Primarily value laden
Social constructivism	Multiple perspectives/ realities	Intersubjective	Qualitative	Ethics important and while externally regulated, ethics are intrinsic to the pursuit of research and the formative construction of meaning and revelation Value laden
Post-modernism	Multiple realities No privileging of position Skepticism towards 'truth' and '-isms'	Relativism	Qualitative	Despite the anathema of external regulation, ethics important albeit they are relative and should be founded on personal codes of ethics Questions all values
Participatory	Realities collectively constructed via interactions between self-other	Embodied and situated, reflexive Hermeneutic	Qualitative Quantitative Mixed method	Ethics important and while externally regulated, are intrinsic to the pursuit of research and the formative co-construction of meaning and revelation Value laden

i A previous version of this table (Jennings, 2009) has examples of tourism research associated with each paradigms

ii Lincoln, Lynham and Guba (2011: 99) noted ethics as "Extrinsic- tilt towards deception"

Although a somewhat dated and sanguine view, Weiss' view has continuing currency. Subsequently, as is already the case, researchers, planners, designers and practitioners need to consider other avenues than policy alone to bring about change with regard to the wicked problem of sustainable tourism development. Other avenues include social action and practice at varying levels of impact in order to bring about adaptation and transformation. Let's return to the question: "are all paradigms suited to contributing to sustainable tourism development, and the principles of collaboration, and resilient action?" Reflecting on each research paradigm using the set of 12 research considerations enables us to filter which paradigm(s) is/are most suited to the task. Table 14.2 (pp 256-262) provides an overview of such reflections. The table was heuristically (see Moustakas, 1990) determined. In the table, readers will note the use of tentative terms, such as 'may', 'possible', 'potential'; these have been applied since an 'exact' determination depends on the researcher, methodological mix and/or "blurring of [paradigmatic] genres" (Denzin & Lincoln, 2018).

As demonstrated in Table 14.2, the paradigmatic guiding elements of positivism and postpositivism preclude them from directly engaging in collaboration and resiliency as defined in this chapter. Similarly, this is the case for critical realism. Based on the text in Table 14.2, of all the paradigms from which we could choose, to varying degrees five are supportive of the 12 research considerations. Those paradigms are pragmatism (mixed methods), chaos and complexity theory, critical theory orientation, constructivism, and the participatory paradigm. Amongst these, the participatory paradigm serves to champion most considerations. Indeed, its very core is predicated on the principles of collaboration and resiliency and its methodologies embrace the majority of considerations. The participatory paradigm is action–oriented stakeholder-wise, communication, collaboration, participation, education and learning-wise, power, agency, empowerment, emancipation, practice, level of impact, adaptation and transformation-wise. The research tradition or approach used in the participatory paradigm is action research in all its various guises (see Jennings, 2018 for discussion of these). In essence,

"[a]ction research is a participatory, democratic process concerned with developing practical knowing in the pursuit of worthwhile human purposes, grounded in a participatory worldview ... It seeks to bring together action and reflection, theory and practice, in participation with others, in the pursuit of practical solutions to issues of pressing concern to people, and more generally the flourishing of individual persons and their communities." (Reason & Bradbury, 2006: 1)

As a consequence of a blurring of research genres, action research has been shaped and fashioned by other paradigms in Table 14.1 to generate, for example, postpositivistic, pragmatic, critical theory, and/or constructivist informed action research (see Jennings, 2018). Again, in Table 14.2, the tentative nature of terms reflects such blurring.

It must be noted that within sustainable tourism development, action research and/or the participatory paradigm have an established history (see for example, respectively research or commentaries by Grybovych and Hafermann, 2010; Jamal & Getz, 1999; Marien & Pizam, 1997; Mowforth & Munt, 1998; Pigram and Wahab, 1997). This chapter reinforces the use of the participatory paradigm in its totality—its ontology, epistemology, methodology and axiology. Why? Because of its ability to engender collaboration and resiliency through democratic dialogue, power sharing, participation in mutual inquiry, critical thinking, reflection, creativity, practical knowing, action learning, Level II, III and double loop learning, to enable agency, empowerment, emancipation as well as transformation and adaptation of practice and more sustainable liveli-hoods. To engage fully and generatively with the participatory paradigm may require researcher, planner, designer and practitioner upskilling, capacity building, and/or further development. Of particular concern are competencies in communication, teamwork, leadership, facilitation and participatory processes and the ability to coach stakeholders to be similarly skilled. Such skill sets will enable all stakeholders to effectively engage in democratic dialogue regarding the wicked problem of sustainable tourism development and super wicked problem of sustainability.

Importantly, wicked problems need to be addressed holistically. Following Rittel (1967 in Churchman, 1967), Churchman (1967) cautions against "carving off" a piece of a wicked problem to study as irresponsible and duplicitous in that only part of the problem is addressed and this may subsequently generate a "mutated wicked problem" (Xiang, 2013:1). For Churchman, this "is morally wrong" (1967: B-142). Xiang also emphasises holism as well as a "process ori-ented approach that is by nature *adaptive, participatory*, and *transdisciplinary* (APT for short)" … [in order to produce] better and more satisfying results" (Xiang, 2013,: 2). Elsewhere, a modular approach to addressing sustainablity transitions have been advocated by Manning and Reinecke (2016). My stance supports holistic, multidisciplinary, interdisciplinary and transdisciplinary sustainable tourism development research informed by the participatory paradigm.

Table 14.2: Reflections on research paradigms and the 12 research considerations

Paradigms	Positivism	Postpositivism							Naturalistic inquiry
	Positivism	**Postpositivism**							
	Positivism	Scientific Post-Positivism	Critical Realism	Pragmatism (Mixed methods)	Chaos and complexity theory orientation	Critical Theory	Social Constructivism	Postmodern	Participatory
1. Values	Value free approach to research processes pursued	Researcher/s essay/s to be value free during research processes	May have value laden elements	Values also play a role in selection of explanation/s that facilitate outcomes	Researcher/s acknowledge/s values in qualitative approach	Researcher/s acknowledge/s their values influence research processes	Researcher/s acknowledge/s the role of their values in research processes	Researchers question all values	(Co-)/Researcher/s acknowledge/s the role of their values in the research process
2. Researcher positionality and stakeholder relationships	Objectivity as researcher concerned with usability of research — Acknowledges the potential for researcher bias (subjectivity)	Subjectivity with regard to explanation			Objectivity and subjectivity	Subjective-intersubjective-objective	Intersubjective	Relativism	Subjective - embodied and intersubjective - situated

Paradigms	Positivism	Scientific Post-Positivism	Critical Realism	Pragmatism (Mixed methods)	Chaos and complexity theory orientation	Critical Theory	Social Constructivism	Postmodern	Participatory
3. Collaboration with stakeholders - in research proposal/ research design	Collaboration associated with funding agencies, private, public, not for profit, industry sectors					May have some collaboration associated with funding agencies, private, public, not for profit, industry sectors		Leaning to individualism	Collaboration embedded in paradigm principles
				May have some collaboration depending on the nature of qualitative research used		Collaboration with marginalized, oppressed and disempowered stakeholders		Rejection of collaboration with institutional stakeholders	Collaboration associated with all respective stakeholders – dependent on which type of participatory research utilised
								No privileging of stakeholder position	
	Inter-researcher collaboration					Inter-researcher and co-researcher collaboration		Inter-researcher collaboration	
4. Democratic dialogue and collaboration with stakeholders in research process	Primarily nil democratic dialogue	Nil or limited 'democratic dialogue. 'Collaboration'/ consultation essentially associated with feedback on research questions, data collection tools and distribution				Potential for democratic dialogue associated with all respective stakeholders:		Skeptical of democratic dialogue	Founded on principles of democratic dialogue and mutuality
						- dependent on nature of critical theory orientation utilised	- especially, if participatory research is used to inform research	Language may be 'collaborative'	
	Collaboration with partner/ collaborative researchers	Primarily, collaboration with partner/collaborative researchers				Inter-researcher collaboration		Leaning to individualism	Co-stakeholder collaboration inherent in paradigm

Paradigms	Positivism	Scientific Post-Positivism	Critical Realism	Pragmatism (Mixed methods)	Chaos and complexity theory orientation	Critical Theory	Social Constructivism	Postmodern	Participatory
4. Democratic dialogue and collaboration with stakeholders in research process (continued)	Research expertise is vested in the 'researcher/s'	Limited collaboration with research participants since research expertise is vested in the 'researchers'				Co-researcher collaboration		Rejection of collaboration/consultation with mainstream stakeholders and power brokers	Collaboration associated with all respective stakeholders
Partnerships related to:	Possibly social justice		Social justice		Possibly social justice			Social justice	Co-researcher interests
	Funding	Researcher interests			Possibly funding			Environmental justice	
		Possibly environmental justice							
Stakeholder participation as:	Possible research "subjects"	Advisory/reference committee				Possible advisory/reference committee		Leaning to individualism	Stakeholder involvement embedded in participatory principles
		Possible research "subjects"		Possible research "subjects" or "participants"			Co-researchers, participants		
		Recipient of findings						Potential readers/viewers of text productions	
7. Education/Learning	Intra-, inter-personal and cross-cultural communication skills required across paradigms and within research processes.								
7a. Communication skills	Evaluate, determine, implement 'capacity building' requirements as on-going processes								

Paradigms	Positivism	Scientific Post-Positivism	Critical Realism	Pragmatism (Mixed methods)	Chaos and complexity theory orientation	Critical Theory	Social Constructivism	Postmodern	Participatory
7b. Team, leadership and facilitation skills	Team building, leadership and facilitation skills required to varying degrees across the paradigms and within research processes. Evaluate, determine, implement 'capacity building' requirements as an on-going process								Potential for all stakeholders - dependent on skills and expertise, may be need for 'capacity building'
7c. Critical thinking	Primarily, used by researchers					Primarily, used by researchers and co-researchers and/or research participants		Primarily, used by researchers	
	Potentially by reference committees, ethics committees, and reviewers - if engaged, as well as other users of the research and, possibly some (interested) stakeholders								
7d. Reflection and/or reflexivity	Researcher(s may use reflection during research design, implementation and reporting. Participants may use reflection during responses				For quantitative research, (self) reflection may occur during various research processes		Possible (self) reflection by co-researchers and/or participants	Continuous deconstruction and reflection	Use of self-reflection and group reflection practices
			Depending on nature of qualitative methods:		For qualitative research oriented research:				
			- use of reflexive practices may be integrated		- reflexivity expected in research	- reflexivity embedded in research	Reflexive practices embedded in research processes		Reflexive practices may be included depending on nature of approach
7e. Types of Learning	Researcher learning	Primarily researcher learning			Individual learning by co-researchers or researchers and research participants	Co-researcher learning or researchers and research participants	Co-researcher learning or researcher and research participant learning	Individuated self-reasoning and justification	Learning is inherent in research processes
	Possible stakeholder learning from research findings and recommendations				Possible interested other 'stakeholder' learning from research 'findings' and/or 'recommendations'				
	Didactic learning (Level 1/single loop learning) associated with transfer of knowledge presented in research								
		Strategic learning	Potential for strategic and practical learning		Potential for Level II learning		Strategic and practical learning if participatory oriented research		Level II and III, double loop learning
									Strategic and practical learning

Paradigms	Positivism	Scientific Post-Positivism	Critical Realism	Pragmatism (Mixed methods)	Chaos and complexity theory orientation	Critical Theory	Social Constructivism	Postmodern	Participatory
7f. Creativity, Innovation, imaginivity	If not theory driven, potential for use by researcher/s during design phase					Potential for use by (co-)researcher/s during design phase		Deconstruction	Use by co-researcher(s)/ stakeholders throughout research phases
	Potential for use during research processes given:			- non-linear research design in qual phase/s	- non-linear approach to research design	- emergent nature of qual research if used	- emergent nature of qualitative research design		
8. Power	Primarily with researcher/s, and potentially funding bodies and some stakeholders					Primarily with researchers or co-researchers – researchers and research participants		Skeptical of power	All stakeholders given participatory, democratic, mutual processes used
						Possibly with funding bodies and some vested interest stakeholders			
9. Agency	Nil agency for all stakeholders during research processes			Possible agency during research processes for researchers and research participants		Potential for agency during research processes for (co-)/researchers or researchers and research participants		Skeptical of agency albeit potential for researcher agency	Potential for agency during research processes for all stakeholders
	Potential for end-point users and possibly researchers			Not for all, possibly for research participants depending on nature of research		Potential for end-point users			
10. Empowerment of stakeholders	Nil throughout research process					Potential through research and research outcomes	Democratic focus of inquiries may generate co-researcher empowerment during research process	Skeptical of empowerment for stakeholders	Empowerment principles embedded in paradigm –throughout and post research process
						Potential for end-point users			

Paradigms	Positivism	Scientific Post-Positivism	Critical Realism	Pragmatism (Mixed methods)	Chaos and complexity theory orientation	Critical Theory	Social Constructivism	Postmodern	Participatory
11. Emancipation	Not through research process		Consideration of emancipatory role of research		Concerned with prediction	Concerned with political cal agendas and emancipation	Consideration of social emancipatory role of research	Skeptical of emancipation	Concerned with emancipation
12. Research action outcomes									
12a. Action	Undermines objectivity		Limited due to paradigm-atic principles	Possible		Predicated to social action	Interpretation/understand-ing leads to social action	Individual action	Individual and collective social action
12b. Policy	Has potential to inform or influence policy							Debates and critiques policy	Potential to inform, influence and generate policy during participatory processes
12c. Practice	Use of research informed policy may influence practice							Debates and critiques practice	Informs and influences practice as a lived consequence of the research experience
12d. Level of impact – local, regional, international	Use of research may influence practice. Depending on utilisation of findings with regard to policy and practice the level of impact will be dependent on:							Individual levels	Impact is immediate and 'lived' – level depends on scope of participatory research

Paradigms	Positivism	Scientific Post-Positivism	Critical Realism	Pragmatism (Mixed methods)	Chaos and complexity theory orientation	Critical Theory	Social Constructivism	Postmodern	Participatory
12d. Level of impact – (continued)	- limitations associated with the research			- limitations/boundness of quant/qual or boundedness/limitations of qual/quant research used			- boundedness associated with the research		
12e. Adaptation	Nil or limited adaptation because of respective paradigmatic guidelines - replication issues with quantitative research can preclude adaptation		Possible adaptation depending on use of qualitative research		Adaptation		Due to emergent nature of research, adaptation is possible	Individually determined	Due to research processes involved in participatory research adaptation is possible
12f. Transformation	Not through the research process of an in itself - research findings may be used to influence policy and practice which may influence transformative practices and strategies			Possibly transformative	Transformative	Personal transformation, social justice	Transformation – social action	Skeptical of transformation	Transformation is a requisite of participatory research
Potential for impact	Depending on nature of research - local to international							'Truth' is for the individual to determine	Depending on nature of research - local to international
Sustainable tourism development	Depending on politics and stakeholder power relations - may inform policy and practice			Potential to contribute to sustainable tourism development				Skeptical of the achievement of sustainable tourism development	Immediacy in contributing to sustainable tourism development

Note: Presentation of content in rows adjacent to the 12 research considerations is not necessarily in any particular priority order. In some instances, the shorthand version of 'qual' has been used for qualitative research and 'quant' for quantitative research.

(Co-)researchers implies researchers and stakeholders/participants researching together.

Into the future

Creating the future we want requires all hands on deck given the sheer magnitude and speed of the required changes" (Rifai, 2017:7).

As Rittel and Webber (1973:164) remind us, " the set of feasible plans of action relies on realistic judgment, the capability to appraise 'exotic' ideas and on the amount of trust and credibility between ... [stakeholders] ...that will lead to the conclusion, "OK, let's try that"". There is not a 'one size fits all' research agenda – there are only multiple, flexible, and mutable processes. Each sustainable tourism development research project is a snapshot in time, space, and place – each is responsible for socio-cultural, environmental and prosperity agendas for human and non-human entities.

The time to act is now! Time is running out – researchers, planners, designers and practitioners –all stakeholders need to appraise their knowledge, practices, values and beliefs, they need to take stock of their skill sets with regard to sustainable livelihoods and their daily life practices, to engage in first person action research and to embrace and pursue action learning by themselves and in collaboration with others in order to harness resilient action to support and practise not just sustainable tourism development but also sustainable development to 'transform our world'. It is time for political action, and here I mean in an Aristotelian sense, which Gee describes as "anything and anyplace where human social interactions and relationships have implications for how 'social goods' are or ought to be distributed" (Gee, 1999:2). Doing nothing is a political act. Ignoring the future is a political act. Living only with regard to the present is a political act. Not changing practices is a political act. Being concerned for future generations is a political act. Speaking and writing are political acts since a "particular *perspective*" (Gee, 1999:2) is adopted by the speaker or the writer.

And so I come to outlining my particular perspective, my politics so to speak – I care about sustaining the world for future generations. I care about sustaining the world for current livelihoods be they human, or non-human. I care about engaging with others to create new futures, and design new research strategies to transform our world with a view to fulfilling the UN 2030 Sustainable Development Agenda. I care that the past is unable to predict the future. I care that dominant research hegemonies constrict the possibility for development of alternate perspectives. I care that novel and different research approaches need to be designed and created. I care that there are obstructions to enabling us to always "walk the talk". I care that the world is socially constructed and that meaning-making and sense-making are critical to engaging in collaborative acts. I care that people do not move beyond single loop learning in their interactions with others. I care that there are political – particular perspectives that work against being able to effectively address the seemingly super wicked problems of poverty, health and wellbeing, equality, climate change, refugee crises, and sustainability. These cares are the impetus for writing this chapter and the championing of the participatory paradigm.

We continue to be faced with the challenges for sustainable development, and sustainable tourism development. The aspirations of sustainability are manifold: "people, planet, partnerships and prosperity" as well as "peace" (World Tourism Organization and United Nations, 2017). Collaboration for sustainable tourism development related research needs to critically consider and reflect on the impact of researcher values and positionalities; levels of and competencies in communication skills; nature of collaboration processes, role and nature of partnerships, and stakeholder participation; role of education and learning—critical thinking, reflection and reflexivity, types of learning, creativity, innovation, and imaginivity; nature of power relationships; potential for agency, empowerment, and emancipation; expected research outcomes—social action, policy, practice, level of impact, adaptation, and transformation. As a sentient being, as a researcher, are you ready to embrace and enact first person, second person and third person research/practice with regard to sustainable tourism development in both your daily personal and professional lives? What role will you play in using collaboration and engendering resiliency to address the wicked problem of sustainable tourism development and the super wicked problem of sustainable development? Why? And remember, sustainable research processes need to incorporate sustainable research practices, ethics, socio-cultural, environmental and aesthetic responsibility and accountability as well as integration of evaluative research processes. How will you 'walk' the sustainable development 'talk' and engender it into your daily life?

References

Argyris, C. & Schön, D. A. (1978). *Organizational Learning: A theory of action perspective* (Vol. 173): Addison-Wesley Reading, MA.

Akyeampong, O.A. (2011) Pro-poor tourism: residents' expectations, experiences and perceptions in the Kakum National Park Area of Ghana, *Journal of Sustainable Tourism*, **19**(2), 197-213, DOI: 10.1080/09669582.2010.509508

Bateson, G. (1972). *Steps to an Ecology of Mind*. San Francisco: Chandler.

Bevir, M. (2009). *Key Concepts in Governance*. London: Sage.

Bradbury, H. & Reason, P. (2006). Conclusion: Broadening the bandwidth of validity: Issues and choice-points for improving the quality of action research. In P. Reason and H. Bradbury (eds) *Handbook of Action Research* (pp. 343-352). London: Sage.

Bramwell, B. and Lane, B. (1999). Editorial, *Journal of Sustainable Tourism*, **7**(3-4), 179-181,

Bramwell, B., & Lane, B. (2000). Collaboration and partnerships in tourism planning. In B. Bramwell & B. Lane (Eds.), *Tourism collaboration and partnerships: Politics, practice and sustainability* (pp. 1–19). Clevedon: Channel View.

Bramwell, B. & Lane, B. (2006). Policy relevance and sustainable tourism research: Liberal, radical and post-structuralist perspectives. *Journal of Sustainable Tourism*, **14**(1), 1–5.

Bramwell, B. & Lane, B. (2011) Critical research on the governance of tourism and sustainability. *Journal of Sustainable Tourism*, **19**(4-5), 411-421.

Bramwell, B., & Pomfret, G. (2007). Planning for lake and lake shore tourism: Complexity, coordi- nation and adaptation. *Anatolia: An International Journal of Tourism and Hospitality Research*, **18**(1), 43–66.

Brundiers, K., Wiek, A. & Redman, C.L. (2010). Real-world learning opportunities in sustainability: from classroom into the real world. *International Journal of Sustainability in Higher Education*, **11**(4), 308-324, https://doi.org/10.1108/14676371011077540

Churchman, C. W. (1967). Free for all: wicked problems. *Management Science* **14**(4), B-141-B-146.

Denzin, N.K. & Lincoln, Y.S. (2000). Introduction: The discipline and practice of qualitative research. In N.K. Denzin & Y.S. Lincoln. (Eds.), *Handbook of Qualitative Research*, 2nd ed. (pp. 1-28). Thousand Oaks, CA: Sage Publications.

Denzin, N.K. & Lincoln, Y.S. (2018). Introduction: The discipline and practice of qualitative research. In N.K. Denzin & Y.S. Lincoln. (Eds.), *Handbook of Qualitative Research*, 5th ed., (Digital). Thousand Oaks, CA: Sage Publications.

Dredge, D. & Jenkins, J. (2007). *Tourism Planning and Policy*. Milton: Wiley.

Evans, B. & Reid, J. (2015) Exhausted by resilience: response to the commentaries, *Resilience*, **3**(2), 154-159.

Garoian, C. R. (2013). *The Prosthetic Pedagogy of Art: Embodied research and practice*. Albany, NY: State University of New York.

Grybovych, O. and Hafermann, D. (2010) Sustainable practices of community tourism planning: lessons from a remote community. *Community Development*, **41**(3), 354-369,

Gee, J.P. (1999). *An Introduction to Discourse Analysis: Theory and method*. London: Routledge.

Guba, E.G. (1990). The alternative paradigm dialog. In Guba, E.G. *The Paradigm Dialog* (pp. 17-27). Newbury Park: Sage.

Guba, E.G. & Lincoln, Y.S. (1994). Competing paradigms in qualitative research. In N.K. Denzin & Y.S. Lincoln, (Eds.). *Handbook of Qualitative Research* (pp. 105-117). Thousand Oaks: Sage.

Healey, P. (2006). Transforming governance: Challenges of institutional adaptation and a new politics of space. *European Planning Studies*, **14**(3), 299–320.

IUCN, WWF and UNEP (1990). *Caring for the World: A strategy for sustainability* (2nd draft). Gland, Switerland.

Jamal, T. & Getz, D. (1999) Community roundtables for tourism- related conflicts: the dialectics of consensus and process structures, *Journal of Sustainable Tourism*, **7**(3-4), 290-313, DOI: 10.1080/09669589908667341

Jamal, T., & Watt, E. M. (2011). Climate change pedagogy and performative action: Towards community-based destination governance. *Journal of Sustainable Tourism*, **19**(4–5), 571–588.

Jennings, G. R. (2001). *Tourism Research*. Brisbane: John Wiley.

Jennings, G.R. (2007a). Advances in tourism research: Theoretical paradigms and accountability. In Matias, Á., Nijkamp, P. & Neto, P. (eds.). *Advances in Modern Tourism Research, Economic Perspectives* (pp. 9-35), Springer, Physica-Verlag Heidelberg.

Jennings, G.R. (2007b). Tourism perspectives towards 'Regional Development and Asia's Values'. *Research Journal of Dong-Eui University: Regional Development and Asia's Values*, Special Issue on the 30th anniversary of Dong-Eui University: October, pp. 259-288.

Jennings, G. R. (2007c). Sustainability and future directions. In Jennings, G.R. (ed.). *Water-Based Tourism, Sport, Leisure and Recreation Experiences* (pp. 223-251). Burlington, MA: Butterworth Heinemann Elsevier.

Jennings, G.R. (2009). Methodologies and methods. In T. Jamal & M. Robinson (eds.). *The Sage Handbook of Tourism Studies* (pp. 672-692). Los Angeles, CA: Sage.

Jennings, G. R. (2010). *Tourism Research*, 2nd Ed. Brisbane: John Wiley.

Jennings, G. R. (2018a) Qualitative research approaches to tourism. In Cooper, C., Gartner, B., Scott, N. & Volo, S. (Eds.)., *The Sage Handbook of Tourism Management*. London: Sage.

Jennings, G. R. (2018b) Action research and tourism studies. In Hillman, W. & Radel, K. (eds.). *Qualitative Methods in Tourism Research: Theory and Practice* (pp. 96-128). Channel View Publications.

Ki-Moon, B. (2013). Preface. In *World Economic and Social Survey 2013*. New York: United Nations Secretariat, Department of Economic and Social Affair (UN/DESA).

Koutsouris, A. (2009). Social learning and sustainable tourism development; local quality conventions in tourism: A Greek case study. *Journal of Sustainable Tourism*, **17**(5), 567–581.

Kuhn, T.S. (1962). *The Structure of Scientific Revolutions*. 1st ed. Chicago, IL: University of Chicago Press.

Kuhn, T.S. (2012). *The Structure of Scientific Revolutions. 4th ed. With an Introductory Essay by Ian Hacking. 50th Anniversary edition*. Chicago, IL: University of Chicago Press.

Levin, K., Cashore, B., Berstein, S. & Auld, G. (2012). Overcoming the tragedy of super wicked problems: constraining our future selves to ameliorate global climate change. *Policy Sciences*, **45**, 123-152.

Levy, D. L. (2000). Applications and limitations of complexity theory in organization theory and strategy. In J. Rabin, G.J. Miller & W. B. Hildreth (Eds.), *Handbook of Strategic Management*, 2nd ed. (pp. 67-87). Newy York, NY: Marcel Dekker, Inc.

Lincoln, Y.S. and Guba, E.G. (2000) Paradigmatic controversies, contradictions, and emerging confluences. In N.K. Denzin and Y.S. Lincoln, (Eds.). *Handbook of Qualitative Research*. 2nd ed. (pp. 163-188). Thousand Oaks: Sage.

Lincoln, Y.S., Lynham, S.A. and Guba, E.G. (2011). Paradigmatic controversies, contradictions, and emerging confluences, revisited. In N.K. Denzin & Y.S. Lincoln. *Handbook of Qualitative Research*, 4th ed., (pp. 97-128). Thousand Oaks, CA: Sage Publications.

Lincoln, Y.S., Lynham, S.A. and Guba, E.G. (2018). Paradigmatic controversies, contradictions, and emerging confluences, revisited. In N.K. Denzin & Y.S. Lincoln. *Handbook of Qualitative Research*, 5th ed. Thousand Oaks, CA: Sage Publications.

Liburd J. & Edwards, D. (Eds.) (2010). *Understanding the Sustainable Development of Tourism*. Oxford: Goodfellow Publishers.

Liburd, J. (2013) *Towards the Collaborative University. Lessons from Tourism Education and Research*. (Professorial dissertation) Odense: Print & Sign

Manning, S. & Reinecke, J. (2016). A modular governance architecture in-the-making: How transnational standard-setters govern sustainability transitions. *Research Policy*, **45**, 618-633.

Marien, C. & Pizam, A. (1997). Implementing sustainable tourism development through citizen participation in the planning process. In S.Wahab, & J.J. Pigram (Eds.), *Tourism, Development and Growth* (pp. 164-178). London: Routledge.

Matarrita-Cascante, D., Brennan, M.A. and Luloff, A.E. (2010). Community agency and sustainable tourism development: the case of La Fortuna, Costa Rica, *Journal of Sustainable Tourism*, **18**(6), 735-756.

Meadows, D., Meadows, D.L., Randers, J. & Behrens III, W.W. (1972). *Limits to Growth*: A report to the Club of Rome's project on the predicament of mankind. New York: Potomac Associates - Universe Books.

Moscardo, G. (2011). Exploring social representations of tourism planning: Issues for governance. *Journal of Sustainable Tourism*, **19**(4–5), 423–436.

Mowforth, M. & Munt, I. (1998). *Tourism and sustainability: New tourism in the Third World*. London: Routledge.

Pigram, J.J. & Wahab, S. (1997). The challenge of sustainable tourism growth. In S. Wahab, & J. Pigram (Eds.), *Tourism, Development and Growth* (pp. 3-13). London: Routledge.

Powell, T. C. (2001) Competitive advantage: logical and philosophical considerations, *Strategic Management Journal*, **22**(9), 875-88.

Reason, P. & Bradbury, H. (2006). Introduction: Inquiry and participation in search of a world worthy of human aspiration. In P. Reason and H. Bradbury (eds) *Handbook of Action Research, Concise Paperback Version* (pp. 1-14). London: Sage Publications.

Reason, P. & Torbert, W.R. (2001). The action turn: Towards transformational social science. *Concepts and Transformations*, **6** (1), 1-37.

Rifai, T. (2017). In World Tourism Organization and United Nations Development Programme, *Tourism and the Sustainable Development Goals – Journey to 2030*. Madrid: UNWTO.

Rittel, H.W.J. & Webber, M.M. (1973). Dilemmas in a general theory of planning. *Policy Sciences*, **4**(2), 155-169.

Rolling, J.H. (2015). Swarm intelligence as a prosthetic capacity. *Qualitative Inquiry*, **21**(6) 539-545.

Schilcher, D. (2007). Growth versus equity: the continuum of pro-poor tourism and neoliberal governance. In Hall, C.M., *Pro-Poor Tourism: Who benefits?: Perspectives on tourism and poverty reduction*. (pp. 56-83). Clevedon, UK: Channel View Publications.

Schwandt, T.A. (2000). Three epistemological stances for qualitative inquiry: interpretivism, hermeneutics, and social constructionism. In N.K. Denzin & Y.S. Lincoln, (Eds.). *Handbook of Qualitative Research*, 2nd ed. (pp.189-213). Thousand Oaks, CA: Sage.

Sofield, T. (2003). *Empowerment for Sustainable Tourism Development*. Oxford. Elsevier.

Stone, M.T. (2015) Community-based ecotourism: a collaborative partnerships perspective, *Journal of Ecotourism*, **14**(2-3), 166-184.

Tashakkori, A. & Teddlie, C. (1998) *Mixed Methodology: Combining Qualitative and Quantitative Approaches*. Applied Social Science Research Methods Series, Volume 46. Sage, Thousand Oaks, CA.

Tashakkori, A. & Teddlie, C. (2003) *Handbook of Mixed Methods in Social and Behavioral Research.* Sage, Thousand Oaks, CA.

Teddlie, C. & Tashakkori, A. (2009). *Foundations of Mixed Methods Research: Integrating quantitative and qualitative approaches in the social and behavioral sciences*. Thousand Oaks, CA: Sage.

UN Department of Economic and Social Affairs. (2015). *Transforming our world: The 2030 Agenda for sustainable development*, A/Res/70/1. Accessed 12/01/2018, from https://sustainabledevelopment.un.org/post2015/transformingourworld

UN Department of Economic and Social Affairs. (n.d.-a). *Sustainable development knowledge platform*. Accessed 31/01/2018, https://sustainabledevelopment.un.org

UN Department of Economic and Social Affairs. (n.d.-b). *Sustainable development knowledge platform: National Capacity Building*. Accessed 31/01/2018, URL: https://sustainabledevelopment.un.org/majorgroups/national-capacity-building.

Xiang, W. (2013). Working with wicked problems in socio-ecological systems: Awareness, acceptance, and adaptation. Editorial. *Landscape and Urban Planning*, **110**, 1-4.

Walker, K. & Weiler, B. (2017) A new model for guide training and transformative outcomes: a case study in sustainable marine-wildlife ecotourism, *Journal of Ecotourism*, **16**(3), 269-290, DOI: 10.1080/14724049.2016.1245736

Wall, G. (1997). Sustainable tourism – Unsustainable development. In S. Wahab, & J. Pigram (Eds.), *Tourism, Development and Growth* (pp. 33–49). London: Routledge.

Weiler, B. & Ham, S.H. (2002) Tour guide training: a model for sustainable capacity building in developing countries, *Journal of Sustainable Tourism*, **10**(1), 52-69.

Weiss, C. (1986). Research and policy-making: a limited partnership. In F. Heller, (ed.). *The Use and Abuse of Social Science*. Newbury Park, CA: Sage.

Wikipedia (2018). Partnership. Accessed 30/01/2018, https://en.wikipedia.org/wiki/Partnership

World Commission on Environment and Development, (1987). *Our Common Future*. Oxford, UK: Oxford University Press.

World Tourism Organization. (1998). *Guide for Local Authorities on Developing Sustainable Tourism*. Madrid: WTO.

World Tourism Organization and United Nations Development Programme. (2017). *Tourism and the Sustainable Development Goals – Journey to 2030*. Madrid: UNWTO.

Wray, M. (2011). Adopting and implementing a transactive approach to sustainable tourism planning: Translating theory into practice. *Journal of Sustainable Tourism*, **19**(4–5), 605–627.

Zebrowski, Chris. (2013) The nature of resilience, *Resilience*, **1**(3), 159-173,

Zhoa, W. & Ritchie, J.R.B. (2007). Tourism and poverty alleviation: An integrative research framework. In Hall C. M., *Pro-Poor Tourism: Who benefits?: Perspectives on tourism and poverty reduction*. Current themes in tourism series. Clevedon, UK: Channel View Publications, pp. 9-33.

15 Imagining Collaborative Tourism Futures

Janne Liburd and Deborah Edwards

> *"The greatest danger for most of us is not that our aim is too high and we miss it, but it is too low and we reach it"*

(Attributed to Michelangelo (1475-1564), cited in Robinson & Aronica, 2009: 260).

The journey of *Collaboration for Sustainable Tourism Development* has aimed high by keeping heads in the clouds and feet on the ground, to visit critical and optimistic possibilities for what sustainable tourism development was, is, and may become. This chapter gives substance to the potential of collaboration for sustainable tourism development by indicating the significance of imagination. Envisaging tourism futures implies that tourism researchers, students, practitioners, policy makers – all stakeholders – engender other kinds of relationships, interactions and conversations to imagine what could be. It is a feasible process of *designing with* as an ethical, ongoing involvement of others through a respect for their ways of being in the world, their sense of values and aspirations for better tourism futures in a better world. In this chapter, we do so by leveraging the variations of interpretation represented in the making of this book and the previous fourteen chapters. This book encompasses philosophical, conceptual and empirical research to expose conditions, empirical circumstances and underpinning values. The contributions meet in the application of the concept of collaboration to uncover what sustainable tourism development was, and presently is, and signposts how unknown futures can be imagined.

Imagining collaborative tourism futures is predicated on epistemological and mutually shared responsibilities. These obligations cannot alone be captured by academics engaged in a persistent quest for knowledge, critical dialogue and thinking tourism into the future. Responsibilities are intimately connected to a holistic understanding of collaborative engagements with the wider world in shaping desirable futures. Imaginations of collaborative tourism futures are a response to current limitations of sustainable tourism development, where we charter the contours of tourism futures to tackle wider societal problems.

Striving for a future orientation for sustainable tourism development is indicative of a proactive attitude. We seek to actively influence future developments, as opposed to being grounded in the past, or simply reacting to external pressures. Mindful that "dreams require optimism and a sense that one's hopes can be fulfilled" (Rifkin, 2005: 348), our imaginations are not castles-in-the-air ideas, but strive towards improvement based on reality and a care for the world. In 1793, Kant argued that "an idea is nothing other than the concept of a perfection which has not as yet been experienced" ([1793] 1963: 12). It may be seen as feasible, as our attempts of perfection rest on what lies behind and in current sustainable tourism development practices and conceptualisations to expose its "being-possible" (Heidegger, 1998: 183). The empirical positioning based on the previous chapters furthermore serves to ensure that the imaginative considerations are not out of touch with the world but that an 'in-touch' with the world is established. They help provide a corrective against potentially harmful imaginations of tourism, by indicating not only the power of the imagination, but assuming a position of intellectual responsibility for actual and future practice. Sensitive to the possibilities on these terms, we address tourism collaboration by not merely thinking tourism into the future but also look to advance desirable futures. Our endeavour towards desirable futures rests on Kant's (1793) moral philosophy of doing good and bringing about gradual improvement in the world. Kant's quadruple key tasks of education (discipline, culture, civilisation, and moralisation) in their original terms denote a commitment to a future world ethic, which Aristotle articulated as 'other-regarding'.

To maintain empirical grounding, the practicality of imagining the being-possible of tourism futures is gleaned from examples of this volume and philosophically based on Liburd's (2013) professorial dissertation about the being of the university. Collectively, the contributions to this volume highlight both issues and opportunities for research, education and practice in sustainable tourism development, including enhancing adaptability to respond to and engage change with others. We strive to identify "the forces and resources within the present that are capable of transforming it for the better in the future, so as to provide a significant dynamic for action in the here and now" (Halpin, 2003: 58).

Future practices and research efforts in sustainable tourism development should entail developing a shared cognition, effective agency, and trust in individuals, businesses and organisations engaged in collaboration with and across different dimensions, including the state, with communities, and other forms and norms of knowledge (Liburd, 2012). A complex, anthropological sense of exchange and reciprocity can feasibly be worked into ideas for further reflection on the way in which collaboration actually brings into being the persons and resources.

Looking back in order to progress, Mauss' ([1923] 1990) analysis of *The Gift* is informative. The traditional gift economy is guided by cultural forms reproducing the social norms and organisation of the group. Goods and services are rendered without any market exchange taking place. Gift-based transactions have a much broader focus than short-term, utilitarian exchanges (Mauss, [1923] 1990). Their primary function is often not related to the achievements of individual gains, or leadership roles, but they do not exclude this. The traditional gift economy is substantiated by reciprocal norms and exchanges that require trust for their consummation. At the same time, they also create it (Boisot, 1998: 141), which ensures possibilities for re-engagement and fair leadership. Mauss ([1923] 1990) explains how the original gift exchange can never be repeated and how it cannot be avoided. Herein lays the duty towards others, who are brought together, for both a return and a failure to return compromise the original status of the gift (Strathern, 1996; Liburd, 2013).

The point about giving and reciprocity in collaboration entails a shift from a self-serving, inside-out approach that currently characterizes tourism as a driver of economic growth: Who will support us to continue doing the excellent things that we do? To reciprocal considerations of collaborative tourism futures: How can tourism enhance its distinctive capabilities and engagements to create value at multiple levels with others, and thereby sustain its being and contribute to better world-making?

Hergesell, Edwards and Zins' (Chapter 5) account of tourists' irresponsible environmental behaviour provides a sobering contrast, where sustainability and value creation are limited to personal, if not outright selfish, interest. Jennings (Chapter 14) reminds us that "Doing nothing is a political act. Ignoring the future is a political act. Living only with regard to the present is a political act. Not changing practices is a political act. Being concerned for future generations is a political act." Heape and Liburd (Chapter 13) argue that attention to the self entails critically seeing into oneself in ontological and epistemological terms to cultivating deeper self-awareness to open up for the possibility of seeing beyond the self. In Kantian terms, collaboration offers opportunity for re-engagement and a duty to others – not only the self. It calls for a sense of care, or stewardship with others, beyond selfish concerns (Liburd, Chapter 2; Liburd & Becken, 2017). How ma y individual and collective doings by tourists enable tourism that is inherently other-regarding?

Devereux and Holmes (Chapter 6) identify the potentials of volunteer tourism in realizing the UN Sustainable Development Goals (SDGs), which they see as under-promoted and lacking ownership. They refer to the "SDGs as a transformative people centred vision", which resonates with Hughes and Morrison-Saunders (Chapter 7), who argue that tourists' wants can function as a lever for sustainable tourism development when combined with an identified need for conservation of forests or a species (Hughes, 2013). Whereas Devereux and Holmes point to the future potential of more tourists volunteering at home and abroad, Hughes and Morrison-Saunders place tourism as only one amid a range of sustainable development alternatives.

While we fully agree that it is people who protect the planet, or not, we question whether such an anthropocentric approach is sufficient in the context of desirable futures? Should 'other-regarding' be limited to human beings in the Anthropocene, while acknowledging that inter- and intra-generational equity is still a much-neglected issue in sustainability research and practice? From an eco-centric position, we would argue that all life has intrinsic value and that nature has value aside from its usefulness to humans (Kortenkamp & Moore, 2001). Indeed, as we impact the environment, we impact ourselves and unless we view ourselves as part of nature we will sacrifice our own needs and wants now and into the future. If we do not value nature, will we have futures to value? For Liburd and Becken (2017) such questions have underpinned empirical research about how humans construct the values and meanings of nature, which in turn influences stewardship.

The extent to which governments are responding to the challenge and engaging with the SDGs varies enormously (Higham & Miller, 2017), if even addressed, in the Anthropocene and the context of desirable futures. While government at the local level will often take responsibility for a sustainable tourism agenda ,this is frequently counterbalanced by self-interested agendas, power struggles and tokenistic involvement of the community. How can we enable governments to be inherently other-regarding? Guia (Chapter 4) presents a conceptual framework of how uncertainties at substantive, strategic and institutional levels can be managed in governance networks for sustainable tourism. He discusses how meta-governance, defined as the governance of (self)governance, transpires in local practices and networks where complex and continuous processes of interpretation, reconciliation, and sustainability meanings enable change. The role and power of the state is implicitly acknowledged, but governance networks hinge on negotiating skills, skills to bring actors together, and skills to identify latent opportunities that appeal to those involved and whose resources are required for implementation. Interestingly, Blichfeldt (Chapter 3) similarly points to the centrality of collaborative meaning making processes, albeit in the context of tourism organizations and businesses engaged in the seeing, making and doings of sustainable tourism development.

Whether the doings of the collaborative economy might be more sustainable and less damaging to the planet than other forms of tourism consumption are thoroughly questioned by Dredge and Meehan (Chapter 10). They draw attention to the intangible but often world-making role of collaborative sociality, which rarely enters public tourism discourses because they are often seen as too intangible or 'fluffy' for economists and policy makers to grasp and incorporate in their work. The rise of collaborative economies have been linked to an expanding ecosystem of micro-entrepreneurial activities, such as apartment cleaning services or key deposit services, often requiring an on-site, multiple job occupation strategy. At the other end of the spectrum we find the mobile dwelling of high-skilled, non-routine, middle-income jobs whose work comprises complex problem-solving activities (Goos et al, 2009). These workers can work in the cloud from almost anywhere and their jobs are not at risk from automation. This blurring of work-life balance (Deery, Jago, Harris & Liburd, Chapter 9) is evident in the increasing number of digital nomads, but is still far from replacing a stable workforce in the tourism and hospitality industries. Future research and collaborative experimentation should focus on how work-life balance can be enhanced through ensuring work task (rather than workforce) stability, trust in sharing jobs, and new value-creation through personal services and experiences to underpin sustainable tourism development. In other words, tourism is much more than a hedonistic phenomenon. Tourism is a lens through which we can begin to understand contemporary society, our (ethical) practice at home and away, while boundaries are increasingly blurred.

The case of the International Convention Centre Sydney (Foley, Edwards & Harrison, Chapter 12) and supported by Hjalager (Chapter 11) is indicative of how tourism businesses can take a proactive, co-developing and/or co-branding role with their suppliers whereby they create value at multiple levels while enhancing competitive advantage. Collaboration with the supply chain represents an opportunity to deliver significant climate, water, and waste benefits not only in our upstream supply chain, but also in the manufacturing, distribution, and use of sustainable tourism products and services. Laudable as business practice, which captures the essence of corporate social responsibility, as discussed by Dwyer and Lund-Durlacher (Chapter 8), tourism's business value and value to society should never be addressed purely in economic terms. Values appear in plural and can be co-designed with others at multiple levels – whether for the individual, for businesses, organizations, the state and through meta-governance.

We believe that knowledge, values and ethics can guide our actions for better futures. The "for" is a carefully chosen word. Collaboration affords human agency to help direct change so that we can redress own consumption and ingrained institutional patterns to avoid blind reproduction of the past (Liburd, 2013; Guia, Chapter 4). More of the same will not change the trajectory of long-term planetary degradation, nor engage the multitude of 'wicked' problems.

Collaborative value creation at multiple levels opens new perspectives on how the situating of sustainable tourism development learning, content and practices in lifewide perspectives can be enabled. Lifewide leaning may be collaborative and still maintain the essence of individuality through the student's personal development and self-directed learning in an infinite range of environments (Jackson, 2010). Learning is not only attributed to teaching (Stergiou, Airey and Riley, 2008: 634) or the acquisition of scientific knowledge in the classroom, but it remains a possibility (Hooks, 1994: 207).

Heape and Liburd (Chapter 13) explain how collaborative learning for sustainable tourism development helps individual students develop a heightened attention to, and perception of the nuance of their process of inquiry, their relating to others involved, both group members and stakeholders, and develop a greater understanding and empowerment of themselves. In present and future tourism higher education for sustainable tourism development teachers should engage with students in a variety of learning environments and processes in which they are challenged in how they see and understand, as opposed to merely capturing what they should see. Questioning the taken-for-granted, including the self, and discovering new ways of knowing and being are vested on ontological aspects and an emancipatory conception of higher education. The formative process of higher education aims both at 'meaningful freedom' and 'transformation of the whole man' (Jaspers, [1946] 1965: 64-65). This implies that both contribute to holistic and potentially transformative learning processes. For the student, tourism higher education heralds changes at the individual level and at the societal level in the forms of collaborative engagement in creating better futures. As the future remains indeterminate, collaborative learning and reciprocal exchanges should facilitate engagement and reengagement to help conceive positive and creative possibilities. Re-engagement across different dimensions implies nothing more than that each collaborative act contains the possibility of other collaborations without specifying what they may be.

We end by pointing to a limitation of this volume in the form of lacking analysis of the power of tourism in marginalisation, oppression, market hegemony, and unequal and unjust labour practices (Higgins-Desbiolles & Whyte, 2012). They should not be left unmentioned in the context of sustainable tourism education and dominating, privileged tourism research. We could choose to reject critique by reference to a politicising of tourism research and higher education. However, as countered by Shor (1992) and Jennings (Chapter 14), refraining from providing critical perspectives in higher education and research is no more political than not questioning knowledge, society and experience, tacitly maintaining the status quo. Indeed, the imagination of tourism education and research aspires to cultivate knowledge, skills, human dispositions, and qualities to critically engage in, and across, different dimensions to help create more desirable and just futures. We imagine future tourism higher education to be "ideologically light" (Barnett, 2011: 3) as it strives to avoid serving specific interests, cognizant that it can never be free of ideology. The value of values is fully accepted and has a place alongside the value freedom of science, which remains at the heart of educational and scientific advancements (Liburd, 2013).

Conclusion

Imaginations of more radical conceptualisations of collaboration are called for. Collaboration for sustainable tourism development is not an aim or a solution. It is a multifaceted phenomenon allowing for reciprocal engagement across endless domains. As mentioned throughout this book, collaboration differs from cooperation, which simply implies a division of labour. The concept of collaboration suggests the creation of joint outcomes that are larger than the individual parts, which could not be generated by a single organisation or individual. The multiplicity of collaborative dimensions, including the relationship to the state, industry, other forms and norms of knowledge, learning and engagements with some, but not others, represents an indefinite number of interest structures permeating desirable tourism futures. The collaborative links and opportunities are not always intuitive or apparent and may also come about through serendipity rather than strategy (Edwards, Foley & Malone, 2017).

Collaborative tourism futures encourage engagement across multiple dimensions without neglecting the fruitfulness of competition in striving for new and more complete domains of knowledge and being-in-the-world. Indeed, collaboration in tourism may represent the epitome of competition. Walsh and Kahn (2010: 197) reminds us that deciding with whom to collaborate also entails the exclusion of other individuals or institutions from the inner circle of collaborative practice. Hence, we argue that collaboration carries intellectual responsibilities, notions of stewardship and sometimes wider issues of virtue and beauty. The philosophical meanings and nature of beauty touch upon both subjective and ontological dimensions of collaboration, as well as how these are framed in the world. Heidegger in *The Question Concerning Technology and Other Essays* (1977) warns us against simply seeing the world as furnishing resources as a standing reserve for exploiting the world. Virtuous engagement therefore signifies stewardship and ethics in collaboration, which are concerned with values and principles of the right conduct, the good life, and considerations of desirable futures. Collaborative tourism futures must be dedicated to creating a world in which "one lives well and for others in just institutions" (Ricoeur, 1992: 330).

References

Barnett, R. (2011). The idea of the university in the twenty-first century: Where's the imagination. *Journal of Higher Education*, **1**(2), 88-94.

Boisot, M. (1998). *Knowledge Assets: Securing competitive advantage in the information economy*. Oxford: Oxford University Press.

Edwards, D., Foley, C. & Malone, C. (2017). *The Power of Conferences: Stories of serendipity, innovation and driving social change*. Sydney: UTS ePress. doi.org/10.5130/978-0-6481242-0-7

Goos, M., Manning, A. & Salomons, A. (2009). Job Polarization in Europe, *American Economic Review*, **99**(2), 58-63.

Halpin, D. (2003). *Hope and Education: The Role of the Utopian Imagination*. London: RoutledgeFalmer.

Heidegger, M. ([1927] 1998). *Being and Time*. Oxford: Blackwell.

Heidegger, M. (1977). *The Question Concerning Technology and Other Essays*. New York: Harper Perennial.

Higgins-Desbiolles, F. & Whyte, K.P. (2012) No high hopes for hopeful tourism: a critical comment. *Annals of Tourism Research* **40**, 428-433.

Higham, J. & Miller, G. (2017). Transforming societies and transforming societies: sustainable tourism in times of change. *Journal of Sustainable Tourism*, **26**(1), 1–8. doi:10.1080/09669582.2018.1407519.

Hooks, B. (1994) *Teaching to Transgress: Education as the Practice of Freedom*. London: Routledge.

Hughes, M. (2013) *Ecocean*: conservation through technological innovation. In J. Liburd, J. Carlsen & D. Edwards (Eds.) *Networks for Sustainable Tourism Innovation: Case studies and cross-case analysis*. Tilde University Press, Australia, pp 25-32.

Jackson, N.J. (2010) From a curriculum that integrates work to a curriculum that integrates life: changing a university's conceptions of curriculum, *Higher Education Research & Development, Work Integrated Learning* Special Issue, **29**(5), 491-505.

Jaspers, K. ([1946] 1965). *The Idea of the University*. London, Peter Owen.

Kant, I. ([1793] 1963). *Ausgewählte Schriften zur Pädagogik und ihrer Begründung*. Paderborn: Schöningh.

Kortenkamp, K. V. & Moore, C. F. (2001). Ecocentrism and anthropocentrism: Moral reasoning about ecological commons dilemmas. *Journal of Environmental Psychology*, 21(3), 261-272.

Liburd, J. (2012). Tourism Research 2.0. *Annals of Tourism Research*, **39**(2), 883–907.

Liburd, J. (2013). *Towards the Collaborative University: Lessons from tourism education and research*. (Professorial Dissertation), University of Southern Denmark, Denmark.

Liburd, J. & Becken, S. (2017). Values in nature conservation, tourism and UNESCO World Heritage Site stewardship. *Journal of Sustainable Tourism* **25**(12), 1719-1735. doi:10.1080/09669582.2017.1293067

Mauss, M. [1923] 1990). *The Gift* transl. by W.D. Halls foreword by Mary Douglas. London & New York: Routledge.

Ricoeur, P. (1992) *Oneself as Another*. (K. Blamey Transl.) Chicago: University of Chicago Press.

Rifkin, J. (2005). *The European Dream: How Europe's Vision of the Future is Quietly Eclipsing the American Dream*. New York: Penguin Group.

Robinson, K. with Aronica, L. (2009) *The Element. How finding your passion changes everything*. London: Penguin Books.

Shor, I. (1992) *Empowering Education: Critical Teaching for Social Change*. Chicago: University of Chicago Press.

Stergiou, D., Airey, D. & Riley, M. (2008). Making sense of tourism teaching. *Annals of Tourism Research,* **35**(3), 631–649.

Strathern, M. (1996). Cutting the Network. *The Journal of the Royal Anthropological Institute,* **2**(3), 517-535.

Walsh, L. & Kahn, P. (eds) (2010) *Collaborative Working in Higher Education. The Social Academy*. New York and London: Routledge.

Index

Printed in the United States
By Bookmasters